Building ASP.NET with Microsoft WebMatrix

Steve Lydford

Building ASP.NET Web Pages with Microsoft WebMatrix

Copyright © 2011 by Steve Lydford

ISBN-13 (pbk): 978-1-4302-4020-4

ISBN-13 (electronic): 978-1-4302-4021-1

President and Publisher: Paul Manning
Lead Editor: Ewan Buckingham
Technical Reviewer: Andy Olsen
Editorial Board: Steve Anglin, Mark Beckner, Ewan Buckingham, Gary Cornell, Morgan Ertel,
    Jonathan Gennick, Jonathan Hassell, Robert Hutchinson, Michelle Lowman, James Markham,
    Matthew Moodie, Jeff Olson, Jeffrey Pepper, Douglas Pundick, Ben Renow-Clarke, Dominic
    Shakeshaft, Gwenan Spearing, Matt Wade, Tom Welsh
Coordinating Editor: Adam Heath
Copy Editor: Chandra Clarke
Compositor: Apress Production (Christine Ricketts)
Indexer: SPI Global
Artist: SPI Global
Cover Designer: Anna Ishchenko

Distributed to the book trade worldwide by Springer Science+Business Media, LLC., 233 Spring Street, 6th Floor, New York, NY 10013. Phone 1-800-SPRINGER, fax (201) 348-4505, e-mail orders-ny@springer-sbm.com, or visit www.springeronline.com.

For information on translations, please e-mail rights@apress.com, or visit www.apress.com.

Apress and friends of ED books may be purchased in bulk for academic, corporate, or promotional use. eBook versions and licenses are also available for most titles. For more information, reference our Special Bulk Sales–eBook Licensing web page at www.apress.com/bulk-sales.

Any source code or other supplementary materials referenced by the author in this text is available to readers at www.apress.com. For detailed information about how to locate your book's source code, go to http://www.apress.com/source-code/.

To my wonderful wife Wendy (WWW) for her love and unending support,
and our four amazing kids Tomos, Wiliam, Amy, and Isabel who make us both so very proud.

-Steve Lydford

Contents at a Glance

Contents

About the Author

■ **Steve Lydford** had been a professional software developer since 1999, although he first learnt to program computers at the age of seven, when his father brought home a Sinclair Spectrum with a black and white portable television and a massive 16Kb of RAM! The countless hours spent typing in listings from Sinclair User magazine sparked an enthusiasm for programming that has stayed with him for life.

During his career, Steve has worked for a variety of small companies, web startups, and corporations, developing systems on an assortment of—mostly web-based—platforms. Currently, he develops almost exclusively on the ASP.NET platform and has worked on many successful projects using Web Forms, MVC, and WebMatrix, which he has followed with great interest since its initial beta release. He enjoys writing and speaking to fellow developers, particularly about emerging web technologies.

Steve lives with his family in mid-Wales where he loves to walk in the mountains and spends far too much time in front of a computer, usually working on his next "big idea."

About the Technical Reviewer

Andy is a freelance consultant/developer/instructor based in the UK. Andy has been working with .NET since Beta 1 days and has worked on numerous book projects with Apress over the last ten years. Andy lives by the seaside in Swansea with his family, and enjoys running (with mandatory coffee stops en route), skiing (of a fashion), and watching the Swans!

Acknowledgments

Huge thanks to all the team at Apress who have guided me through this, my first book. Thanks to Ewan Buckingham for getting the whole thing going and working with me to produce the initial table of contents. Thanks also to Adam Heath for guiding the project to its successful conclusion and answering my countless emails and questions on the whole publishing process—most of which is still largely a mystery to me! And massive thanks to the Technical Reviewer, Andy Olsen, who did an outstanding job, meticulously checking all the code and technical details. The excellent feedback he provided has greatly enhanced the final copy.

Most importantly, I would like to thank my beautiful wife Wendy and our four great kids Tomos, Wiliam, Amy, and Isabel. Without their love and support this book would never have seen the light of day. I'll take next weekend off, I promise!

–Steve

Introduction

Microsoft WebMatrix is a free web development tool that includes everything required to create small and medium-sized web applications. The tool includes a web server, a powerful server-side scripting language, and a database, all of which can be used from within its own customized, lightweight development environment.From the outset, it has been designed to provide developers with an easy-to-learn, easy-to-use, rapid web development platform.

By the end of this book, you will have learned all the skills necessary to develop dynamic, data-driven web sites using the tools provided as part of the WebMatrix platform. We will cover every part of the toolset in detail and see how each can be best used to provide real-world solutions to common web development tasks. Later in the book (in Chapters 9, 10, and 11), we will use the skills learned to develop a fully-functional e-commerce web site, which includes a data-driven product catalog, membership system, shopping cart, and checkout process as well as site administration pages and other features.

In the text, I have assumed that the reader has no prior knowledge of WebMatrix, or the other Microsoft ASP.NET web development platforms. In order to follow the examples in the book you will simply need a working knowledge of HTML and Cascading Style Sheets (CSS); however, readers with previous experience of another framework, such as PHP or Rails, will certainly find this beneficial. For readers with little previous programming experience, I have, wherever possible, provided links and references to online information and books to help you broaden your knowledge.

Code Samples

Sample code from the book is available for download from the Apress web site. To obtain the files, visit **www.apress.com** and search for the book. Once you have found it you can download the files from the Source Code/Downloads tab.

The sample files are compressed into a single ZIP file, which contains folders for each of the chapters for which source code is available.

Errata

While the author, technical reviewer, copy editors, and many other members of Apress staff have reviewed the content of this book in a bid to eliminate all errors, it is possible that some small mistakes have slipped through the net.

Details of any known errata can be found on the book's page on the Apress web site. If you do happen to find any errors, in the text or code examples, that have not already been reported please let us know via email at **support@apress.com**. By doing this, we can keep other readers informed and provide corrections where necessary.

Contacting the Author

Please feel free to contact me directly at `webmatrix@stevelydford.com`, or via my blog at
`http://blog.stevelydford.com`. If you wish to, you can also follow me (`@stevelydford`) on Twitter. I'll do
my best to reply to any messages as soon as I possibly can.

If you have general WebMatrix development questions the best place to get a quick response is via
the official online forum at `http://forums.asp.net/1224.aspx`.

CHAPTER 1

Introducing Microsoft WebMatrix

WebMatrix is a web development platform from Microsoft aimed at providing a fast and lightweight way to develop dynamic web content. The WebMatrix platform consists of many individual component parts that go together to create a complete web development environment. Throughout the course of this book you will learn about each of these component parts in some detail.

This chapter is not concerned with the inner-workings of the platform or its individual components, but is focused on explaining the landscape in which WebMatrix exists. It will aim to explain the intent behind the design of WebMatrix and the problems it sets out to solve.

What is WebMatrix?

WebMatrix is a set of free development tools that designed to allow users to easily create dynamic, data-driven web sites and publish them on the Internet.

The tools and technologies included as part of the WebMatrix platform include among others, a database, web server, deployment tool, Search Engine Optimization (SEO) tool and a server-side scripting language. Although all of these tools and technologies are available for download and use as separate entities, Microsoft has combined them into a single stack known as WebMatrix. By doing this a web developer can control the development of all aspects of a web site from within a single environment, greatly reducing complexity. This reduction in complexity realizes many benefits, not least of which are the shortening of development times and a greatly reduced entry barrier – the developer must learn to use just one integrated environment, rather than five or six separate tools.

To further reduce the learning curve, many of the component parts are simplified when presented as part of WebMatrix. For example, the web server supplied by Microsoft as part of WebMatrix is a smaller, development-friendly version of their full-blown Internet Information Services web server application and the database is the Compact Edition of SQL Server, their enterprise-level relational database server. This is a great advantage to new developers. WebMatrix presents you only with what you absolutely need to create web sites, cutting away the myriad of features that are used rarely, often only by advanced users.

To the more advanced developer this simplification of the development environment can be a refreshing change, especially with the current trend of huge monolithic web development frameworks and architectures. You can after all still access the component parts through their native tools should the need arise.

What WebMatrix offers above all else is simplicity, ease of use and rapid development.

What is a Dynamic, Data-Driven Web Site?

So far we have learnt that Microsoft WebMatrix is a great tool for creating "dynamic, data-driven web sites", but what exactly does that mean? Well let's take the dynamic bit first.

Dynamic Web Pages

In simple terms website content can be provided in one of two ways. The first, more traditional way is to store the content in static files like documents and serve them whole to the client browser. If you were to take each page of this book and store it as an HTML page which was displayed back to the user in its entirety when they requested it, you would be providing static content. A static web page retrieved by different users at different times will always be displayed in exactly the same way.

A dynamic page is one that freshly produces at least some of its content programmatically when a request is made to the web server. In other words, when a user requests a page from the web server some code is run which is used to construct the output to be returned to the user. This dynamic creation of content is the polar opposite of the traditional static website. WebMatrix uses ASP.NET Web Pages to execute C# or Visual Basic .NET code on the server to create dynamic content.

Dynamic pages can also be used to accept input from users, which is then used for some kind of computation. For example, a page may request a monetary value in one currency, which is then converted to another currency on the server and the result displayed back to the user.

Data-Driven Pages

Data-driven pages are those that interact with some kind of data store. For example, input from the user may be used to create or update database records or data may be retrieved from an XML file and formatted by code for output. By using the data stores in database tables and records we are able to produce custom page content, whether on a user-by-user or some other basis.

The typical database operations conducted by web pages are Create, Read, Update and Delete, typically abbreviated as CRUD. We can produce user interfaces and server-side code which will allow site users to carry out these operations on the database in a very controlled fashion.

A Pragmatic Solution

In reality most web pages produced by WebMatrix, or any of the other server-side dynamic frameworks such as PHP or Ruby on Rails, are a mix of static and dynamic content. This is done primarily for two reasons; speed and simplicity.

It is much simpler for a developer to create static content and it is quicker to produce and serve. Therefore it is common practice to mix the two techniques within a single page, returning dynamic, data-driven content only where necessary, amongst the rest of the static markup.

Figure 1-1 demonstrates this concept by identifying the areas of static and dynamic content on a typical page from the example ecommerce web site, "TechieTogs" that we will design and build in chapters 9, 10 and 11. Content that has been created dynamically in code is highlighted; the rest of the page is constructed using static HTML:

Figure 1-1. Mixing static and dynamically (highlighted) produced content within a single web page

Why Use WebMatrix?

There are many great web frameworks available for developing dynamic sites, why should you choose to use WebMatrix? Well it has a lot of advantages; let's have a look at a few of the major benefits here:

- **Simplicity** – Simplicity is the key behind the success of WebMatrix. This is achieved largely by steering clear of some of the massive and hugely-complex architectures that have become prevalent in the last few years. You can add uncomplicated, dynamic server-side code straight inside your web pages, in a way that will be familiar to developers with previous experience of Classic ASP or PHP. There is absolutely nothing stopping you from creating a site architecture which is efficient and useful to you, but in the vast majority of small and medium-sized web applications there is simply no need to add complexity by designing some convoluted cathedral-like code structure which provides no real benefit and slows down development.

- **It's easy to learn** – The learning curve for WebMatrix is much less steep than the majority of modern web platforms. As you will see as you progress through this book, the simplicity of the framework makes it easy to learn and master. As long as you have a working knowledge of HTML and have done some basic programming in the past, you should have few problems learning WebMatrix.

- **It's complete and integrated** – Everything you need to develop a complete web site is contained within WebMatrix, a point we will prove when we develop the TechieTogs sample ecommerce application in chapters 9, 10 and 11. This includes a database, scripting language,

3

web server, deployment tool and development environment (the tool you will use to create the site); and they all play nicely together! This is one of the strongest selling points and very unusual amongst other platforms.

- **It's all free and easy to install** – As you will see in Chapter 2 – Getting Started, the whole platform is really simple to download and install using the Web Platform Installer and is absolutely free of charge.

- **It is part of the ASP.NET platform** – ASP.NET is Microsoft's mature and well-proven web platform. It has been around since the early nineties and has grown into a very capable technology. ASP.NET is built on the .NET Framework which means you can write code in any .NET language (C# is the most popular and is what we will use exclusively in this book) and take full advantage of the vast .NET class library to simplify many of your programming tasks.

- **You have complete control over the rendered output** – In the past some criticism has been leveled at the ASP.NET Web Forms model for the lack of control over the final markup rendered to the client browser. WebMatrix has none of these issues. By using ASP.NET Web Pages, with the ground-breaking Razor syntax, the developer has total control over the output sent to the client. This means that rendered pages can comply with web standards and page elements are easily accessible to developers who wish to use client-side scripting in their application.

- **It is flexible and open** – The WebMatrix development environment is equally suitable for development of PHP and ASP.NET Web Pages. Using WebMatrix you can find, download, install, configure and customize a wide variety of free open source web applications quickly and easily. These include many of the web's most popular open source applications, including WordPress, Umbraco, Drupal, Joomla!, Moodle and DotNetNuke.

- **It is designed to be scalable** – Two of the major parts of the WebMatrix platform are the integrated web server and database. Both of these components can easily be upgraded to higher-performance production systems should the need arise, in fact it is encouraged. The facilities to accomplish this are provided out-of-the box as part of the development environment.

- **It can be extended** – As we'll see later in the book, WebMatrix includes a Package Manager which allows you to download, install and customize helper code to easily add specific features to your site and simplify integration with third-party providers such as Twitter, FaceBook, Amazon, PayPal, Groupon, Windows Azure and Foursquare.

The ASP.NET Platform

We have mentioned that WebMatrix uses ASP.NET Web Pages to create dynamic content by executing code on the web server. ASP.NET Web Pages is the latest addition to the ASP.NET platform, which has been around since 2002. As a result the designers of the ASP.NET Web Pages platform have been able to draw on vast experience, gained over nearly a decade, to design a lightweight and fully-functional web development platform. In designing WebMatrix, Microsoft have really listened to the users in the ASP.NET and wider web-development communities, many of whom have been asking for the power of .NET and its associated libraries and infrastructure in a platform which allows simple rapid-development, ease of use, extensibility and total control over the output sent to users.

The Trend Towards Simplicity

In the past few years there has been an explosion in new web development frameworks and methodologies. However, many of these new frameworks require a huge amount of infrastructure and code that is complete overkill for the development of most small websites. This unsuitability for simple web development tasks and the programming and scientific knowledge required to get started using many of these frameworks, has driven an ever-increasing trend towards simplicity.

Platforms such as ASP.NET Web Pages and Sinatra, aimed at Ruby developers, are beginning to gain serious market share from the "full-stack" platforms as developers realise the benefits of using a simple framework to develop simple web sites and newcomers discover the lower barriers to entry.

Figure 1-2 shows how ASP.NET Web Pages fits into the ASP.NET technology stack:

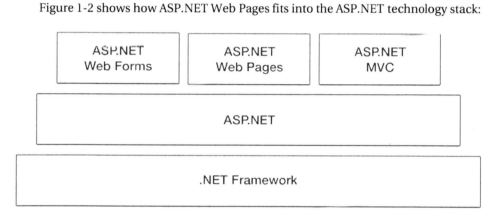

Figure 1-2. *The ASP.NET stack*

From this diagram it is clear to see that ASP.NET Web Pages is built on top of ASP.NET in the same way as ASP.NET Web Forms and ASP.NET MVC (Model View Controller). ASP.NET is in turn built on the .NET Framework. This architecture means that ASP.NET Web Pages can take full advantage of the huge .NET Class libraries which exist to enable developers to perform a wide variety of common programming tasks, which would otherwise be cumbersome, complex and time-consuming.

The other advantage that becomes apparent from the architecture is that the transition for .NET developers from one platform to another is relatively straightforward. A .NET developer will have many transferable skills between the various web, desktop and mobile development frameworks, due to the fact that they are all built on the .NET Framework with which they are already familiar.

Who Should Use WebMatrix?

WebMatrix is absolutely ideal for anyone wishing to create a small to medium-sized dynamic, data-driven site for deployment on a Microsoft Windows web server. Examples of people who may find WebMatrix useful include:

- Web developers with previous experience of some other platform, such as ASP.NET Web Forms, PHP, Ruby on Rails or Classic ASP, who want to use a simple, modern framework for developing web applications on the ASP.NET platform.

- Developers of Windows desktop applications who want to extend their existing skill set to develop a web-based application using a programming language with which they are already familiar.

- Web designers who want to include some dynamic content in otherwise static web sites with a minimum of fuss.

- Hobbyists, enthusiasts and students who are interested in learning how to develop web applications. They will find WebMatrix easy to learn, with rapid results and all the features they require in one place.

This is by no means an exhaustive list, but does go some way to demonstrate the diverse groups of people who could benefit from this platform. This book is aimed at all of these groups and assumes no previous knowledge other than a basic understanding of HTML and Cascading Style Sheets (CSS), although some previous programming experience, however minimal, will certainly be of benefit.

What Will I Learn?

Over the course of the book you will learn everything you need to create fully-functional, dynamic, data-driven websites; a fact that will be proved in chapters 9, 10 and 11 when we use the skills and techniques learnt in the first part of the book to develop a fully-working ecommerce web site.

The following list describes some of the major topics covered in the text:

- **Installation** - The first step to using WebMatrix is downloading and installing it. We'll see in Chapter 2 exactly how to achieve that to get you up and running.

- **The tools** – We'll take an in depth look at all of the tools supplied as part of the WebMatrix development environment. We'll cover these throughout the course of the book as we come to use each of them.

- **The language** – WebMatrix web sites can be developed using any of the .NET languages. In this book we will be focusing on the most popular of these, C#. Chapter 3 contains a C# Primer, designed to give you enough knowledge about the language to enable you to complete the examples in the rest of the book.

- **ASP.NET Web Pages** – In Chapter 4 we'll see how we can use the fabulous Razor syntax model to develop ASP.NET Web Pages. These pages allow the execution of server-side C# code to produce dynamic pages with which the user can fully interact.

- **Forms and validation** – HTML forms are the most popular method with which web sites gather information from users. In Chapter 5 We'll learn how to make use of that information and how to implement code to check that the user input is valid.

- **SQL Server Compact Edition** – WebMatrix ships with an integrated file-based database; SQL Server Compact Edition, which we'll take a detailed look at in Chapter 6. We'll learn how to use the built-in tools to create and administer these databases and how we can connect to and use other existing data sources.

- **Interacting with databases** – Also in Chapter 6 we'll see how ASP.NET Web Pages can be used to interact with databases. We'll see how to perform create, read, update and delete operations from with a web page. In this chapter we'll also learn how to use the built-in helpers to display data in graphs and tables.

- **Security and web site membership** – In most reasonably complex web sites it is desirable that some areas are visible only to logged in users. In Chapter 7 we will see how the comprehensive ASP.NET Web Pages security and membership system can be used to achieve this goal.

- **Social Network integration** – WebMatrix has a built-in package manager which enables you to find, download and install helper packages into your web application that facilitate integration with social networks and other third-party web sites. We'll spend the whole of Chapter 8 looking at the Package Manager and some of the more commonly used web helper packages.

- **Real-World Development** – Throughout Chapters 9, 10 and 11 we will develop a fully-featured ecommerce application using the skills and techniques learnt in the previous chapters.

- **Debugging** – Although you will always seek to minimize them, in any reasonably complex application bugs and errors will inevitably creep in. We'll look at ways to identify and fix them before the site goes live in Chapter 13.

- **Search Engine Optimization (SEO)** – With search engine traffic being so important, particularly to start-up web sites, it is vital that you optimize your site for search engine placement. WebMatrix can help you achieve this by helping you to ensure your site is indexed correctly by search engines such as Google, Yahoo and Bing. We'll learn how to make the most of this tool in Chapter 13.

- **Deployment** – Once your web site is finished you will need to deploy it from your development PC to a public-facing web server. In Chapter 13 we'll see how WebMatrix makes this easy for you, and can even help you choose a suitable web hosting provider.

The WebMatrix Community

WebMatrix has an active and vibrant on-line community, made up of a wide range of beginners, students, hobbyists and professional developers, where new members are always warmly welcomed. There are several excellent on-line forums available, which are a good place to ask any questions you may have; these include:

- The Official ASP.NET WebMatrix Forums - *http://forums.asp.net/1224.aspx*

- The IIS. NET WebMatrix Forum - *http://forums.iis.net/t/1169334.aspx*

- Stack Overflow - *http://stackoverflow.com/questions/tagged/webmatrix*

■ **Tip**   Please remember to follow normal forum etiquette by always using the forum's search facility to see if your question has been asked previously by another user before you post.

I would also recommend that you visit the following sites regularly to keep yourself up-to-date with developments in WebMatrix as well as details of future releases, updates and events:

- The Official ASP.NET Web Pages Site - *http://www.asp.net/web-pages*

- The Microsoft.com WebMatrix Site - *http://www.microsoft.com/web/webmatrix/*

- Web Camps - *http://www.webcamps.ms/*

Finally, there are a number of experts whose blogs who I would recommend to any WebMatrix developer. Here I have listed a few interesting articles:

- Scott Guthrie – Introducing WebMatrix
  http://weblogs.asp.net/scottgu/archive/2010/07/06/introducing-webmatrix.aspx

- Rob Conery – Thoughts on WebMatrix
  http://blog.wekeroad.com/microsoft/someone-hit-their-head

- Scott Hanselman – On WebMatrix (with Rob Conery) – Hanselminutes Podcast 249
  http://www.hanselman.com/blog/HanseminutesPodcast249OnWebMatrixWithRobConery.aspx

- James Senior – WebMatrix Blog Posts
  http://www.jamessenior.com/?cat=13

- Joe Stagner – WebMatrix Blog Posts
  http://www.misfitgeek.com/category/webmatrix/

Prerequisites

There are some personal and hardware requirements which you must be able to meet before you can progress through this book.

Previous Knowledge

You will be able to complete and understand all the chapters in this book as long as you have a basic working knowledge of HTML and CSS. However, some previous programming experience of any kind and a general working knowledge of internet technologies would be of benefit.

Links and references to useful web pages and publications are provided throughout the text to help you read around the subject and really gain a full in-depth knowledge of the concepts discussed.

System Requirements

To install and use WebMatrix you must have a PC running one of the following supported Microsoft Operating Systems:

- Windows XP Service Pack 3
- Windows Vista Service Pack 2
- Windows 7
- Windows Server 2003 Service Pack 2,
- Windows Server 2008
- Windows Server 2008 R2

Summary

In this chapter you have had a brief overview of WebMatrix, what it can do and why it has become so incredibly popular with beginners and experts alike. Now I've whetted your appetite let's move on to the next chapter where we dive straight in by installing WebMatrix and writing our first web application.

Good luck!

CHAPTER 2

Getting Started

In this chapter, we are going to jump right in the deep end and create our first site using Microsoft WebMatrix.

We will start by installing the WebMatrix toolbox on to your Windows PC using the Microsoft Web Platform Installer, a kind of all–in–one download manager and installer. Next, we'll take a look at the major parts of the WebMatrix Integrated Development Environment (IDE) and the options we have for opening existing projects and creating new sites. Finally, we'll create our first site and add some dynamic content with some simple server-side functionality.

■ **Note** The purpose of this chapter is to serve as an introduction to the environment and concepts involved with developing web sites with Microsoft WebMatrix—the in-depth technical discussions will come at a later stage; therefore, to avoid confusion, we will pass over some technical details in this chapter. Wherever a feature is used without explanation, I will provide a reference to a later section of the book, where a more detailed explanation can be found.

Installing WebMatrix

The easiest and best way to install WebMatrix is to use the Microsoft Web Platform Installer.

The Microsoft Web Platform Installer 3.0 is a free tool designed to greatly simplify the process of downloading and installing the components of the Microsoft Web Platform, including WebMatrix. Although separate installations of all the Web Platform components can still be downloaded individually from the Microsoft web site, the use of the Web Platform Installer is the preferred method and makes the whole procedure much more straightforward and reliable.

The actual process of installing WebMatrix will differ slightly depending whether or not you already have the Web Platform Installer available on your machine; we will look at both scenarios here.

Getting WebMatrix If You Don't Already Have the Web Platform Installer

If you don't already have the Web Platform Installer 3.0, you can easily download it and automatically set it and WebMatrix up in one process. To do this, go to

`http://www.microsoft.com/web/`

This will take you to the Microsoft Web Platform home page, as seen in Figure 2-1.

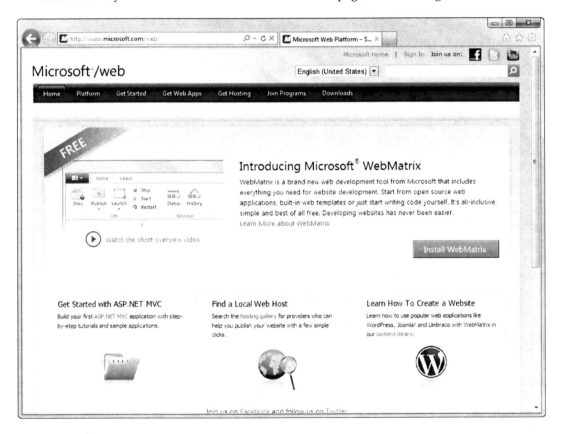

Figure 2-1. *The Microsoft Web Platform home page*

■ **Tip** This site also has some great additional information about Microsoft WebMatrix and links to further tutorials, forums, and other resources on the ASP.NET web site.

Click the green `Install WebMatrix` button on this page and `Install Now` on the next and you will be directed to the Web Platform Installer 3.0 installation page. At this point, depending on your choice of browser and Windows settings, you may be prompted for permission to run the installer; or, as shown in Figure 2-2, you may receive a notification from Windows User Account Control, which you should accept.

Figure 2-2. Choose 'Yes' if presented with the User Account Control dialog box.

Once the Web Platform Installer has launched, it will automatically prompt you to install Microsoft WebMatrix. Click `Install` and read and accept the terms of the license. Again, the installer may take 5–10 minutes to complete, depending on your PC hardware and Internet connection speed.

Getting WebMatrix via the Web Platform Installer

If you have previously installed the Web Platform Installer, you can open it via the Windows Start Menu from Start All Programs Microsoft Web Platform Installer, using the shortcut shown in Figure 2-3.

Figure 2-3. The Web Platform Installer shortcut in the Windows Start menu

Once the Web Platform Installer has fired up, you can find the option to install WebMatrix either by using the built-in search facility or choosing the Products menu at the top of the screen, selecting the Tools submenu on the left, and scrolling down to Microsoft WebMatrix. It's then simply a matter of clicking the `Add` button (see Figure 2-4) and then `Install`.

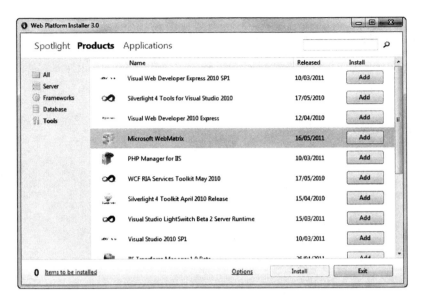

***Figure 2-4.** The Microsoft Web Platform Installer 3.0*

After you click Install, you will be directed to the license screen, where you will need to read and accept the license terms of each of the products about to be installed (see Figure 2-5). Click I Accept and all the components of WebMatrix that you do not already have installed, or that you have installed but require updating, will be downloaded to your machine and set up.

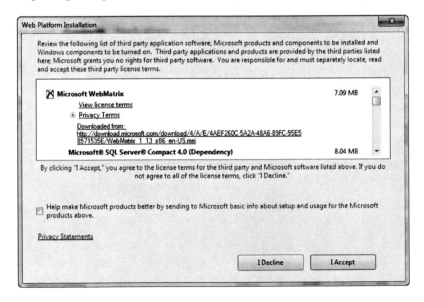

***Figure 2-5.** Accepting the license terms*

The installer may take 5–10 minutes to complete, depending on your PC hardware and Internet connection speed. Once the install has successfully completed, you will be shown the congratulations message, seen here in Figure 2-6.

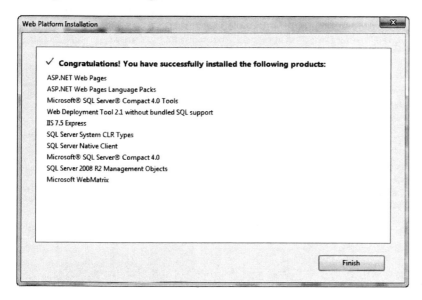

Figure 2-6. A successful install of WebMatrix

Once the installation is complete, click Finish to be taken directly to the WebMatrix QuickStart page, as shown in Figure 2-7.

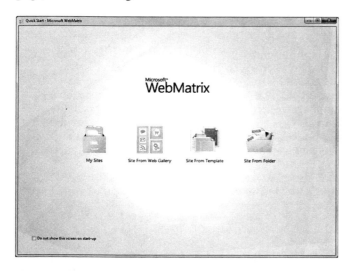

Figure 2-7. The Microsoft WebMatrix QuickStart page

What's in the box?

WebMatrix can be described as a web development stack, or toolset, in that it is a collection of separate components that combine to create a single, integrated development experience. Rather than being a distinct application or programming framework, it combines a web server with a database and ASP.NET Web Pages, all of which are manipulated via a single Integrated Development Environment (IDE). Figure 2-8 shows this relationship.

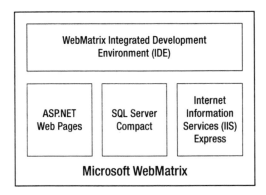

Figure 2-8. The WebMatrix toolset

The four major components of WebMatrix are the IDE, ASP.NET Web Pages, IIS 7.5 Express, and Microsoft SQL Server Compact 4.0. However, the Web Platform Installer actually installs 10 different components as part of the WebMatrix package. Let's take a look at each of these 10 components to help us fully understand our toolbox.

ASP.NET Web Pages

ASP.NET Web Pages provide the programmable User Interface (UI) for your web application. Web Page output is created dynamically on the server for display in any Web browser or mobile device using a combination of client-side and server-side code and markup.

ASP.NET Web Pages are built on the Microsoft .NET Framework, a managed environment that provides important services, such as memory management, security, type safety, and access to the .NET Base Class Library, a standard library available to all .NET languages that encapsulates a large number of common programming functions. Although this book concentrates on writing this server-side code in C#, ASP.NET Web Pages are compatible with any language supported by the .NET Common Language Runtime (CLR), such as Visual Basic.

Over the course of this book, you will learn to design and create your own web sites using ASP.NET Web Pages to deliver dynamic content to the user's web browser.

IIS 7.5 Express

IIS 7.5 Express is a lightweight, desktop version of Microsoft Internet Information Services that is optimized for use on a standalone machine during development. Internet Information Services is a web server application used to deliver ASP.NET and PHP pages to browsers. IIS Express is a scaled-down version: it does not require administrator user rights and is designed to run locally on the web developer's machine for testing and debugging purposes. As IIS Express contains all the core capabilities of the full version of IIS, you can be confident that, barring configuration differences, a site that runs locally under IIS Express will also work on a web host running the full version.

IIS 7.5 Express is a seamlessly integrated part of the WebMatrix platform. As you develop web sites using WebMatrix, you will use IIS 7.5 Express for testing and debugging. It starts automatically when you first run your site from the IDE and very little (if any) configuration is usually required. Once the web site is complete, it can be moved to a production server with a full IIS installation or published to a web host using the Web Deployment Tool.

SQL Server Compact 4.0

Microsoft SQL Server Compact 4.0 is the default database for WebMatrix. It has been optimized and tuned for ASP.NET web applications and can scale up to a database size of 4 GB. The database is file-based (.sdf files) and does not require a separate database engine—SQL Server Compact automatically runs when your application runs and shuts down when your application shuts down. SQL Server Compact databases are created and administered directly from within the WebMatrix IDE.

The file-based database is entirely self-contained and runs in memory, so SQL Server Compact databases do not require any configuration on the server and can be uploaded as part of the site. SQL Server Compact is fit for use in a live web application and can be easily migrated to different versions of the SQL Server family of products, should the need arise.

You will use SQL Server Compact extensively throughout this book as you learn to create custom dynamic data-driven web sites with Microsoft WebMatrix.

Microsoft WebMatrix

The Microsoft WebMatrix installation refers to the WebMatrix Integrated Development Environment (IDE). The IDE provides a functional and seamless interface for creating ASP.NET Web Pages; administering IIS Express and SQL Server Compact; installing third-party open source web applications, such as WordPress, Joomla!, and Umbraco; deploying to web hosting providers; and much more.

By the end of this book, you will have become very well acquainted with the WebMatrix IDE and all of its functionality.

Other Components

ASP.NET Web Pages, IIS Express, SQL Server Compact, and the WebMatrix IDE are the four main components of the WebMatrix toolbox. The rest of the following components, which are installed by the Web Platform Installer, are there to support them and enable them to interact:

- The *Microsoft SQL Server Compact 4.0 Tools* component provides the tooling within the WebMatrix IDE for creating and administering SQL Server Compact 4.0 databases.

- The *SQL Server System CLR Types* package contains the components for implementing the geometry, geography, and hierarchyid types in SQL Server.

- The *SQL Server Native Client* is the component containing the database driver.

- The *SQL Server Management Objects* component is a collection of objects that automates the management of the SQL Server. WebMatrix uses this component to perform administrative tasks on the database.

- The *ASP.NET Web Pages Language Packs* contain translated text, such as error messages, for languages other than English. Without the Language Pack, these messages are displayed in English by default.

- The *Web Deployment Tool* manages the deployment and synchronization of WebMatrix web sites to IIS hosting providers from within the IDE.

Getting Started with WebMatrix Web Sites

In this section, we'll get our hands dirty and build our first WebMatrix application. The application we create here will use three of the four major components of the WebMatrix toolbox: ASP.NET Web Pages, IIS 7.5 Express, and the WebMatrix IDE (Chapter 6: "Working with Data" contains detailed information on the use of the SQL Server Compact component).

Enter the Matrix: Creating Your First Site

When you run the WebMatrix application, you are presented with the WebMatrix QuickStart page (see Figure 2-7). Figure 2-9 shows the four options for working with a WebMatrix project from the QuickStart page.

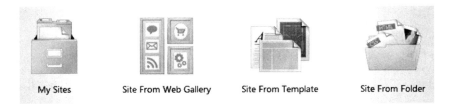

Figure 2-9. *The four options available on the QuickStart page*

Each of these options presents a different way to either open an existing web site or create a new one. Generally, when creating a bespoke WebMatrix application, you will either create a Site from Template or open My Sites to view a list of previously created projects. However, in the interest of completeness, we will look at all four available options here, as each one offers unique features and benefits.

My Sites

This option opens a dialog box that allows you to browse through your existing sites to choose the one you wish to work on. WebMatrix stores web sites by default in the My Web Sites folder of the user's documents library (C:\Users\[username]\Documents\My Web Sites on Windows 7); however, the My

Sites dialog box will list all the sites that you have ever opened in WebMatrix, regardless of their actual location(s).

As you learn WebMatrix, you will doubtless create tens (or even hundreds!) of web sites to test code and ideas. Your My Sites list can very quickly become cluttered, making it difficult to find the project you wish to open. To remove a site from the My Sites dialog box, you can right-click the relevant site and choose delete from the context menu. You will then be shown the Delete Site dialog box, as seen in Figure 2-10.

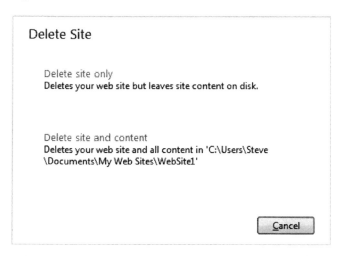

Figure 2-10. *The Delete Site dialog box*

The Delete Site dialog box gives you the opportunity to simply remove the site from the choices in the My Sites dialog, or delete the site and content completely, erasing both the entry in the My Sites dialog box and the physical files from disk.

▓ **Tip** The web sites that you create for testing code and ideas will seldom be more than a few hundred kilobytes each, often less. Unless you are particularly short of disk space, or are certain that you will never need to refer to your test code again, it is often worth choosing to delete the site only; this way, you will keep your My Sites list free of clutter, but you will always be able to open your site in the future using the Site from Folder option on the QuickStart page.

Site from Web Gallery

WebMatrix contains a built-in Web Gallery that allows you to choose one of many free, open-source web applications that can be automatically downloaded and installed locally. The open-source applications offered in the Web Gallery include a wide variety of the most popular PHP- and ASP.NET-based open-source projects, such as WordPress, Umbraco, Moodle, Joomla!, Dot Net Nuke, ScrewTurn, Wiki, and

Orchard. At the time of writing, over 50 free, open-source web applications are available to download, install, and configure via WebMatrix. The Web Gallery can be seen in Figure 2-11 and offers a great way to kick-start a project by customizing or extending an already-developed application.

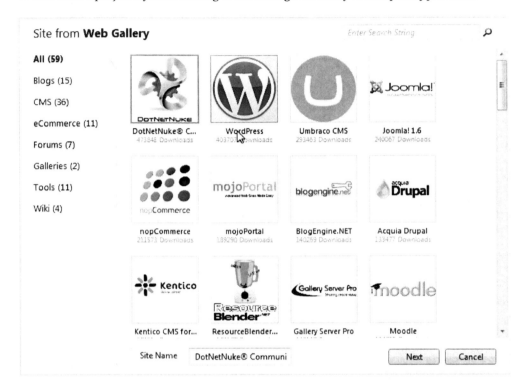

Figure 2-11. The WebMatrix Web Gallery

Once the open-source web application of choice has been downloaded and installed, WebMatrix provides tools to configure the site to your specifications.

As an example, we will install and configure a web site using the popular, PHP-based blogging engine, WordPress. Select WordPress from the `Site from the Web Gallery` screen, enter a site name, and click `Next`. The following screen, shown here in Figure 2-12, is used to choose a database instance.

Figure 2-12. Choosing the database for a WordPress installation

Select install MySQL on your machine and click **Next**. Specify a password for the root user on the following screen, then click **Next** and accept the license agreement. WebMatrix will now automatically download and install all of the components necessary for the WordPress installation; this may take several minutes, depending on your PC and internet connection speed.

Figure 2-13 shows the configuration screen presented by WebMatrix for the configuration of a new WordPress installation. Enter the necessary information and click **Next** to complete the installation.

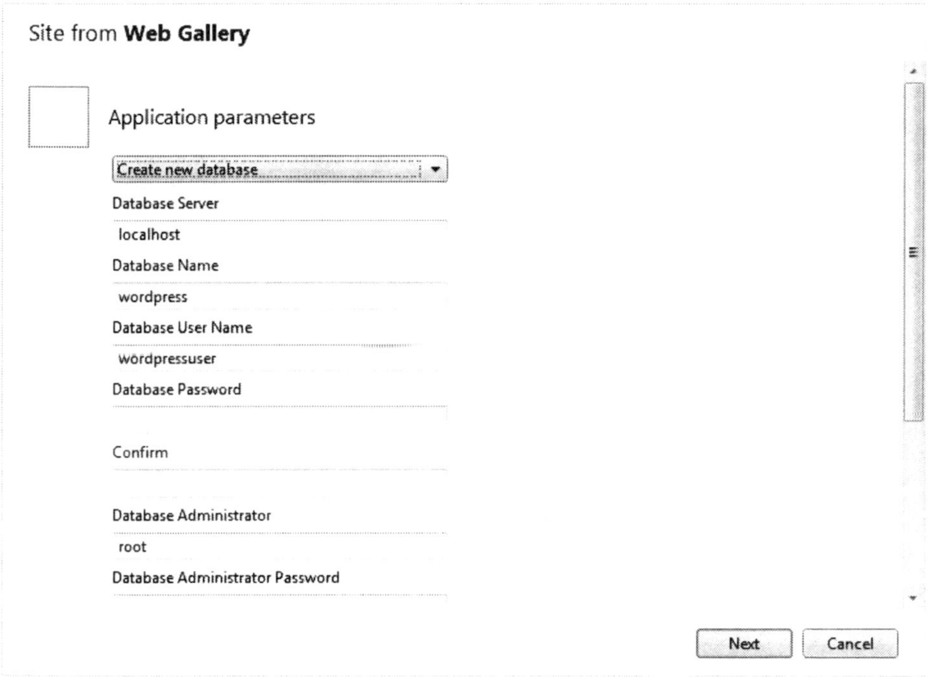

Figure 2-13. Configuring a site from the Web Gallery

Once WebMatrix has finished installing and configuring the application, it will present the confirmation screen, shown here in Figure 2-14.

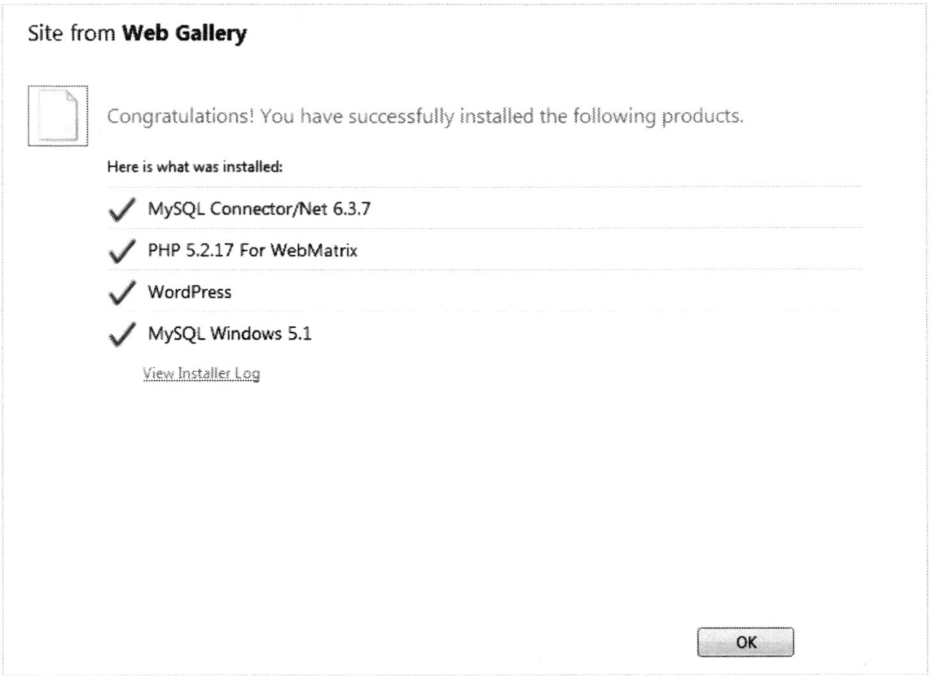

Site from **Web Gallery**

Congratulations! You have successfully installed the following products.

Here is what was installed:

✓ MySQL Connector/Net 6.3.7

✓ PHP 5.2.17 For WebMatrix

✓ WordPress

✓ MySQL Windows 5.1

View Installer Log

OK

Figure 2-14. *Confirmation of a successful WordPress installation*

Finally, click the OK button to open the site in WebMatrix, where it can be run in the browser by clicking the Run button on the Ribbon Control located in the top-left of the screen. Figure 2-15 shows the WordPress application running for the first time in the browser.

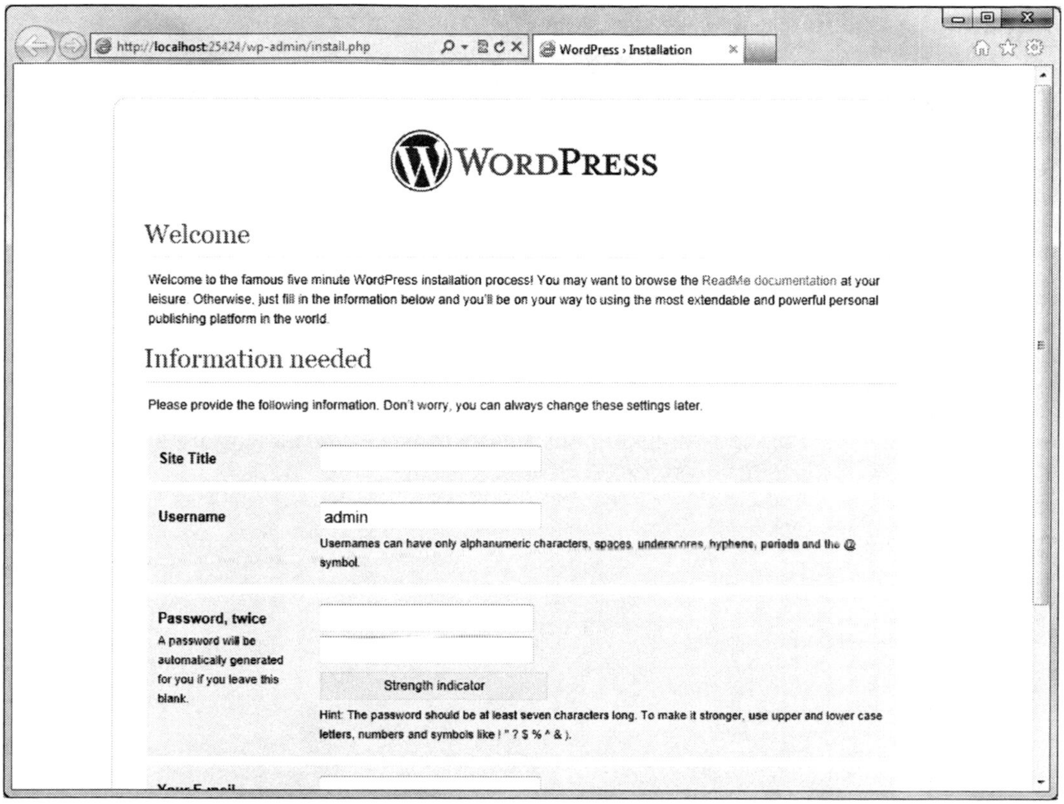

Figure 2-15. *WordPress running in the browser for the first time*

Sites downloaded from the Web Gallery can be run directly on the local machine from the WebMatrix IDE, because IIS Express inherits the ability to serve PHP as well as ASP.NET sites from the full version of Internet Information Services (IIS). This means that WebMatrix can be used to construct both PHP and ASP.NET web sites—a powerful feature!

This process is very simple and requires little (if any) further explanation, so we will not go into it in any more detail. The rest of this book is focused exclusively on teaching you how to create bespoke web sites by creating your own ASP.NET Web Pages.

■ **Tip**　The Windows Web App Gallery can be browsed at http://www.microsoft.com/web/gallery/. The online gallery allows you to see much more information about the applications than you have access to through the Web Gallery built into WebMatrix. The material in the online gallery includes ratings, reviews, screenshots, and links to further resources, such as forums and tutorials. The online gallery is well worth checking out before you make an irreversible decision on the open-source platform you are going to use for your project.

Site from Folder

The Site from Folder option allows you to create a WebMatrix site from any specified folder on disk. This option is particularly useful when a WebMatrix site already physically exists, but has not yet been opened using WebMatrix on the current machine; for example, suppose that a site has been created by another developer and passed on to you for further development, or you wish to use WebMatrix to add some dynamic content to an existing static HTML site.

Another common use for this option involves forcing WebMatrix to create a new site in a location other than the default (C:\Users\[username]\Documents\My Web Sites); for example, on a network drive. If you often find yourself wishing to create a site in a location other than the My Web Sites folder, the default site location can be changed in the Options menu in the WebMatrix IDE.

Site from Template

To create a new WebMatrix site in the default location, choose the Site from Template option. This will open the Site from Template dialog box, shown in Figure 2-16.

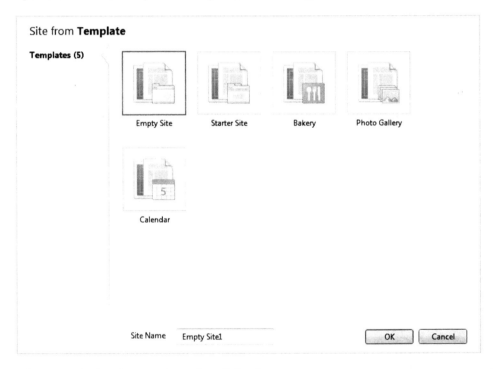

Figure 2-16. *The Site From Template dialog box*

Templates are, as the name suggests, pre-built starting points for developing new ASP.NET Web Page applications. As we will see, a template can contain any number of files, folders, and features. A template can be anything from a bare-bones set of folders to a functional web application. The important thing to remember is that they are intended only as starting points for developing custom applications, not as ready–to–deploy applications in their own right. We will now explore WebMatrix's five default templates.

Empty Site

The Empty Site template sets up a folder with the name you specify in the Site from Template dialog box in the default site location. The new folder contains only one file, robots.txt. This template is ideal if you do not wish to implement any of the functionality provided by the other templates, or you just want to test some code without the overhead or distraction of one of the larger templates. We will use this template throughout the course of this book, as it will help you gain a more complete knowledge of building web applications in WebMatrix.

Robots.txt

Robots.txt is a text file that restricts access to all or part of your web site via search engine robots. The file contains instructions in a specific format that robots can follow when fetching data from the site. For example, a robots.txt file may instruct web crawling robots not to visit—and therefore not to index in a search engine—parts of a web site that contain temporary pages for proofreading or testing, or personal images.

It is very important to note that search engine spiders' and other web robots' adherence to the Robots Exclusion Protocol by is purely advisory and in no way guarantees privacy. You must still ensure that all confidential information is password protected.

Visit http://www.robotstxt.org for more information about Robots.txt and the Robots Exclusion Protocol.

Starter Site

Back in the Site Template window, click the Starter Site icon and then click OK. This will create a small example web site, based on the Starter Site template, which you can use as a starting point for your own applications. Clicking the Run button in the Ribbon Control at the top left-hand side of the screen (see Figure 2-17) will open the site in your default web browser, shown in Figure 2-18. The template produces a web site that has a pre-built membership and authentication system alongside a professionally designed layout and navigation structure.

Run

Figure 2-17. Click the Run button in WebMatrix to open the site in your default browser.

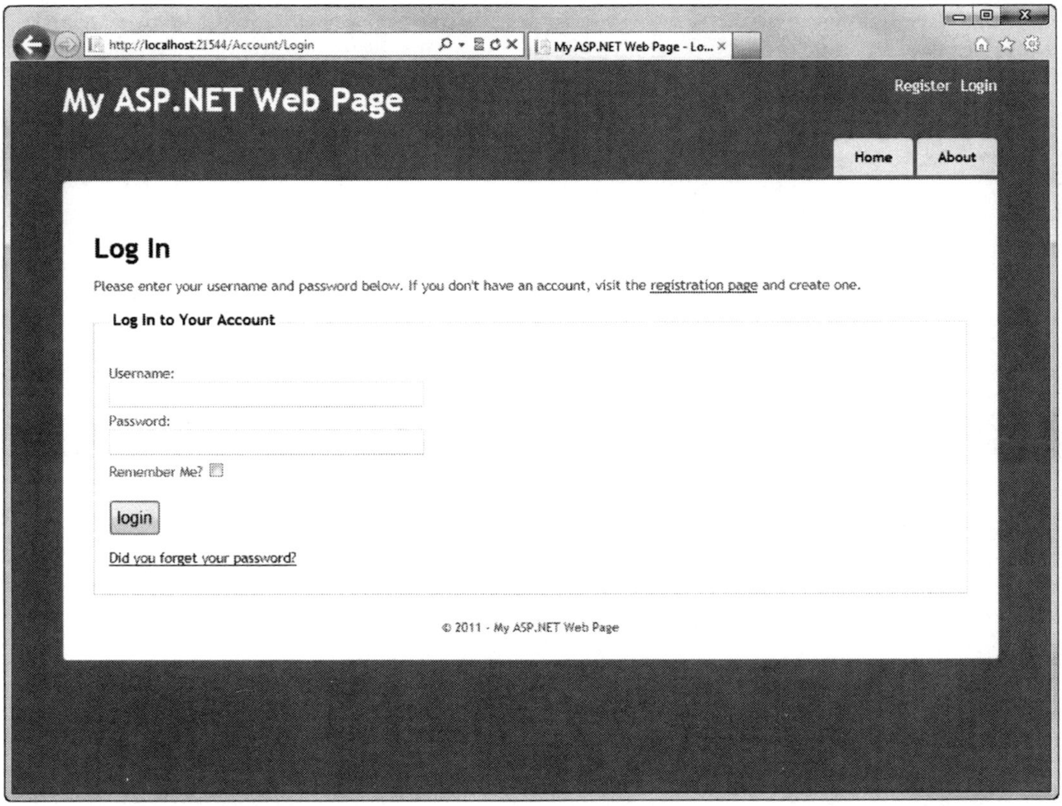

Figure 2-18. *The Starter Site template*

To previous users of ASP.NET Web Forms or ASP.NET MVC, the Starter Site template will probably look very familiar. The template contains Home and About pages, as well as nine pages in a folder named Account, which provide sample code related to membership, registration, and authentication. The Starter Site template also includes an SQL Server Compact database used to store membership, role, and profile information (see Chapter 7: "Security and Membership"). The site layout is controlled using layout pages (see Chapter 4: "Working with Razor and ASP.NET Web Pages"), which can be customized easily using Cascading Style Sheets (CSS).

Bakery, Photo Gallery, and Calendar Templates

The remaining three templates found in the `Site From Template` screen (see Figure 2-16)—Bakery, Photo Gallery, and Calendar—create sample web sites that include code to perform various common tasks. They serve as valuable learning aids to assist developers who wish to implement similar ideas and features.

As with the Starter Site template, WebMatrix makes creating sites based on these templates a very simple process. In each case, you simply need to select the required template from the `Site From`

Template screen, name the site, and click Next. Once WebMatrix has created the site, it can be run in the browser by clicking the Run button in the Ribbon Control, located in the top left-hand side of the screen.

The Bakery template (shown in Figure 2-19) creates a sample e-commerce web site that includes a database of products the user can "purchase" through an order processing system. The order processing system also features some basic forms of validation code and code to send emails to customers for order confirmation. The web site also includes some social networking integration via Twitter.

The Photo Gallery template (see Figure 2-20) creates a site that allows users to upload and display images in galleries. The site also makes extensive use of the membership system and includes an SQL Server Compact database to store user details, comments, and galleries. Some more advanced code is included to perform various image manipulations, such as rotation and thumbnail generation.

The Calendar template (see Figure 2-21) generates a site that allows registered users to create and share calendars online. Site users can create calendars and events, choose other users to share their calendars with, and even download their entire calendars or individual events in iCalendar format for import into other scheduling applications, such as Microsoft Outlook, Google Calendar, or Apple iCal. The Calendar template also demonstrates the use of themes to style an application.

■ **Tip**   Generate sites based on the Bakery, Photo Gallery, and Calendar templates and study them in detail. This way, you'll know instantly where to go to grab some sample code to help you implement similar features in a future project of your own.

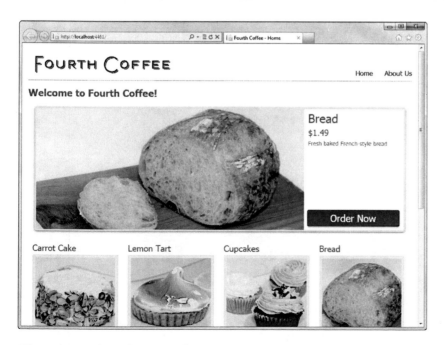

Figure 2-19. The Bakery Template—an example e-commerce site

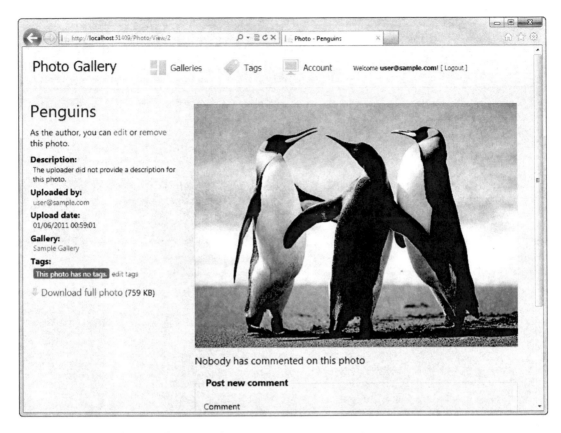

Figure 2-20. The Photo Gallery Template

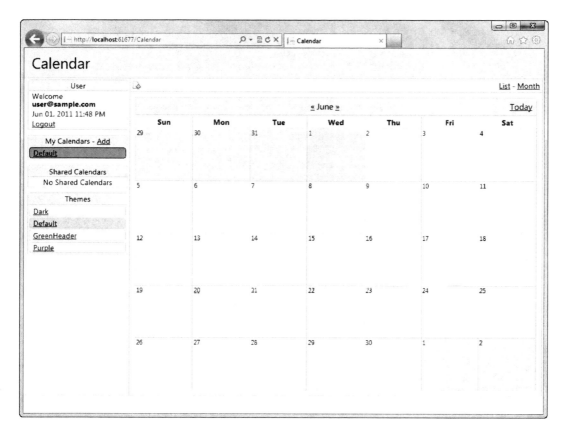

Figure 2-21. *The Calendar Template*

Our First WebMatrix Application

We are going to create our first web site using the Empty Site template to avoid any of the distractions of the other templates. Choose the Empty Site template, enter the name of your site as "Hello World" in the Site Name textbox, and click the OK button.

■ **Note** When naming a project, it is important to use a name that describes the contents and functionality of the site. In six-month's time, you will not remember what "Empty Site27" does, but you will remember the purpose of "Hello World" or "BlogEngine." The same rule applies when naming pages within your site and elements within the pages themselves. A good naming convention can make a site much more maintainable in the future.

The WebMatrix IDE: A Quick Tour

Once you have created your "Hello World" site, the WebMatrix IDE will open. Before we move on with the development of our first application, let's take a few minutes to familiarize ourselves with the WebMatrix IDE.

The WebMatrix Integrated Development Environment (IDE) is, as the name suggests, a software application that allows the developer to interact with all of the different components of WebMatrix from a single user interface. The concept of an IDE has been around since the 1970s on many different platforms, and is a well-developed and proven way to increase developer productivity and efficiency. The WebMatrix IDE is quite basic compared to some (see the "Alternatives to the WebMatrix IDE" section later in this chapter); however, this is not necessarily a bad thing—it is fully functional and contains everything you need to develop and deploy WebMatrix applications. The following screenshot in Figure 2-22 shows the WebMatrix IDE, as you will see it upon the creation of a new empty site:

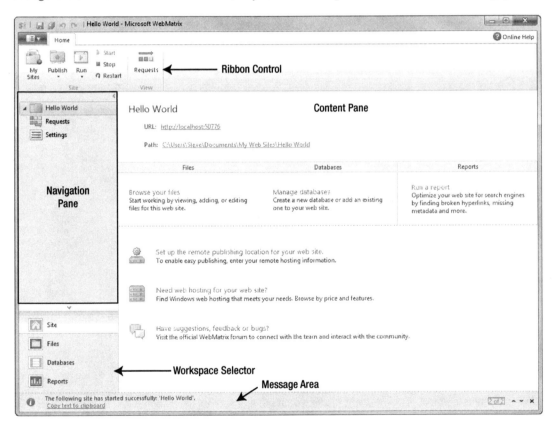

Figure 2-22. The WebMatrix IDE

■ **Tip**   There is a well-known phrase among experienced developers: "Know Your IDE." Everything you need to create a web application can be accomplished through the WebMatrix IDE; you are going to spend a lot of time using it. Therefore, if you know how to use it efficiently and effectively, you can really increase your productivity. Taking the time to learn keyboard shortcuts, where to go to perform specific common tasks, and how to customize the IDE according to your preferences will pay dividends.

The IDE contains five distinct areas. Let's look at them in more detail.

The Workspace Selector

The Workspace Selector (see Figure 2-23) is located in the lower left-hand side of the IDE by default. It allows you to choose one of the four workspaces available within the IDE: Site, Files, Databases, or Reports. Workspaces are used to group the tasks involved in creating WebMatrix sites into areas of common functionality within the IDE. Each workspace contains a set of tools specifically designed for each task. Almost every task that you can conduct within the WebMatrix IDE will be found inside one of these workspaces.

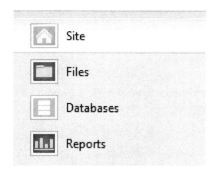

Figure 2-23. The Workspace Selector

The contents of the other elements in the IDE will change according to your workspace selection. Therefore, it is important to know which workspace you require to perform a particular task.

- **Site**: When you open a new or existing site in WebMatrix, the IDE will always start in the Site workspace. The Site workspace lets you perform site-wide tasks, such as managing server settings and monitoring HTTP requests.

- **Files:** The Files workspace is where you will spend the majority of your time in WebMatrix. The Files workspace displays the site's file and folder structure in the Navigation Pane (located in the top left-hand side of the IDE by default). Double-clicking an individual file in the Navigation Pane opens the file for editing in the Content Pane (the main area in the center of the IDE).

- **Databases:** All activity regarding database management is carried out within the Databases workspace; here, you can connect to existing databases, create and view databases and tables, and edit their contents directly.

- **Reports:** The final workspace is the Reports workspace. The Reports workspace enables you to create and view site analysis reports to provide you with useful information about the performance of your site and Search Engine Optimization (SEO).

The Ribbon Control

Across the full width of the window at the top of the page is the Ribbon control (see Figure 2-24), which gives quick access to common tasks and will be familiar to users of other Microsoft products, particularly Microsoft Office. The content of the Ribbon control changes contextually, based on the current selection in the Workspace Selector and Navigation Pane (see the following), with the exception of the Site panel on the far left of the Ribbon Control, which remains constant.

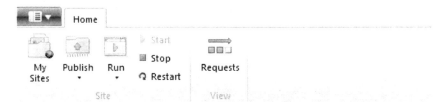

Figure 2-24. *The content of the Ribbon Control changes contextually.*

On the far right-hand side of the Ribbon Control is a small button labeled "Online Help." This button will open the online help documentation on the Microsoft web site.

The Navigation and Content Panes

Below the Ribbon control are the Navigation and Content Panes (see Figure 2-25).

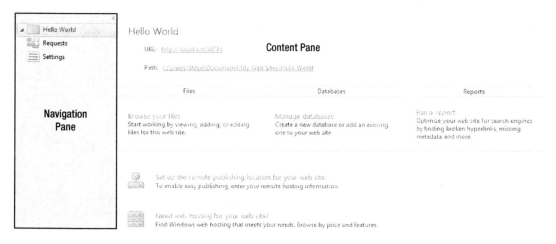

Figure 2-25. *The Navigation Pane (left) and Content Pane (right)*

The contents of the Navigation Pane change automatically, according to the current selection in the Workspace Selector. For instance, in the Files workspace, the Navigation Pane lists all the files within the current site, whereas in the Database workspace, the Navigation Pane allows you to navigate through database connections and tables.

The Content Pane takes up the majority of the screen real-estate. The contents of the Content Pane are determined by the selection in the Workspace Selector, Ribbon Control, and Navigation Pane. The Content Pane is where you will actually carry out the tasks involved in developing your web sites; for instance, the Content Pane can display a code editor for editing code and markup, a database table designer, or a performance report, depending on the current activity.

The Notifications Area

The final area of the IDE worth noting is the Notifications Area, which appears from time to time as a yellow bar across the bottom of the screen with any system messages, as shown in Figure 2-26. The Notifications Area is not a permanent fixture and disappears after a short delay once messages have been displayed.

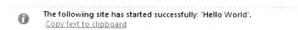

Figure 2-26. *The Notifications Area*

Alternatives to the WebMatrix IDE

Although it is an excellent tool, you are not restricted to using only the WebMatrix IDE to edit ASP.NET Web Pages. If you have Microsoft Visual Studio or Visual Web Developer installed, you will notice a Visual Studio button on the Ribbon Control when working in the Files workspace. Clicking this button will launch the site in Visual Studio or Visual Web Developer, where you will be able to take advantage of its more sophisticated features including debugging and IntelliSense. Experienced Visual Studio users will probably find this approach beneficial. It is worth noting that Visual Studio opens the project as a Web Site rather than as a Web Application.

You can also edit ASP.NET Web Pages in any text editor, such as Notepad or Notepad++. However, the WebMatrix IDE has the advantage of providing integrated access to all the WebMatrix components and is free to download (as is Visual Web Developer). We will be using the WebMatrix IDE throughout this book.

Adding a Page to Your Site

To view your web site in a browser, you can click the Run button in the Ribbon Control. This will open your default browser and display the web site. Clicking the down arrow underneath the word "Run" will drop down a list of all the browsers you have installed on your development machine (see Figure 2-27). You will also have the option to open the site in all installed browsers. This is an incredibly useful feature for ensuring that your site is compatible with all the major web browsers.

■ **Note** Cross-browser compatibility issues can be a real headache, even for experienced web developers. Historically, different browsers have implemented web "standards" in HTML, JavaScript, and CSS in slightly different ways, leading to situations where a single page could look dramatically different from browser to browser, or even not work at all. The situation has improved a great deal in recent years and many strategies have been developed to minimize its impact, but some differences do remain. Therefore, it is essential that you fully test your sites in all popular browsers before deployment; otherwise, you could find yourself in a situation where your site simply doesn't work for a large percentage of your intended audience.

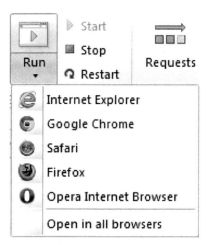

Figure 2-27. WebMatrix makes it easy to run your web site in any browser.

If you click the Run button now, you will see that IIS Express generates a 404 Not Found error (similar to the one shown in Figure 2-28), which is displayed by the browser.

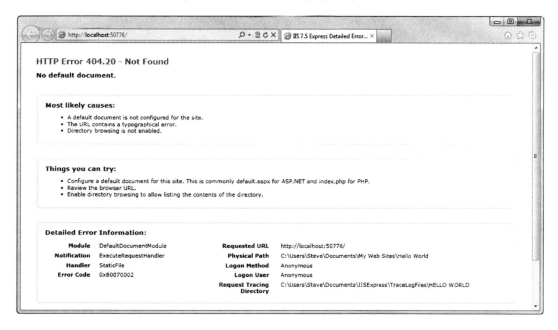

Figure 2-28. The browser displays a 404 Not Found error, as no default page currently exists in our site.

The browser is displaying this error because we don't have any pages to display in our web site. By default, if no specific page is requested from a URL, IIS will attempt to find and display a page named

35

something like `Default.cshtml` or `Index.htm`. Let's create our default page. Back in the WebMatrix IDE, select the `Files` workspace in the Workspace Selector and choose `New` from the Ribbon Control or click the `Create a new file` button in the centre of the Content Pane. This will open the Choose a File Type dialog box (see Figure 2-29).

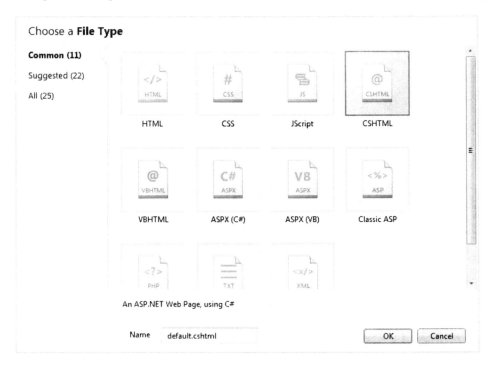

Figure 2-29. *The Choose a File Type dialog box is displayed when adding a new file to the web site.*

There are 25 different types of files that WebMatrix can add to your site; although, there are only seven that you will commonly add to your site through this dialog.

- HTML: A simple, static HyperText Markup Language (HTML) page
- CSHTML: A C# based ASP.NET Web Page page (more on this in Chapter 4: "Working with Razor and ASP.NET Web Pages")
- VBHTML: A VB.NET based ASP.NET Web Page
- CSS: A Cascading Style Sheet (CSS) file
- Jscript: A JavaScript file
- TXT: A blank text file
- XML: An eXtensible Markup Language file

Choose to add a CSHTML file and name it `Default.cshtml` and click OK. The page will be created and displayed in the text editor in the Content Pane.

▓ **Note** You may have noticed the options for creating ASP.NET Web Forms (.aspx) and Classic ASP (.asp) files in the screenshot in Figure 2-29. These are included for compatibility reasons. All dynamic ASP.NET Web Pages' files have a .cshtml or .vbhtml file extension.

Working with the HTML

You will notice that the page created for you contains just the usual HTML elements that you would expect to see in any static HTML page—<html>, <head>, <title>, <body>, etc.

```
<!DOCTYPE html>

<html lang="en">
    <head>
        <meta charset="utf-8" />
        <title></title>
    </head>
    <body>

    </body>
</html>
```

What about the .cshtml file extension? Well, the .cshtml file extension tells the web server that this page contains Razor code. Razor code is simply C# (or VB) code, placed inline within standard HTML markup. The code is inserted using a special Razor syntax (more in Chapter 4: "Working with Razor and ASP.NET Web Pages"), wherever we want the server to perform a dynamic action, such as displaying a table of data from a database or calculating values based on user input. Put simply, you can layout an HTML page the same way you always have and just insert some Razor code wherever you want the server to produce some dynamic content. This will become clearer as we move through this example. In the meantime, just to prove that we still use plain old HTML for presentation, let's add a title to the <head> and some markup to the page.

```
<!DOCTYPE html>

<html lang="en">
    <head>
        <meta charset="utf-8" />
        <title>Hello World</title>
    </head>
    <body>
        <h1>Hello World!</h1>
        <ul>
            <li>
                Bonjour tout le monde
```

```
            </li>
            <li>
                Hallo Welt
            </li>
            <li>
                Ciao mondo
            </li>
            <li>
                Hola mundo
            </li>
        </ul>
    </body>
</html>
```

You will notice that as you type the opening tag of an HTML element, a small popup menu, like the one shown in Figure 2-30, appears next to the cursor.

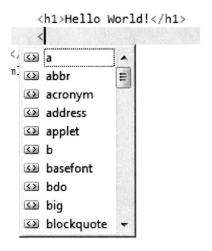

Figure 2-30. *Hint menus are designed to aid developer productivity.*

This menu, also known as *hinting*, displays a list of all the valid HTML tags that can be displayed at the current cursor position. For instance, if you are inside a pair of <ul>...</ul> tags, the only option in the hint menu when you type an opening angle bracket will be <li>, as this is the only legal tag within an un-ordered list according to World Wide Web Consortium (W3C) HTML specifications.

This list will narrow as you continue typing; or, you can scroll through the list using the scrollbar or the up/down arrows on your keyboard. Once you have found the element you want to use, it can be inserted into the page by pressing `return`, `tab`, the `spacebar`, or double-clicking with the mouse.

If you enter a space directly after a tag name, a second hint menu will be displayed, like the one in Figure 2-31. This menu displays all the possible attributes for the tag you have just entered, which can be chosen in the same way as the previous hint menu.

■ **Tip**   If you move the selection cursor over an item in the hint menu, or single-click an item with the mouse, a tooltip will be displayed; it provides more information about the item, including the name of the element, a brief description, and the URL of the HTML namespace.

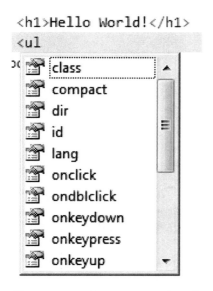

Figure 2-31. The HTML attribute hint menu

Notice also that closing tags are automatically created when you close the opening tag, and that the markup in the Content Pane's code editor is colored. This colorization of the markup in the code editor is known as *syntax highlighting*. Syntax highlighting is a useful aid that helps you quickly navigate the code and spot mistakes in the markup, such as malformed or incorrectly nested tags. All of these added features in the WebMatrix IDE's code editor make it much more fun to use and contribute to a marked increase in developer productivity over a plain text editor.

Now, let's run the page again by clicking the Run button on the Ribbon Control (or by pressing F12 or Alt + H, then R; see the following Keyboard Shortcuts). You will see the page displayed, as seen in Figure 2-32.

Figure 2-32. Hello World!

Well, this is hardly ground-breaking stuff, but it does prove that the presentation markup within a Razor-based page is simply HTML.

Keyboard Shortcuts

Many developers like to use keyboard shortcuts in their IDE to perform common tasks. It makes total sense—your hands are likely already on it—so you can save quite a bit of time and effort: instead of hunting through the user interface (UI) with the mouse, all you need to do is memorize the keyboard shortcuts. The following is a list of the keyboard shortcuts available in the WebMatrix IDE.

Launch Site in Browser	F12
Close Site	Control + Shift + F4
Switch to Sites Workspace	Control + Shift + 1
Switch to Files Workspace	Control + Shift + 2
Switch to Databases Workspace	Control + Shift + 3
Switch to Reports Workspace	Control + Shift + 4
Switch to Next Workspace	Control + Shift + W
Close Current Tab	Control + F4 or Control + W
Cycle to Next Tab	Control + Tab
Cycle to Previous Tab	Control + Shift + Tab
Tab Well Drop Down Menu	Control + Shift + T
(displays a list of currently open tabs)	
Add New File from Template	Control + N
Add Existing File	Control + Alt + A

Open	`Control + O`
Find	`Control + F`
Find Next	`F3`
Find Previous	`Shift + F3`
Replace	`Control + H`
Go To Line	`Control + G`
Select All	`Control + A`
Copy	`Control + C` or `Control + Insert`
Cut	`Control + X` or `Shift + Delete`
Paste	`Control + V` or `Shift + Insert`
Undo	`Control + Z` or `Alt + Backspace`
Redo	`Control + Shift + Z` or `Control + Y`
Refresh	`F5`
Save	`Control + S`
Save All	`Control + Shift + S`
Launch Online Help	`F1`

Alternatively, you can press the `Alt` key to display top-level key tips on the Ribbon Control, which can then be activated using the indicated keys. This will be familiar to users of Microsoft Office, where the same functionality exists in the Ribbon Control.

Adding Some Razor Code

Now that we have a static page working and displaying correctly, let's add some dynamic content by inserting some in-line C# Razor code. Add this markup in `Default.cshtml` between the `</h1>` end tag and the `<ul>` start tag:

```
<p>The date and time here is @DateTime.Now</p>
```

When you run the site, you will see something similar to the output shown in Figure 2-33, but with the current date and time set to wherever you are in the world.

Figure 2-33. *The output of your first line of Razor code*

■ **Note** Razor code can be written using C# or Visual Basic .NET. In this book, all the code samples will be written exclusively in C#.

To display dynamic content, Razor code is inserted in-line with the HTML using the @ character to denote the start of a block of code. One of the things that makes Razor really stand out from other in-line code models, such as Classic ASP or PHP, is the lack of a closing tag. Razor has semantic knowledge of C# and VB.NET code and is able to use that knowledge to identify where the code finishes and the markup begins.

You will learn much more about Razor in Chapter 4; for now, you just need to know that the use of the @ symbol in a .cshtml or .vbhtml file tells the Razor parser that this is the start of a code block.

So what does the line we added to our Default.cshtml actually do? Well, the majority of it is just a simple HTML paragraph; the interesting bit is shown here in bold:

```
<p>The date and time here is @DateTime.Now</p>
```

As we know, the @ symbol tells the Razor parser that this is the start of a code statement. Since this is a .cshtml file, the parser knows that any code following an @ character will be in C# (although in this simple case, the code is actually identical in VB.NET), so the parser reads in the next set of characters: DateTime.Now. When the parser looks at the next character, which in this case is an angle bracket from the closing paragraph tag, it identifies that this is not valid C#, so it outputs the current date and time to the browser and switches back to HTML mode. The parser will continue outputting HTML until it parses the next @ symbol.

This code is run every time the page is requested from the server. If you refresh the page in the browser by pressing F5, you will notice that the time updates, and it will do so every time the page is served.

It is also worth noting that the web server's date and time is output to the response stream, as this code is running on the server as opposed to the client machine. This is important to take into account, since it is possible that the user may be in a time zone different from the web server.

Let's add some more C# Razor code to our page to provide a little more interaction. First, let's add a simple HTML form to accept our user's name.

```
<!DOCTYPE html>

<html lang="en">
    <head>
        <meta charset="utf-8" />
        <title>Hello World</title>
    </head>
    <body>
        <h1>Hello World!</h1>
        <p>The date and time here is @DateTime.Now</p>
        <form method="post" action="">
            <div>
                <label for="Username">Please enter your name:</label>
                <input type="text" name="Username" />
                <input type="submit" value="Go" />
            </div>
        </form>
        <ul>
            <li>
                Bonjour tout le monde
            </li>
            <li>
                Hallo Welt
            </li>
            <li>
                Ciao mondo
            </li>
            <li>
                Hola mundo
            </li>
        </ul>
    </body>
</html>
```

The page now uses a standard HTML form to gather the username. The `form` tag has its `method` attribute set to `post` and its action left as an empty string, which tells WebMatrix to post the user input back to the same page (`Default.cshtml`) for processing when the user clicks the form's submit button.

Now we'll declare and initialize some variables to hold our greetings. Insert the following code at the very top of the page, above the `<!DOCTYPE html>` tag:

```
@{
    var english = "World";
    var french = "tout le monde";
    var german = "Welt";
    var italian = "mondo";
    var spanish = "mundo";
}
```

43

This code simply declares and initializes five variables, one for each of the languages in our list of greetings, using the **var** keyword. We will use these variables to hold the second part of the greeting for each language for output into our page.

■ **Note** If you have no previous programming experience and the last sentence has left you puzzled, do not panic! The next chapter is a C# Primer where all will be explained—for now, you'll just have to trust me and follow along. Don't worry, I'll keep it simple.

You will notice that the code is enclosed in a pair of braces {...} immediately following the @ symbol, which denotes the start of some Razor code. This is known as a *multi-statement block* and is used to tell the Razor parser that everything inside the braces should be processed as C# code, not as output to the browser.

The variables declared within the multi-statement block are available for use in every subsequent line in that page, so we can display the value held within those variables by calling them from within our un-ordered list.

```
@{
    var english = "World";
    var french = "tout le monde";
    var german = "Welt";
    var italian = "mondo";
    var spanish = "mundo";
}

<!DOCTYPE html>

<html lang="en">
    <head>
        <meta charset="utf-8" />
        <title>Hello World</title>
    </head>
    <body>
        <h1>Hello @english</h1>
        <p>The date and time here is @DateTime.Now</p>
        <form method="post" action="">
            <div>
                <label for="Username">Please enter your name:</label>
                <input type="text" name="Username" />
                <input type="submit" value="Go" />
            </div>
        </form>
        <ul>
            <li>
                Bonjour @french
```

```
            </li>
            <li>
                Hallo @german
            </li>
            <li>
                Ciao @italian
            </li>
            <li>
                Hola @spanish
            </li>
        </ul>
    </body>
</html>
```

If you refresh your browser now, you will see that the output hasn't changed (our variables are being output), but they hold the same values as the static text they replaced. Let's add our final piece of Razor code to accept the user input and personalize the greeting.

We'll use the `IsPost()` method to determine if the page has been posted back to the server; i.e., if the user pressed the submit button on the form. The `IsPost()` method is built into ASP.NET Web Pages and returns `true` if the page is a postback (an HTTP POST request) or `false` for any other type of HTTP request (usually HTTP GET).

On postback, our page will change the values of the greetings variables we set up earlier by requesting the value held within the `Username` text box, adding an appropriate greeting, and assigning the result to the relevant variable. We get the value of the `Username` text box by interrogating the ASP.NET `Request` object and specifying the name of the form field we wish to read.

■ **Note** We'll be covering the `IsPost` method and the `Request` object in greater detail in Chapter 5: "Forms and Validation."

Edit the code within the multi-statement block at the top of the page to look like this:

```
{
    var english = "World";
    var french = "tout le monde";
    var german = "Welt";
    var italian = "mondo";
    var spanish = "mundo";

    if (IsPost)
    {
        english = Request["Username"] + ". Welcome to WebMatrix!";
        french = Request["Username"] + ". Bienvenue a WebMatrix!";
        german = Request["Username"] + ". Willkommen auf WebMatrix!";
        italian = Request["Username"] + ". Benvenuti a WebMatrix!" ;
        spanish = Request["Username"] + ". Bienvenido a WebMatrix!";
    }
```

```
}
<!DOCTYPE html>
<html lang="en">
    <head>
        <meta charset="utf-8" />
        <title>Hello World</title>
    </head>
    <body>
        <h1>Hello @english</h1>
        <p>The date and time here is @DateTime.Now</p>
        <form method="post" action="">
            <div>
                <label for="Username">Please enter your name:</label>
                <input type="text" name="Username" />
                <input type="submit" value="Go" />
            </div>
        </form>
        <ul>
            <li>
                Bonjour @french
            </li>
            <li>
                Hallo @german
            </li>
            <li>
                Ciao @italian
            </li>
            <li>
                Hola @spanish
            </li>
        </ul>
    </body>
</html>
```

Now, when you run the page, enter your name in the textbox and click Go. You will see something similar to Figure 2-34.

Figure 2-34. *Our personalized international greetings!*

On the initial load, our page displays the default greetings, but when a name is entered into the Username textbox and the form is posted back to the server, personalized greetings are constructed and output to the browser.

Summary

We have covered a lot of new information in this chapter. We have seen that WebMatrix is not a single product or application; rather, it is made up of many different components, the four most important of these being the WebMatrix IDE, ASP.NET Web Pages, SQL Server Compact 4.0, and IIS 7.5 Express.

You have also installed WebMatrix on your machine using the Microsoft Web Platform Installer and had a brief introduction to the WebMatrix IDE. We will cover the IDE in a lot more detail throughout the course of this book, as we look at all of its various features.

Finally, you have created your first site using WebMatrix to get an introductory look at how a site built using ASP.NET Web Pages actually works. We have barely scratched the surface of ASP.NET Web Pages and we will be spending a considerable amount of time looking more in-depth at its features and implementation details in the following chapters.

In the next two chapters, we will be looking at C# and Razor in more detail. This foundational knowledge will assist you greatly as you plan out and build custom WebMatrix sites.

■ ■ ■

CHAPTER 3

C# Primer

Before we look any further into ASP.NET Web Pages and WebMatrix, it is important that you have a basic familiarity with the C# programming language and that you understand a few elementary programming concepts. In this chapter, we are going to discuss:

- C# types and variables

- Operators

- Collections

- Conditions and loops

- An introduction to Object Oriented Programming

- Dynamics

The Razor code that we will use in this book to create and display dynamic data within ASP.NET Web Pages will all be built upon C#, so it is essential that you have a solid foundation in the language before we move on any further.

If you already have experience of any of the topics covered in this chapter, you might want to skip ahead. For some readers, this chapter will be totally new material; for others, who perhaps have some programming experience in another language, it will just be a matter of converting to the C# syntax. All readers should bear in mind that, due to size limitations, this chapter is only intended as a C# primer and it is by no means proposed as an exhaustive reference. I provide merely enough content to allow you to progress through the rest of the examples in the book and to prompt further research. I will also point you in the direction of useful references at appropriate points in the text.

▓ **Note** The Razor syntax used when developing ASP.NET Web Pages is based on C# and that is the language that we will use throughout this book. The vast majority of online materials are also based on C#. However, although Razor was originally written for C#, since its initial release it has gained support for the Visual Basic language. The Visual Basic language and the resulting Razor syntax are much more verbose than C# but are popular with developers coming from a Visual Basic or VBScript (Classic ASP) background. Both languages work equally well and the use of one or the other makes little or no difference to the user experience achieved in the end result.

A Brief History of C#

C# is a simple, modern, general-purpose, object-oriented language. It is a C-style language and any readers with experience of languages such as C, C++, or Java will doubtless see many similarities. C# was developed at Microsoft in 1999 as part of the .NET project by a team lead by Anders Hejlsberg, who had previously been involved with the design of the Turbo Pascal, Delphi, and J++ languages. The original goal in designing the language was to use it to write the .NET class libraries and ASP.NET runtime, which was achieved.

C# is an excellent language and it's fun to use. It's also one of the big reasons that so many web developers choose to develop their sites on the Microsoft ASP.NET stack.

So let's dive straight into some code by looking at variables and the various types available for the programmer to use in C#.

Types and Variables

When we want to keep a piece of data in the memory of the computer to work with later, we store it in a variable. You can think of the computer's memory as a huge set of shelves that can store anything you like, as long as it's in a box. The only proviso to being able to store anything you like is that the computer needs to know what sort of thing you want to store beforehand—so that it can give you the right box and allocate enough space on the shelf. This essentially explains variables and types: the variable is the actual item you want to store and the type describes the kind of box you are going to put it in (which in turn determines the space required).

As a program executes, the variables are defined and changed as necessary to support the running of the program and any algorithms that may be defined. A variable can only be used within the scope it is declared. For example, if a variable is declared at the class level, it can be used anywhere within that class. However, if a variable is declared within a block of code, such as within a method or an `if` statement structure, it can only be used within that code block. This is known as a local variable.

■ **Note** Classes, methods and code blocks will be explained fully later in the chapter. Do not worry if you did not fully understand the last paragraph; it will become much clearer as we progress.

To define a variable, we use the following pattern to tell the compiler what type of variable we want to use and by what name we are going to refer to it:

```
Type Identifier;
```

For example to declare an integer (a whole number) for storing the total number of employees at a company, we might say:

```
int totalEmployees;
```

Here `int` is the type of the variable and `totalEmployees` is the identifier. We will discuss the built-in variable types that C# provides later in this chapter. Declared in this way, the local variable `totalEmployees` has not been assigned a value. An uninitialized local variable will throw an error if accessed later in code (see Figure 3-1).

■ **Note** All .NET built-in types have a default value that is automatically given to an uninitialized variable declared at the class level. In the case of an `int`, for example, the default value is 0. However, it is good practice to always explicitly initialize your variables because it's important to be certain exactly what is being stored.

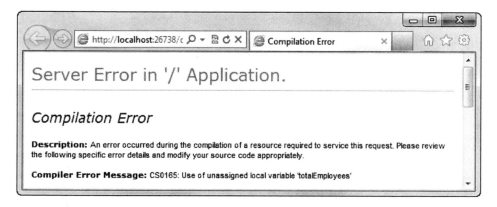

Figure 3-1. Use of an unassigned local variable will cause an error.

We can initialize a variable at the point of declaration by doing the following:

```
int totalEmployees = 100;
```

This code initializes our `totalEmployees` integer with a value of 100. We can change the value of that variable by using an assignment. In this example, we will double the number of employees:

```
totalEmployees = 200;
```

■ **Caution**   As you follow along with these code examples, remember that C# is a case-sensitive language. Therefore, two variables called `totalEmployees` and `TotalEmployees` would be treated as entirely separate entities by the compiler. This same case-sensitivity applies to all C#'s keywords and identifiers.

Naming Identifiers

C# has some strict rules to follow regarding the naming of identifiers (variable names, method names, class names, etc.). When naming an identifier, you must adhere to the following rules:

- Identifiers must start with a letter or an underscore

- It must contain only non-formatting Unicode characters (i.e., letters, numbers, and symbols)

- The identifier must not contain any spaces

- It must not be a C# reserved word (i.e., not a word used as part of the C# language)

In general, as long as you name your variables using only letters and underscores (and numbers after the first character) and avoid reserved words (see Table 3-1), you will be OK.

Table 3-1. *C# Reserved words*

abstract	as	base	bool	break
byte	case	catch	char	checked
class	const	continue	decimal	default
delegate	do	double	else	enum
event	explicit	extern	false	finally
fixed	float	for	foreach	goto
if	implicit	in	int	interface
internal	is	lock	long	namespace
new	null	object	operator	out
override	params	private	protected	public
readonly	ref	return	sbyte	sealed
short	sizeof	stackalloc	static	string
struct	switch	this	throw	true
try	typeof	uint	ulong	unchecked
unsafe	ushort	using	virtual	void
volatile	while			

Choosing good names for your identifiers, more than anything else, will improve the readability of your code. You should always strive to use a name that describes the exact purpose of the identifier in a clear and concise manner.

Always strive to create your programs in such a way that another developer could pick up your code and easily understand it—that programmer may well be you in two or three years, when you come to implement new functionality on your site. The purpose of a variable will be much easier to remember (or work out) if the variable is called `totalPrice` or `shippingAddress1` than if it is named `t`, `x`, or `sa1`.

■ **Tip** A set of guidelines for C# Coding Conventions, including naming conventions, can be found on the Microsoft Developer Network Site at http://msdn.microsoft.com/en-us/library/ff926074.aspx. Defining a set of coding conventions helps to create a consistent look and feel to your code, which will greatly aid readability to help in future development and debugging. This is particularly important if you are working as part of a development team.

In the next few sections we will look at some of the different types built into C# and see some examples of their use.

Booleans

Booleans are the simplest of all the C# .NET types in that they are able to hold only one of two values: true or false. They are declared using the keyword bool:

```
bool isAuthorized = true;
bool messageRead = false;

...

messageRead = true;
```

■ **Note** Unlike languages such as C and C++, the C# bool type will not allow an integer expression such as 0, 1 or –1 for setting a true or false value. The true and false keywords are built into the C# language and they are the only values accepted by the compiler for assignment to a Boolean variable.

Numbers

The numeric types in C# are split into two different categories—integral and floating-point. The integral types can hold only integer values (i.e., whole numbers without a decimal part), whereas the floating-point types hold real numbers represented to a specified number of significant digits.

Integral Types

C# has eight individual integral types available for use when working with and storing integers. The reason for the requirement for so many different integral types has primarily to do with the amount of memory required to store and manipulate each variable. Table 3-2 shows this in some detail.

Table 3-2. *C# Integral Types*

Type	Size (in Bits)	Range
sbyte	8	−128 to 127
byte	8	0 to 255
short	16	−32768 to 32767
ushort	16	0 to 65535
int	32	−2147483648 to 2147483647
uint	32	0 to 4294967295
long	64	−9223372036854775808 to 9223372036854775807
ulong	64	0 to 18446744073709551615

You can see from Table 3.2 that the web server requires eight times more space to hold a long or ulong over a byte or sbyte. Therefore, you should always try to ensure that you use an appropriately sized type wherever possible (i.e., choose one with the minimum size required to hold any likely values), in the same way that you would choose the smallest usable field type when designing a database.

■ **Note** This will become increasingly important as your web site gathers users and as performance becomes an issue when thousands (or even tens of thousands) of browsers are requesting pages from your server. Compared to only a couple of years ago, computer memory and disk space is cheap, but there is no point wasting it!

For more information on optimizing your web site's performance, take a look at the 'Improving Performance using Caching' section in Chapter 12.

As with any other C# type, integral variables are declared by use of the relevant keyword and assignment of a valid identifier. As mentioned previously, all class level numeric types default to 0 (zero), but always specifying an initial value (called initialization) is considered good practice. All local variables must be initialized before use.

```
int variance = -1000;
byte studentCount = 20;
long numberOfBacteria = 0;
```

Floating-Point Types

C# provides three types specifically designed for use when working with floating-point numbers; `float`, `double` and `decimal` (see Table 3-3).

Table 3-3. *C# Floating-Point Types*

Type	Size (in Bits)	Precision	Range	Suffix
float	32	7 digits	$\pm 1.5 \times 10^{-45}$ to $\pm 3.4 \times 10^{38}$	f or F
double	64	15–16 digits	$\pm 5.0 \times 10^{-324}$ to $\pm 1.7 \times 10^{308}$	d or D
decimal	128	28–29 significant digits	$\pm 1.0 \times 10^{-28}$ to $\pm 7.9 \times 10^{28}$	m or M

The major factor when deciding between the use of a `decimal` or `double` is the priority of precision or range. A double has the greatest range, whereas the decimal type is much more precise, making it a good choice, in particular, for financial calculations where rounding errors can be problematic.

Each floating-point type has a literal suffix that is used to ensure that the compiler uses the intended type when evaluating expressions. To avoid the associated—and often very hard to find—bugs and errors, you should always use the appropriate suffix. This has the added benefit of self-documenting your code for future reference. Floating-point variables are declared and initialized as follows:

```
float totalVolume = 46524.23f;
double calculationsPerSecond = 6984725.389277d;
decimal jackpot = 145678289.42m;
```

Floating-point values can also be specified using exponential notation. This allows the programmer to describe extremely large or small numbers more easily than using a lot of zeros in the number, albeit with a trade-off against precision:

```
float averagePopulation = 6.43e35f;
double mass = 3.42e-108d;
decimal annualSales = 93883992e11m;
```

Numeric Conversions

The C# compiler places constraints on the conversion of numeric types in any situation where data loss may occur. All integral types may be implicitly converted to any other integral type, where the type to be converted to has a range larger than the type to be converted from. For example, conversion from a `byte` to a `short` is implicit as a variable of type `short` can contain every possible value of a variable of type byte:

```
byte hoursWorked = 105;
short totalHours = hoursWorked;
```

However, in the reverse direction (i.e. from a short to a byte) an explicit conversion is required. This is achieved by the placing the type name in brackets before the value on assignment; an action known as casting:

```
short hoursWorked = 105;
byte totalHours = (byte)hoursWorked;
```

This tells the compiler that it is OK to force the value of the hoursWorked variable into totalHours even though the range of the variable type is smaller in the case of totalHours. Without this cast, the compiler will display the error seen here in Figure 3-2:

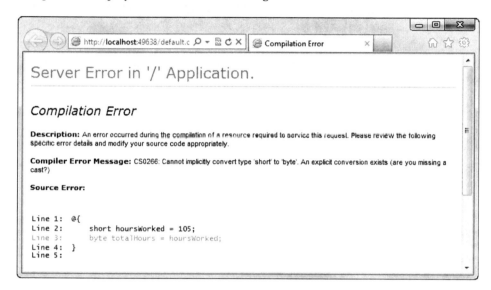

Figure 3-2. Implicit conversion between non-compatible types will generate a compilation error

---

▒ **Caution**   You need to take care when performing casting operations in order to ensure that the type you are casting to can fully hold the intended value. If there is any possibility that the original value may fall outside the permitted range of the intended type, you should implement code to check the value before casting in order to avoid out of range errors or unexpected values (which can be an absolute nightmare to debug).

An implicit conversion from a float to a double is permitted as no information may be lost. However, conversions from double to float and to/from a decimal type must be performed using explicit casts:

```
//float to double - implicit conversion permitted
float deviation = 9378239.2872f;
double totalDeviation = deviation;
```

```
//double to float requires explicit cast
double xPosition = 1.4e37d;
float totalXMovement = (float)xPosition;

//float or double to/from decimal requires explicit cast
decimal departmentalProfit = 2993899.28m;
double totalProfit = (double)departmentalProfit;
```

Code Comments

Adding comments to your code greatly improves readability for yourself and other developers in the future. C# has two standard types of comment; single-line and multi-line.

```
// This is a single-line comment

/* This is
   a multi-line
   comment */
```

Comments should be added wherever it is necessary to provide a clear explanation of complex areas of code, or where code has been revised. However, comments should not be used as an alternative to clear, concise code. Code that is unnecessarily complex should be refactored to improve its readability.

Integral types can be converted to floating-point types implicitly as long as the range of the two types is compatible. However, conversions from floating-point types to integers must always be cast explicitly.

■ **Tip**   For more information on casting in C#, visit the Casting and Type Conversions section of the C# Programming Guide on the Microsoft Developer Network site at: http://msdn.microsoft.com/en-us/library/ms173105.aspx

Strings

Two built-in types exist in C# that are designed to hold exclusively textual, or string, values; char and string. The string type holds a series of Unicode characters, whereas the char type can hold only one.

The value to be stored in a char type must be enclosed by single quotes:

```
char department = 'B';
```

Values assigned to variables of type **string** must be enclosed in double quotes:

```
string firstName = "Steve";
```

Strings and chars can also contain Unicode escape sequences to represent other useful formatting instructions; these are preceded with a backslash. A list of the more common escape sequences can be seen in Table 3-4:

***Table 3-4.** Common Unicode character escape sequences*

Character	Meaning
\ '	Single quote
\ "	Double quote
\\	Backslash
\b	Backspace
\n	New line
\r	Carriage return
\t	Horizontal tab

Therefore, to represent the following file path as a string:

```
C:\Users\Steve\Documents\My Web Sites\Hello World\default.cshtml
```

you must escape all the backslash characters, giving you this:

```
string filePath = "C:\\Users\\Steve\\Documents\\My Web Sites\\Hello World\\default.cshtml";
```

Alternatively you can also create a verbatim string literal using the @ symbol. By placing the @ symbol before the string literal you instruct the compiler to ignore Unicode escape sequences:

```
string filePath = @"C:\Users\Steve\Documents\My Web Sites\Hello World\default.cshtml";
```

ToString()

All data types in C#, including the C# built-in types such as int and float, derive from a base class called **Object**, which enables them to share some common functionality. One such function is the ToString() method, which returns a string representation of the value on which the method is called. For example:

```
int numberOfUsers = 1253;
string userCount = numberOfUsers.ToString();
```

This method is particularly useful when creating a string literal to be output to a screen that contains some calculated numeric or Boolean value.

String.()Format()

The `String.Format()` method is used to insert values into string literals. Any number of values can be inserted into the original string using numbered placeholders contained in curly braces:

```
int numberOfUsers = 1253;
string userCountMessage = String.Format("There are currently {0} users logged ↵
into the  system", numberOfUsers);
```

Notice that use of the `String.Format()` method does not require calling the `ToString()` method on the values to be inserted.

String Length

Ascertaining the length of a string is often useful while programming web sites. For example, you may want to check that a specified username contains more than a set number of characters. This can be achieved by accessing the string's `Length` property, which returns an `int`:

```
string username = "stevelydford";
int usernameLength = username.Length;    // usernameLength = 12
```

Changing Case

Two methods are available to change the case of letters in a string; `ToUpper()` and `ToLower()`. The following example takes a first name, "Steve" and a last name, "Lydford" and creates a new variable called `fullName` which contains the formatted text, "LYDFORD, Steve".

```
string firstName = "Steve";
string lastName = "Lydford";
string fullName = String.Format("{0}, {1}", lastName.ToUpper(), firstName);
```

Other Useful String Methods

Strings have many other methods. We will take quick look at some of the most useful ones here.

■ **Note** As mentioned previously, this chapter is only intended as a "getting started guide," not as an exhaustive manual. For more information on C#, I recommend visiting the Microsoft Developer Network (MSDN) C# Programming Guide at http://msdn.microsoft.com/en-us/library/67ef8sbd.aspx

---

The `Replace()` method allows easy substitution of all or part of a string:

```
string welcome = "Welcome to my world!";
string newWelcome = welcome.Replace("my", "your");        // Becomes "Welcome to your world!"
```

The `Trim()` method removes all whitespace from the beginning and end of a string :

```
string noPadding = "   My Web Site   ".Trim();          // noPadding contains "My Web Site"
```

Methods also exist to remove whitespace at each end of a string literal individually; `TrimStart()` and `TrimEnd()`.

To access specific portions of a string you can use the `Substring()` method. You need to tell the method which character to start at (where 0 (zero) is the first character) and how many characters you require.

```
string title = "Microsoft WebMatrix";
string shortTitle = title.Substring(10, 9);           // shortTitle contains "WebMatrix"
```

The final string methods we are going to consider in this section are concerned with searching within strings - `StartsWith()`, `EndsWith()`, `Contains()` and `IndexOf()`. The following code example shows how these are used and the outcome of the methods:

```
string movieTitle = "Star Wars Episode V: The Empire Strikes Back";

bool startsWithStar = movieTitle.StartsWith("Star");      // Returns true
bool endsWithBack = movieTitle.EndsWith("back");          // Returns false (case-sensitive)
bool containsEmpire = movieTitle.Contains("Empire");      // Returns true
int indexOfEpisode = movieTitle.IndexOf("Episode");       // Returns 10
```

The `endsWithBack` variable contains a false, as all of the methods described in this example are case-sensitive by default. The `IndexOf()` method reports the zero-based index of the first occurrence of a string of one or more characters, within the specified variable. If the string is not found within the specified variable, –1 is returned.

Concatenation and StringBuilder

Strings can be concatenated, or joined, using the string concatenation operator, + as seen here:

```
string firstString = "abcdefg";
string secondString = "hijklmn";
string thirdString = firstString + secondString;      // thirdString contains "abcdefghijklmn"
```

In the following code, the += operator is used to append text onto the end of the original string, which saves the overhead of creating variables to hold the second and third values, if that is appropriate to the program (the original value of the `name` variable will no longer be available after this operation):

```
string name = "Steve";
name += " Lydford";          // name contains the value "Steve Lydford"
```

C# strings are immutable, meaning that the content of the object cannot be changed once it has been created and initialized. The methods that we have seen that perform operations on strings actually create new string objects in memory. When we are performing one action, such as a `Replace()` or single concatenation, this is not generally a problem. However, imagine that you are in looping through 500,000 records and concatenating a string from the value of each record; performance may well become an issue here as hundreds of thousands of redundant string objects are created in memory. In scenarios involving anything more than one or two concatenations, the StringBuilder class should be used to ensure that no performance hit occurs on your web site.

StringBuilder is very easy to use. You simply create a new StringBuilder instance, which can optionally contain the first part of your string, and then call the `Append()` method as necessary to concatenate. The following example demonstrates the correct use of the StringBuilder class:

```
StringBuilder sb = new StringBuilder("The quick");
sb.Append(" brown");
sb.Append(" fox jumps");
sb.Append(" over the");
sb.Append(" lazy");
sb.Append(" dog");
sb.Append('.');
```

The StringBuilder object `sb` now contains the text, "The quick brown fox jumps over the lazy dog." and no redundant string objects have been created.

When we are done appending to our StringBuilder object, we can convert it back to a String using the ToString() method:

```
string message = sb.ToString();
```

Dates and Times

Dates and times are represented in C# by the DateTime type. Dates and times are very complex and can present a number of issues in everyday development, particularly around time zones and Daylight Savings Time (DST). The .NET Framework provides excellent facilities to cope with these complexities, although they are beyond the scope of this chapter (see the following Note).

■ **Note** The MSDN coverage of this topic is excellent and can be found at http://msdn.microsoft.com/en-us/library/system.datetime(v=VS.100).aspx
I would highly recommend reading the information available here before attempting any complex DateTime code.

The usual way to instantiate a `DateTime` is as followings:

```
DateTime appointment = new DateTime(2012, 9, 3, 10, 30, 00);
```

This creates a `DateTime` object and sets its initial value to 10:30:00 (ten thirty and zero seconds on 3rd September 2012). An alternative way to assign a date and time to a `DateTime` object is via its `Parse()` method, using a standard format date and time:

```
DateTime start = DateTime.Parse("31/08/2011 14:25:00");
```

■ **Note** My PC is set up to use the United Kingdom default date formats (dd/MM/yyyy HH:mm:ss). Your PC may give a different result, depending on your Windows settings.

This method can be extremely useful when populating DateTime objects from values stored in input controls (textboxes, drop-down lists, etc.) on web pages and from external data sources, as we will see later in the book.

Let's quickly look at a few common DateTime methods and properties, starting with the Now property, which we used in Chapter 2 to give us the current date and time for our Hello World application.

```
DateTime currentDateTime = DateTime.Now;
```

As well as the usual ToString() method, the DateTime object has a number of methods that output strings in various formats:

```
DateTime start = DateTime.Parse("31/08/2011 14:25:00");

string dateTime1 = start.ToString();                // 31/08/2011 14:25:00
string dateTime2 = start.ToLongDateString();        // 31 August 2011
string dateTime3 = start.ToLongTimeString();        // 14:25:00
string dateTime4 = start.ToShortDateString();       // 31/08/2011
string dateTime5 = start.ToShortTimeString();       // 14:25
```

We can also inspect individual parts of a DateTime by accessing the following properties:

```
DateTime dateJoined = DateTime.Parse("22/11/2009 18:02:24");

string dateElements = String.Format("Year: {0} Month: {1} Day: {2} " +
                                    "Hours: {3} Mins: {4} Secs: {5} " +
                                    "Milliseconds {6} Day of Week: {7} Day of Year: {8}",
                                    dateJoined.Year,
                                    dateJoined.Month,
                                    dateJoined.Day,
                                    dateJoined.Hour,
                                    dateJoined.Minute,
                                    dateJoined.Second,
                                    dateJoined.Millisecond,
                                    dateJoined.DayOfWeek,
                                    dateJoined.DayOfYear        // Days since 1st Jan
                                );
```

Output:

```
Year: 2009 Month: 11 Day: 22 Hours: 18 Mins: 2 Secs: 24 Milliseconds 0 Day of Week: Sunday Day
of Year: 326
```

Finally, we can perform basic addition operations on DateTime objects using the various Add() methods. Subtractions can be achieved by passing a negative integer:

```
DateTime arrival = new DateTime(2011, 02, 24, 09, 30, 42);   // 24/02/2011 09:30:42

DateTime newArrivalYear = arrival.AddYears(1);       // 24/02/2012 09:30:42
DateTime newArrivalMonth = arrival.AddMonths(4);     // 24/06/2011 09:30:42
DateTime newArrivalDay = arrival.AddDays(-20);       // 04/02/2011 09:30:42
DateTime newArrivalHour = arrival.AddHours(2);       // 24/02/2011 11:30:42
DateTime newArrivalMinute = arrival.AddMinutes(-30); // 24/02/2011 09:00:42
DateTime newArrivalSecond = arrival.AddSeconds(-2);  // 24/02/2011 09:30:40
```

Operators

C# provides a series of built-in operators that allow us to perform a number of operations on literals and variables. We will look at the common, more useful, operators in this chapter, broken down into a few sections.

Arithmetic Operators

As the name would suggest, the arithmetic operators allow us to perform mathematical operations on numeric variables and literals (see Table 3-5).

Table 3-5. *Commonly used C# Arithmetic Operators*

Operator	Name	Example
+	Addition	`int result = 48 + 1024;`
-	Subtraction	`int result = 512 - 128;`
/	Division	`float result = 22 / 7;`
*	Multiplication	`int result = 10 * 50;`
%	Modulus	`int result = 5 % 2;`
++	Increment	`count++;`
--	Decrement	`count--;`

All operators can be used to operate on variables as well as literals. Therefore, the two result variables in the following example contain the same value, 25.

```
int result1 = 100 / 4;

int operand1 = 100;
int operand2 = 4;
int result2 = operand1 / operand2;
```

The addition, subtraction, division, and multiplication operators are self-explanatory, except perhaps to say that they are subject to operator precedence. Operator precedence states that multiplicative operators (* and /) will be evaluated before any additive operators (+ and -) in the same expression— this may give some surprising results if not accounted for. Evaluation order can be forced by the use of parentheses, with expressions inside parentheses being evaluated before other expressions.

```
int result1 = 3 + 2 * 4;        // Result = 11
int result2 = (3 + 2) * 4;      // Result = 20
```

64

The modulus operator returns the remainder of the result of the division of the first operand by the second.

```
int result1 = 32 % 20;          // Result = 12
int result2 = 15 % 2;           // Result = 1
```

The increment and decrement operators simply increase or decrease a numeric value by one. The timing of the operator depends on which side of the operand it appears. If it appears after the operand, known as a post-increment/decrement operator, the value is evaluated then incremented/decremented. If the operator appears before the operand, known as a pre-increment/decrement operator, the value is incremented or decremented before it is evaluated. The following code example shows this in operation:

```
// Post-increment operator
int operand1 = 10;
int result1 = operand1++;       // result1 = 10; operand1 = 11

// Pre-increment operator
int operand2 = 20;
int result2 = ++operand2;       // result2 = 21; operand2 = 21

// Post-decrement operator
int operand3 = 30;
int result3 = operand3--;       // result3 = 30; operand3 = 29

// Pre-increment operator
int operand4 = 40;
int result4 = --operand4;       // result4 = 39; operand4 = 39
```

Assignment Operators

C# supports a number of assignment operators which are used to assign a value to a variable. Table 3-6 details the most commonly used of these:

Table 3-6. *Commonly used C# Assignment Operators*

Operator	Name	Example
=	Assignment	index = 128;
+=	Addition Assignment	message += " complete";
-=	Subtraction Assignment	count -= 10;
*=	Multiplication Assignment	profit *= sales;
/=	Division Assignment	share /= employees;
%=	Modulus Assignment	result %= 3;

Let's take a quick look at an example of each of these operators to better understand their behavior.

The assignment operator simply assigns a value to a variable, as we have seen in previous examples in this chapter. The value to be assigned can be either a literal or the value of another variable:

```
int score1 = 10;
int score2 = score1;
```

The addition assignment operator adds the specified value to the original:

```
decimal totalProfit = 100.00m;
decimal sales = 40.50m;
totalProfit += sales;                    // totalProfit is now 140.50
```

This code is equivalent to:

```
decimal totalProfit = 100.00m;
decimal sales = 40.50m;
totalProfit = totalProfit + sales;            // totalProfit is also 140.50 here
```

As we have seen previously, the addition assignment operator can also be used with string variables to concatenate them:

```
string user = "stevelydford";
user += "@example.com";                  // user contains text stevelydford@example.com
```

The subtraction, multiplication, division and modulus assignment operators work in similar ways as you would expect.

```
int result = 100;

result -= 50;                            // result = 50
                                         // Equivalent to: result = result - 50;

result *= 10;                            // result = 500;
                                         // Equivalent to: result = result * 10;

result /= 20;                            // result = 25;
                                         // Equivalent to: result = result / 20;

result %= 3;                             // result = 1;
                                         // Equivalent to: result = result % 3;
```

These operators will not work with string variables.

Equality Operators

The two C# equality operators simply compare two values for equality or inequality and return a Boolean **true** or **false** value depending on the outcome. As you will see later in the chapter, these operators are used extensively when testing variables for conditions and loops. Table 3-7 describes the two equality operators:

Table 3-7. *C# Equality Operators*

Operator	Name	Example
==	Equality	`sales == predicted;`
!=	Inequality	`red != blue;`

In the following code sample we can see the equality and inequality operators in action:

```
int first = 10;
int second = 20;
int third = 30;

bool result1 = first == second;          // false
bool result2 = first + second == third;  // true

bool result3 = first != second;          // true
bool result4 = first + second != third;  // false
```

Relational Operators

The relational operators allow us to compare one value in relation to another. Table 3-8 shows the commonly used relational operators:

Table 3-8. *Commonly used C# Relational Operators*

Operator	Name	Example
<	Less than	`10 < 11`
>	Greater than	`seats > passengers`
<=	Less than or equal to	`120.49 <= 120.50`
>=	Greater than or equal to	`income >= outgoings`

Again, the result of a relational operator is always a Boolean:

```
int first = 10;
int second = 20;
int third = 20;

bool result1 = first > second;          // false
bool result2 = first < second;          // true

bool result3 = second > third;          // false
bool result4 = second >= third;         // true

bool result5 = (first + second) > third;    // true
```

Conditional Operators

The final trio of operators we are going to cover in this chapter are known as conditional operators (see Table 3-9).

Table 3-9. Commonly used C# Relational Operators

Operator	Name	Example
!	NOT	!loggedIn
&&	AND	x > y && a == b
||	OR	(status >= 5) || (username == "admin")

The NOT operator is used to negate its operand. In other words, it will return a Boolean true only if its operand is false.

```
bool isLoggedIn = false;
bool showLoginScreen = !isLoggedIn;         //true
```

For a conditional AND to evaluate as true, **both** sides of the argument must be true. A conditional OR will return true if **either** side, or both sides, of the argument evaluate to a Boolean true.

```
int first = 10;
int second = 20;
int third = 20;

bool result1 = first < second && second == third;       // true
bool result2 = first > second && second == third;       // false

bool result3 = first < second || second == third;       // true
bool result4 = first > second || second == third;       // true
bool result5 = first > second || second != third;       // false
```

Note that the second part of a conditional AND will never be evaluated if the first part returns a false value. Likewise the second part of a conditional OR will not be evaluated if the first part returns true.

Collections

In C#, a collection is a data structure that holds data in an indexed way for ease of storage and retrieval. It can be thought of as a related group of variables that can be accessed individually; examples may include a collection of exam results or a list surnames for a class register. A collection removes the requirement for a separate variable to store each value and most collections provide greatly simplified methods for performing common operations across the collection as a whole, such as sorting, iteration, etc.

Many different types of collection are available to the C# programmer. As I have mentioned before, this chapter has been designed to give you a working knowledge of the language, sufficient only to allow you to progress through the rest of the book, so we will cover just the most commonly used collection types here.

Arrays

An array is a simple collection that contains several values of the same type. The collection is indexed (a zero-based integer index) and each element of the array can be accessed individually by specifying the index of the required element.

A single-dimensional array containing five elements can be declared as follows:

```
string[] names = new string[5];
```

To assign a value to each element, we can refer to them using the index (notice the zero-based index):

```
names[0] = "John";
names[1] = "Bob";
names[2] = "Tom";
names[3] = "Bill";
names[4] = "Jack";
```

If we want to initialize our array at the same time we declare it, we can use one of the shorter alternative syntaxes. The following two lines demonstrate the two types of concise syntax and are equivalent:

```
string[] names = new string[] {"John", "Bob", "Tom", "Bill", "Jack"};
```

```
string[] names = {"John", "Bob", "Tom", "Bill", "Jack"};
```

The value of each element can be retrieved in a similar fashion, specifying the required element by referring to its index, as shown in this example:

```
bool isBob = names[1] == "Bob";        // isBob is true
```

Arrays can also be multi-dimensional, in that they can hold several sets of elements. Imagine you wanted to hold the following table of measurements in an array:

Index	Height	Width	Depth
0	1.44m	2.81m	0.76m
1	4.23m	5.94m	2.32m
2	2.45m	4.40m	1.95m
3	3.0m	4.91m	4.39m
4	2.98m	3.02m	3.15m

A two-dimensional array to hold this data, with 5 rows and 3 columns, would be defined as follows:

```
float[,] measurements = new float[5,3];
```

To then refer to each cell in the table, you would use the index of the row, followed by the index of the column. For example:

```
measurements[0, 0] = 1.44f;
measurements[0, 1] = 2.81f;
measurements[0, 2] = 0.76f;
measurements[1, 0] = 4.23f;
measurements[1, 1] = 5.94f;
measurements[1, 2] = 2.32f;
measurements[2, 0] = 2.45f;
measurements[2, 1] = 4.4f;
measurements[2, 2] = 1.95f;
measurements[3, 0] = 3.0f;
measurements[3, 1] = 4.91f;
measurements[3, 2] = 4.39f;
measurements[4, 0] = 2.98f;
measurements[4, 1] = 3.02f;
measurements[4, 2] = 3.15f;
```

Alternatively you could use either of the following shortcut syntaxes:

```
float[,] measurements = { { 1.44f, 2.81f, 0.76f },
                          { 4.23f, 5.94f, 2.32f },
                          { 2.45f, 4.4f, 1.95f },
                          { 3.0f, 4.91f, 4.39f },
                          { 2.98f, 3.02f, 3.15f }
                        };
```

```
float[,] measurements = new float[5,3] { { 1.44f, 2.81f, 0.76f },
                                         { 4.23f, 5.94f, 2.32f },
                                         { 2.45f, 4.4f, 1.95f },
                                         { 3.0f, 4.91f, 4.39f },
                                         { 2.98f, 3.02f, 3.15f }
                                       };
```

C# also supports jagged arrays. A jagged array is similar to a multi-dimensional array, but each row can contain a different number of columns; they are often referred to as an array of arrays. For more information on arrays, visit the MSDN web site at http://msdn.microsoft.com/en-us/library/9b9dty7d.aspx.

To get the size of an of array dimension, you can access the array's Length property. This property holds the number of columns in the specified dimension. For instance, in the measurements array we declared earlier we have three columns.

```
int columnCount = measurements.Length;          // columnCount = 3
```

An array can be sorted using the Sort() method of the Array object. To order our names array from earlier, we would use the following code:

```
Array.Sort(names);
```

This arranges the elements of our array into alpha-numeric sequence, in this case: Bill, Bob, Jack, John, Tom. It is worth noting here that, unlike the String methods described earlier, the Array methods actually change the original array and do not make a copy.

We can reverse the elements of an array by calling the **Array.Reverse()** method:

```
Array.Reverse(names);
```

Our array is now ordered in reverse: Tom, John, Jack, Bob, Bill.

Two methods are useful in finding elements within an array; IndexOf() and LastIndexOf(). IndexOf() returns an integer containing the index of the first element in the array matching the specified search object; LastIndexOf() returns the index of the last matching element.

```
int jacksIndex = Array.IndexOf(names, "Jack");          // jacksIndex = 2
```

The final thing I want to talk about with regard to arrays is the IndexOutOfRange exception. This exception will be generated if you ever try to access an array element that is outside the bounds of the array. For example, the following line:

```
float boxSize = measurements[1, 6];
```

will cause WebMatrix to display the following error page (Figure 3-3):

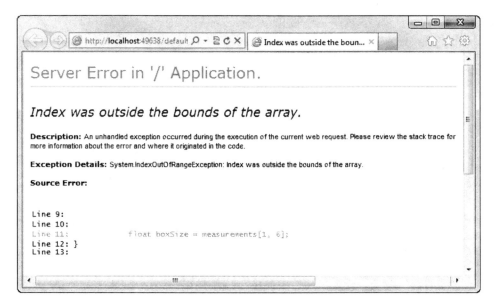

Figure 3-3. An IndexOutOfRangeException error page

■ **Note** The search and order functions of Arrays have been largely superseded by LINQ (Language Integrated Query). We will look at LINQ later in Chapter 6—Working with Data.

Generic Collections-

Generics were introduced into C# in version 2.0, which came along in 2005 as part of Visual Studio 2005. They are a way of defining type-safe data structures without committing to data types until runtime. Generics in C# is a vast subject that could easily fill a chapter of its own, but here we are just interested in the basics. We will look at two commonly used built-in generic collections—List and Dictionary—which will cope well with most situations, and the var keyword. Finally, we will talk briefly about the IEnumerable interface and how it helps us to interact with our generic collections.

■ **Note** We will also be discussing generics in the Object Oriented Programming section later in this chapter.

List<T>

A generic list is very similar in functionality to an array (in fact, it is backed by an array behind-the-scenes), but with a number of useful additional features that make it much more programmer friendly.

The best way to see a generic list in action is to take a look at some code, so let's declare our list. When we refer to List<T>, the T stands for Type. We simply need to tell List<T> what type we wish to create a list of, as it is a generic list remember, which we do inside the angle brackets:

```
List<string> cars = new List<String>();
```

We can also initialize the list with items at the point of declaration by passing the values within curly braces, as we did with arrays.

```
List<string> cars = new List<String>() { "Ferrari", "Aston Martin" };
```

So now the compiler knows that I have a list of strings that I have called cars. I can add items to the end of my list by calling the Add() method and passing it the string I wish to add. Remember that the list is now strongly typed as a list of strings, so if I pass in a value that cannot be implicitly cast to a string, I will receive an error.

```
cars.Add("Lamborghini");
cars.Add("Porsche");
```

This code demonstrates one of the major advantages that List<T> has over an Array. At no point have we told the compiler what size the list should be— it simply does not matter. Unlike an array, which has its size set at the time of declaration, a List<T> can be resized at any time—in fact this process is virtually invisible to the programmer; items can be added and removed at will.

To get the current number of elements, use the Count() method. This is the number of elements, not the index of the last element (which would be Count() -1):

```
int carsCount = cars.Count();          // carsCount = 4
```

To remove an item, call the Remove() method:

```
cars.Remove("Lamborghini");
```

Items can also be accessed using the index, as with an array:

```
string myCar = cars[0];          // myCar = "Ferrari"
```

or, as is more often the case, using a Language Integrated Query(LINQ). We will be taking an introductory look at LINQ in Chapter 6—Working with Data.

Dictionary<TKey, TValue>

The generic dictionary stores key/value pairs. When we declare it, we need to tell the compiler the type of the key and type of the value:

```
Dictionary<string, decimal> prices = new Dictionary<string, decimal>();
```

Again, we can use shortcut syntax to initialize the dictionary at the point of declaration:

```
Dictionary<string, decimal> prices = new Dictionary<string, decimal>()
                                    {
                                        { "Bread", 1.20m },
                                        { "Soup", 1.50m },
                                        { "Butter", 0.95m },
                                        { "Milk", 1.90m }
                                    };
```

We can also add items to our dictionary using the `Add()` method:

```
prices.Add("Orange Juice", 2.60m );
```

Now, to retrieve items, we can simply refer to them by their key:

```
decimal priceOfMilk = prices["Milk"];              // priceOfMilk = 1.90
```

As with `List<T>`, we can find out the number of elements in our dictionary by using the `Count()` method and we can delete items from the dictionary using the `Remove()` method:

```
prices.Remove("Butter");
int numberOfPrices = prices.Count;                 // numberOfPrices = 4
```

The var keyword

The syntax for declaring C# generics can get pretty long-winded. Take a realistic dictionary declaration:

```
Dictionary<string, List<float>> measurements = new Dictionary<string, List<float>>();
```

We can see here that the majority of the declaration is merely a repetition of the type. The **var** keyword allows us to shorten this considerably by instructing the compiler to infer the type:

```
var measurements = new Dictionary<string, List<float>>();
```

This makes the code much more concise and readable. As long as the compiler can infer the type from the right-hand side of the equals sign, then the **var** keyword can be used.

Although originally implemented to deal with the incredibly long declarations required by the introduction of generics to the language, the **var** keyword can be used during any type declaration. The following are all equally valid:

```
var surname = "Lydford";
var pricePerHour = 25.99m;
var count = 3;
var myArray = new string[12];
```

Notice that the variable must be initialized at the time of declaration when using **var,** as its type is not explicitly specified on the right hand side. It is the type of this initial value that the compiler uses to infer the actual type of the variable at compile time.

IEnumerable<T>

`IEnumerable<T>` is not a type of generic collection; rather, it is an interface that defines a number of actions useful for interacting with collections, most importantly the ability to iterate over then. The `IEnumerable<T>` interface requires that any generic collection that implements it provides a core set of functionality. `List<T>` and `Dictionary<TKey, TValue>` both implement `IEnumerable<T>` which means that, along with several other useful functions, we have the ability to iterate over the collection using the C# `foreach` loop (which we will see later in the chapter).

This ability to be iterated over will become very important later in the book, when we move on to displaying dynamic data on our web pages (see Chapter 6 - Working with Data).

Conditions

Conditions are sometimes referred to as Control or Selection statements. They are the part of a program that allows us to branch into separate logical sequences according to decisions based on specific values at runtime.

C# has three major conditional statements—if...else, switch, and try...catch—each of which we will look at now.

if...else

The if statement selects a branch for execution based on the evaluation of a Boolean expression. Although not mandatory, it is often used in conjunction with the else statement to provide an alternative program flow should the if statement evaluate to false.

The code to be executed must be placed in a code block (i.e., within a pair of braces). This tells the compiler where the code to be executed starts and ends.

```
var loggedIn = false;
var message = "";

if (loggedIn)
{
    message = "User logged in successfully.";
}
else
{
    message = "User login failed.";
}
```

It is common practice to use conditional operators here to evaluate more than one expression:

```
var loggedIn = true;
var membershipValid = true;
var message = "";

if (loggedIn && membershipValid)
{
    message = "User logged in successfully.";
}
else
{
    message = "User login failed.";
}
```

Multiple if statements can be nested within each other as necessary, although care should be taken to ensure readability is not compromised.

```
var count = 15;
var message = "";

if (count > 10)
{
```

```
    if (count < 20)
    {
        message = "Count is more than 10 but less than 20";
    }
    else
    {
        message = "Count is 20 or more";
    }
}
else
{
    message = "Count is 10 or less";
}
```

else if can be used to handle multiple conditions if necessary, although in many cases this is better dealt with through use of the switch statement, which we will look at in the next section.

```
int role =2;
string username = "Steve";
string securityLevel = "";

if ((role == 4) && (username == "Steve"))
{
    securityLevel = "Developer";
}
else if (role == 3)
{
    securityLevel = "Administrator";
}
else if (role == 2)
{
    securityLevel = "Moderator";
}
else if (role == 1)
{
    securityLevel = "Member";
}
else
{
    securityLevel = "Guest";
}
```

The Ternary Operator

The ternary operator is provided by the C# language to provide a clear, concise way to write an `if...else` statement, where a single expression is to be evaluated dependent on the outcome of the condition. The ternary operator takes the following form:

```
condition ? first_expression : second_expression
```

Here, if the condition evaluates to `true`, the expression `first_expression` is evaluated; otherwise, the program will evaluate `second_expression`. Here is an example of the ternary operator in use:

```
int i = 18;
string message = (i > 10) ? "Greater than 10" : "10 or less";
```

The outcome of this code is that the `message` variable is set to have a value of "Greater than 10".

switch

The switch statement is used to evaluate an expression against a number of possible values and pass program control to one of the case statements within it if required. The following code evaluates the value of the `primaryColor` string variable and executes code accordingly:

```
var primaryColor = "red";
var hexValue = "";

switch (primaryColor)
{
    case "blue":
        hexValue = "#0000FF";
        break;
    case "red":
        hexValue = "#FF0000";
        break;
    case "green":
        hexValue = "#00FF00";
        break;
    case "yellow":
        hexValue = "#FFFF00";
        break;
    default:
        hexValue = "#FFFFFF";
        break;
}
```

In this example, the `hexValue` variable will be set to "#FF0000".

The **break** keyword halts execution of the **switch** statement and transfers program flow to the next statement. Any value of **primaryColor** that is not met by one of the **case** statements is handled by the **default** code block.

The **switch** statement can handle any number of cases, but no two cases can have the same value. In addition to this, each **case** instance can only have a single value. However, by using multiple **case** statements without a **break** between them, you can achieve the same result:

```
var animal = "lizard";
var animalType = "";

switch (animal)
{
    case "dog":
    case "cat":
    case "cow":
        animalType = "Mammal";
        break;
    case "eagle":
    case "hawk":
    case "sparrow":
        animalType = "Bird";
        break;
    case "lizard":
    case "snake":
        animalType = "Reptile";
        break;
    default:
        animalType = "Unknown";
        break;
}
```

At the end of execution, the variable **animalType** holds the string "Reptile".

■ **Note** You must have a break statement at the end of each non-empty case branch; otherwise, a compilation error will occur.

try…catch

The **try..catch** block basically says to the compiler, "Try and execute this code and if it fails, catch the exception here and execute this code instead." In C# that looks like this:

```
var sports = new List<string> {"Football", "Cricket", "Rugby", "Golf"};
var output = "";

try
{
    output = sports[7];
```

```
}
catch(Exception e)
{
    output = "Try block failed - " + e.Message;
}
```

When this example is executed, the try block fails so the catch block is executed. This takes the exception raised and concatenates the exception message to the output, which in this case reads as: "Try block failed – Index was out of range. Must be non-negative and less than the size of the collection. Parameter name: index"

It is worth noting that this is a superficial example designed to explain the use of the try...catch block. In reality, we would write code to check that the index was valid before trying to access the element in the array.

▓ **Note** We will look at error handling and try..catch in much more depth in Chapter 12—Advanced WebMatrix.

The try..catch block has one other code construct, called finally. The finally block is placed after the catch block and is always run, whether the try block fails or not. This is a useful place to put code that is used to release resources—for example, a database connection or file stream.

```
var output = "";

try
{
    output += "Executing try statement. ";
}
catch (Exception e)
{
    output += "Executing catch. ";
}
finally
{
    output += "Executing finally.";
}
```

The value of output after execution of this example would be, "Executing try statement. Executing finally." However, if for some reason the try block had failed and the catch block was run, the code inside finally would still be executed.

Loops

A loop is a code construct designed to allow a statement, or sequence of statements, to be performed multiple times. The C# language specifies four different types of loop— while, do, for, and foreach— which we will look at in turn here.

The while loop

A while loop is a condition controlled loop that tests the condition at the start of the loop and continues to iterate while the condition is true. As seen earlier with the if and try…catch statements, the code to be executed is placed with a pair of braces.

```
int count = 1;
string message = "";

while (count <= 10)
{
    message += count + " ";
    count++;
}
```

After the loop has completed all its cycles, the string value of message will be, "1 2 3 4 5 6 7 8 9 10 ".

■ **Caution**   In the above example, note that the count integer is incremented each time the body of the loop is executed, using the statement count++;

If we had failed to increment the count integer on each iteration, the condition of the loop would always be evaluated to true and the loop would continue to run. In other words, we would have an infinite loop.

If the initial condition is not met, the code inside the body of the loop will never run, as in this example:

```
int studentIndex = 0;

while (studentIndex > 10)
{
    // This will never be run
    studentIndex++;
}
```

Exiting Loops

You can instruct the runtime to exit any of the C# loops at any point using the break keyword. When the break keyword is encountered, control of the program is passed directly to the next statement outside of the loop.

If you just need to exit a particular iteration of the loop, you can use the continue keyword. When the runtime encounters a continue statement the program steps directly to the next iteration, as long as any condition on the loop is still met.

The do loop

The do loop is also a conditional loop and works in a way similar to while, except that the condition is evaluated at the end of the loop. This means that, unlike the while loop, the code in the body of a do loop will always execute at least once.

```
var recordCount = 0;
var output = "";

do
{
    output += recordCount + " ";
    recordCount++;
} while ( recordCount < 10 );
```

In this example, following the successful completion of the loop, the value of the output string is set to "0 1 2 3 4 5 6 7 8 9 ".

The for loop

The for loop iterates over a series of statements until the specified expression evaluates to a Boolean false value. The for loop is commonly used for iterating over arrays (i.e., visiting every element in an array dimension) or performing sequential processing.

The following example iterates over an array of integers, adding ten to every value:

```
int[] values = {1, 2, 3, 4, 5, 6, 7, 8, 9, 10};

for (int i = 0; i < values.Length; i++)
{
    values[i] += 10;
}
```

Let's take a look at this in a little more detail. First, the for loop declares a loop counter variable, i, and initializes it to 0:

```
for (int i = 0; i <= values.GetUpperBound(0); i++)
```

Then, while the value of i is less than or equal to the number of the last index in our array (in this case 9), the code inside the curly braces executes:

```
for (int i = 0; i <= values.GetUpperBound(0); i++)
```

Each time the loop iterates the value of i is altered as specified. In this case (and in most common scenarios), we simply add one to it using the increment operator:

```
for (int i = 0; i <= values.GetUpperBound(0); i++)
```

When the test evaluates as false, i.e. the index i is no longer less than or equal to the upper bound of the array, execution stops and program control is transferred to the next statement outside the loop.

■ **Note** Whereas the value of the index is altered (in our case incremented) immediately after each iteration of the loop, the condition is evaluated immediately before. Therefore, the statements inside a for loop code block may not execute at all if the condition is initially evaluated as true.

For example, in the following code the contents of the loop will never be executed:

```
int minimum = 5;
int maximum = 5;

for (int i = minimum; i < maximum; i++)
{
    // Code in here will never be executed...
}
```

The foreach loop

The foreach loop can be used to easily iterate over any collection that implements the IEnumerable or IEnumerable<T> interface. This means that it can be used to iterate over both arrays and the generic collections we looked at previously; List and Dictionary.

In fact, the ability to iterate over collections is why we will use the foreach loop most often as we continue with our coverage of WebMatrix. It is a natural fit for iterating over the results of a database query for display on an ASP.NET Web Page using Razor.

The following example shows how to iterate over a generic List using a foreach loop:

```
var cities = new List<string>() {"London", "Paris", "New York", "Seattle", "Sydney"};
var output = "";

foreach (var city in cities)
{
    output += city + " ";
}
```

The value of the string variable `output`, once the `foreach` loop has completed its iterations, is "London Paris New York Seattle Sydney".

■ **Tip**   Items cannot be added to or removed from the collection being iterated over using a `foreach` loop. If you need to perform that function, it must be achieved using a `for` loop.

Object Oriented Programming

This section will provide only a very basic introduction to Object Oriented Programming (OOP), as a full in-depth investigation into OOP is well beyond the scope of this book (and could easily fill it). I will give a very brief overview of the guiding principles behind OOP and how they can be implemented using C#, but space allows only just that—a very brief overview.

Should you wish to gain a greater knowledge of OOP, and C# in general, than I can impart here, you should consider taking a look at Adam Freeman's book, "Introducing C#" available from Apress.com.

Principles and Terminology

The three core principles behind OOP support in the .NET framework are encapsulation, abstraction, inheritance, and polymorphism.

Encapsulation is the inclusion of all related properties, methods, and data about a program entity into a single unit or class. The encapsulated class hides its internal implementation and instead exposes a series of methods and properties to the outside world to provide its functionality. This process of exposing external methods and properties while hiding the inner workings of the object is called abstraction. By following the principles of abstraction and encapsulation, the internal implementation of a class can change without affecting the way it is used by other objects.

The principle of inheritance describes the ability to create new classes based on existing ones. The newly created class would automatically inherit all the members of the base class (except constructors), and can also define additional members. Where allowed, inherited classes can override the members of the base class and specify additional ones.

Polymorphism is the ability to create a class or method that has more than one form. The objects created based on these classes and their member methods can then be used interchangeably, even though they may have wildly different implementations. Polymorphism in C# is commonly implemented through the use of interfaces. For example, a number of classes implementing a single interface must all implement the set of methods and properties specified by the interface, but each can do so in their own way. This means that we can safely use any of the classes which implement the interface interchangeably in our program.

.NET languages, such as C# and VB.NET, fully support these three OO principles.

Classes and Objects

Classes are all about encapsulation—they are a bunch of related data and functionality that describes an object. A class can be described as a blueprint or specification for a type of object, whereas an object created from that specification is referred to as being an instance of that class. When we create an object in C# it is called instantiation.

A class is defined using the `class` keyword and in WebMatrix is defined within a separate class file with a .cs file extension, which can be selected from the 'New File' dialog .

```
class Person
{
}
```

Objects based on that class can then be instantiated using the new keyword:

```
var employee = new Person();
var customer = new Person();
```

These objects are independent instances of the `Person` class and changes made to one instance will not affect any other instances of the same class.

Fields and Properties

The fields and properties of a class describe the data held and used by it. A field is defined simply by declaring a variable at the top level within the class:

```
class Person
{
    public DateTime DateOfBirth;
}
```

Notice that before the field declaration there is the keyword `public`. This is known as an access modifier and is used to determine who and what has access to this field. In this case the access modifier `public` means that any other code can read or set the value of the `DateOfBirth` field directly. Table 3-10 lists the different access modifiers available in C#:

Table 3-10. C# Access Modifiers

Access Modifier	Can be accessed by...
public	Any other code that references it
private	Only code in the same class
protected	Only code in the same class or a class derived from it
internal	Any code in the same assembly, but not from another assembly
protected internal	Any code in the same assembly or from within a derived class in another assembly that references it

These access modifiers can be attached to classes and all their member fields, properties and methods.

Properties have get and set methods which provide access to the underlying data field. These methods allow you to determine how values are set or returned, and validate those values if necessary. This is good programming practice as the underlying data fields are not directly accessible outside the class. For this reason they are much the preferred way of exposing data outside the class. It is usual to have a private field within the class that is used internally, with a property controlling access to it from the outside world:

```csharp
class Person
{
    public DateTime DateOfBirth;
    private string _surname;

    public string Surname
    {
        get { return _surname; }
        set { _surname = value; }
    }
}
```

The set method accesses the data to be written by using a hidden parameter called value.

By omitting the get or set statement, a property can be made read-only or write-only. As the implementation of properties is so common a more concise syntax is available for creating properties which deals with the creation of a private field and the basic logic behind the scenes.

```csharp
class Person
{
    public DateTime DateOfBirth;

    public string Surname { get; set; }
}
```

The Surname property can now be accessed in code once a new object of type Person has been instantiated:

```csharp
var student = new Person();
student.Surname = "Smith";
string surnameInitial = student.Surname.Substring(0, 1);        //surnameInitial = "S"
```

Alternatively, the values of an object's fields and properties can be set during instantiation using object initializers:

```csharp
var student = new Person { Surname = "Smith" };
var employee = new Person { DateOfBirth = new DateTime(1976, 5, 20), Surname = "Williams"};
```

Methods

A method is an action that can be performed by an object. Methods are defined using the following format:

```csharp
[access modifier] [return type] MethodName ([parameters]) { }
```

The access modifier must be one of the values detailed in Table 3-10. The return type describes the type returned as a result of the method. If the method does not return a result the return type should be specified as void.

A comma-separated list of parameters can be specified in parentheses after the method name. If the method does not require any parameters to be passed to it the parentheses should be left empty. A method also has access to all the members in the class, such as fields, properties and other methods.

The following code example declares two methods. The method called GetFullName() takes no parameters and returns a string. The AgeAtDate() method accepts a single DateTime parameter and returns a double.

```
class Person
{
    public DateTime DateOfBirth;

    public string Surname { get; set; }
    public string Forenames { get; set; }

    public string GetFullName()
    {
        var fullName = String.Format("{0} {1}", Forenames, Surname);
        return fullName;
    }

    public double AgeAtDate(DateTime calculationDate)
    {
        double ageInDays = (calculationDate - DateOfBirth).TotalDays;
        return ageInDays / 365.25;
    }
}
```

These methods can be called from code as follows:

```
var student = new Person();
student.Surname = "Smith";
student.Forenames = "Joe";
student.DateOfBirth = new DateTime(1990, 1, 1);

string fullName = student.GetFullName();        // Returns "Joe Smith"
double age = student.AgeAtDate(DateTime.Now);   // Returns age at current date
```

Two methods with the same name may be declared as long as they have different parameter types or number of parameters—this is known as overloading.

Definition of optional parameters is also possible. Optional parameters must be defined at the end of the parameter list and they need to set a default value, which must be a constant. If the parameter is not passed to the method specifically, then the default value is used.

```
public void exampleMethod (int requiredInteger, string optionalString = "default")
```

Constructors

A constructor is a special type of method that is called every time an object is instantiated. Constructors are commonly used to initialize the object's member fields and properties. The code in the constructor is guaranteed to run before any other code in a class and, as with any other method, they can optionally receive parameters and be overloaded. Constructors cannot be declared with a return type, not even void.

To define a method as a constructor, simply name the method the same as the class it is contained within. Constructor definitions can also contain parameters. The following code example shows an example of both a parameterless and parameterized constructor:

```
public class Vehicle
{
    public Vehicle()    // Parameterless Constructor
    {
        // Add initialization code here...
    }

    Public Vehicle(string color)    //Parameterized Constructor
    {
        // Add initialization code here...
    }
}
```

Events and Delegates

An event is a class member that is used to notify other classes or objects of a particular occurrence. Although an event is a valid C# class member, ASP.NET Web Pages does not make use of them so their inclusion here is merely in the interest of completeness. Much more information about handling and raising events can be found at http://msdn.microsoft.com/en-us/library/edzehd2t.aspx.

Delegates are declared using the delegate keyword and most commonly used with events in event-driven programming, although they do have some use on their own. A delegate is essentially a type that defines only a method signature that can then provide a reference to any other method with a compatible signature. This is useful for passing methods as arguments to other methods. As with events, delegates are rarely used in ASP.NET Web Pages but further information can be found via MSDN at http://msdn.microsoft.com/en-us/library/ms173171.aspx.

Static Classes and Members

A static member is a member that is shared across all instances of a class. For example, a property marked as static represents a single value that applies across the whole class, rather than a separate value per object.

The following code sample declares the field BookingCount as static and uses a constructor method to increment its value every time an object is instantiated from the class:

```
public class Booking
{
    public static int BookingCount { get; private set; }

    public Booking()
    {
        BookingCount++;
    }
}
```

Now, each time a new object of type Booking is created, the BookingCount field is incremented. We can inspect the value of BookingCount by referring to its class name.

```
var booking1 = new Booking();
var booking2 = new Booking();
var booking3 = new Booking();

int totalBookings = Booking.BookingCount;       // Returns 3
```

Entire classes can also be marked as static. Static classes can only have static members and cannot be instantiated.

```
public static class Conversions
{
    public static double kilogramsToPounds(double kg)
    {
        return (kg * 2.2d);
    }

    public static double poundsToKilograms(double pounds)
    {
        return (pounds / 2.2d);
    }
}
```

To call a static methodfrom code, we simply refer to the name of the class followed by the name of the method using standard .NET dot notation:

```
double weightInPounds = Conversions.kilogramsToPounds(100d);
double weightInKilos = Conversions.poundsToKilograms(100d);
```

Inheritance

In OOP, inheritance describes the principle of defining a new class type based on an existing one and having the ability to modify and extend its behavior. The class that the new type inherits from is called the base class and the class that inherits from the base class is called the derived class.

In the following example, the Circle class derives from the Shape class and extends its functionality with the addition of a Circumference property. We use a colon (:) followed by the base class name to let the compiler know which base class we are deriving from:

```
public class Shape
{
    public double Width { get; set; }
    public double Height { get; set; }
    public string FillColor { get; set; }
}

public class Circle : Shape
{
    public double Circumference { get; set; }
}
```

Objects instantiated from the Circle class have access to all members of the Circle and Shape classes, according to the access modifiers of the members of the base classes. To specify that a class cannot be used as a base class, you must use the **sealed** keyword in the class definition:

```
public sealed class Shape { }
```

To specify that a class can only be used as a base class and cannot be instantiated, you can use the **abstract** keyword:

```
public abstract class Shape { }
```

Namespaces

Namespaces are simply a way of organizing classes—they are used extensively in C#, in part due to the enormous size of the .NET Framework Base Class Library. The use of namespaces allows developers to organize their classes into a logical structure and helps to prevent duplication of class names.

In this example:

```
WebMatrix.Data.Database.Open("myDB");
```

`WebMatrix.Data` is a namespace, and `Database` is a class within that namespace. The `Database` class has a static `Open()` method that takes a string parameter.

When creating classes within your own projects, you can organize them within your own namespaces by using the `namespace` keyword:

```
namespace Geometry
{
    public class Shape
    {
        public double Width { get; set; }
        public double Height { get; set; }
        public string FillColor { get; set; }
    }
}
```

The `Height` property of the shape class can now be accessed like this:

```
Geometry.Shape.Height = 22.9d;
```

If we want to use classes from within the `Geometry` namespace throughout our code, without specifying it every time, we can use the `using` keyword. We will then be able to access the classes within that namespace directly:

```
@using Geometry;

var hexagon = new Shape();
```

Interfaces

An interface is a contract to which other classes must comply. Interfaces are separate entities that define properties, methods and events, but do not provide an implementation and cannot be instantiated. A class that implements an interface must implement every one of these properties, methods and events. The purpose of an interface is to ensure that all classes that implement it expose the same set of public members, although their specific implementation may differ.

We briefly mentioned interfaces earlier in this chapter when we discussed `IEnumerable<T>`. `IEnumerable<T>` is an interface (by convention all interface names are prefixed with a capital I) that defines the set of members necessary for other code constructs to be able to enumerate, and hence iterate over, a set of data. The `foreach` loop then, for example, will only accept a type that implements this interface (or its non-generic equivalent `IEnumerable`).

You define an interface with the keyword `interface`. All members are then declared without implementations:

```
interface IVehicle
{
    // Properties
    string manufacturer { get; set; }
    string model { get; set; }

    // Methods
    void Move(int x, int y);
}
```

A class can declare that it implements an interface by using the same colon notation we used to signify inheritance. The implementing class must contain at least an implementation of every member specified in the interface, although additional members may be added:

```
public class SportsCar : IVehicle
{
    private string _manufacturer;
    private string _model;
    private int _currentXPosition;
    private int _currentYPosition;

    public string manufacturer
    {
        get { return _manufacturer; }
        set { _manufacturer = value; }
```

```
    }

    public string model
    {
        get { return _model; }
        set { _model = value; }
    }

    public void Move(int x, int y)
    {
        _currentXPosition += x;
        _currentYPosition += y;
    }
}
```

Anonymous Types

Anonymous types in C# provide a way to quickly create objects which encapsulate a set of read-only properties without the need to write an explicit class definition. The compiler automatically generates a class which contains only the properties you define in the initializer. As the type of object is not pre-defined, anonymous types must be declared using the **var** keyword:

```
var motorcycle = new { Manufacturer = "Honda", Year = 2010, Mileage = 1569.3d };
```

Generics

We have already looked at generic collections earlier in the chapter, which is by far their most common use, but generics can also be applied to methods and types. This is useful when we want to declare a class but defer the specification of the type until runtime, when the class or method is instantiated. We can achieve this by the use of a generic type parameter <T>. Consider the following class definition:

```
public class GenericClass<T>
{
    public T GenericField;
}
```

Use of the generic type parameter T allows us to specify the exact type at runtime. The following two lines of code are equally valid and declare and instantiate objects based on the same generic class:

```
var generic1 = new GenericClass<string>();
var generic2 = new GenericClass<int>();
```

The chosen type is substituted everywhere that the type parameter appears in the class definition:

```
generic1.GenericField = "Indiana Jones";
generic2.GenericField = 1024;
```

OOP Conclusion

Well, that concludes our whistle-stop tour of Object Oriented Programming in C#. Please remember that this is only a very brief introduction and was designed only to help you understand the code samples in the rest of the book. I would highly recommend further reading on the subject of OOP as it forms the basis for everything in C#.

Dynamics

The C# dynamic type allows the developer to bypass compile-time type checking, instead passing the responsibility of type resolution to the Dynamic Language Runtime (DLR). Dynamics are used extensively within ASP.NET Web Pages, and are at the heart of the standard data access strategy.

A dynamic variable can essentially store any value and will not be checked by the compiler during the build process; the DLR will deal with the resolution of types at runtime. The following code may look a bit strange to anyone used to programming in a strongly-typed, type-safe environment such as C#, but it is valid code and will compile and run successfully:

```
dynamic myDynamic = "hello";
myDynamic = 2.94e-56d;
myDynamic = DateTime.Today.Year;
```

This ability to store any type makes them really convenient for use in collections where you don't necessarily want to store the same data type in each index. The following code will demonstrate this further:

```
var myList = new List<dynamic>();

myList.Add(DateTime.Now);
myList.Add("This is a string");
myList.Add(29.45f);
myList.Add(new Dictionary<string, double>());
```

Here we have a generic list of dynamics where we are able to store any valid .NET data type. This concept is in widespread use in ASP.NET Web Pages and we will re-visit it several times in later chapters.

ExpandoObject()

The last item I want to touch on with regards dynamics in C# is the very coolly named `ExpandoObject()` class. `ExpandoObject()` lives in the `System.Dynamic` namespace and allows you to create an object that can have its members dynamically added and removed at runtime. The following code creates an ExpandoObject called product and adds four members at runtime:

```
dynamic product = new System.Dynamic.ExpandoObject();

product.Name = "Widget";
product.Description = "The best widget money can buy!";
product.Price = 2.99m;
product.StockID = 92102;
```

ExpandoObjects can even contain other ExpandoObjects as members:

```
using System.Dynamic;

dynamic product = new ExpandoObject();
product.Name = "Widget";
product.Description = "The best widget money can buy!";
product.Price = 2.99m;
product.StockID = 92102;

product.Dimensions = new ExpandoObject();
product.Dimensions.Height = 42;
product.Dimensions.Width = 96;
```

The same overall effect could be achieved using a generic dictionary inside a generic dictionary, but the code would soon become very ugly and hard to read. `ExpandoObject()` provides an elegant and efficient solution.

Summary

In this chapter we have had a very quick introduction to the C# programming language. A good understanding of the concepts outlined in this chapter will arm you with enough knowledge to be able to follow all the code in the rest of this book.

Please bear in mind that this chapter has barely scratched the surface of the C# language and the .NET Framework. As you grow in experience with ASP.NET Web Pages, your knowledge and understanding of C# will also grow. An in-depth working knowledge of C# is essential if you are to consider yourself a competent WebMatrix developer

CHAPTER 4

■ ■ ■

Working with Razor and ASP.NET Web Pages

In the "Hello World" application in Chapter 2, Razor, C#, and ASP.NET Web Pages were used to perform relatively complex server-side tasks with ease. Now that you have a base knowledge of C#, either from experience or from the previous chapter, it is time to take a more in-depth look at Razor and ASP.NET Web Pages.

C#, Razor, and ASP.NET Web Pages combine perfectly to create an extremely powerful framework for creating sophisticated and dynamic web pages. In this chapter, some of the features of this framework that have been designed to provide a lightweight, fast, and scalable way to build web applications will be looked at. Topics covered in this chapter include:

- Razor syntax

- Layout

- Helpers

- Functions

- Maintaining state

- Uniform Resource Locators (URLs) and Routing

Razor Syntax

Razor is a simple to use, yet extremely powerful, programming syntax for inserting server-side code into web pages. When you create a new ASP.NET Web Page (.CSHTML or .VBHTML) in WebMatrix, you are creating a file that has two totally separate types of content: client-side and server-side. The client-side content of an ASP.NET Web Page can contain any of the usual code and markup that you would expect to see in a normal HTML page, including HTML, JavaScript, and CSS. The server-side content contains instructions to the web server in C# (or VB.NET), which are used to create dynamic content and interact with other resources, such as databases and file systems.

The server-side code is inserted directly into the page amongst the client-side content; use of the Razor syntax is your way of telling the web server where the client-side content ends and where the server-side content begins, and vice-versa.

The most common use of Razor is to dynamically create HTML and other client-side content. When IIS receives a request for a .CSHTML or .VBHTML page it recognizes it as an ASP.NET Web Page, executes any server-side instructions marked with the Razor syntax, and then returns the generated page to the browser.

■ **Note** The Razor syntax was actually invented for WebMatrix. However, it proved to be so popular amongst developers and such a great improvement over previous syntaxes, that it has now also been adopted as the default view engine for ASP.NET MVC.

Adding a single line of server-side code

A single line of server-side code can be added to an ASP.NET Web Page using the @ symbol. The code is added in-line with the client-side content, such as HTML, etc., and is recognised and processed automatically by the web server, substituting the Razor code with relevant dynamic content wherever this is the intention, such as

```
<p>The current date and time is: @DateTime.Now</p>
```

The parser has an intimate in-built knowledge of C# syntax, which makes it able to recognize where a C# statement ends and the HTML begins.

When a single-line expression is used in this way, the output is rendered directly to the page. If the single line of server-side code is there to perform some other function and is not intended for display, you can inform the parser by wrapping the statement in a pair or curly braces, thereby creating a statement block. This is seen in the following code

```
@{ var PageTitle = "My Home Page"; }

<!DOCTYPE html>

<html lang="en">
    <head>
        <meta charset="utf-8" />
        <title>@PageTitle</title>
    </head>
    <body>
        <h1>@PageTitle</h1>
        <p>The current date and time is: @DateTime.Now</p>
    </body>
</html>
```

This mix of code and HTML markup would output the result, as seen in Figure 4-1.

Figure 4-1. The result of the combination of Razor code and HTML.

As far as the browser is concerned, the server is returning plain old HTML and is no different from a normal static page. The following code is the HTML returned to the browser in the previous example.

```
<!DOCTYPE html>

<html lang="en">
    <head>
        <meta charset="utf-8" />
        <title>My Home Page</title>
    </head>
    <body>
        <h1>My Home Page</h1>
        <p>The current date and time is: 07/07/2011 01:18:41</p>
    </body>
</html>
```

The final type of single-line expression in Razor is known as a multi-token statement. Here, you want the output to be the result to the page, but need multiple items within the expression to be evaluated beforehand. The syntax for a multi-token expression is to enclose the expression in parentheses. In this example, the two integer variables are multiplied then output.

```
<p>The number is: @( 12 * 4 )</p>
```

The result of this code is seen in Figure 4-2.

Figure 4-2. The result of a calculation performed inside a multi-token statement.

Adding more complex code

Multiple lines of C# code can be added using a multi-statement block. Unlike in-line expressions, each line of code inside a code block, whether single or multi-statement, must end with a semi-colon. The following code shows an example of a multi-statement block.

```
@{
    var movies = new List<string>();
    movies.Add("The Shawshank Redemption");
    movies.Add("The Godfather");
    movies.Add("The Godfather: Part II");
    movies.Add("The Good, the Bad and the Ugly");
    movies.Add("Pulp Fiction");
}
```

To display the data held within your `movies` list, you could use a `foreach` loop to iterate over the collection and output each item to an HTML list. This is actually a really useful pattern, as the page emitted by IIS and sent to the browser will contain just a simple HTML unordered list, meaning that it can be easily styled with CSS by a designer to achieve the desired look and feel. Figure 4-3 shows the un-styled HTML page returned to the browser.

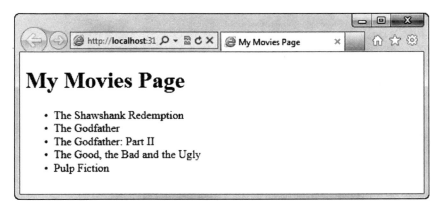

Figure 4-3. *The un-styled HTML list rendered in the page.*

The Razor code to achieve this is pretty interesting; let's take a look at it.

```
@{ var PageTitle = "My Movies Page"; }

@{
    var movies = new List<string>();
    movies.Add("The Shawshank Redemption");
    movies.Add("The Godfather");
    movies.Add("The Godfather: Part II");
    movies.Add("The Good, the Bad and the Ugly");
    movies.Add("Pulp Fiction");
}
```

```
<!DOCTYPE html>

<html lang="en">
    <head>
        <meta charset="utf-8" />
        <title>@PageTitle</title>
    </head>
    <body>

        <h1>@PageTitle</h1>

        <ul id="movies">

            @foreach (var movie in movies)
            {
                <li>@movie</li>
            }

        </ul>

    </body>
</html>
```

You can see here that, due to its semantic knowledge of the C# language, Razor is able to recognize that the <li> and </li> within the **foreach** loop are actually HTML tags and should be output to the page, along with the value of the local variable, **movie**.

Note also that Razor recognizes the curly braces { } as the start and end of the **foreach** loop, without the requirement for additional @ characters in the markup. This is a huge improvement over many other syntaxes, and helps to create code with a good standard of readability. The body of the same page that you have just created using Razor, for example, written using the traditional ASP <% ... %> Web Forms syntax would look like this

```
<body>

    <h1><%= PageTitle %></h1>

    <ul>

        <% foreach (var movie in movies)
        } %>
            <li><%= movie %></li>
        <% } %>

    </ul>

</body>
```

Even in this simple nine line example, you can see just how much of an improvement the Razor syntax offers, in terms of readability and ease of coding.

Comments

As mentioned in Chapter 3, adding comments to your code greatly improves readability for yourself and other developers in the future. Razor only has one type of comment, which can be used in a single or multi-line fashion.

```
@* This is a Razor comment. *@

@*
    This is a multi-line
    Razor comment.
*@
```

Unlike comments made directly in HTML, Razor comments are not sent to the browser and cannot be viewed by users.

Mixing it up

There are times when an @ symbol is not intended as a token to identify the text immediately following it as server-side code. Take for instance an email address.

```
<p>Please contact support@example.com</p>
```

The Razor parser is clever enough to recognise this as an email address because it evaluates the text to the right-hand side of the @ symbol to determine if it is a valid C# code. It will also recognise where an email address ends and code begins. The following code renders the email address as plain text and the telephoneNumber variable as code.

```
@{ var telephoneNumber = "01632 567890"; }
<p>Please contact support@example.com or @telephoneNumber</p>
```

In the vast majority of cases, Razor works just exactly as you would expect. Once you have used it a few times, you will find that it becomes second nature and you use it without really thinking. However, there are bound to be a few edge cases where the Razor parser could potentially interpret the markup in a way that was not originally intended by the developer. In order to cope with this, there are a couple of ways to clarify your intent to the parser.

In cases where an @ symbol is intended for display on the page, but is also valid code, you can escape the @ symbol with @@.

```
@{ var stevelydford = "me"; }
<p>Follow me on twitter: @@stevelydford</p>
```

If you are nesting a block of client-side content within a server-side code block, it is necessary to wrap the content within an HTML element such as a <p>, <span>, or <div> to clarify the intent of the code to the Razor parser. The following example demonstrates this technique using <div> tags inside an if ... else statement.

```
@{ var loggedIn = false; }

<!DOCTYPE html>

<html lang="en">
    <head>
        <meta charset="utf-8" />
        <title>Example Page</title>
    </head>
    <body>
        @if (loggedIn)
        {
            <div>
                <h1>Welcome</h1>
                The time now is:
                @DateTime.Now.ToShortTimeString()<br />
                Have a nice day!
            </div>
        }
        else
        {
            <div>
                <h1>Please Log In</h1>
                You are not currently logged in<br />
                to this site. Please log in or register.
            </div>
        }
    </body>
</html>
```

Notice that there is also a single-line expression within the first <div>, declared using the @ symbol.

If you wish to send the content of the relevant code block in the if statement to the browser, without wrapping it within an HTML element, you can use the special tag, <text>.

```
<text>
    <h1>Welcome</h1>
    The time now is:
    @DateTime.Now.ToShortTimeString()<br />
    Have a nice day!
</text>
```

The <text> tag will not be sent to the browser, and exists purely to help the Razor parser in these circumstances. In this example, the following HTML is sent to the browser.

```
<h1>Welcome</h1>
The time now is:
17:45<br />
Have a nice day!
```

If you only need to output a single line of content within a code block, you can use the @: operator instead of wrapping it in <text> tags.

```
@if (loggedIn)
```

```
{
    @:Welcome, user!
}
else
{
    @:Please log in or register.
}
```

If the @: operator is omitted from the previous code example, the web server will display the following error page (see Figure 4-4).

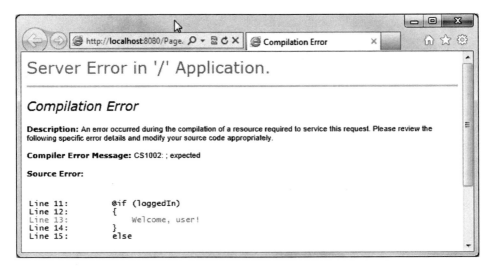

Figure 4-4. The error message displayed when the @: operators are omitted. They are required to provide clarification to the Razor parser.

■ **Tip**   All content output to the browser, using Razor, is HTML encoded for security purposes. This helps prevent Cross-Site Scripting (XSS) attacks. This means that reserved HTML characters are converted to their equivalent codes for display on the page (for example, a < symbol is converted to &lt). For example, if your page contains the following code

```
@{
    var message = "You must be <a href='login.cshtml'>logged in</a><br />to use this site.";
}
<p>@message</p>
```

the server will send the following encoded HTML to the browser

```
<p>You must be &lt;a href=&#39;login.cshtml&#39;&gt;logged in&lt;/a&gt; to use this site.</p>
```

To prevent this encoding, use the Html.Raw() method.

```
@{
    var message = "You must be <a href='login.cshtml'>logged in</a> to use this site.";
}
<p>@Html.Raw(message)</p>
```

For more information on XSS attacks and HTML encoding, see Chapter 5.

Layout

The look and feel of your site is very important when you are aiming to provide a great user experience; WebMatrix has lots of great features to help you achieve this. Perhaps, one of the most important of these, is the fact that the server-side Razor code produces clean standards-compliant HTML, which can be easily styled by a competent web designer using CSS and other techniques with which they are already familiar. The importance of this cannot be over-emphasised. Over the years, many web development frameworks have been heavily criticised for producing non-standard client-side content that is extremely difficult, or even impossible, to style and make work consistently across all browsers. With Razor, you have complete control over exactly what is sent to the users' browser–there are no "server controls" or "ViewStates" that will insert unwieldy HTML, scripts, and data into your page at runtime.

In addition to rendering clean standards-compliant content in a very controllable way, Razor has the ability to create layout templates to make designated sections of markup reusable across your site.

Staying DRY

"Don't Repeat Yourself", commonly known as DRY, is a software engineering principle that aims to minimise, or even remove entirely, the duplication of effort. The principle states that every piece of knowledge must have a single, unambiguous, authoritative representation within the system. This approach has many benefits, including reductions in initial development time, ease of maintenance, testing and debugging, and an improved ability to reuse code and assets in other projects.

If a system has completely implemented the DRY approach, the modification of any component of the system should have no effect on any unrelated parts. Likewise, any changes will only need to be made once–in the single, unambiguous, authoritative representation.

Whenever you sit down to carry out the initial design of a new system, you should always keep the principle of DRY at the forefront of your mind. The layout techniques covered in the rest of this section are an excellent place to start, as they facilitate the creation of sections of markup that can be reused across the entire site.

Most websites have at least some content that is displayed on every page. This helps in the consistency of the design and user experience. It may include common items such as headers, footers, and navigation, as well as other content areas specific to the user or application. When you are using WebMatrix, it is possible to define these items as templates and reuse them across all or selected pages.

RenderPage()

The first technique that you are going to look at to help reuse content in multiple places in your site is the use of the RenderPage() method. This method basically takes the content of another file in your site, often referred to as a partial page, and renders it in the exact place where the RenderPage() method is placed in the calling code. Once all calls to RenderPage() (and the other layout methods that you will look at later in this chapter) have been completed, the finished page is assembled by WebMatrix and sent to the client's browser. To the client, this process will be seamless.

The easiest way to fully understand the steps involved in using the RenderPage() method is to create a working example, so go ahead and fire up WebMatrix. Once the IDE has loaded, create a new 'Site From Template', choose the 'Empty Site' template, and call it 'Layouts'.

The first thing you'll need is a page from which to call the RenderPage() method. Select the Files tab in the Workspace Selector, and from the Ribbon Control choose New New File. Select CSHTML in the 'Choose a File Type' dialog, name the page Default.cshtml, and click OK.

Let's add some content to your default page.

```
@{ var PageTitle = "Layout Example"; }
<!DOCTYPE html>

<html lang="en">
    <head>
        <meta charset="utf-8" />
        <title>@PageTitle</title>
    </head>
    <body>
        <h2>@PageTitle</h2>
        <p>This is the main page content.</p>
    </body>
</html>
```

Next, add your partial page. It is a common convention amongst web developers that files intended to be shared across multiple pages in a site are stored in a folder named Shared. In the Navigation Pane, right-click the root folder (i.e. Layouts), and choose 'New Folder' from the context menu (see Figure 4-5). By default, WebMatrix will name the folder 'New Folder', so rename it to 'Shared' by overtyping the name or right-clicking and choosing 'Rename'.

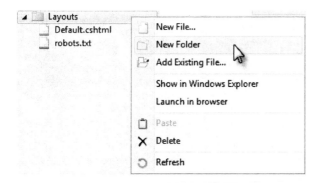

Figure 4-5. *Adding a new folder to your site.*

Add two new CSHTML files to this folder and call them `_Header.cshtml` and `_Footer.cshtml`.

■ **Note** By default, WebMatrix will not serve pages to the client's browser that are named with a leading underscore. You can use this to your advantage here, as you don't want users to request your partial pages unintentionally or otherwise.

Remove all the default HTML from `_Header.cshtml` and replace it with the following

```
<div id="header">
    <h1>.: Company Logo :.</h1>
    <hr />
</div>
```

Similarly, remove the HTML that was automatically created by WebMatrix in `_Footer.cshtml` and substitute it with the following content.

```
<div id="footer">
    <hr />
    <p>
        For all support enquiries, please contact
        <a href="mailto:support@example.com">support@example.com</a>
    </p>
</div>
```

Finally, you need to add calls to the `RenderPage()` method in `Default.cshtml` to insert the header and footer exactly where you want them to appear. You need to pass the `RenderPage()` method the exact location and filename of the shared file that you wish to render.

```
@{ var PageTitle = "Layout Example"; }
<!DOCTYPE html>

<html lang="en">
```

105

```
<head>
    <meta charset="utf-8" />
    <title>@PageTitle</title>
</head>
<body>

    @RenderPage("/Shared/_Header.cshtml")

    <h2>@PageTitle</h2>
    <p>This is the main page content.</p>

    @RenderPage("/Shared/_Footer.cshtml")

</body>
</html>
```

When you run the page, you will see that the header and footer have been inserted (see Figure 4-6).

Figure 4-6. *The default page, with the shared header and footer inserted, using the RenderPage() method.*

As far as the browser is concerned, it has just been served a single page by WebMatrix, as described in Figure 4-7.

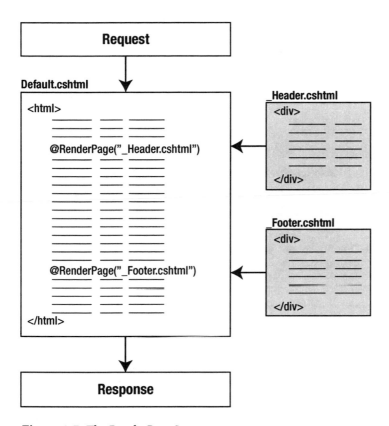

Figure 4-7. *The RenderPage() process.*

This is the code that you will see if you right-click the browser and choose 'View Source'.

```
<!DOCTYPE html>

<html lang="en">
    <head>
        <meta charset="utf-8" />
        <title>Layout Example</title>
    </head>
    <body>
        <div id="header">
            <h1>.: Company Logo :.</h1>
            <hr />
        </div>
        <h2>Layout Example</h2>
        <p>This is the main page content.</p>
        <div id="footer">
            <hr />
            <p>
```

```
            For all support enquiries, please contact
            <a href="mailto:support@example.com">support@example.com</a>
        </p>
    </div>
</body>
</html>
```

■ **Tip** When running the site from the WebMatrix IDE, it will always attempt to run the page that was currently (or most recently) selected in the Navigation Pane. Unfortunately, there is no way to set the page you wish to run by default, so you will need to remember to select the page you wish to view before clicking run, particularly if you have been editing a file that will not render, such as a partial page with an underscore prefix or a CSS file.

Alternatively, you can keep the browser open after the first run, and instead of running the site every time from within the WebMatrix IDE, just save all pages in WebMatrix (Ctrl + Shift + S) and refresh the browser (by pressing F5 in most browsers) to see any changes.

Layout Pages

The RenderPage() method is great for inserting a piece of common user interface (UI) into multiple pages, but what if you want to create a common whole-page design to be used throughout your site? In this situation, a good solution is the use of layout pages.

A layout page contains the template for a web page. Once a layout page has been defined, you can create content pages that specify that their layout is inherited from your layout page. Each layout page has a single call to the RenderBody() method that fetches the content and merges it with the layout page. If you have any previous experience with ASP.NET Web Forms, you will recognise this as being a similar concept to ContentPlaceHolders in Master Pages.

Layout pages can still include Razor code, and calls to the RenderPage() method as you did in the previous section. In fact, let's modify your existing Default.cshtml to use a layout page.

Create a new file in the Shared folder called _Layout.cshtml, and modify the generated HTML, as shown here

```
<!DOCTYPE html>

<html lang="en">
    <head>
        <meta charset="utf-8" />
        <title>Layout Page Example</title>
    </head>
    <body>
        @RenderPage("/Shared/_Header.cshtml")

        <div id="content">
            @RenderBody()
        </div>
```

```
        @RenderPage("/Shared/_Footer.cshtml")
    </body>
</html>
```

Now, open `Default.cshtml` and amend it to look like the following

```
@{
    Layout = "/Shared/_Layout.cshtml";
    var PageTitle = "Layout Example";
}
```

```
<h2>@PageTitle</h2>
<p>This is the main page content.</p>
```

Notice that in `Default.cshtml`, you have removed all the page level HTMLs (head tags, body tags, etc.), as this is now being provided by the layout page. All you need to do is to specify which layout page you wish to use by setting the `Layout` property at the top of the page before any markup is defined. In this case, you have set the Layout property equal to `"/Shared/_Layout.cshtml"`, the location of your layout page. The layout page then generates further calls to the `RenderPage()` method to pull in the header and footer and the finished page, is sent to the browser. Figure 4-8 shows how this process works.

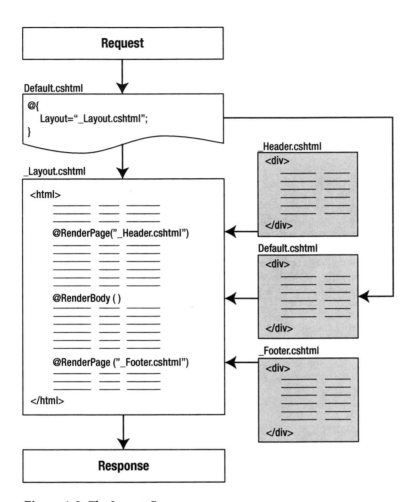

Figure 4-8. *The Layout Page process.*

The final result in this case will be identical to that seen previously in Figure 4-5. However, now you could go on to create any number of content pages, all by using your layout page to create a consistent look and feel to your site. Additionally, if you wanted to change the design at any point, you could do that once in the layout page and have that instantly reflected across your whole site.

RenderSection()

You can identify multiple content sections within a layout page, which is useful if you want to design layouts that have more than one area of replaceable content. This technique involves naming sections within your layout page, using the RenderSection() method, and providing content sections with a matching name in your content pages, as shown in Figure 4-9. Each named section within the content page is contained within a @section block.

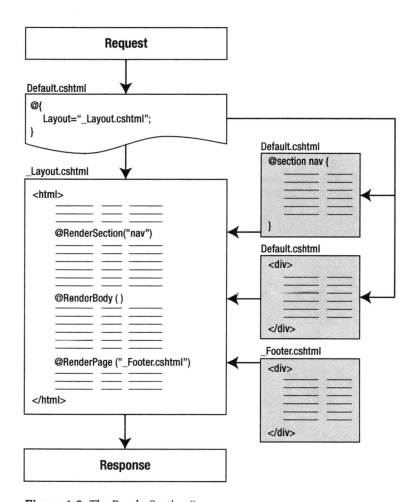

Figure 4-9. *The RenderSection() process.*

Let's demonstrate this process with an example. To begin, modify your layout page to include some calls to RenderSection(). These are the changes that you will make to /Shared/_Layout.cshtml

```
<!DOCTYPE html>

<html lang="en">
    <head>
        <meta charset="utf-8" />
        <title>@RenderSection("title")</title>
    </head>
    <body>
        @RenderPage("/Shared/_Header.cshtml")

        <div content="links">
```

111

```
        @RenderSection("links")
    </div>

    <div id="content">
        @RenderBody()
    </div>

    @RenderPage("/Shared/_Footer.cshtml")
    </body>
</html>
```

Two new sections called `title` and `links` have been defined. You'll need to define these sections in your content page (`Default.cshtml`) now, as running the site in its current state will produce the error page shown in Figure 4-10.

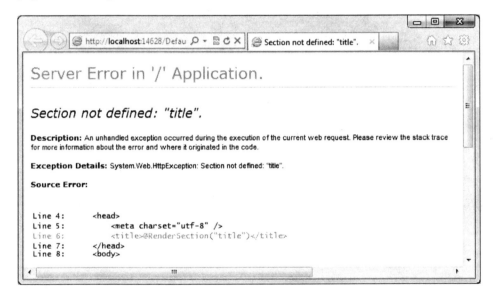

Figure 4-10. *Content sections are mandatory by default, if defined by using the RenderSection() method in the layout page.*

▓ **Caution**   WebMatrix will generate an error if the layout page contains a section that is not matched in the content page, and vice versa. It will also throw an exception if the layout page contains method calls that try to render the same section multiple times.

How to prevent this error will be discussed later in this section. For now, let's just add the required sections to your Default.cshtml page.

```
@{
    Layout = "/Shared/_Layout.cshtml";
    var PageTitle = "RenderSection Example";
}

@section title {
    @PageTitle
}

@section links {
    <ul>
        <li><a href="#">Home</a></li>
        <li><a href="#">Products</a></li>
        <li><a href="#">Clients</a></li>
        <li><a href="#">Contact Us</a></li>
    </ul>
}

<h2>@PageTitle</h2>
<p>This is the main page content.</p>
```

Now when you run the page, the content is correctly rendered (see Figure 4-11). The content within the named section blocks are rendered in place of the related RenderSection() method calls, and the RenderBody() call fetches the remaining content not held within the named sections.

Figure 4-11. Content correctly rendered within the named sections.

Making a section optional

In Layout.cshtml, notice how the `<title>` tag has a call to `RenderSection()`. This is a particularly useful technique, because without it, the title of the page would be set within the layout page and become essentially immutable. In a similar way, it is also useful to render a section within the document `<head>` tags to allow the content page to access to them, perhaps to register some CSS or JavaScript that is individual to that page. However, you do not want sections such as this to be mandatory, as you may not wish to use them on every occasion. To make the section optional, you can set the `required` parameter of the `RenderSection()` method equal to `false`, using C# named parameters, like so

```
@RenderSection("head", required: false)
```

Passing Data to Layout and Partial Pages

Often, you will require the actual rendered content of a layout or partial page to be based on some contextual data from the calling page. Examples of this include displaying a list of products depending on which category is chosen in an online store, or displaying a different piece of UI depending on whether a user is currently logged into the site or not.

In order to achieve this, you will need some way of passing data from the content page (i.e. the page requested by the user) to the relevant layout or partial pages. ASP.NET Web Pages delivers this functionality through the provision of the `PageData` property of the content page. The `PageData` property is a dictionary object that is shared between pages, layout pages, and partial pages, and can be used to pass data as required. To pass data from the content page, it is simply a matter of adding a key/value pair to the `PageData` property in the content page, which can then be accessed from any layout or partial pages that are called. This process is shown in Figure 4-12.

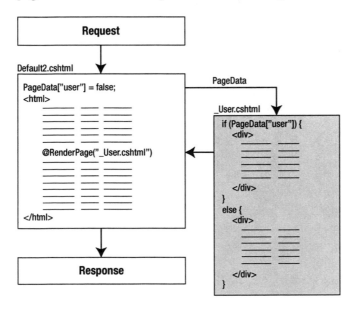

Figure 4-12. Passing data to a partial page.

Create a new page called Default2.cshtml. At the top of this page, add a value to the PageData dictionary. The following code shows this technique in practice.

```
@{
    PageData["user"] = false;
    var PageTitle = "PageData Example";
}

<!DOCTYPE html>

<html lang="en">
    <head>
        <meta charset="utf-8" />
        <title>@PageTitle</title>
    </head>
    <body>
        <h1>@PageTitle</h1>
        @RenderPage("/Shared/_User.cshtml")
    </body>
</html>
```

Next, create a partial page called _User.cshtml in the Shared folder. In this partial page, check the value of PageData["user"] to decide whether to display a welcome message or a login form.

```
@if (PageData["user"]) {
    <div>
        <h2>Welcome!</h2>]
        <!-- More info about user here -->
    </div>
}
else {
    <div>
        <form method="post" action="login.cshtml">
            <h2>Login:</h2>
            <div>
                <label for="username">Username: </label>
                <input type="text" name="username" />
            </div>
            <div>
                <label for="password">Password: </label>
                <input type="password" name="password" />
            </div>
            <div>
                <input type="submit" value="Login" />
            </div>
        </form>
    </div>
}
```

The key/value pairs stored in the PageData dictionary are not restricted to just .NET primitive types. The PageData dictionary is actually declared as

115

IDictionary<object, dynamic>

So, it is quite common to see custom objects, generic collections, etc. being passed in the PageData dictionary. To see this in action, create a new page called Catalog.cshtml and amend the default markup to match the code example below, which adds a notional list of categories to the PageData dictionary.

```
@{
    var categories = new List<string>() { "Books", "Films", "Music", "Games", "Toys" };
    PageData["categories"] = categories;
}

<!DOCTYPE html>

<html lang="en">
    <head>
        <meta charset="utf-8" />
        <title>PageData Example</title>
    </head>
    <body>
        <h1>PageData Example</h1>
        @RenderPage("/Shared/_Categories.cshtml")
    </body>
</html>
```

The following example code shows how a partial page named Categories.cshtml can access the categories page data passed in from the calling page.

```
<div>
    <h2>Categories</h2>
    <ul>
        @{
            foreach (var category in PageData["categories"])
            {
                <li>@category</li>
            }
        }
    </ul>
</div>
```

This renders the output to the browser, as seen in Figure 4-13.

Figure 4-13. Passing a generic list to a partial page using PageData.

Helpers

Helpers are another way to help you achieve DRYness in your site design. A helper is a custom component that can receive a list of parameters in a way similar to a method call, and return HTML (or any kind of client-content) to be rendered on the page.

Helpers have an enormous number of potential uses. In the example in this section, you will use a helper to display a common piece of UI that presents information about a product. This is a very simple example, but in reality, helpers can contain any markup and client-side or server-side code that you need. You will make extensive use of helpers of varying complexity throughout the examples in this book.

Helpers (and functions that will be covered in the next section) must be created within a folder in the root of your website called **App_Code**. This folder name is an ASP.NET convention that automatically makes all code within it available for use in the rest of your application. The **App_Code** folder can contain sub-folders, the contents of which will also be accessible to the code in the rest of your site.

Tip   There are many pre-written helpers available for download that you can use to add functionality to your site. Some of these, including Twitter, Facebook, and other helpers, will be discussed in more detail in Chapter 8.

In order to see an example of helpers in action, you will create a new site called HelperExample, using the Empty Site template. You will need to add an **App_Code** folder to the root of your web site, which you can do by right-clicking the root folder in the Navigation Pane and choosing the New Folder option. Once the folder has been created and named, right-click it and choose New File. Add a CSHTML file called **ProductHelpers.cshtml**. The site structure in your Navigation Pane should look like the one shown in Figure 4-14.

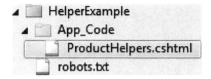

Figure 4-14. The App_Code folder.

Note   By default, WebMatrix will not serve any pages in the App_Code folder directly to the user's browser, so you do not need to prefix the filename with an underscore.

Replace the default content that WebMatrix has automatically generated inside the new file with the following

```
@helper ProductInfo(string title, string description, decimal price)
{
    <div style="border:2px solid #666; background-color:#ffffcc; padding:10px; width:10em;">
        <strong>@title</strong><br />
        @description<br />
        <em>£@price</em>
    </div>
}
```

A call to this helper method can be made within any page by using an @ symbol followed by the filename and helper name, separated by a dot. Add a file named Product.cshtml to the root folder in your application. In the body of the page, add the following code.

```
@ProductHelpers.ProductInfo("Widget", "This is the product description", 2.99m)
```

If you had created folders within App_Code, you would be able to call the helper using the following syntax.

```
@FolderName.FileName.HelperName
```

When called, your example product helper renders, as seen in Figure 4-15.

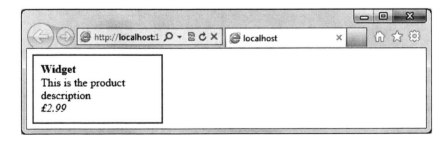

Figure 4-15. An example ProductInfo helper.

Functions

WebMatrix functions are static methods that can be called from anywhere in your WebMatrix application. Unlike helpers, which can return only a block of HTML for rendering in the browser, a function can return any valid C# type.

Let's create a function that accepts a date of birth as a parameter and returns the person's current age as an integer.

If your site doesn't already have an App_Code folder, create one, and inside it create a file called DateFunctions.cshtml. Add the following code to DateFunctions.cshtml.

```
@functions {

    public static int CurrentAge (DateTime dateOfBirth)
    {
        DateTime today = DateTime.Today;
        int years = today.Year - dateOfBirth.Year;
        // Subtract a year if this year's birthday hasn't happened yet
        if (today.Month < dateOfBirth.Month || (today.Month == dateOfBirth.Month && 
            today.Day < dateOfBirth.Day))
        {
            years--;
        }
        return years;
    }
}
```

As you can see from this code snippet, functions are simply standard C# static methods enclosed within a @functions {...} code block. In this example, you have declared a function called CurrentAge, which accepts a DateTime and returns an int. The function simply subtracts the year of the date of birth passed to the function from the current year and then decrements this by a further year, if this year's birthday hasn't yet happened.

You can add any number of functions to your DateFunctions.cshtml file, as long as they all appear within the @functions {...} code block.

```
@functions {

    public static int CurrentAge (DateTime dateOfBirth)
    {
        DateTime today = DateTime.Today;
        int years = today.Year - dateOfBirth.Year;
        // Subtract a year if this year's birthday hasn't happened yet
        if (today.Month < dateOfBirth.Month || (today.Month == dateOfBirth.Month && 
            today.Day < dateOfBirth.Day))
        {
            years--;
        }
        return years;
    }

    public static int DaysToNextBirthday (DateTime dateOfBirth)
    {
```

```
    DateTime today = DateTime.Today;
    DateTime next = new DateTime(today.Year, dateOfBirth.Month, dateOfBirth.Day);

    // Add a year if this years birthday has already happened
    if (next < today)
    {
        next = next.AddYears(1);
    }

    int days = (next - today).Days;

    return days;
    }
}
```

To call your functions from within any Razor page in your project, simply give the filename followed by the function name in the standard .NET dot-separated format.

```
@{
    DateTime birthday = new DateTime(1981, 12, 8);
    int age = @DateFunctions.CurrentAge(birthday);
    int daysToBirthday = @DateFunctions.DaysToNextBirthday(birthday);
}

<p>Your current age is @age</p>
<p>@daysToBirthday days until you are @(age + 1)</p>
```

Tip As you build more and more WebMatrix web applications, you will gather a whole library of common functions and helpers that can help to vastly reduce the development time of future projects.

Maintaining State

The HyperText Transfer Protocol (HTTP),which is the networking protocol used as the foundation of data communication on the World Wide Web, is a stateless protocol. When using HTTP, a request is made to the web server by the client, and a response is constructed and then returned. After the response has been returned, the web server has no further links to the client browser. In other words, each individual HTTP request has no knowledge of previous requests, and future requests will have no knowledge of the requests made today.

This concept works well for the disconnected and distributed nature of the World Wide Web, but it does cause some problems for web developers when trying to perform tasks that require data to be maintained across requests. Even relatively simple and common tasks, such as tracking the status of a user's authentication or keeping track of the items in a shopping cart, require some sort of state to be maintained.

HTTP and ASP.NET Web Pages provide several ways for us to maintain state in web applications. In this chapter, you will look at sessions and cookies.

Session State

The ASP.NET session state enables you to store and retrieve data per user, as they browse your application. A session is started when the user first lands on a page in your web site and ends either when they close their browser, or when the session "times out" due to inactivity after a predetermined period of time (set in IIS as twenty minutes, by default).

Session Variables

The most common use of the session for maintaining state is for storing user specific data in session variables. Session variables are stored in a dictionary on the server, and are unique to each visitor per session.

The session variable collection is indexed by a string or an integer index. Session variables do not have to be explicitly added to the collection, they can simply be added or retrieved by referring to their name or index.

```
@{
    Session["username"] = "Bond007";
    Session["membershipLevel"] = 3;
}

<h1>Welcome @Session["username"]!</h1>
```

By default, session variables can hold any valid .NET data type, including generic collections and custom objects.

Session Identifiers

All sessions created and maintained by the server are given a unique identifier, which is stored in the SessionID property of the page. Each new request for a page is examined to see if it already has a valid SessionID–if one is not present; the server starts a new session and assigns a new SessionID.

A session is considered to be active if the user has requested a page within the session "time out" period. If the time between requests exceeds the time out period, the session is dropped and a new SessionID is assigned, and by default, stored in a cookie. The SessionID can be accessed directly in code, and returns a randomly generated sequence of numbers and letters, an example of which is shown here

```
@Session.SessionID       // wxjzybjnnkur0qrgf5wjs2ko
```

The SessionID is generated in memory, on the server, and is not persisted to disk. Therefore, while a SessionID is unique at the time it is created, it cannot be guaranteed to be unique over an extended period. A server reset, for example, may cause duplicate SessionID's to be produced.

If your application design requires that you determine whether the session was created during the current request, you can interrogate the Session.IsNewSession property, which returns a Boolean true or false.

Cookies

A cookie is a small text file kept on the user's machine that can be used to store data specific to that user. The advantage of using cookies is that they are not necessarily deleted when a session closes, so they can persist on the users machine and be retrieved or amended the next time they visit the site. The disadvantages are that they have a very limited size, are text-only, are browser-specific, and might be disabled in the users' browser settings.

Cookies are written using the page's Response property, and can contain only strings. When writing a cookie, you can also set some other properties, the most common being the expiration date.

```
@{
    Response.Cookies["username"].Value = "Bond007";
    Response.Cookies["username"].Expires = DateTime.Now.AddDays(7);
}
```

If you do not set the expiration date, the cookie will expire at the end of the current session. Cookies can also contain subkeys, which help the developer to keep the site's cookies organised and treat groups of them as a single object when convenient. For example

```
@{
    Response.Cookies["user"]["username"] = "Bond007";
    Response.Cookies["user"]["membershipLevel"] = "3";
    Response.Cookies["user"].Expires = DateTime.Now.AddDays(7);
}
```

To retrieve the value of a cookie, you use the Request property of the page. You need to check that the cookie exists before you retrieve its value, because if it does not, ASP.NET will throw a NullReferenceException.

```
@{
    string username = "";

    if(Request.Cookies["username"] != null)
    {
        username = Request.Cookies["username"].Value;
    }
}
```

Cookies containing subkeys are also interrogated using the Request property, and must be checked for existence before accessing.

```
@{
    string username = "";
    int userLevel = 0;

    if(Request.Cookies["user"] != null)
    {
        username = Request.Cookies["user"]["username"];
        userLevel = int.Parse(Request.Cookies["user"]["membershipLevel"]);
    }
}
```

Limitations of Cookies

When designing a web application that uses cookies, it is important to bear in mind that individual users can delete, or altogether refuse, cookies on their machine–in fact, a user may not even be on the same machine when they re-visit the site, whether they accept cookies or not. Therefore, although cookies are very useful, you should never rely on them, and should use them only for non-essential features. The same rule applies to session variables, as they too rely on cookies by default.

If you attempt to write a cookie to a browser that will not accept them, no exception will be thrown. Checking to see if a browser can accept cookies is actually a fairly straightforward task. You just need to attempt to write a cookie and read it back on another page. If you cannot read the value of the cookie you have just set, you can assume that cookies are unavailable to you.

▓ **Caution**   In order to ensure the security of your application, it is important that you validate any data that you receive from a user. This includes cookies, which are stored on a user's machine and could potentially be open to tampering, and thereby inject malicious data into your site.

Startup Code

ASP.NET Web Pages provide ways to run code before a page loads. There are various scenarios in which this pattern can be advantageous– error handling and the setting of global site wide variables are to name but two.

You can run code the first time the web site is accessed and before and after any page in a particular folder is loaded. This section will describe the methods of doing this.

Application Level Code

When a site is first accessed, WebMatrix checks to see if the `_AppStart.cshtml` page has been run. If this check returns false, then the `_AppStart.cshtml` page is executed before the actual page requested is dealt with.

The `_AppStart.cshtml` file must be created in the root of the website, which is an excellent place to set global variables–in fact ASP.NET Web Pages provides the `AppState` dictionary specifically for this task.

In this example, you will add an item to the `AppState` dictionary to store the application's name. Create a new site, add an `_AppStart.cshtml` file to the site root, and replace the contents of the file with the following

```
@{
    AppState["appName"] = "My Custom Web Site";
}
```

You now have access to the `AppState` dictionary from everywhere within your site. To see this in action, create a new file called Default.cshtml, and enter the following code

```
<!DOCTYPE html>
<html>
    <head>
```

```
        <title>@AppState["appName"]</title>
    </head>
    <body>
        <h1>@AppState["appName"]</h1>
    </body>
</html>
```

This code interrogates the `AppState` dictionary, in order to display the name of the application inside the `<title>` and `<h1>` tags.

A common use for the `_AppStart.cshtml` file is to initialize values for helpers that you use in your site–many of the available third-party helpers require initialization with API keys, usernames, etc.

░ **Caution**   You should take extra care to ensure that the code inside your _AppStart file is bug free, because if it fails to run the website won't start.

Folder Level Code

ASP.NET Web Pages checks for the presence of a `_PageStart.cshtml` in the folder containing the requested file, or any of the folders above it, and if found, runs them all, starting at the root folder, before the requested page is executed. If the `_AppStart.cshtml` file has not been run when a page is requested, it is run first; this is then followed by the execution of the relevant `_PageStart.cshtml` files, if they exist. Finally, the requested page is executed.

If a hierarchy of folders exists, each can contain a `_PageStart.cshtml` file. WebMatrix will start at the root folder level and run every `_PageStart.cshtml` file it encounters as it navigates its way down the folder hierarchy to the requested page.

Within the `_PageStart.cshtml` file, you make a call to the `RunPage()` method, which tells the server where in the `_PageStart.cshtml` file you want the requested page to run, as shown in Figure 4-16.

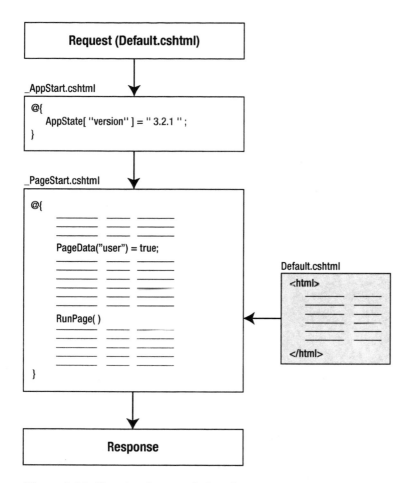

Figure 4-16. *The _AppStart and _PageStart process.*

As you can see in this diagram, `_PageStart.cshtml` can include code that is run before and after every page in a folder. The diagram also shows that if the `_AppStart.cshtml` file needs to be run, this will always happen first.

The most common use for the `_PageStart.cshtml` file is to set the layout page for every file in a particular folder. By declaring the location of the layout page in the `_PageStart.cshtml` file, it will be inherited by all other pages in that folder and those below. Other common uses include error handling and folder-level access restriction; you will look at all these techniques during the course of the book.

URLs and Routing

The URLs of the pages in your site can have a huge impact on the usability of your site and how it is indexed by the major search engines.

WebMatrix provides several tools for working with URLs, both in terms of making them human readable and search engine friendly, and for passing data between pages within the URL itself. This section will identify the most common of these methods, and how they can benefit your site.

Routing

ASP.NET Web Pages have built-in support for working with friendly URLS. Consider the following two URLs.

```
http://www.example.com/store/showProducts.cshtml?catID=12
http://www.example.com/store/categories/books
```

Clearly, the second one is easier for a human user to read, making it more likely to be hacked (i.e. it visualizes the site structure and allows users to move to higher levels of the information architecture by hacking off the end of the URL), but it is also much friendlier to search engine spiders, and can help improve your site's ranking on search engines such as Google. So how can you achieve this with WebMatrix?

If you have used ASP.NET MVC in the past (or possibly ASP.NET Web Forms), you will have used System.Web.Routing to provide a detailed routing table matching URL elements to controllers or files. In ASP.NET Web Pages, the built-in routing requires that URLs ultimately map to a physical file on the server. This sounds complicated, but in reality it is actually a simple concept. Take the second URL in the previous example– WebMatrix will take the URL and attempt to match the individual elements of the URL, from left to right, to physical files and folders on disk. If a match is found, the remaining elements are passed to the page as URLData (which will be discussed in more detail at the end of this section).

The search for a matching file in this case would adhere to the following steps:

1. Is there a file at `/store/categories/books.cshtml` or `/store/categories/books.vbhtml`? If so, run this page.
2. Is there a file at `/store/categories.cshtml` or `/store/categories.vbhtml`? If so, run this page, and pass "books" in the URLData.
3. Is there a file at `/store.cshtml` or `/store.vbhtml`? If so, run this page, and pass "categories" and "books" in the URLData.
4. Is there a file at `/store/categories/books/default.cshtml` or `/store/categories/books/default.vbhtml`? If so, run this page.
5. Is there a file at `/store/categories/books/index.cshtml` or `/store/categories/books/index.cshtml`? If so, run this page.

If no match is found during this search, an HTTP 404– File Not Found error page is returned.

Passing Data in the URL

There are two types of data that can be passed in a URL. If WebMatrix performs the routing search described in the last section and has data to be passed to the page, it will pass it in the URLData collection.

Data can be retrieved from the URLData collection using an integral, zero-based index. For example, imagine you had a file at /store/categories.cshtml and a user browsed to

```
http://www.example.com/store/categories/music
```

Web Pages would execute /store/categories.cshtml and pass the value "music" in the URLData, which you could retrieve in the categories.cshtml page with the following code

```
<!DOCTYPE html>
<html>
    <head>
        <title>URLData Example</title>
    </head>
    <body>
        <h1>Category: @UrlData[0].ToString()</h1>
    </body>
</html>
```

Data can also be passed in the URL in the form of a QueryString. A QueryString is a standard web format where name/value pairs are passed at the end of the URL following a question mark (?) character. Multiple name/value pairs can be passed, separated by an ampersand (&). For example

```
http://www.example.com/store/showProduct.cshtml?catID=B12&productID=CD20199
```

This data can then be retrieved using the pages' Request property, like so

```
@{
    string categoryID = "";
    string productID = "";

    if (Request.QueryString["catID"] != null)
    {
        categoryID = Request.QueryString["catID"].ToString();
    }

    if (Request.QueryString["productID"] != null)
    {
        productID = Request.QueryString["productID"].ToString();
    }
}
```

Notice that you are performing a check to see if the QueryString parameter exists before you try to access its value, to avoid a potential NullReferenceException.

■ **Caution** It is important that you never trust the data being sent to you as part of a URL. It can easily be changed by the user, which can cause serious security issues. This type of vulnerability is known as an "Insecure Direct Object Reference," and was exploited famously in 2011, to unlawfully gain access to accounts on a major banking web site by hackers who altered the account number passed in the URL, having previously logged in to a valid account.

Summary

In this chapter, you have expanded your knowledge of WebMatrix by learning about ASP.NET Web Pages and the Razor syntax. You have learned how the Razor syntax is used to insert C# server-side code into ASP.NET Web Pages and how to use helpers and functions to maximize code reuse in your project. You have also seen how easy it is to achieve a consistent look and feel throughout your site using layout pages and partial pages. Finally, you learned different ways to maintain state in your application, run code before your pages execute, and made use of the ASP.NET Web Pages built-in routing system.

In the next chapter, you are going to look at ways to build some user interaction into your site through the use of HTML forms, and learn how to validate that interaction.

Forms and Validation

Until now, our server-side code has provided dynamic content but it also has been a one-way operation—we have only been concerned with presenting content to the user. In this chapter we will learn how to make our sites much more interactive by taking user input and performing operations based on it.

User input is commonly gathered through the use of HTML forms; we can interrogate the form contents using Razor code once the form has been submitted. When we have learned how to retrieve the data from the submitted form, we will look at ways of validating the data submitted by users, both to ensure that they have submitted the required data and that any data they have supplied is in the format we are expecting.

The first section in this chapter deals with the mechanics and semantics of HTML forms. If you have little or no previous experience with creating dynamic interactive web pages, and consequently have not have spent much time working with HTML forms, this section is for you. If you are already an experienced web developer, perhaps currently using a different server-side technology such as Rails or PHP, you may wish to simply skim over this section.

■ **Note** A good understanding of HTML forms is fundamental to the content in the rest of the book. Although prior knowledge of HTML is assumed, I have included the brief revision section on HTML forms at the beginning of this chapter as it is very possible for even an experienced web designer to have very little actual working knowledge of forms if they have no previous server-side coding experience.

HTML Forms

HTML forms use a `<form>` tag to act as a container for an assortment of input controls to gather data from the user. The `<form>` tag has attributes that determine where the data captured by the controls in the form will be sent for processing (the `action` attribute) and how those data are sent (the `method` attribute).

The action attribute contains the URL of the page which will handle the submitted form data; in the majority of cases this will be the same page that contains the form. By default, if the action attribute contains an empty string, WebMatrix will pass the data back to the sending page. Nevertheless, it is good to be explicit to help keep your code readable.

The method attribute specifies the HTTP method that is to be used to send the form to the processing page. The attribute can contain one of two values: `get` or `post`. The get method appends the form data to the URI as a `QueryString`, whereas the post method includes the form data in the HTTP request and is not visible to the user. The get method has the advantage that the resulting URI (including the form data in the `QueryString`) can be bookmarked by the user—this is useful for bookmarking search results, for example. However, if the server-side code uses the submitted form data to make changes to persisted data (in a database for example), then the post method should be used to ensure security as the `QueryString` can be easily changed by the user in the browser's address bar.

```
<form action="page.cshtml" method="post">
    ...
</form>
```

Form Controls

Any HTML tag, except that defining another form, can be nested within a `<form>` start tag and a `</form>` end tag. The tags we are interested in here are the group of HTML elements known as controls—input, button, select, textarea, label, and fieldset.

The input tag

The `<input>` tag can display a number of different UI elements that are designed to gather data from the user in different ways; it is the most commonly used element by far. The exact characteristics of the control to be rendered by the input element are determined by the values of its various attributes. The most important attributes when working with `<input>` tags in WebMatrix are listed in Table 5-1:

Table 5-1. Important HTML input tag attributes

Attribute	Definition	Possible Values
type	The type of control to create.	Required. Accepted values are: text, password, checkbox, radio, submit, reset, file, image, button, hidden
name	The name of the control.	Any character string
value	The initial value of the control.	Any character string. Mandatory only for "radio" and "checkbox" controls.
size	The width of the control.	Given in pixels (or number of characters for "text" or "password" controls).
maxlength	The maximum number of characters which can be entered in a "text" or "password" control.	Unlimited number of characters for "text" and "password" controls by default.

Table 5-1 cont.

checked	Indicates whether a "radio" or "checkbox" control is checked (i.e. true).	The checkbox or radio button is unchecked by default. If you want it to be checked, set the attribute checked="checked".
src	The location of the images to be used for "image" controls.	Any valid URI
readonly	Specifies whether the control can be modified by the user.	Boolean
disabled	When set, disables the control for user input.	Boolean

As you can see, the value of the type attribute actually determines which control is rendered to the page. The text and password input controls render a single-line textbox to the page designed to capture keyboard input. The two controls are essentially the same, except that the password control masks the user's input (see Figure 5-1).

```
<form action="page.cshtml" method="post">
    Username: <input type="text" name="username" maxlength="20" /><br />
    Password: <input type="password" name="password"  />
</form>
```

Figure 5-1. *The text and password input controls showing user input*

As you would expect, Razor code can be used to set the initial value of a control. Here, we set the initial value of a text control called **startdate** to the current date:

```
<form action="page.cshtml" method="post">
    Start Date:
    <input type="text" name="startdate" value="@DateTime.Now.ToShortDateString()" />
</form>
```

■ **Note** If you have previous experience with ASP.NET Web Forms, you will know that, due to the architecture of the ASP.NET Web Forms model, it is restricted to a single form per page. The same is not true of ASP.NET Web Pages. With ASP.NET Web Pages, multiple, non-nested forms are perfectly acceptable within the same CSHTML page.

Checkbox controls are designed to collect Boolean data. The string specified in the value attribute is the literal that will be sent as part of the forms data if the checkbox is checked when the form is submitted. If the checked attribute is set to a value of "checked", the checkbox will be checked on the initial rendering of the form (see Figure 5-2).

```
<form action="page.cshtml" method="post">
    Correct? <input type="checkbox" name="correct" value="true" checked="checked" /><br />
    Opt in? <input type="checkbox" name="opt_in" value="true" />
</form>
```

Figure 5-2. The checkbox control

Unlike checkbox controls, which work independently of each other, radio buttons are intended to be used in situations where a user ideally selects only one of a number of options. All options are given the same name and the string in the value attribute of the chosen option is passed to the form handler on submission. Because the radio button group might possibly be submitted with no value selected, prevent this behavior by ensuring that one of the options has the checked attribute set in the initial markup (see Figure 5-3).

```
<form action="page.cshtml" method="post">
    Color: <br/>
    <input type="radio" name="color" value="red" checked="checked" /> Red<br />
    <input type="radio" name="color" value="green" /> Green<br />
    <input type="radio" name="color" value="blue" /> Blue<br />
    <input type="radio" name="color" value="yellow" /> Yellow
</form>
```

Figure 5-3. *A group of radio button controls*

The next code sample and screenshot (see Figure 5-4) show the various types of button control, listed here:

- The `file` control displays a file selection dialog box that allows the user to choose a file on their machine; this control is commonly used as part of a file upload process.

- The `button` control simply renders a push button on the page. The push button has no default behavior and is designed to be used in conjunction with client-side scripting to react to events (when clicked, released, etc.).

- The `reset` button control simply resets all of the controls in the form to their initial values.

- The `submit` and `image` buttons fulfill the same purpose; they both send the form data to the server. Every form must have at least one submit or image button that, when clicked, will send the form data to the server using the method and action specified in the form tags attributes. The submit control renders a standard button with the text specified in the `value` attribute as the button's label. The image button uses an image, whose URI is specified in the `src` attribute, to decorate the button. For accessibility reasons, providing an alternate text, using the alt attribute, is important for image buttons.

```
<form action="page.cshtml" method="post">
    File control: <input type="file" name="userfile" /><br />
    Button control: <input type="button" value="Click Here" /><br />
    Reset control: <input type="reset" value="Reset Form" /><br />
    Submit control: <input type="submit" value="Submit Form" /><br />
    Image control: <input type="image" src="images/button.png" alt="click me" />
</form>
```

Figure 5-4. *HTML button controls*

The final type of input control is the hidden control. The hidden control is not rendered but its value is submitted with the form. This is generally used to store data that are meaningless to the user but are necessary for the server-side functionality of the form handler, such as an individual record's unique identifier. It is important to note that the hidden control is not secure and the value can be easily read by the user viewing the source of the page.

```
<form action="page.cshtml" method="post">
    <input type="hidden" name="id" value="abcd1234" />
</form>
```

The select tag

The `<select>` element is used to render a drop-down list. Each choice within the drop-down list is represented by an `<option>` element, whose content is rendered in the drop-down section of the drop-down list. The `<option>` element also contains an attribute called value, which is the actual data to be posted back to the web server as part of the form. The following code example and screenshot (see Figure 5-5) demonstrates the use of a `<select>` tag, where the name of each airport is displayed to the user, but the unique three-letter international code is sent to the server for processing:

```
<form action="page.cshtml" method="post">
    Choose an airport:
    <select name="airport">
        <option value="LHR">London Heathrow</option>
        <option value="LAX">Los Angeles International</option>
        <option value="SIN">Changi International</option>
        <option value="JFK">John F. Kennedy International</option>
        <option value="HND">Tokyo International</option>
        <option value="MIA">Miami International</option>
        <option value="FRA">Frankfurt International</option>
        <option value="CDG">Charles De Gaulle International</option>
        <option value="HKG">Hong Kong International</option>
        <option value="PEK">Beijing Capital International</option>
    </select>
</form>
```

Figure 5-5. The select element

To set an initial value, the selected attribute can be applied to any one of the options with a value of selected (i.e. `selected="selected"`). Groups of options can also be brought together into logical clusters using the `<optgroup>` tag. The following code sample and screenshot, Figure 5-6, shows our airport drop-down list grouped by continent:

```
<form action="page.cshtml" method="post">
    Choose an airport:
    <select name="airport">
        <optgroup label="Europe">
            <option value="LHR" selected="selected">London Heathrow</option>
            <option value="FRA">Frankfurt International</option>
            <option value="CDG">Charles De Gaulle International</option>
        </optgroup>
        <optgroup label="North America">
            <option value="LAX">Los Angeles International</option>
            <option value="JFK">John F. Kennedy International</option>
            <option value="MIA">Miami International</option>
        </optgroup>
        <optgroup label="Asia">
            <option value="SIN">Changi International</option>
            <option value="HND">Tokyo International</option>
            <option value="HKG">Hong Kong International</option>
            <option value="PEK">Beijing Capital International</option>
        </optgroup>
    </select>
</form>
```

Figure 5-6. Clustering menu options using the optgroup tag

As you can see, the use of the `<optgroup>` tag makes the list much easier for the user to navigate; only the options, not the option groups, can be selected.

A common programming requirement is to want to populate the contents of a `<select>` tag with a list of values held in a collection, whether that collection has itself been populated as the result of a database query or by other means. Assuming that the collection you are iterating implements either IEnumerable or IEnumerable<T>, the easiest way to add the contents of a collection to a drop-down list is to use a **foreach** loop. In the following example we declare and initialize a generic list of months and add them as options to a select control:

```
@using System.Globalization;
@{
    Dictionary<int, string> months = new Dictionary<int, string>();

    // Populate the months dictionary with the month number and name
    for (int i = 1; i <= 12; i++)
    {
        months.Add(i, DateTimeFormatInfo.CurrentInfo.GetMonthName(i));
    }
}

<!DOCTYPE html>
<html lang="en">
<head>
    <meta charset="utf-8" />
    <title></title>
</head>
<body>
    <form action="page.cshtml" method="post">
    Month:
    <select name="month">
        @foreach (var month in months)
        {
            <option value="@month.Key">@month.Value</option>
        }
    </select>
    </form>
</body>
</html>
```

Although not often used, the <select> tag has a size attribute, which indicates the number of items to be shown in your list. When set, the browser will render a fixed list, or list box, instead of a drop-down menu. The list box works in every other way identically to the drop-down list.

The button tag

The <button> element creates a push button that operates in exactly the same way as the <input> element button control type; the only difference between the two control types is the <button> element's ability to contain HTML content—most usually, but not restricted to, styled text or images. The button's type attribute determines whether it is a submit, reset, or push button type.

The following markup renders the button shown in Figure 5-7:

```
<form action="page.cshtml" method="post">
    <button name="submit" type="submit">
        Submit
        <img src="images/tick.png" alt="Submit the form" />
    </button>
</form>
```

Figure 5-7. The button control has richer rendering possibilities than the input button types.

The textarea tag

The `<textarea>` element renders a multi-line text input control. The control is sized by specifying the number of rows and columns of text, using the rows and cols attributes. Unlike the `<input>` text controls, the initial value of the `<textarea>` element is contained between the `<textarea>` start tag and the `</textarea>` end tag, rather than in a value attribute.

The following code example and screenshot (see Figure 5-8) renders a `textarea` 40 columns by 10 rows in size, with some initial sample content. The actual textual content of the `textarea` has been shortened in the code example for clarity:

```
<form action="page.cshtml" method="post">
    Notes:<br/>
    <textarea name="notes" cols="40" rows="10">Lorem ipsum... </textarea></form>
```

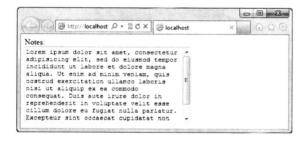

Figure 5-8. The textarea element renders a multi-line text box.

As with the `<input>` control types, the `<textarea>` has Boolean flags, `readonly` and `disabled`, which can be used to stop users from making changes to the content of the `textarea`, or to disable it completely.

The label and fieldset tags

The final two types of HTML form control that we are going to look at here are the `<label>` and `<fieldset>`. These controls are purely read-only controls that are designed to convey information to our users and organize our UI.

The `<fieldset>` tag is used to visually group controls on the page to aid users' understanding and navigation of the form. A `<legend>` tag can be added as the first child element of the `<fieldset>` tag to assign a caption to the fieldset.

The `<label>` tag is explicitly related to an individual form control (such as a textbox) via its `for` attribute, which must match exactly the value contained in the `id` attribute of the associated control. It is

137

used to attach information to a control to present a visually improved user experience and to aid navigation and accessibility.

The following code sample and screenshot (see Figure 5-9) demonstrate the correct use of the `<fieldset>`, `<legend>`, and `<label>` elements to provide visual cues to the users of our forms:

```
<form action="page.cshtml" method="post">
    <fieldset>
        <legend>Personal Details</legend>
        <div>
            <label for="surname">Surname: </label>
            <input type="text" name="surname" id="surname" />
        </div>
        <div>
            <label for="forenames">Forenames: </label>
            <input type="text" name="forenames" id="forenames" />
        </div>
        <div>
            <label for="license">Current Driving License: </label>
            <input type="checkbox" name="license" id="license" />
        </div>
    </fieldset>
    <fieldset>
        <legend>Vehicle Details</legend>
        <div>
            <label for="make">Make: </label>
            <input type="text" name="make" id="make" />
        </div>
        <div>
            <label for="model">Model: </label>
            <input type="text" name="model" id="model" />
        </div>
    </fieldset>
    <div>
        <input type="reset" value="Reset Form" />
        <input type="submit" value="Save Details" />
    </div>
</form>
```

Figure 5-9. *Improving the user interface using* `fieldset`, `legend`, *and* `label` *elements*

You will notice that all of the `<input>` tags have `id` and `name` attributes. The `id` attribute is used to identify all HTML elements for style and scripting purposes, whereas the `name` attribute is used to access the value of form controls (see the Accessing Submitted Form Data section later in the chapter).

■ **Tip**   The World Wide Web Consortium (W3C) is the organization responsible for the development of web standards and they have excellent information on all aspects of HTML available on their web site. The section containing information specific to HTML forms can be found at: `www.w3.org/TR/html5/forms.html`

HTML Form Helpers

As you can imagine, creating forms in HTML can soon become a tedious and repetitive process. Fortunately, ASP.NET Web Pages provides us with some useful HTML helper methods for displaying form fields. The methods are all part of the HtmlHelper class and can save a considerable amount of development time when creating forms, as they offer a much terser, neater syntax.

For example, to create an input text control, instead of writing the following HTML:

```
<input id="description" name="description" type="text" value="" />
```

you can simply call the `Html.Textbox()` helper method and pass in the name, like so:

```
@Html.TextBox("description")
```

In this section, we'll take a quick tour of the form helpers and see some examples of use. They each share some common parameters, some obvious such as `name` and `value` and others that are not so obvious, such as `htmlAttributes` that defines the names and values of any other custom HTML attribute we wish to assign to the control we are creating. In the course of going over the following examples, I will explain any method parameters that may be less than apparent.

Html.TextBox(), Html.Password() and Html.Hidden()

The `Textbox()` helper renders a text input element with the specified name, value, and HTML attributes. It has the following four signatures:

```
public IHtmlString TextBox(string name)

public IHtmlString TextBox(string name,
                           Object value)

public IHtmlString TextBox(string name,
                           Object value,
                           Object htmlAttributes)

public IHtmlString TextBox(string name,
                           Object value,
                           IDictionary<string, Object> htmlAttributes)
```

The following code sample demonstrates the use of the `Textbox()` helper method and shows the actual HTML generated by the helper and emitted to the page:

```
@Html.TextBox("description")
@Html.TextBox("description", "Description goes here")
@Html.TextBox("description", "Description goes here", new { maxlength = "50",
                                                    @class = "valid-style" } )

@* Actual HTML sent to client... *@

<input id="description" name="description" type="text" value="" />
<input id="description" name="description" type="text" value="Description goes here" />
<input class="valid-style" id="description" maxlength="50" name="description"
    type="text" value="Description goes here" />
```

Note that in the last example, when creating the `htmlAttributes` object, we used the @ operator to indicate a verbatim string because `class` is a reserved word in C#.

The `Html.Password` and `Html.Hidden` helpers have the same set of overloads and work in exactly the same way, but they render either a password input control or a hidden input control, respectively.

Html.CheckBox()

The `CheckBox()` helper renders an HTML checkbox input control to the page and has the following six signatures:

```
public IHtmlString CheckBox(string name)

public IHtmlString CheckBox(string name, bool isChecked)

public IHtmlString CheckBox(string name, IDictionary<string, Object> htmlAttrributes)

public IHtmlString CheckBox(string name, Object htmlAttributes)

public IHtmlString CheckBox(string name, bool isChecked, Object htmlAttributes)

public IHtmlString CheckBox(string name, bool isChecked,
                            IDictionary<string, Object> htmlAttrributes)
```

The code sample below shows typical usage of the helper, followed by the actual HTML rendered:

```
@Html.CheckBox("approved")
@Html.CheckBox("approved", true)

@* Actual HTML sent to client... *@
<input id="approved" name="approved" type="checkbox" />
<input checked="checked" id="approved" name="approved" type="checkbox" />
```

Unfortunately, the HTML rendered by the CheckBox helper does not include a value attribute, which means that when the box is checked and the form is submitted the CheckBox returns the default value of "on". In order to use the AsBool() extension method, which we will discuss later in this chapter, we need the CheckBox's value attribute to be set to "true". We can accomplish this using the htmlAttributes parameter:

```
@Html.CheckBox("approved", true, new { value = "true" })
```

which renders the HTML that we require:

```
<input checked="checked" id="approved" name="approved" type="checkbox" value="true" />
```

Html.RadioButton()

The RadioButton helper returns an HTML radio input control with the specified name, value, and other attributes. It has six overloads:

```
public IHtmlString RadioButton(string name, Object value)

public IHtmlString RadioButton(string name, Object value, bool isChecked)

public IHtmlString RadioButton(string name, Object value,
                          IDictionary<string, Object> htmlAttributes)

public IHtmlString RadioButton(string name, Object value, Object htmlAttributes)

public IHtmlString RadioButton(string name, Object value, bool isChecked,
                          IDictionary<string, Object> htmlAttributes)

public IHtmlString RadioButton(string name, Object value, bool isChecked,
                        Object htmlAttributes)
```

The following code sample demonstrates use of the helper and the resulting HTML output:

```
@Html.RadioButton("vehicleType", "car", true)
@Html.RadioButton("vehicleType", "truck")
@Html.RadioButton("vehicleType", "motorcycle")

@* Actual HTML sent to client... *@
<input id="vehicleType" name="vehicleType" type="radio" value="car" checked="checked" />
<input id="vehicleType" name="vehicleType" type="radio" value="truck" />
<input id="vehicleType" name="vehicleType" type="radio" value="motorcycle" />
```

Html.TextArea()

The TextArea() helper is very similar to the TextBox() helper, but it includes additional overloads to allow the developer to specify the row and col attributes:

```
public IHtmlString TextArea(string name)

public IHtmlString TextArea(string name,
```

141

```
                                            Object htmlAttributes)

public IHtmlString TextArea(string name,
                            IDictionary<string, Object> htmlAttributes)

public IHtmlString TextArea(string name,
                            string value)

public IHtmlString TextArea(string name,
                            string value,
                            Object htmlAttributes)

public IHtmlString TextArea(string name,
                            string value,
                            IDictionary<string, Object> htmlAttributes)

public IHtmlString TextArea(string name,
                            string value,
                            int rows,
                            int columns,
                            Object htmlAttributes)

public IHtmlString TextArea(string name,
                            string value,
                            int rows,
                            int columns,
                            IDictionary<string, Object> htmlAttributes)
```

The following code shows the TextArea() helper method in use and the resulting HTML sent to the client:

```
@Html.TextArea("description", "", 10, 40, null)
@Html.TextArea("comment", "Please enter your comments")

@* Actual HTML sent to client... *@
<textarea cols="40" id="description" name="description" rows="10"></textarea>
<textarea cols="20" id="comment" name="comment" rows="2">Please enter your comments</textarea>
```

Html.DropDownList()

The DropDownList() helper method renders an HTML select control to the page. It has the following signatures:

```
public IHtmlString DropDownList(string name,
                                IEnumerable<SelectListItem> selectList)

public IHtmlString DropDownList(string name,
                                IEnumerable<SelectListItem> selectList,
                                IDictionary<string, Object> htmlAttributes)

public IHtmlString DropDownList(string name,
```

```
                           IEnumerable<SelectListItem> selectList,
                           Object htmlAttributes)

public IHtmlString DropDownList(string name,
                           string defaultOption,
                           IEnumerable<SelectListItem> selectList)

public IHtmlString DropDownList(string name,
                           string defaultOption,
                           IEnumerable<SelectListItem> selectList,
                           IDictionary<string, Object> htmlAttributes)

public IHtmlString DropDownList(string name,
                           string defaultOption,
                           IEnumerable<SelectListItem> selectList,
                           Object htmlAttributes)

public IHtmlString DropDownList(string name,
                           string defaultOption,
                           IEnumerable<SelectListItem> selectList,
                           Object selectedValue,
                           IDictionary<string, Object> htmlAttributes)

public IHtmlString DropDownList(string name,
                           string defaultOption,
                           IEnumerable<SelectListItem> selectList,
                           Object selectedValue,
                           Object htmlAttributes)
```

The selectList parameter accepts an IEnumerable collection of SelectListItem objects. The SelectListItem object is used to create an HTML option element and as such, it represents an item in an HTML select list (a drop-down list or list box). The SelectListItem class has three properties; Selected—which indicates whether the SelectListItem is currently selected; Text—which is the text to be displayed to the user; and Value—which is the content of the HTML value attribute of the HTML option element to be rendered.

The selectedValue parameter of the DropDownList() helper specifies the item in the list that is selected by default. The helper will select the first item in the list with a matching value, or if the item has no value, matching text.

The defaultOption parameter inserts an option tag with no value as the first item in the list and is used to communicate that no option has been chosen, either for optional fields or to facilitate the development of required field validation.

The following code sample shows typical use of the DropDownList() helper method and the resulting HTML:

```
@{
    var optionList = new List<SelectListItem>()
    {
        new SelectListItem { Value = "C", Text = "Cyan" },
        new SelectListItem { Value = "M", Text = "Magenta" },
        new SelectListItem { Value = "Y", Text = "Yellow" },
        new SelectListItem { Value = "K", Text = "Black" }
```

143

```
    };
}
@Html.DropDownList("color", "Not selected", optionList, "M", null)

@* Actual HTML sent to client... *@
<select id="color" name="color">
    <option value="">Not selected</option>
    <option value="C">Cyan</option>
    <option selected="selected" value="M">Magenta</option>
    <option value="Y">Yellow</option>
    <option value="K">Black</option>
</select>
```

This may seem a little long-winded at this stage for populating a list with static values, but in a later chapter you will see how this helper can be used to easily populate drop-down lists from a database.

Html.ListBox()

The ListBox() helper works in essentially the same way as the DropDownList() helper, but includes additional overloaded methods to give access to the size and multiple attributes of the rendered HTML select control:

```
@Html.ListBox("color", "Not selected", optionList, "M", 5, true)
```

These attributes can, of course, also be set using the htmlAttributes parameter:

```
@Html.DropDownList("color", "Not selected", optionList, "M",
                   new { size = 5, multiple = "multiple" })
```

Html.Label()

The final HTML helper method that we are going to look at in this section is Html.Label(), which simply renders an HTML label control to the page output. It has five signatures:

```
public IHtmlString Label(string labelText)

public IHtmlString Label(string labelText,
                         Object attributes)

public IHtmlString Label(string labelText,
                         string labelFor)

public IHtmlString Label(string labelText,
                         string labelFor
                         IDictionary<string, Object> attributes)
public IHtmlString Label(string labelText,
                         string labelFor
                         Object attributes)
```

The use of the `Label()` helper method and the resulting HTML output are shown here:

```
@Html.Label("Username: ", "username")
@Html.TextBox("username")

@* Actual HTML sent to client... *@
<label for="username">Username: </label>
<input id="username" name="username" type="text" value="" />
```

■ **Note** The HTML helper methods we have seen in this section are all extension methods of the HtmlHelper class. Extension methods are a special kind of static method used to "add" methods to existing types, without the need to modify the existing type or derive a new one. Further information on extension methods can be found on the MSDN web site at: `http://msdn.microsoft.com/en-us/library/bb383977.aspx`

The MSDN web site also has further information on the HtmlHelper class at:
`http://msdn.microsoft.com/en-us/library/system.web.webpages.html.htmlhelper.aspx`

Handling Forms with WebMatrix

Now that we have a good understanding of HTML forms, we can look at ways of processing the form data submitted to the web server using WebMatrix. The first part of this process is identifying when a form has been submitted and displaying dynamic UI accordingly. This is accomplished in ASP.NET Web Pages through the use of the `IsPost` property.

In order to fully understand this process, it is important that we understand the entire form lifecycle; from initial request, through user submission to form data processing:

- Initially a browser requests a .cshtml web page

- The server executes the requested .cshtml web page. This generates a form with empty input controls, which is returned to the browser and displayed to the user.

- At the browser, the user fills in the form, and clicks a button to submit the form data to the server.

- At the server, the web page is executed again. Here we can use the `IsPost` property to detect that the page has been posted back, and can therefore process the form data posted from the user.

The diagram in Figure 5-10 demonstrates this process:

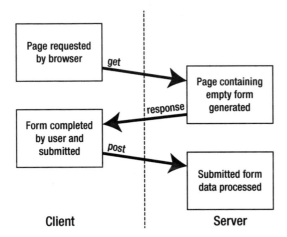

Figure 5-10. *The form lifecycle*

Identifying Form Submissions

The Boolean `IsPost` property of a WebMatrix page provides us with a simple and effective way to determine whether a form has been submitted by the user. Up to this point, clicking the submit button on a form has done nothing except post the page back to itself and restore the default values of any form controls. By interrogating the `IsPost` property, we can now ascertain whether the page has been requested as part of a form action and perform server-side processing as necessary. Typically, this server-side code would perform some calculation or data access function, but in the following code we will simply display a message to the user to inform them that the form has been processed.

___

■ **Note** We will be looking at ways to implement data access code in the next chapter: Chapter 6 - Working with Data.

___

```
@{
    if (IsPost){
        <div>
            <em>Product details added.</em>
        </div>
    }
}

<!DOCTYPE html>
```

```
<html lang="en">
<head>
    <meta charset="utf-8" />
    <title>Add Product</title>
</head>
<body>
    <form action="" method="post">
        <fieldset>
            <legend>Add New Product</legend>
            <div>
                @Html.Label("Name: ", "name")
                @Html.TextBox("name")
            </div>
            <div>
                @Html.Label("Description: ", "description")
                @Html.TextArea("description", "", 5, 40, null)
            </div>
            <div>
                @Html.Label("Price: ", "price")
                @Html.TextBox("price")
            </div>
            <div>
                @Html.Label("Discount Available? ", "discount")
                @Html.CheckBox("discount", new { value = "true" })
            </div>
        </fieldset>
        <div>
            <input type="submit" value="Submit Form" />
        </div>
    </form>
</body>
</html>
```

If you take a look at the code block at the very top of this example, you can see that when the page is run for the first time the if(IsPost) conditional returns false (as the page is not being executed as the result of an HTTP POST request). Therefore, the code inside the if block, in this case the code displaying the success message, is not executed.

However, when the submit button is clicked and the form is posted back to the same server, the page will run again (due the value in the action attribute of the form), the IsPost property will evaluate to true, and the message will be displayed, as in Figure 5-11:

Figure 5-11. *The message returned to the user when the IsPost property is true.*

We can now determine when a form has been submitted and execute specific code accordingly. Our next task is to read the data sent to the server by the form as part of the HTTP POST request.

Accessing Submitted Form Data

The values of submitted form fields can be accessed via the Request object. Each item within the Request object is identified by a key that corresponds to the value of the name attribute of each of the fields within the form. For example, to access the value of the following input text control after a postback:

```
<input type="text" name="username" />
```

You would access the value stored in the Request object with a key of username:

```
Request["username"]
```

Let's make some changes to the code at the top of our page to provide some confirmation to the user when they click the Submit Form button, by pulling the data back out of the Request object. We'll do this by assigning the relevant values of the Request object to four string variables and then displaying the content of those variables:

```
@{
    if (IsPost){
        string name = Request["name"];
        string description = Request["description"];
        string price = Request["price"];
        string discount = Request["discount"];

        <div>
            <em>Product details added.</em><br />
            Product Name: @name<br />
            Description: @description<br />
            Price: @price<br />
            Discount Available? @discount<br />
        </div>
    }
}
```

Now, when the user fills in the form and clicks the submit button, they will see the confirmation text just above the form, as shown in Figure 5-12:

Figure 5-12. *The confirmation seen by the user on postback.*

Form values are stored within the Request object as strings. Therefore, if we need to work with the value of the field as a DateTime, Boolean, or some other type we will need to convert it first. Web Pages provides five type conversion extension methods (defined in the StringExtensions class), as detailed in Table 5-2:

Table 5-2. *ASP.NET Web Pages type conversion extension methods*

Method	Description
AsBool(), AsBool(value)	Converts a string value to a Boolean value. Returns false, or the specified value, if conversion is not possible.
AsDateTime(), AsDateTime(value)	Converts a string value to a DateTime. Returns DateTime.MinValue, or the specified value, if unable to convert the supplied string.
AsDecimal(), AsDecimal(value)	Converts a string value to a decimal value. Returns 0.0, or the specified value, if the string value cannot be converted.
AsFloat(), AsFloat(value)	Converts a string value to a float value. Returns 0.0, or the specified value, if unable to convert.
AsInt(), AsInt(value)	Converts a string value to an integer. Returns 0 (zero), or the specified value, if conversion is not possible.

149

As an example, we can use these methods to determine whether a discount is available on our product and display to the user the discounted price, which in our case will be a 50% reduction.

We will accomplish this by using the `AsBool()` and `AsDecimal()` methods to convert the string value returned from the discount checkbox (which will return the string `"true"` if checked) and the price textbox. Once we have converted these values we can use them to test if a discount is available and, if so, display the discounted price (see Figure 5-13):

```
@{
    if (IsPost){
        string name = Request["name"];
        string description = Request["description"];
        decimal price = Request["price"].AsDecimal();
        bool discount = Request["discount"].AsBool();

        <div>
            <em>Product details added.</em><br />
            Product Name: @name<br />
            Description: @description<br />
            Price: @price<br />
            Discount Available? @discount<br />
            @if(discount)
            {
                <text>
                    Discounted Price: @(price / 2)
                </text>
            }
        </div>
    }
}
```

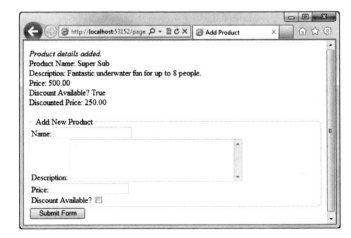

Figure 5-13. *Showing the discounted price*

> ▓ **Note** By interrogating the Request object in the way we have (e.g. the Request["key"]), we are actually interrogating the posted form for values as well as the URL for QueryString values. Therefore it is important that you do not introduce any ambiguity by having form fields and QueryString values of the same name. If this is unavoidable, or you wish to be more explicit in your code, you can call the Request.Form or Request.QueryString methods separately. For example:
>
> ```
> Request.Form["productName"]
> Request.QueryString["productName"]
> ```

Validating User Input

In an ideal world, we would present the user with a form and they would fill it in correctly, in its entirety, before pressing the submit button. However, in reality, this often does not happen. People make mistakes, misunderstand what is being asked for, bypass fields, or in the worst case deliberately try to damage your site or its data by submitting potentially harmful values (see the section in this chapter on Form Security). To counter this, we can check the submitted form field values before we use them in our application and prompt the user to enter correct values and re-submit the form. This process is known as form validation.

Note the important difference between correct data and valid data. Just because data have passed our checks, and are therefore seen as valid, the data are not necessarily correct. In the majority of cases, we can only reasonably expect to check that data are within permitted ranges and are properly formatted. For instance, if a user is entering a Date of Birth, we can check that the date is within a reasonable date range, say between DateTime.Today and DateTime.Today.AddYears(-120), but we do not know if the date they have entered is factually correct. It is your job, when writing your validation logic, to ensure that data are valid and reasonable, and usable for successful completion of any subsequent operations. It is virtually impossible in most cases to check for absolute accuracy. After all, if we know what the value should be, why would we need to ask the user to supply it?

When to validate?

Form validation code can be written to take place either on the client browser or on the web server. Both techniques have advantages and disadvantages, which we will look at here before we discuss the ideal solution.

Server-side validation

Server-side validation is accomplished in ASP.NET Web Pages by writing Razor code, which is executed after the page is submitted by the user. If the validation passes, the data are processed as necessary and the program flow continues. However, if the validation fails the data are not processed; instead a response is sent back to the client, the page containing the form is refreshed and information is displayed to the user asking them to correct the relevant data and re-submit the form.

Server-side validation has two significant benefits to us as programmers. Firstly, we can write the validation logic in C#, which we know and love, and as such we can take full advantage of the classes and methods available to us in the .NET Framework as part of ASP.NET. Secondly, and more importantly, server-side validation is secure—it will always be executed, unlike client-side validation, which can be bypassed by the user.

The only real disadvantage to the server-side approach lies in the fact that the data must be submitted to the server before any validation occurs. This means that the user must fill in and submit the whole form before they get a response, which can in some cases provide a less than ideal user experience, particularly over a slow connection.

The diagram in Figure 5-14 describes the process flow involved in server-side validation. In the diagram, every time the process crosses the dashed line between client and server-side, an HTTP request is sent and a page refresh occurs.

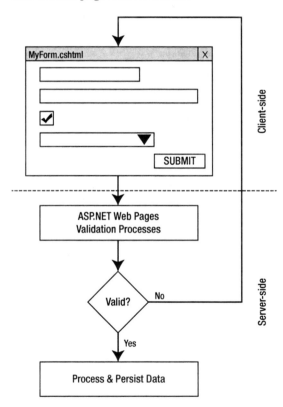

Figure 5-14. The server-side validation process

Client-side validation

Client-side validation is carried out in the browser before the data are submitted to the client. This is achieved using a client-side scripting language, such as JavaScript, or by the use of a combination of client-side technologies, commonly referred to as AJAX (Asynchronous JavaScript and XML). Taking this approach allows validation of a user's input as they type, rather than requiring a page refresh, which means a richer and more responsive user experience.

The big disadvantage to client-side scripting is that it can be easily bypassed by the user, who, by disabling JavaScript in their browser settings, also disables our client-side validation. For this reason, most developers choose to only use client-side scripts to provide guidance and feedback to the user, through features such as input masking, dynamic help, and tooltips, rather than relying on it for full input validation.

Figure 5-15 outlines the process flow involved in client-side validation. We can see that building the validation into the page results in only one trip to the server and instant feedback for the user.

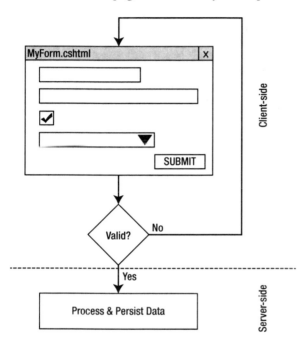

Figure 5-15. *The client-side validation process*

The best of both worlds

The best approach is clearly to use a 'belt and braces' combination of the two. Ideally, you would use JavaScript to provide rich, responsive validation and feedback and back that up with server-side code to carry out a final comprehensive check before any data processing takes place. Using this design pattern means that, in the vast majority of cases, when JavaScript is enabled, the user gets the very best user experience. At the same time, when JavaScript is disabled on the client, validation and security are not compromised.

As this book is about ASP.NET Web Pages, a server-side technology, we will be concentrating on server-side validation. In any case, server-side validation cannot be 'turned off', so it is the only choice if one must be made. Client-side is for vanity; server-side for sanity.

Figure 5-16 shows the process involved in this ideal method. The page is validated using JavaScript and, when deemed valid, passed to ASP.NET Web Pages for final validation before any data processing takes place. As I say, this is the ideal method, but it does require a lot of work. You should always ensure that your server-side validation routines are 'watertight' before adding the JavaScript client-side functionality, as the server-side code that is your ultimate security checkpoint.

Client-Side Validation Frameworks

Although this is a book about ASP.NET Web Pages and WebMatrix, a server-side technology, it is worth mentioning at least the existence of the numerous client-side validation frameworks that are available for web developers to take advantage of. Validation can be a very time-consuming task and, as such, it is often tempting to just carry out all of your form validation on the server. However, the existence of client-side validation greatly improves the user experience of your web site and can really make a site stand out among its competitors. With this is mind, it is worth investigating the use of one of the many open-source client-side validation frameworks available, as a lot can be achieved with them for very little effort.

One of the most popular of these frameworks is the jQuery Validation Plugin, which can be found at: http://bassistance.de/jquery-plugins/jquery-plugin-validation/

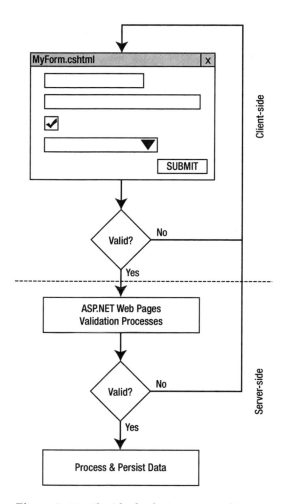

Figure 5-16. *The ideal solution—a combination of client and server-side validation*

Form Security

A malicious user could try to attack your web site in a number of ways, usually in an attempt to gain information or to submit falsified data. Two common types of attack targeted at HTML forms are Cross-site Scripting (XSS) and Cross-site Request Forgery (XSRF). In this section, we'll look at the ways that ASP.NET Web Pages can help you to secure your site against these types of attacks.

Cross-site Scripting (XSS))

Cross-site scripting (XSS) attacks exploit vulnerabilities in web page validation by injecting client-side code into form fields on web pages viewed by other users.

155

Whenever you accept some input from the user and redisplay it (as we have in this chapter with our 'Add New Product' form), you are opening your site to potential XSS attacks. By default, ASP.NET prevents people from posting potentially dangerous values via a `get` or `post` request. Imagine that a user was to enter the following text into our forms product name field:

```
<script>alert('All your base are belong to us!')</script>
```

When they click the submit button they would, by default, be presented with an error similar to the one shown in Figure 5-17:

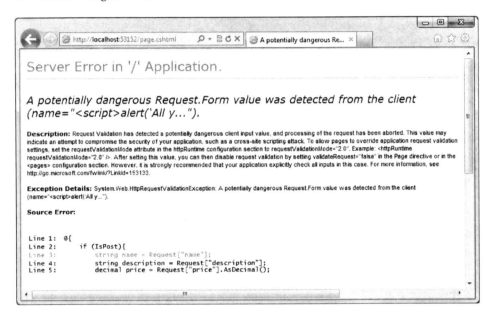

Figure 5-17. *The error page seen on submission of potentially unsafe data*

This may seem a little excessive for the example we have just seen that, if allowed to pass, would simply display a browser message box on the client. However, client-side scripts can be used in much more malicious ways; for example, to gain access to cookies storing important, sensitive information about the user, to steal an authenticated session, to manipulate files on the client computer, or even to record the keystrokes that a user makes while using a web site.

In some cases, you may want to allow your users to enter HTML into a form field; this is a common requirement in content management systems, for example. We can use the `Request.Unvalidated()` method to switch off the ASP.NET validation for individual form fields. For example, if we wanted to allow the user to enter HTML into our description field, we could do the following:

```
@{
    if (IsPost){
        string name = Request["name"];
        string description = Request.Unvalidated("description");
        decimal price = Request["price"].AsDecimal();
        bool discount = Request["discount"].AsBool();
```

CHAPTER 5 ■ FORMS AND VALIDATION

```
        <div>
            <em>Product details added.</em><br />
            Product Name: @name<br />
            Description: @description<br />
            Price: @price<br />
            Discount Available?: @discount<br />
            @if(discount)
            {
                <text>
                    Discounted Price: @(price / 2)
                </text>
            }
        </div>
    }
}
```

This would be fine if we wanted simply to validate the HTML for potentially harmful values and then store it away in a database, for example, but if we were to display it back to the user, as in the code sample above, they would see the encoded HTML returned, as shown in Figure 5-18:

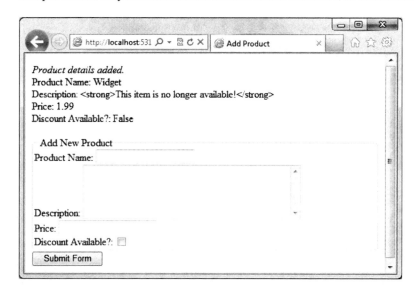

Figure 5-18. The result of calling the `Request.Unvalidated()` *method*

If we were happy that the submitted HTML was suitable, we could display it as intended in the browser by using the `Html.Raw()` helper method:

```
Description: @Html.Raw(description)<br />
```

157

This method prevents ASP.NET encoding the HTML and outputs it directly to the browser, as seen in Figure 5-19:

Figure 5-19. HTML encoding is prevented by using the HTML.Raw helper method.

Cross-site Request Forgery (XSRF)

Cross-site Request Forgery (XSRF) attacks occur when a user visits a malicious web site, often via an email or instant message. The web site covertly submits a harmful request on a site where the user is already authenticated. The malicious site carries out its attack by sending a forged request, which appears to come from a legitimately authenticated user, to the form handling code of a page. Real world examples of attacks carried out by this method range from gaining access to account information to submitting false orders and stealing money.

The most effective way to prevent an XSRF attack is to check that the HTTP POST request originates from the expected form within your site and does not come from an unknown source. ASP.NET Web Pages provides the AntiForgery class to help accomplish this.

The AntiForgery helper class has two public methods; GetHtml() and Validate(). The GetHtml() method creates an encrypted token, stores it in a cookie, and also adds it to the form within a hidden field. The Validate() method is called within the form handler and checks that the value within the hidden field matches the value stored within the cookie. If they do not match the form, processing stops and an exception is generated. This simple measure ensures that the request has come from the correct, legitimate form and has therefore not been forged.

The following code sample demonstrates the use of the AntiForgery class:

```
@{
    var username = "";

    if(IsPost) {
        AntiForgery.Validate();
        username = Request["username"];
    }
}
<!DOCTYPE html>
<html lang="en">
<head>
    <meta charset="utf-8" />
    <title>AntiForgery Example</title>
</head>
<body>
```

```
@if (IsPost)
{
    <text>
        <h1>Welcome, @username</h1>
    </text>
}
<form method="post" action="">
    @Html.Label("Username: ", "username")
    @Html.TextBox("username")
    @AntiForgery.GetHtml()
    <input type="submit" value="Submit" />
</form>
</body>
</html>
```

Performing Form Validation

In this section, we will see how we can use ASP.NET Web Pages to perform server-side form validation. First off, let's create a form to validate. Our form will gather information about an employee:

```
<!DOCTYPE html>
<html lang="en">
<head>
    <meta charset="utf-8" />
    <title>Add Employee</title>
</head>
<body>
    <h1>Add Employee</h1>
    <form action="" method="post">
        <fieldset>
            <legend>Personal Details</legend>
            <div>
                @Html.Label("Forenames: ", "forenames")
                @Html.TextBox("forenames")
            </div>
            <div>
                @Html.Label("Surname: ", "surname")
                @Html.TextBox("surname")
            </div>
            <div>
                @Html.Label("Date of Birth: ", "dateOfBirth")
                @Html.TextBox("dateOfBirth")
            </div>
        </fieldset>
        <fieldset>
            <legend>Company Details</legend>
                <div>
                    @Html.Label("Department: ", "department")
                    @{
                        var departmentList = new List<SelectListItem>()
```

159

```
                    {
                        new SelectListItem { Value = "admin", Text = "Administration" },
                        new SelectListItem { Value = "hr", Text = "Human Resources" },
                        new SelectListItem { Value = "catering", Text = "Catering" },
                        new SelectListItem { Value = "dev",
                                               Text = "Product Development" },
                        new SelectListItem { Value = "sales",
                                               Text = "Sales and Marketing" },
                    };
                }
                @Html.DropDownList("department", "Not selected", departmentList)
            </div>
            <div>
                <div>
                    @Html.Label("Employee ID: ", "employeeID")
                    @Html.TextBox("employeeID", "", new { maxlength = 4 })
                </div>
            </div>
        </fieldset>
        <div>
            <input type="submit" value="Add Employee" />
        </div>
    </form>
</body>
</html>
```

Next, we'll add a code block to the top of our page to test the IsPost property and, if true, perform our data processing. For the purposes of this demonstration, we'll send the user to a "success" page using the Response.Redirect() method:

```
@{
    if (IsPost)
    {
        Response.Redirect("Success.cshtml");
    }
}
```

If we run the page in the browser, we can see that an empty form is displayed and if we click on the 'Add Employee' button we will be redirected to Success.cshtml. However, we do not want an empty form to be submitted for processing, which at the moment is perfectly possible. In this example, we'll assume that the minimum information that we require about a new employee is their surname and employee ID, so our first piece of validation code will make these fields mandatory.

At the very top of the page, we will add some variables to store the values of our form fields. As we have seen in previous examples, when the submit button is pushed, the page is refreshed and the form fields are cleared. Clearly, we need to show the submitted data back to the user in the form to allow them to make corrections, so we will pass these variables to the value parameters of the various HTML form helpers we have used.

```
@{
    var forenames = "";
    var surname = "";
    var dateOfBirth = DateTime.MinValue;
```

```
    var department = "";
    var employeeId = "";

    if (IsPost)
    {
        forenames = Request["forenames"];
        surname = Request["surname"];
        dateOfBirth = Request["dateOfBirth"].AsDateTime();
        department = Request["department"];
        employeeId = Request["employeeId"];

        @*Response.Redirect("Success.cshtml");*@
    }
}
<!DOCTYPE html>
<html lang="en">
<head>
    <meta charset="utf-8" />
    <title>Add Employee</title>
</head>
<body>
    <h1>Add Employee</h1>
    <form action="" method="post">
        <fieldset>
            <legend>Personal Details</legend>
            <div>
                @Html.Label("Forenames: ", "forenames")
                @Html.TextBox("forenames", forenames)
            </div>
            <div>
                @Html.Label("Surname: ", "surname")
                @Html.TextBox("surname", surname)
            </div>
            <div>
                @Html.Label("Date of Birth: ", "dateOfBirth")
                @Html.TextBox("dateOfBirth", dateOfBirth.ToShortDateString())
            </div>
        </fieldset>
        <fieldset>
            <legend>Company Details</legend>
                <div>
                    @Html.Label("Department: ", "department")
                    @{
                        var departmentList = new List<SelectListItem>()
                        {
                            new SelectListItem { Value = "admin", Text = "Administration" },
                            new SelectListItem { Value = "hr", Text = "Human Resources" },
                            new SelectListItem { Value = "catering", Text = "Catering" },
                            new SelectListItem { Value = "dev",
                                                 Text = "Product Development" },
```

161

```
                           new SelectListItem { Value = "sales",
                                              Text = "Sales and Marketing" },
                    };
                }
                @Html.DropDownList("department", "Not selected", departmentList,
                              department, null)
            </div>
            <div>
                <div>
                    @Html.Label("Employee ID: ", "employeeID")
                    @Html.TextBox("employeeID", employeeId, new { maxlength = 4 })
                </div>
            </div>
        </fieldset>
        <div>
            <input type="submit" value="Add Employee" />
        </div>
    </form>
</body>
</html>
```

Note that we have set the initial value of the Date of Birth field to `DateTime.MinValue`. By doing this, we help indicate to the user the format of the input we are expecting in this field. Also note that we have temporarily commented out the call to the `Response.Redirect()` method to allow us to test the functionality so far.

ModelState

Now we are in a position to carry out our first piece of validation, which will be to check that the surname and employee ID fields are not empty. If a field is empty, we simply want to record that fact and move on to the next part of the validation process; it would be a terrible user experience if we only told the user about validation errors one at a time and expected a fresh form submission for each. Once all the validations checks have been processed, we will then report back all of our findings to the user.

In order to achieve this, we will use the page's ModelState object to store a dictionary of errors (in the ModelStateDictionary). In ASP.NET the model refers to the entity represented in your form, which in our case is an employee; the ModelState object stores the state (i.e. the validity) of the data stored in our model. Once all the validations are complete we can interrogate the `ModelState.IsValid` property to determine whether the form contains entirely valid data—`ModelState.IsValid` will be set to false if any errors have been added to the `ModelStateDictionary`. We add validation errors to the ModelStateDictionary using the `ModelState.AddError` method, passing in a key (usually corresponding to the name of the control) and the relevant error message.

```
if (IsPost)
{
    forenames = Request["forenames"];
    surname = Request["surname"];
    dateOfBirth = Request["dateOfBirth"].AsDateTime();
    department = Request["department"];
    employeeId = Request["employeeId"];
```

```
    if (surname.IsEmpty())
    {
        ModelState.AddError("surname", "The Surname field is required");
    }
    if (employeeId.IsEmpty())
    {
        ModelState.AddError("employeeID", "The Employee ID field is required");
    }

    if (ModelState.IsValid)
    {
        Response.Redirect("Success.cshtml");
    }
}
```

Displaying Validation Results

ASP.NET Web Pages provides us with a couple of helper methods designed to display validation feedback to users. The first of these methods, Html.ValidationSummary(), displays an HTML unordered list of all validation error messages held within the ModelStateDictionary. The second method, ValidationMessage(), displays the first error message found in the ModelStateDictionary which corresponds to the specified key.

We'll insert a ValidationSummary at the top of our page and a ValidationMessage next to the relevant form fields.

The validation helpers also assign a CSS class to the HTML regions they render. The CSS styles defined in the <head> of this code sample will help the users to identify the feedback by highlighting the relevant fields and validation error messages. As well as the ValidationSummary and ValidationMessage helpers, any form fields identified as keys within the ModelStateDictionary also get assigned a CSS class which can be used to alter the appearance of the relevant HTML tags.

■ **Tip** The ValidationSummary gets rendered as an HTML <div> element with a class attribute of "validation-summary-errors". The ValidationMessage helper renders a <span> element with a class attribute of "field-validation-error", which is also assigned to the corresponding form control if the name of the control matches the key in the ModelStateDictionary.

While we are adding some CSS styles for our validation helpers, we'll take the opportunity to add some very basic styles to make our form a bit neater:

```
@{
    ... validation code, as before ...
}

<!DOCTYPE html>
```

```
<html lang="en">
<head>
    <meta charset="utf-8" />
    <title>Add Employee</title>
    <style>
        /* Form styles */
        fieldset { margin: 0.5em 0; padding: 0.4em; }
        fieldset div { clear: left; padding: 0.3em 0; }
        fieldset label { float: left; width: 7em; text-align: right; padding-right: 0.4em;}
        legend { text-transform:uppercase; font-weight:bold; }

        /* Validation styles */
        .validation-summary-errors { font-weight: bold; color: #FF0000; }
        span.field-validation-error { color: #FF0000; }
        input.field-validation-error { border: 1px solid #FF0000; background-color: #FFCCCC; }
    </style>
</head>
<body>
    <h1>Add Employee</h1>
    @Html.ValidationSummary("Please correct the following errors:")
    <form action="" method="post">
        <fieldset>
            <legend>Personal Details</legend>
            <div>
                @Html.Label("Forenames: ", "forenames")
                @Html.TextBox("forenames", forenames)
            </div>
            <div>
                @Html.Label("Surname: ", "surname")
                @Html.TextBox("surname", surname)
                @Html.ValidationMessage("surname")
            </div>
            <div>
                @Html.Label("Date of Birth: ", "dateOfBirth")
                @Html.TextBox("dateOfBirth", dateOfBirth.ToShortDateString())
            </div>
        </fieldset>
        <fieldset>
            <legend>Company Details</legend>
                <div>
                    @Html.Label("Department: ", "department")
                    @{
                        var departmentList = new List<SelectListItem>()
                        {
                            new SelectListItem { Value = "admin", Text = "Administration" },
                            new SelectListItem { Value = "hr", Text = "Human Resources" },
                            new SelectListItem { Value = "catering", Text = "Catering" },
                            new SelectListItem { Value = "dev",
                                                 Text = "Product Development" },
                            new SelectListItem { Value = "sales",
```

```
                                          Text = "Sales and Marketing" },
                    };
                }
                @Html.DropDownList("department", "Not selected", departmentList,
                                    department, null)
            </div>
            <div>
                <div>
                    @Html.Label("Employee ID: ", "employeeID")
                    @Html.TextBox("employeeID", employeeId, new { maxlength = 4 })
                    @Html.ValidationMessage("employeeID")
                </div>
            </div>
        </fieldset>
        <div>
            <input type="submit" value="Add Employee" />
        </div>
    </form>
</body>
</html>
```

The form and validation feedback now look like this (see Figure 5-20):

Figure 5-20. *The ValidationSummary and ValidationMessage helpers*

Building a validation library

Most validation routines fall into one of four categories; required field, comparison to a value, range checking, and pattern matching. Due to their capacity for reuse, form validations are ideally suited for

165

implementation using functions. By using functions instead of re-writing the same, or similar, validation code in every page within our site, we can write a set of universal methods and call them whenever we need them, passing parameters to suit the situation.

The first category of validation routine—the required field—is implemented through the ASP.NET Web Pages IsEmpty() method, as demonstrated previously. So let's move straight to the second category: comparison.

In validation terms, comparisons are concerned with relating the value of a form field to another specified value. Our functions must allow us to apply the equality and relational operators (see Chapter 3) to submitted form field values. In order to do this, we'll create a series of public, static methods that take two parameters—the field value and the comparator—and return the result of the comparison as a Boolean.

We'll add a file called Validation.cshtml to the App_Code folder of the project and create a series of methods with generic parameters that will allow us to compare any data types that implement the IComparable interface:

■ **Note** Any type that implements the IComparable interface can be compared with any other instance. The interface requires that any implementing types define a single method: CompareTo(Object). The use of the `where` keyword in the following code sample simply ensures that any type passed into the method implements the IComparable interface.

This is a relatively advanced concept. If you are new to C#, do not be overly concerned with the syntax below; you should just understand that all native numeric types, `Strings`, `Chars` and `DateTimes` all implement IComparable, which means that we can compare them using the `CompareTo()` method.

Much more detailed information about the IComparable interface can be found on the MSDN web site at: `http://msdn.microsoft.com/en-us/library/ey2t2ys5.aspx`

```
@* Validation Functions *@
@functions {

    @* Comparisons *@
    public static bool IsEqualTo<T>(T value, T comparator) where T : IComparable
    {
        return value.Equals(comparator);
    }

    public static bool IsGreaterThan<T>(T value, T comparator) where T : IComparable
    {
        return value.CompareTo(comparator) > 0;
    }

    public static bool IsLessThan<T>(T value, T comparator) where T : IComparable
```

```
    {
        return value.CompareTo(comparator) < 0;
    }

    public static bool IsGreaterThanOrEqualTo<T>(T value, T comparator) where T : IComparable
    {
        return value.CompareTo(comparator) >= 0;
    }

    public static bool IsLessThanOrEqualTo<T>(T value, T comparator) where T : IComparable
    {
        return value.CompareTo(comparator) <= 0;
    }

}
```

Next we'll add some range validation. This method will require three generic parameters; the form field value, the minimum acceptable value (i.e. the bottom of the range) and the maximum acceptable value (i.e. the top of the range). The method will return a Boolean indicating whether the value is greater than or equal to (>=) the minimum value and (&&) less than or equal to (<=) the maximum.

```
@* Range Validation *@
public static bool IsBetween<T>(T value, T minValue, T maxValue) where T : IComparable
{
    return (value.CompareTo(minValue) >= 0 && value.CompareTo(maxValue) <= 0);
}
```

The final addition to our validation library, for the time being, will be involved with pattern matching. Our pattern matching functions will use regular expressions to match strings to common patterns, such as email addresses and URLs. These methods will simply accept a single string parameter and return a Boolean indicating the success of the match. Here we will implement four pattern matching functions; `IsNumbersOnly()`, `IsLettersOnly()`, `IsAlphaNumeric()` and `IsValidEmail()`. You may wish to add additional functions here in the future by replacing the regular expressions with your own.

■ **Tip** Regular expressions are incredibly useful, but can be very long and laborious to design and test. A single expression can be hundreds of characters long (a popular one for checking URLs is over 500 characters for example). Fortunately a simple web search will provide you with an example regular expression for just about any common scenario, which you can then test and use within your validation library.

More information on Regular Expressions can be found on the MSDN web site at:
`http://msdn.microsoft.com/en-us/library/hs600312.aspx`

Here are our pattern matching methods:

```
@* Pattern Matching *@
```

```
public static bool IsNumbersOnly(string value)
{
    string expression = @"^[0-9]+$";

    return System.Text.RegularExpressions.Regex.IsMatch(value, expression);
}

public static bool IsLettersOnly(string value)
{
    string expression = @"^[A-Za-z]+$";

    return System.Text.RegularExpressions.Regex.IsMatch(value, expression);
}

public static bool IsAlphaNumeric(string value)
{
    string expression = @"^[A-Za-z0-9]+$";

    return System.Text.RegularExpressions.Regex.IsMatch(value, expression);
}

public static bool IsValidEmail(string value)
{
    string expression = @"^([a-zA-Z0-9_\-\.]+)@((\[[0-9]{1,3}" +
            @"\.[0-9]{1,3}\.[0-9]{1,3}\.)|(([a-zA-Z0-9\-]+\." +
            @".)+))([a-zA-Z]{2,4}|[0-9]{1,3})(\]?)$";

    return System.Text.RegularExpressions.Regex.IsMatch(value, expression);
}
```

Using our validation functions

Your validation library will grow over time, but this first iteration will cope with the vast majority of validation requirements. To use the library, we can call the functions from directly from any page, as Validation.cshtml resides in the App_Code folder. The following example checks that the Employee ID submitted in our form falls within a range of 100 to 9999 and adds an error into the ModelStateDictionary if it does not:

```
if (!Validation.IsBetween(employeeId.AsInt(), 100, 9999))
{
    ModelState.AddError("employeeID",
        "The Employee ID must be between 100 and 9999 inclusive");
}
```

Because our comparison methods have generic parameters, we can call the same function to check that the date of birth falls between today and 100 years ago:

```
if (!Validation.IsBetween(dateOfBirth, DateTime.Now.AddYears(-100), DateTime.Now))
{
    ModelState.AddError("dateOfBirth", "Invalid Date of Birth");
}
```

If we use the `AsDateTime()` method to convert the string input from the textbox to a `DateTime` before we call our validation, any non-date formatted input, including a blank field, will be converted to `DateTime.MinValue`. Therefore, by using our validation function in this way, we can deal with an empty field and check that a date is valid and between ranges; three validations in one and no redundant checks.

It pays to plan your validation carefully to ensure that all bases are covered, not only for expected values, but also for the expected data types. There will always be someone who types "yesterday" into a date field or "three" into a numeric field; you must ensure that you can cope with all of these scenarios gracefully.

Summary

This chapter demonstrated how to create forms using both standard HTML and the helper functions supplied by ASP.NET Web Pages. We also learned how to detect form submission and interrogate HTTP POST requests to gain access to submitted form field values. Finally, we looked at ways of validating user input and created a universal validation library, using Razor functions, which we can use in future projects.

The next chapter deals with persistence—making use of the SQL Server Compact database provided as part of WebMatrix. This will combine with the lessons learned in this chapter to enable the building of interactive, data-driven web applications where users can create, edit, and store data for later use.

CHAPTER 6

■ ■ ■

Working with Data

By combining ASP.NET Web Pages with SQL Server Compact Edition, Microsoft WebMatrix provides a powerful framework for building data-driven, dynamic web applications.

In previous chapters, we have worked with sessions, cookies, forms, and HTTP requests, all of which allow us to maintain state for a period of time, but which are not useful for permanent data storage. In a data-driven web site, a database—SQL Server Compact in our case—provides a permanent store to allow the development of web applications that require stable data persistence as an integral part of the design.

There is a vast scope for database use within a web application; a database is particularly useful wherever content changes frequently or originates from a number of sources, or where large quantities of information must be managed and presented.

This chapter covers the creation and administration of SQL Server Compact Edition databases and looks at how users can interact with them through ASP.NET Web Pages. We will start by creating a database of employees for a fictional company and then use the functionality built into WebMatrix to develop web pages to facilitate the common Create, Read, Update, and Delete (CRUD) operations.

SQL Server Compact Edition

WebMatrix ships with version 4.0 of the SQL Server Compact Edition database, which is installed by the Web Platform Installer as an integral part of the platform. It is a file-based database, where all data is stored within our site in a single file with an .sdf file extension, which makes for easy deployment as no additional install is required on the web server. As the database file is stored within our site, it can be deployed automatically when we deploy the site to the production server using the tools provided by WebMatrix (see Chapter 13 for more information on deployment).

SQL Server Compact databases are limited to a maximum size of 4 GB, although an upgrade path is provided to allow easy migration to another member of the SQL Server family of products if scalability should become an issue. We will look at ways of upgrading the database later in the chapter.

Creating a Database

Although it is perfectly possible to create and administer an SQL Compact database using text commands, the WebMatrix IDE provides a graphical design tool to make this job easier for us. To access the database features of the IDE, first select the **Databases** tab in the Workspace Selector. A WebMatrix project can contain multiple databases, although in this simple example we will only need one. To create a new database, click either the New Database button in the Ribbon Control or the Add a database to our site button in the center of the Content Pane. An empty database will be created and appear in the Navigation Pane, where it can be renamed, if necessary. By default, the database will be given the same name as our project, suffixed with a .sdf file extension.

■ **Note**   The database file itself is stored in the App_Data folder within our project. If the App_Data folder does not already exist, WebMatrix will create it for us.

Creating Tables

Now that we have an empty database to work with, we will need to add some tables in which to store our data. To create a table, either click the New Table button in the Ribbon Control or right-click the Tables node under our database in the Navigation Pane and choose New Table.

With the new table open in the designer, columns can be added by clicking the New Column button in the Ribbon Control. The designer is split into two halves: the top half contains an overview of the entire table, while the bottom half displays the properties of the selected column (see Figure 6-1).

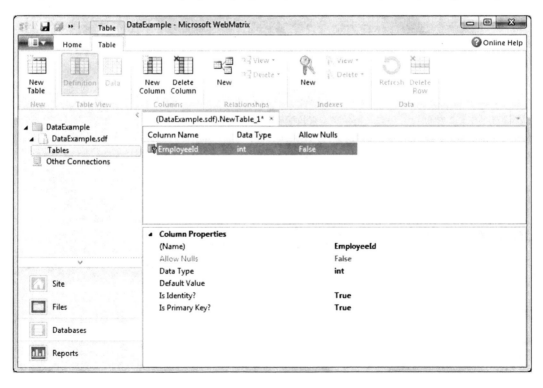

Figure 6-1. The table design tool within the WebMatrix IDE

The following, Table 6-1, describes the six default properties, which can be edited for each column within the WebMatrix design tool.

Table 6-1. Column Properties

Property	Description
(Name)	The name of the column. This is the name by which we will refer to the column within our code. It must be unique within a table.
Allow Nulls	Specifies whether a column can contain a null value.
Data Type	The type of data to be stored in the column. SQL Server Compact allows the following values: bigint, binary, bit, datetime, float, image, int, money, nchar, ntext, numeric, nvarchar, real, rowversion, smallint, tinyint, uniqueidentifier, varbinary (see Table 6-2).
Default Value	The value inserted into the column by default when a new row is created.
Is Identity?	A Boolean value that determines whether the column is to be used as an identity. If set to true, the value of the column will be set to a unique identity by SQL Server Compact when a new row is created.
Is Primary Key?	Specifies whether this column is to be used as a Primary Key for the table.

As shown in Table 6-1, the Data Type property can be set to one of eighteen different data types as defined by SQL Server Compact. The following, Table 6-2, details these types and their use.

Table 6-2. Data Types

Data Type	Size	Description
bigint	8 bytes	Integer values from –9,223,372,036,854,775,808 to 9,223,372,036,854,775,807.
binary	Specified (max 8000 bytes)	Fixed-length binary data with a maximum length of 8000 bytes. Default length = 1 byte. When the binary type is chosen, an additional property (Length) becomes available in the designer to allow specification of the desired length.

Table 6-2 cont.

bit	1 bit	Integer value of either 1 or 0. Commonly used to store Boolean values.
datetime	8 bytes (two 4-byte integers)	Date and time values from January 1, 1753 to December 31, 9999.
float	8 bytes	Floating point numeric data from –1.79E +308 to 1.79E+308.
image	Variable	Variable-length binary data with a maximum length of 1,073,741,823 bytes.
int	4 bytes	Integer values from –2,147,483,648 to 2,147,483,647.
money	8 bytes	Monetary data values from –922,337,203,685,477.5808 to 922,337,203,685,477.5807, with accuracy to a ten-thousandth of a monetary unit.
nchar	2 × length in bytes	Fixed-length Unicode character data of specified length between 1 and 4000. When the nchar type is chosen, an additional property (Length) becomes available in the designer to allow specification of the desired length.
ntext	2 × length in bytes	Variable-length Unicode data with a maximum length of 536,870,911 characters. When the ntext type is chosen, an additional property (Length) becomes available in the designer to allow specification of the desired length.
numeric	19 bytes	Fixed-precision and scale numeric data from $-10^{38}+1$ through $10^{38}-1$. When the numeric type is chosen, two additional properties (Scale and Precision) become available in the designer. The precision can be set to a value between 1 and 38, whereas the scale can be between 0 and the precision.
nvarchar	2 × length in bytes	Variable-length Unicode data with a length between 1 and 4000 characters. Default length = 1. When the nvarchar type is chosen, an additional property (Length) becomes available in the designer to allow specification of the desired length.

Table 6-2 cont.

`real`	4 bytes	Floating precision number data between –3.40E+38 and 3.40E+38.
`rowversion`	8 bytes	An automatically generated unique binary number.
`smallint`	2 bytes	Integer values from –32,768 to 32,767.
`tinyint`	1 byte	Integer values from 0 to 255.
`uniqueidentifier`	16 bytes	A globally unique identifier (GUID).
`varbinary`	Variable	Variable-length binary data with a maximum length of 8000 bytes. Default length = 1.

To add the details of the first column, we simply need to type the details into the empty properties panel, as shown in Figure 6-1. Note that we can only enter values in the properties panel in the bottom half of the designer; the top half is entirely read-only (this may come as a surprise to readers who have previous experience with other SQL Server design tools). Once we have entered the details, press the New Column button on the Ribbon Control and enter the details of the next column; repeat this until all the columns have been added.

Table 6-3 shows the details of the columns to be added to our first table.

Table 6-3. *Employees Table Columns*

Column Name	Data Type	Allow Nulls?	Other Properties
EmployeeId	int	False	Is Identity = True; Is Primary Key = True;
Forenames	nvarchar	False	Length = 50
Surname	nvarchar	False	Length = 20
DateOfBirth	datetime	False	
EmailAddress	nvarchar	False	Length = 100
Role	nvarchar	False	Length = 100

Once we have added all the columns, click the Save button in the top left-hand side of the screen, or click Ctrl+S and enter the name of the table as "Employees" in the box provided (see Figure 6-2).

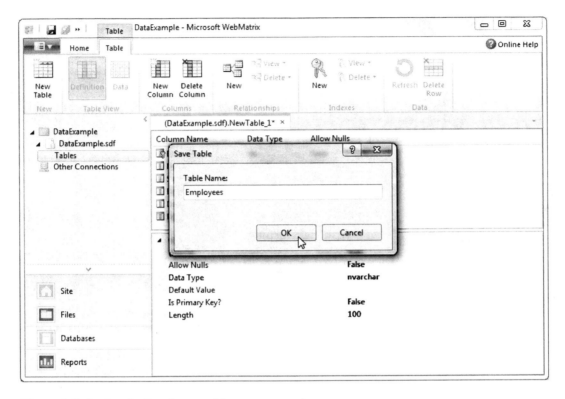

Figure 6-2. Saving the Employees table

Once we have saved the table, the Data button on the Ribbon Control will become available. Click the button and enter some test data, such as that shown here in Figure 6-3.

■ **Note** Do not try to enter data into the EmployeeID column, as it is an identity field that SQL Server Compact will fill in for we with unique values, in our case integers. If we do try to enter data into the column, either here through the designer or later through code in an ASP.NET Web Page, we will encounter an error.

If we do enter a value into this column by mistake in the designer, it can sometimes be difficult to progress, as every time we try to move to a new column we receive an 'invalid format' or similar error. Click OK to any error messages and press the Esc key to cancel our changes. This will return the value to null.

EmployeeId	Forenames	Surname	DateOfBirth	EmailAddress	Role
2	Robert	Harewood	29/03/1973	bob@example.com	Sales Consultant
4	Howard	Ripley	16/08/1964	howard@example.com	Sales Manager
5	Jane	Millbrook	20/02/1980	jane@example.com	Engineer
6	Patrick	Hart	08/12/1959	p.hart@example.com	Production Manager
7	Rachel	Cross	28/05/1978	rachel@example.com	Accountant
8	Nicholas	Hurst	19/09/1962	n.hurst@example.com	Engineer
9	Julie	Williams	10/10/1971	julie@example.com	Secretary
10	Richard	Procter	04/05/1969	r.procter@example.com	Managing Director
▶* NULL	NULL	NULL	NULL	NULL	NULL

Figure 6-3. Sample test data entered into the Employees table

■ **Caution**   The date format for the DateOfBirth column will depend on the local date format settings for our development machine. In the screenshot in Figure 6-3, they are set to the date format of my machine, which is the standard United Kingdom format of dd/mm/yyyy.

Now that we know how to create databases and tables, we can look at ways of interacting with that data through code. First, we need to ensure that we have a basic understanding of Structured Query Language (SQL), the language that SQL Server uses to interact with data.

■ **Note** Experienced users of SQL Server will no-doubt notice that there is no facility to create other types of database objects, such as stored procedures, triggers, views, etc. SQL Server Compact Edition is a vastly scaled-down, file-based version of SQL Server and, as such, offers only a subset of the functionality. If we do need this functionality, we can use WebMatrix with a different version of SQL Server (see the Working with Other Databases section at the end of this chapter).

Interacting with Data

Structured Query Language (SQL) is a tried and tested way of interacting with data and databases through code. It was developed at IBM in the early 1970s and is used today by most relational database systems for data retrieval and manipulation. Several versions of SQL exist, which have slightly differing functionality, although the core features of the language, including those seen in this chapter, are generally common across all versions. This means that the same SQL can be used across different databases, usually with only minor syntactical changes. SQL Server databases use a version of SQL called Transact-SQL, commonly referred to as T-SQL.

SQL can be run against our database from within the WebMatrix IDE by closing any open tables, switching to the "Home" tab in the Ribbon Control and clicking the New Query button. To run the query, use the Execute button in the Ribbon Control, located immediately to the right of the New Query button.

■ **Note** This section is only intended for novices to serve as a very basic introduction to SQL, which will enable a good understanding of the code in the rest of the book. If we already have a good working knowledge of SQL, we may want to skip to the next section.

For a much more detailed source of information on using T-SQL, take a look at the MSDN Transact-SQL Reference, which can be found at http://msdn.microsoft.com/en-us/library/bb510741.aspx.

Fetching Data

To read data from a database (the R in CRUD), we use the SQL `select` command. The `select` command searches for specific records, depending on a set of criteria that we specify as part of the command. When the command is executed, the database will return zero, one, or multiple matching rows.

The simplest form of the `select` statement is as follows:

```
SELECT <column names> FROM <table name>
```

The column names are listed, separated by commas, or can be replaced with an asterisk (*) if we wish to return all columns. The following SQL statement returns the data shown in Figure 6-4.

```
SELECT Forenames, Surname, Role FROM Employees
```

Forenames	Surname	Role
Robert	Harewood	Sales Consultant
Howard	Ripley	Sales Manager
Jane	Millbrook	Engineer
Patrick	Hart	Production Manager
Rachel	Cross	Accountant
Nicholas	Hurst	Engineer
Julie	Williams	Secretary
Richard	Procter	Managing Director

Figure 6-4. *The result of a simple SQL select statement*

■ **Note** T-SQL is not case sensitive, yet we will note that in the preceding SQL statements I have entered the SQL keywords (SELECT and FROM) in block capitals. This is merely a convention that helps to distinguish the SQL from the names of tables, columns, etc. T-SQL also pays no attention to white space, except within literal values.

The set of rows returned by a select statement can be further distilled through the use of the where clause. The where clause is used to specify the value, or range of values, by which we wish to filter a column. For example, the following two statements return just the engineers and everyone but the Managing Director, respectively.

```
SELECT Forenames, Surname, Role FROM Employees WHERE Role = 'Engineer'

SELECT * FROM Employees WHERE Role != 'Managing Director'
```

Note that in a T-SQL string, literals are surrounded by single quotes, not double quotes as we have grown accustomed to in C#.

Several filters can be applied as part of the where clause using standard Boolean operators. For example, this SQL returns the records shown in Figure 6-5.

```
SELECT Forenames, Surname, Role
FROM Employees
WHERE Role = 'Engineer' OR Role = 'Production Manager'
```

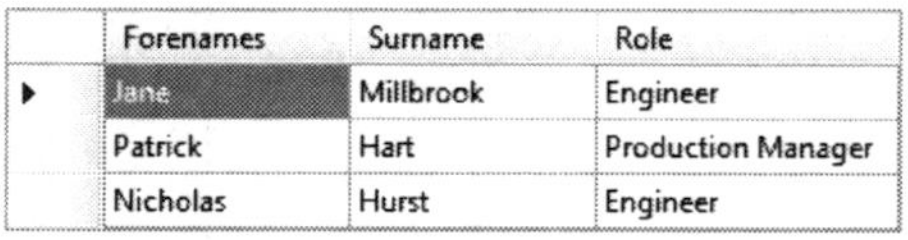

Forenames	Surname	Role
Jane	Millbrook	Engineer
Patrick	Hart	Production Manager
Nicholas	Hurst	Engineer

Figure 6-5. Selecting engineers and production managers

If we only want to look for a partial match against a string literal, we can use the like statement in combination with any of the four wildcard characters described in Table 6-4.

Table 6-4. T-SQL Wildcard Characters

Wildcard Character	Description
%	Matches any string of zero or more characters.
_ (underscore)	Matches any single character.
[]	Matches any single character within a specified range [v-z] or set [vwxyz].
[^]	Matches any single character **not** within a specified range [^v-z] or set [^vwxyz].

The following SQL example uses the like statement to return all managers, as shown in Figure 6-6.

```
SELECT Forenames, Surname, Role FROM Employees WHERE Role LIKE '%Manager'
```

	Forenames	Surname	Role
▶	Howard	Ripley	Sales Manager
	Patrick	Hart	Production Manager

Figure 6-6. *Use of the % wildcard character to return all managers*

It is perfectly acceptable to use multiple wildcard characters within the same statement. For example, if we want to include the Managing Director in the results set, we can use a multicharacter wildcard character on either side of the string literal, which returns the results shown in Figure 6-7.

```
SELECT Forenames, Surname, Role FROM Employees WHERE Role LIKE '%Manag%'
```

	Forenames	Surname	Role
▶	Howard	Ripley	Sales Manager
	Patrick	Hart	Production Manager
	Richard	Procter	Managing Director

Figure 6-7. *Using multiple wildcard characters to include the managing director in the result set*

Finally, we can choose how the result set is ordered by specifying column names and directions using the order by statement. The statement is followed by a comma-separated list of column names, which can be sorted in either ascending (asc) or descending (desc) order. If no sort direction is given, the default setting of asc is implied.

The following statement returns the result set seen in Figure 6-8.

```
SELECT Surname, Forenames FROM Employees WHERE Surname LIKE 'H%' ORDER BY Surname DESC
```

	Surname	Forenames
▶	Hurst	Nicholas
	Hart	Patrick
	Harewood	Robert

Figure 6-8. *Sorting the results in reverse-alphabetical order*

The results can be sorted by more than one column. For example, the following code sorts first by Role and then by Surname and returns the results seen in Figure 6-9.

```
SELECT Surname, Forenames, Role FROM Employees ORDER BY Role, Surname
```

Surname	Forenames	Role
Cross	Rachel	Accountant
Hurst	Nicholas	Engineer
Millbrook	Jane	Engineer
Procter	Richard	Managing Director
Hart	Patrick	Production Manager
Harewood	Robert	Sales Consultant
Ripley	Howard	Sales Manager
Williams	Julie	Secretary

Figure 6-9. Sorting the results by multiple columns—in this case, Role followed by Surname

Here we can see that the two engineers are listed in alphabetical order by surname.

Inserting Data

To create a new row in a table (the C in CRUD), we use the SQL `insert` statement in conjunction with the `into` and `values` keywords. In its simplest form, the `insert` statement can be written using the following syntax.

```
INSERT INTO <table name> VALUES (<column values>)
```

However, it is more usual to specify the column names as well as the column values; this greatly aids readability and prevents the need to refer to the database schema to understand the code. This syntax can also be used to insert data into specific fields only, which is useful if the table has some non-nullable columns.

```
INSERT INTO <table name> (<column names>) VALUES (<column values>)
```

In this case, it is absolutely necessary to specify the column names, because our first column, EmployeeId, is an automatically generated Identity column, which will cause an error in SQL Server if we attempt to stipulate a value for it. To add a row of data to our Employees table, we could use the following SQL to add the record seen in Figure 6-10.

```
INSERT INTO Employees (Forenames, Surname, DateOfBirth, EmailAddress, Role)
VALUES ('Roger', 'Smith', '02/03/1975', 'r.smith@example.com', 'IT Technician')
```

EmployeeId	Forenames	Surname	DateOfBirth	EmailAddress	Role
24	Roger	Smith	03/02/1975 00:00:00	r.smith@example.com	IT Technician

Figure 6-10. Our new employee added to the Employees table

Note that the EmployeeId of the record we have added will probably be different from the one shown here. Each time a new row is added to the table, the value of the EmployeeId field is automatically generated by SQL Server, so the value assigned will depend on how many rows are already in the table.

Updating Data

The SQL update command is used to change existing data in a table. The update command is used with the set keyword to specify the columns to be effected and their new values.

```
UPDATE <table name> SET <column name> = <value>
```

Used in this way, the command will update every row in a table. Therefore, it is usual to specify criteria for the rows to be updated using an SQL where clause.

```
UPDATE <table name> SET <column name> = <value> WHERE <criteria>
```

For example, assuming that we know the EmployeeId, we could change the e-mail address and role of the record we added in the previous example using the following SQL.

```
UPDATE Employees
SET EmailAddress = 'roger@example.com', Role = 'Systems Engineer'
WHERE EmployeeId = 24
```

Deleting Data

The SQL delete command is used to remove existing row(s) from a database table. To use the delete command, we simply need to specify the table name and the row, or rows, to be deleted.

```
DELETE FROM <table name> WHERE <criteria>
```

To remove a row from the Employees table, we can use the following statement.

```
DELETE FROM Employees WHERE Forenames = 'Roger' AND Surname = 'Smith'
```

▓ **Caution**   Be careful when writing code to delete records from a database table while using SQL. The WHERE clause is actually optional, but by omitting it, we will delete every record in the table. We should take extra care not to do this unintentionally—it has caught many an experienced developer!

Also, pay particular attention to the criteria used within our WHERE clause. If we are intending to delete only one row, ensure that our criteria are absolutely specific and could not apply to more than one record, which typically means specifying the unique primary key value of the row concerned. This is particularly easy to fall foul of if the criteria for the command are being dynamically generated within code.

Now that we have a grasp of the basic SQL required to conduct CRUD operations against an SQL Server database, we can learn how to connect ASP.NET Web Pages to a database and start to create really useful, dynamic, data-driven web pages that interact with the objects within our database.

Data Access with WebMatrix

Data access in WebMatrix has been designed from the ground up to provide a simple, quick, and effective way to perform SQL-based database operations. Following the WebMatrix ethos, ASP.NET Web Pages provides classes that facilitate database interaction in an incredibly easy way, steering clear of the Object-Relational Mapping (ORM) solutions and other colossal code constructs and abstractions that have become widespread in many other frameworks. WebMatrix is about agility and rapid development, and that is exactly what the classes within the `WebMatrix.Data` namespace give us.

In this section, we will create a small web site, based on the employee database created earlier in the chapter, to enable the user to carry out the most commonly required operations—creating new records, reading and displaying data, updating existing records, and deleting them. This example will give us the basis for creating our own feature-rich, data-driven, dynamic pages.

Making the Connection

Before we can perform any database operations from an ASP.NET Web Page, we need to provide the page with a database connection. The database connection lets ASP.NET know which database we are intending to operate on and is made using the Open method of the `Database` object.

```
Database.Open(filename)
```

▨ **Note** Seasoned .NET developers should note that this is not the same as creating an ADO.NET connection.

This method opens a connection to the database file whose filename is specified as a parameter. WebMatrix assumes that the .sdf file containing the database is held within the App_Data folder of our site—we should not specify the .sdf file extension in the filename parameter, just the name of the file. For example, to open a connection to an SQL Server Compact database called EmployeeData.sdf stored in the App_Data folder of our website, we call the `Database.Open` method as follows:

```
Database.Open("EmployeeData")
```

▨ **Note** By convention, the Database.Open method will look for an SQL Server Compact database, stored with a .sdf file extension in the default App_Data folder. However, it is perfectly possible, and often necessary, to connect to different types of databases or those stored in a location outside the App_Data folder. I will cover the methods for achieving this in the Working with Other Databases section later in the chapter.

Now that we have established a connection between the page and the database, we can start to retrieve data and display it to the user.

Retrieving and Displaying Data

ASP.NET Web Pages provides the `WebMatrix.Data` namespace that contains classes that simplify database interaction. The `Database` class within the `WebMatrix.Data` namespace exposes three methods designed for the execution of SQL `select` commands: `Query`, `QuerySingle`, and `QueryValue`. The `Query` method returns a collection of records, `QuerySingle` returns a single record, and `QueryValue` returns a single scalar value as the result of an SQL aggregate or scalar function (such as count, avg, min, max, len, etc.).

To fetch all the employee records from the database, we will use the `Query` method of the `Database` class. The `Query` method executes an SQL query against the specified database and returns a generic collection of dynamics (specifically `IEnumerable<dynamic>`) containing the resulting rows of data.

So let's create a new page called default.cshtml and list the contents of the database in an HTML table. We'll do this by first opening a connection to our database (in this example, my database is called DataExample.sdf; we should change this to whatever we called our database) and defining the necessary SQL `select` statement in a code block at the top of the page.

```
@{
    var db = Database.Open("DataExample");
    var sqlCommand = "SELECT * FROM Employees ORDER BY Surname";
}
```

Now we'll take advantage of the fact that the return type of the `Query()` method is `IEnumerable<dynamic>`, by iterating through the results using a `foreach` loop and dynamically building a table containing the employee data at runtime.

```
@{
    var db = Database.Open("DataExample");
    var sqlCommand = "SELECT * FROM Employees ORDER BY Surname";
}
<!DOCTYPE html>

<html lang="en">
    <head>
        <meta charset="utf-8" />
        <title>Employees</title>
    <style>
        table { border-spacing: 0px; border-collapse: collapse; }
        th, td { border: 1px solid #CCC; padding: 10px; }
    </style>
    </head>
    <body>
        <h1>Employees</h1>
        <table>
            <thead>
                <tr>
                    <th>Employee Id</th>
                    <th>Forenames</th>
                    <th>Surname</th>
                    <th>Date Of Birth</th>
                    <th>Email Address</th>
                    <th>Role</th>
```

```
            </tr>
        </thead>
        <tbody>
            @foreach (var row in db.Query(sqlCommand))
            {
                <tr>
                    <td>@row.EmployeeId</td>
                    <td>@row.Forenames</td>
                    <td>@row.Surname</td>
                    <td>@row.DateOfBirth</td>
                    <td>@row.EmailAddress</td>
                    <td>@row.Role</td>
                </tr>
            }
        </tbody>
    </table>
</body>
</html>
```

The foreach statement simply executes the command against the database opened at the top of the page and iterates through each row of the results. On each iteration, i.e. for each new record returned, we'll emit a set of HTML <tr> tags and six sets of <td> tags, one for each column within the returned set of data.

It is important to remember that the Query() method returns IEnumerable<dynamic>. The advantage of this is that we can carry out any legal action with any of the dynamic properties returned. For example, ASP.NET has no idea, and frankly doesn't care, what data type each column contains. However, we know that DateOfBirth is a DateTime, so we can do the following without any complaints from the compiler, as the statement will be resolved at runtime by the DLR.

```
<td>@row.DateOfBirth.ToLongDateString()</td>
```

When we run this code, we will see that, when the page is rendered in the browser, the DateOfBirth field is formatted as intended (see Figure 6-11).

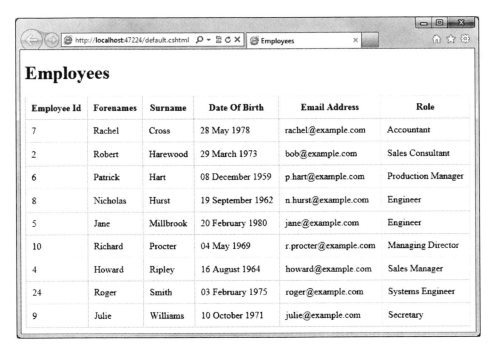

Figure 6-11. The contents of the Employees table, rendered with a formatted Date Of Birth column.

Now that we can fetch and display our existing database records, let's see how we can go about adding some new ones.

Adding Records

Before we worry about how to use `WebMatrix.Data` to execute an SQL insert statement, we will need a page containing an HTML form for the user to fill in and submit. So, we will create a new page called add.cshtml and add a form for data capture.

■ **Caution**   As we are performing a data persistence function, we must ensure that we are using the HTTP post method in our form to help prevent the possibility of a cross-site attack by someone injecting malicious form field values or SQL into the URL.

```html
<!DOCTYPE html>

<html lang="en">
    <head>
        <meta charset="utf-8" />
        <title>Add an Employee</title>
        <style>
            fieldset { margin: 0.5em 0; padding: 0.4em; }
            fieldset div { clear: left; padding: 0.3em 0; }
            fieldset label { float: left; width: 7em; text-align: right;
                             padding-right: 0.4em; }
            legend { text-transform:uppercase; font-weight:bold; }
        </style>
    </head>
    <body>
        <h1>Add an Employee</h1>
        <form action="add.cshtml" method="post">
            <fieldset>
                <legend>Employee Details</legend>
                 <div>
                    @Html.Label("Forenames: ", "forenames")
                    @Html.TextBox("forenames")
                </div>
                <div>
                    @Html.Label("Surname: ", "surname")
                    @Html.TextBox("surname")
                </div>
                <div>
                    @Html.Label("Date of Birth: ", "dateOfBirth")
                    @Html.TextBox("dateOfBirth")
                </div>
                <div>
                    @Html.Label("Email Address: ", "emailAddress")
                    @Html.TextBox("emailAddress")
                </div>
                <div>
                    @Html.Label("Role: ", "role")
                    @Html.TextBox("role")
                </div>
            </fieldset>
            <div>
                <input type="submit" value="Add Employee" />
            </div>
        </form>
    </body>
</html>
```

This will present the user with the form shown here in Figure 6-12.

Figure 6-12. The 'Add an Employee' page.

Note that there is not a field here for the EmployeeId, as it is an identity field which will be generated by SQL Server when we insert a new record.

Next, we'll add some code to the very top of the page to detect a post back from the form and insert the submitted form data into the database.

■ **Caution**   In order to keep the examples in this chapter clear and focused, the code examples given contain no input validation. It is absolutely essential that all user input is validated thoroughly before being committed to the database. Failure to carry out this validation correctly will, in the best case, lead to bugs and errors, but may also expose significant security flaws that could prove damaging and costly if exploited.

For more information on form validation using ASP.NET Web Pages, see Chapter 5.

```
@{
    if (IsPost) {

        var forenames = Request["forenames"];
        var surname = Request["surname"];
        var dateOfBirth = Request["dateOfBirth"];
        var emailAddress = Request["emailAddress"];
        var role = Request["role"];

        var db = Database.Open("DataExample");
        var sqlCommand = "INSERT INTO Employees " +
                "(Forenames, Surname, DateOfBirth, EmailAddress, Role) " +
```

```
                    "VALUES (@0, @1, @2, @3, @4)";
        db.Execute(sqlCommand, forenames, surname, dateOfBirth, emailAddress, role);

        Response.Redirect("~/default");
    }
}
```

Let's take a closer look at exactly how this code works. If the code is being executed as the result of a page postback, we declare some variables and populate them with the values of the submitted forms. Next, we open a connection to the database and construct your SQL insert query using parameter placeholders (@0, @1, @2, @3, @4) in place of the values to be inserted.

```
var sqlCommand = "INSERT INTO Employees " +
                 "(Forenames, Surname, DateOfBirth, EmailAddress, Role) " +
                 "VALUES (@0, @1, @2, @3, @4)";
```

▓ **Tip**   We should always use parameters to pass values to an SQL command, as seen in this example. This helps to ensure that the data is passed into the query in the correct format and takes advantage of ASP.NET's built-in safeguards to help protect against SQL injection attacks.

More information on SQL injection attacks and how to guard against them can be found on the MSDN web site: http://msdn.microsoft.com/en-us/library/ms161953.aspx

---

Once we have constructed your SQL insert statement using parameter place holders, we call the Execute() method, passing in the variables that contain the values to substitute for the placeholders.

```
db.Execute(sqlCommand, forenames, surname, dateOfBirth, emailAddress, role);
```

▓ **Note**   Although I chose to ignore it here, the Execute() method actually returns an integer containing the number of rows affected by the command, in a way similar to the ADO.NET ExecuteNonQuery() method.

Finally, we redirect the user to default.cshtml using the Redirect method of the Response object.

```
Response.Redirect("~/default");
```

Note that we do not need to declare the .cshtml file extension here, as the built-in routing system will deal with that for us. For more information on the ASP.NET Web Pages Routing System, see the URLs and Routing section in Chapter 4.

Your last job is to provide a link on the default page to take us to the Add New Employee page. Add the following to default.cshtml directly under the header.

```
<p>
    <a href="add">Add an Employee</a>
</p>
```

Editing Existing Data

We need to provide a way for our users to be able to edit existing employee records. We will achieve this by adding a new page (edit.cshtml) containing a form populated from the database. We will also need to add a link against each row in the employee list on the default page to redirect the user to our edit form, passing the EmployeeId in the URL.

We'll construct the link to our edit page first, by adding an extra column to the existing table in default.cshtml.

```
<table>
    <thead>
        <tr>
            <th>Employee Id</th>
            <th>Forenames</th>
            <th>Surname</th>
            <th>Date Of Birth</th>
            <th>Email Address</th>
            <th>Role</th>
            <th> </th>
        </tr>
    </thead>
    <tbody>
        @foreach (var row in db.Query(sqlCommand))
        {
            <tr>
                <td>@row.EmployeeId</td>
                <td>@row.Forenames</td>
                <td>@row.Surname</td>
                <td>@row.DateOfBirth.ToLongDateString()</td>
                <td>@row.EmailAddress</td>
                <td>@row.Role</td>
                <td><a href="edit/@row.EmployeeId">Edit</a></td>
            </tr>
        }
    </tbody>
</table>
```

This code renders a link to the edit page for each employee passing the EmployeeId as part of the URL (see Figure 6-13). The actual HTML emitted to the browser by ASP.NET Web Pages will look something like this.

```
<a href="edit/5">Edit</a>
```

When a user clicks on this link, the ASP.NET Web Pages routing system will redirect the browser to edit.cshtml, as there is no such page as 5.cshtml within a folder called edit (see Chapter 4 for further explanation). We can then use Razor code in the edit page to interrogate the URL and extract the particular EmployeeId we are interested in.

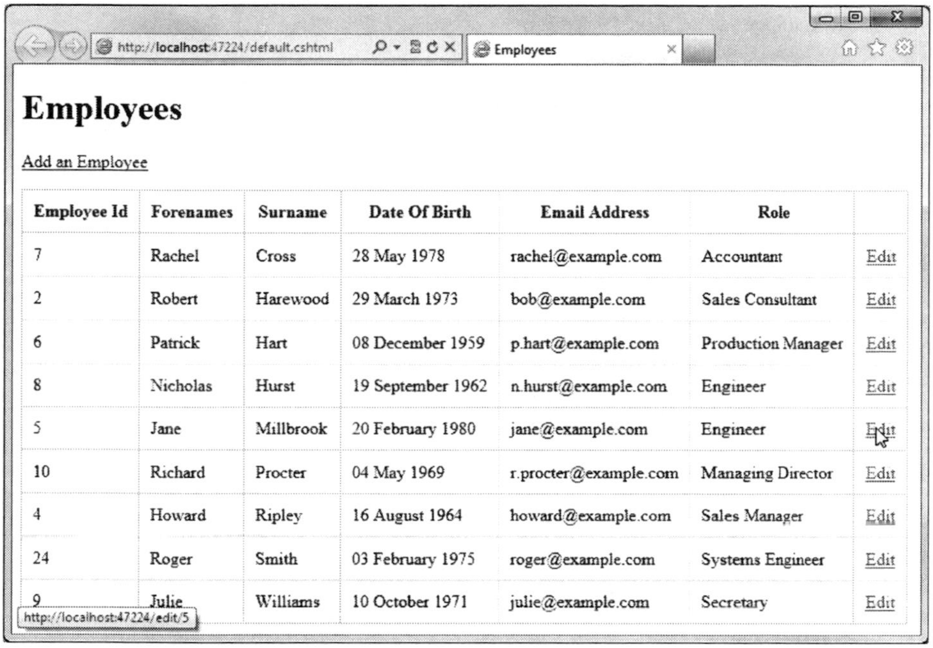

Figure 6-13. *The Edit links added to the employee list*

Next we'll add a new page, called edit.cshtml, and create a form for editing. We'll get the record relating to the EmployeeId passed to the page in the UrlData and populate the form controls.

```
@{
    var employeeId  = UrlData[0];
    if (employeeId.IsEmpty()) {
        Response.Redirect(@Href("~/default"));
    }

    var forenames = "";
    var surname = "";
    var dateOfBirth = "";
    var emailAddress = "";
    var role = "";

    var db = Database.Open("DataExample");

    var sqlSelect = "SELECT * FROM Employees WHERE EmployeeId=@0";

    var row = db.QuerySingle(sqlSelect, employeeId);

    forenames = row.Forenames;
    surname = row.Surname;
    dateOfBirth = row.DateOfBirth.ToShortDateString();
```

```
        emailAddress = row.EmailAddress;
        role = row.Role;
}

<!DOCTYPE html>

<html lang="en">
    <head>
        <meta charset="utf-8" />
        <title>Edit Employee Record</title>
        <style>
            fieldset { margin: 0.5em 0; padding: 0.4em; }
            fieldset div { clear: left; padding: 0.3em 0; }
            fieldset label { float: left; width: 7em; text-align: right;
                             padding-right: 0.4em; }
            legend { text-transform:uppercase; font-weight:bold; }
        </style>
    </head>
    <body>
        <h1>Edit Employee Record</h1>
        <form action="" method="post">
            <fieldset>
                <legend>Employee Details</legend>
                 <div>
                    @Html.Label("Forenames: ", "forenames")
                    @Html.TextBox("forenames", forenames)
                </div>
                <div>
                    @Html.Label("Surname: ", "surname")
                    @Html.TextBox("surname", surname)
                </div>
                <div>
                    @Html.Label("Date of Birth: ", "dateOfBirth")
                    @Html.TextBox("dateOfBirth", dateOfBirth)
                </div>
                <div>
                    @Html.Label("Email Address: ", "emailAddress")
                    @Html.TextBox("emailAddress", emailAddress)
                </div>
                <div>
                    @Html.Label("Role: ", "role")
                    @Html.TextBox("role", role)
                </div>
            </fieldset>
            <div>
                <input type="submit" value="Update Employee Record" />
            </div>
        </form>
    </body>
</html>
```

The first part of this code gets the EmployeeId from the UrlData, passed in from the link we added to the default page. We then check the value of the EmployeeId and pass the browser back to the default page if it is blank. This handles the situation where a user may just browse directly to the edit page without specifying an EmployeeId in the URL.

```
var employeeId = UrlData[0];
if (employeeId.IsEmpty()) {
    Response.Redirect(@Href("~/default"));
}
```

In the call to the Redirect method of the Response object, we will notice that we have used the Href helper. The Href helper builds a URL from a local file path, which means we can use the ASP.NET tilde (~) symbol to reference the default page from the root of the application. This has the advantage that wherever we move this page or site to in the future, as long as the location of the destination page remains the same, the URL will still be built correctly; this solves a common problem in web sites where pages or sites move and references to relative or absolute URLs are broken.

The next part of the code declares some variables to hold the data retrieved from the database. We then simply open the database, execute our SQL, passing in the EmployeeId as a parameter, and assign the returned values to our variables. Notice here that we are using the QuerySingle() method as we are only retrieving a single row.

The final job is to pass in the values of the variables containing the employee data to the Html helper methods used to display the form controls.

■ **Note** For more information on the use of Html helper controls to render HTML form controls, see the HTML Form Helpers section in Chapter 5.

As we can see here in Figure 6-14, if we run the default page now and click the Edit link against one of the rows, the edit page will be displayed with the form controls populated with data from the database, according to the EmployeeId passed in the URL.

Figure 6-14. The populated edit form: Notice the URL in the address bar containing the EmployeeId.

193

Now we need to write some code to handle the form submission. We'll want to update the record in the database and redirect the user back to the default page when the Update Employee Record button is clicked. Amend the code block at the top of the page to include the code highlighted in bold in this listing.

```
@{
    var employeeId  = UrlData[0];
    if (employeeId.IsEmpty()) {
        Response.Redirect(@Href("~/default"));
    }

    var forenames = "";
    var surname = "";
    var dateOfBirth = "";
    var emailAddress = "";
    var role = "";

    var db = Database.Open("DataExample");

    if (IsPost) {

        forenames = Request["forenames"];
        surname = Request["surname"];
        dateOfBirth = Request["dateOfBirth"];
        emailAddress = Request["emailAddress"];
        role = Request["role"];

        var sqlCommand = "UPDATE Employees SET Forenames = @0, Surname = @1, " +
                "DateOfBirth = @2, EmailAddress = @3, Role = @4 " +
                "WHERE EmployeeId = @5";
        db.Execute(sqlCommand, forenames, surname, dateOfBirth, emailAddress, ↵
role, employeeId);

        Response.Redirect(@Href("~/default"));
    }

    var sqlSelect = "SELECT * FROM Employees WHERE EmployeeId=@0";

    var row = db.QuerySingle(sqlSelect, employeeId);

    forenames = row.Forenames;
    surname = row.Surname;
    dateOfBirth = row.DateOfBirth.ToShortDateString();
    emailAddress = row.EmailAddress;
    role = row.Role;
}
```

Here, inside the If(IsPost) code block, we assign the values of the submitted form fields to our variables and execute an SQL update command against the database, passing in the variables as parameters. This is done using the Execute() method of the Database object in the same way as we did when inserting records earlier. Once the record has been updated, we redirect the user back to the default page.

Now that we have implemented the Create, Read, and Update parts of CRUD, we are left with just the Delete, which we'll deal with in the next section.

Deleting Records

To implement our delete functionality, we will add a delete link for each employee to the employee list on the default page. Clicking this link will take the user to a page requesting confirmation before the actual delete operation takes place. As an HTML hyperlink always issues an HTTP GET request, this is an important step, as it is against W3C guidelines to perform a delete operation (or any operation which affects persisted data) through an HTTP GET request.

First, let's add a delete link to the default page for each employee in the employee list. Amend the last column in the table to include a link to delete.cshtml, passing the EmployeeId in the UrlData.

```
<tbody>
    @foreach (var row in db.Query(sqlCommand))
    {
        <tr>
            <td>@row.EmployeeId</td>
            <td>@row.Forenames</td>
            <td>@row.Surname</td>
            <td>@row.DateOfBirth.ToLongDateString()</td>
            <td>@row.EmailAddress</td>
            <td>@row.Role</td>
            <td>
                <a href="edit/@row.EmployeeId">Edit</a> |
                <a href="delete/@row.EmployeeId">Delete</a>
            </td>
        </tr>
    }
</tbody>
```

Next, we'll create delete.cshtml and write code to get the relevant record from the database and display some confirmation text to the user.

```
@{
    var employeeId  = UrlData[0];
    if (employeeId.IsEmpty()) {
        Response.Redirect(@Href("~/default"));
    }

    var db = Database.Open("DataExample");

    var sqlSelect = "SELECT Forenames, Surname FROM Employees WHERE EmployeeId=@0";
    var row = db.QuerySingle(sqlSelect, employeeId);
}
<!DOCTYPE html>

<html lang="en">
    <head>
```

```
        <meta charset="utf-8" />
        <title>Delete Employee Record</title>
    </head>
    <body>
        <h1>Delete Employee Record</h1>
        <p>
            Are we sure we want to delete employee @employeeId, @row.Forenames @row.Surname?
        </p>
        <p>
            <form action="" method="post">
                <input type="button"
                onclick="document.location.href='default.cshtml';"
                value="Cancel" />
                <input type="submit" value="Delete" />
            </form>
        </p>
    </body>
</html>
```

The first part of this code gets the EmployeeId from the UrlData and stores it in a variable for later use. If the UrlData is empty, the user is returned to the default page. Next, we use the `QuerySingle()` method of the Database object to select a single row from the database, passing in the EmployeeId as a parameter.

■ **Note** As is the nature of web-based applications, there is the always the possibility (albeit slim) that the employee record could be deleted by another user between the employee list being created and the delete page being displayed, or between the delete confirmation form being displayed and submitted. In the interests of clarity, this code example carries out no checks to ensure that the employee to be deleted actually exists. However, in a production environment, our code must take all these possibilities into account to avoid potential errors.

Confirmation text is then displayed to the user, showing the name and EmployeeId of the employee to be deleted. This helps to ensure that the correct record is deleted (see Figure 6-15). We supply a standard submit button to confirm the deletion as well as a second HTML button to cancel the operation. The cancel button uses JavaScript in the `onclick` event, which will redirect the user back to the default page without submitting the form.

```
<input type="button"
 onclick="document.location.href='default.cshtml';"
 value="Cancel" />
<input type="submit" value="Delete" />
```

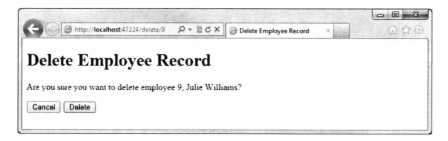

Figure 6-15. *The delete confirmation page*

Finally, we'll add some code to detect an HTTP POST request and perform the SQL delete operation on the Employees table, which conforms to the W3C guidelines mentioned earlier. If the site had been set up to delete straight from the link on the default page, without requiring an HTTP POST request from the confirmation page, anyone could delete records from the database just by browsing to a correctly formed URL, like http://<servername>/delete/4.

Amend the code block at the top of the page to include the POST request handler shown in bold in the listing that follows, which deletes the row on postback and returns the user to the default page.

```
@{
    var employeeId = UrlData[0];
    if (employeeId.IsEmpty()) {
        Response.Redirect(@Href("~/default"));
    }

    var db = Database.Open("DataExample");

    if (IsPost)
    {
        var sqlDelete = "DELETE FROM Employees WHERE EmployeeId=@0";
        db.Execute(sqlDelete, employeeId);
        Response.Redirect("~/default");
    }

    var sqlSelect = "SELECT Forenames, Surname FROM Employees WHERE EmployeeId=@0";
    var row = db.QuerySingle(sqlSelect, employeeId);
}
```

Now that we can Create, Read, Update, and Delete database records, let's take a look at a couple of handy features that can help us to display useful data to our users; the WebGrid and Chart helpers.

Displaying Data with WebMatrix Helpers

Out of the box, WebMatrix ships with two helpers designed to facilitate the easy development of two common data display scenarios: grids (or tabular data) and graphs. In this section, We will look at both of these and discuss common examples of their use.

The WebGrid Helper

The WebGrid helper is used to render tabular data. Earlier in the chapter, in the Retrieving and Displaying Data section, we used a `foreach` loop to iterate through a set of database records and construct a table. This is a very common requirement in the development of web pages, which the WebGrid aims to simplify and accelerate. The helper also provides support for formatting, paging, and sorting, all of which we will see examples of in this section. The examples will all use the Employees database we constructed earlier in the chapter.

Displaying Data

Start by creating a new file in the root of our web site, called EmployeeGrid.cshtml. Next, replace the existing default markup with the following:

```
@{
    var db = Database.Open("DataExample");
    var sqlCommand = "SELECT * FROM Employees ORDER BY Surname";
    var result = db.Query(sqlCommand);
    var employeeGrid = new WebGrid(result);
}
<!DOCTYPE html>

<html lang="en">
    <head>
        <meta charset="utf-8" />
        <title>Employee Grid</title>
    </head>
    <body>
        <h1>Employee Grid</h1>
        <div id="grid">
            @employeeGrid.GetHtml()
        </div>
    </body>
</html>
```

The first three lines of the code block at the top of the page will probably look quite familiar by now. They simply open a connection to the database, define an SQL query to return all the records in the database in alphabetical order by surname, and finally execute that query against the database and store the returned records in the `result` variable.

The final, fourth line of the initial code block is where we start to actually use the WebGrid helper.

```
var employeeGrid = new WebGrid(result);
```

Here, we create a new WebGrid object and assign it to a variable called `employeeGrid`. We then just need to call the `GetHtml()` method of the WebGrid within the page to render it. We render the grid inside an HTML `div` element with its `id` attribute set to "grid," which we'll use later for styling.

```
<div id="grid">
    @employeeGrid.GetHtml()
</div>
```

Run the page, and we will see the rendered WebGrid, as seen here in Figure 6-16. We will notice that the WebGrid's column headers are hyperlinks. Clicking these hyperlinks will sort the table by the data in those columns.

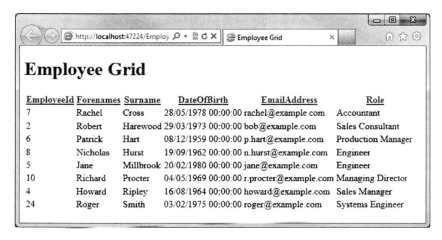

Figure 6-16. *The Employee Grid, rendered by the WebGrid helper*

Clearly, the WebMatrix WebGrid helper presents quite a usable UI straight out of the box, with an absolute minimum of code; it is reasonably formatted with headers and sortable columns and emits markup that complies with the HTML5 standard. However, there are several ways we can further improve the formatting and functionality, which we will look at in the next three sections.

Formatting Columns

As we have seen, by default the WebGrid helper displays all the data columns returned by the SQL query, using the column names defined in the database as the column headers in the grid. We can customize this behavior by displaying only a subset of the data columns that are returned by the query and by specifying how the data in the columns within the WebGrid should be displayed.

In reality, a WebGrid is actually constructed from one or more WebGridColumns. To specify the columns to be displayed and how they are formatted, we need to pass in a collection of WebGridColumns to the GetHtml() method of the WebGrid. Each WebGridColumn has five properties that can be set (see Table 6-5).

Table 6-5. *WebGridColumn Properties*

Property	Description
CanSort	Gets or sets a Boolean value that indicates whether the WebGridColumn can be sorted.
ColumnName	Gets or sets the name of the data item that is associated with the column.
Format	Gets or sets a function that is used to format the data item associated with the column.
Header	Gets or sets the text that is to be displayed in the header row of the column.
Style	Gets or sets the CSS class attribute that is rendered as part of the HTML table cells that form the column.

Replace the existing code and markup in EmployeeGrid.cshtml with the following, which I'll explain in detail afterwards.

```
@{
    var db = Database.Open("DataExample");
    var sqlCommand = "SELECT Forenames, Surname, EmailAddress, Role FROM Employees⤸
ORDER BY Surname";
    var result = db.Query(sqlCommand);
    var employeeGrid = new WebGrid(result);
}
<!DOCTYPE html>

<html lang="en">
    <head>
        <meta charset="utf-8" />
        <title>Employee Grid</title>
        <style type="text/css">
            .name { width: 150px; }
            .role { font-style: italic; }
        </style>
    </head>
    <body>
        <h1>Employee Grid</h1>
        <div id="grid">
            @employeeGrid.GetHtml(
                columns: employeeGrid.Columns(
                    employeeGrid.Column("Surname",
                                        style: "name",
                                        format: @<text>
                                                    @item.Surname.ToUpper()
                                                </text>),
                    employeeGrid.Column("Forenames",
```

```
                                    style: "name"),
            employeeGrid.Column("EmailAddress",
                                "Email Address",
                                format: @<text>
                                            <a href="mailto:@item.EmailAddress">
                                                @item.EmailAddress
                                            </a>
                                         </text>),
            employeeGrid.Column("Role",
                                "Job Title",
                                style: "role")
            )
        )
    </div>
    </body>
</html>
```

We will notice, first of all, that the SQL query has changed. As we only want to display a subset of columns, there is no point in returning all of them, as it would waste system resources on the web server. This may not be a huge problem when we are working with the small amounts of data in this sample, but it could cause significant performance issues when working with larger production data sets.

We have also added some CSS styles into the head section of the page, which we will use to style the table cells.

The GetHtml() method call has changed significantly, both to specify columns and to format them. If we run the page, we will see the following (see Figure 6-17):

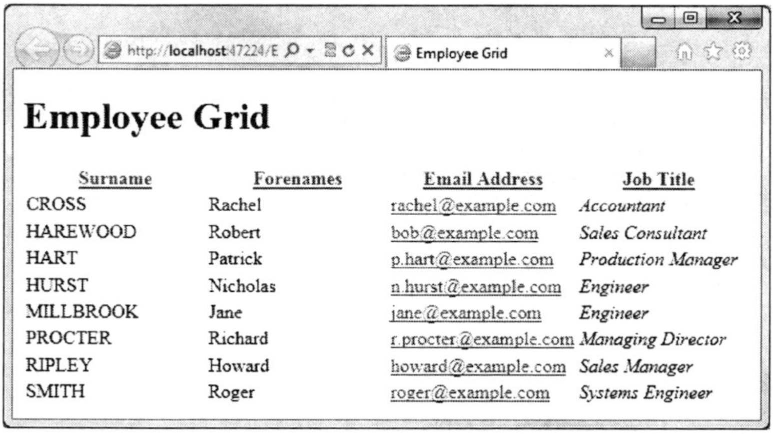

Figure 6-17. The formatted grid

The GetHtml() method call is not actually as complicated as it looks! In the call, we are simply specifying the value of the columns parameter. The columns parameter is actually an array of WebGridColumn objects, which is what we are creating in this code.

The WebGridColumn class defines objects that represent columns in a WebGrid instance. The class has five properties, which can be set as named parameters when calling the WebGridColumn constructor.

201

Table 6-6 describes these properties, their names, types, and the name of the respective `WebGridColumn` constructor parameter.

Table 6-6. *WebGridColumn Properties*

Property Name	Type	Constructor Parameter	Description
CanSort	bool	canSort	Gets or sets a value that indicates whether this particular column in the `WebGrid` can be sorted.
ColumnName	string	columnName	Gets or sets the name of the data item that is associated with the `WebGrid` column.
Format	Func<T, TResult>	format	Used to format the data item that is associated with the `WebGrid` column.
Header	string	header	Gets or sets the text that is rendered in the header row of the `WebGrid` column.
Style	string	style	The name of the CSS class to be applied to the `WebGrid` column.

These are all fairly straightforward, except perhaps for the `format` property. This property is used to reformat values into an easily readable form and to add HTML markup to provide custom formatting for the `WebGrid` column's data. The value of any item in the current row can be retrieved through a dynamic object called `item`. For example, `@item.Role` would retrieve the value of the `Role` column in the current row. If we wanted to display the `Role` in bold type, we could simply include some HTML within the `format` property for the `Role` column: for example, `<strong>@item.Role</strong>`.

The first column is populated from the Surname field. It has its CSS style set to "name," which is declared in the head section and sets the column width to 150 pixels, by setting the property using a named parameter. The format parameter is set to return the surname in upper case, using the `ToUpper()` method of the `String` type, which we are able to do, as the `Database.Query()` method returns `IEnumerable<dynamic>`.

```
employeeGrid.Column("Surname",
                    style: "name",
                    format: @<text>
                                @item.Surname.ToUpper()
                            </text>),
```

The second column displays the Forenames field and is again styled using the "name" style specified in the document head.

```
employeeGrid.Column("Forenames",
                    style: "name"),
```

The third column contains the EmailAddress field. Here, we specify that the header should display the text "Email Address" rather than the field name, and we specify the format of the field by setting the format parameter. The format parameter is passed a template for an HTML `mailto` hyperlink, which will be populated with `item.EmailAddress`. As described earlier, the data in each individual row can be accessed using the `item` collection.

```
employeeGrid.Column("EmailAddress",
                    "Email Address",
                    format: @<text>
                                <a href="mailto:@item.EmailAddress">
                                    @item.EmailAddress
                                </a>
                             </text>),
```

The final column displays the contents of the Role database field, with the column header set to "Job Title." The column is assigned the "role" CSS style, by specifying it using the style parameter.

```
employeeGrid.Column("Role",
                    "Job Title",
                    style: "role")
```

Applying Grid-Wide Styles

In addition to specifying the styles for individual table cells, the `GetHtml()` method of the WebGrid also allows us to set a number of CSS styles that apply to the grid as a whole. These are listed as follows in Table 6-7.

Table 6-7. *WebGrid.GetHtml Style Parameters*

Parameter	Description
tableStyle	The name of the CSS class to be applied to the whole grid (table).
headerStyle	The name of the CSS class to be applied to the table header.
footerStyle	The name of the CSS class to be applied to the table footer.
rowStyle	The name of the CSS class to be applied to each table row.
alternatingRowStyle	The name of the CSS class to be applied to even-numbered table rows.
selectedRowStyle	The name of the CSS class to be applied to the selected table row. Only one row can be selected at any one time.

We'll now use the GetHtml() method to apply some CSS styles across the whole grid to improve the presentation. Amend the style tag in the page header to the following:

```
<style type="text/css">
    .grid { margin: 4px; border-collapse: collapse; width: 600px; }
    .grid th, .grid td { border: 1px solid #CCC; padding: 5px; }
    .header { background-color: #DDD; font-weight: bold; }
    .header a { text-decoration: none; }
    .alt { background-color: #EEE; color: #000; }
    .name { width: 150px; }
    .role { width: 200px; font-style: italic; }
</style>
```

Next, we'll apply those styles to the relevant elements of our table, using named parameters. Amend our call to the GetHtml() method in the body of the page to look like the following:

```
@employeeGrid.GetHtml(
    tableStyle: "grid",
    headerStyle: "header",
    alternatingRowStyle: "alt",
    columns: employeeGrid.Columns(
        employeeGrid.Column("Surname",
                            style: "name",
                            format: @<text>
                                        @item.Surname.ToUpper()
                                    </text>),
        employeeGrid.Column("Forenames",
                            style: "name"),
        employeeGrid.Column("EmailAddress",
                            "Email Address",
                            format: @<text>
                                        <a href="mailto:@item.EmailAddress">
                                            @item.EmailAddress
                                        </a>
                                    </text>),
        employeeGrid.Column("Role",
                            "Job Title",
                            style: "role")
    )
)
```

Now, when we run the EmployeeGrid.cshtml page or refresh the page in the browser, the grid will look like the example shown in Figure 6-18.

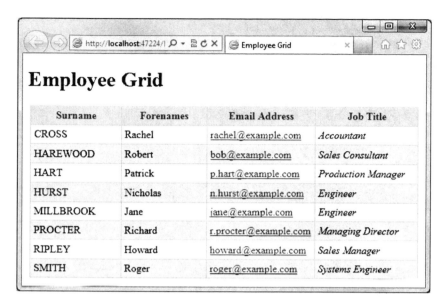

Surname	Forenames	Email Address	Job Title
CROSS	Rachel	rachel@example.com	*Accountant*
HAREWOOD	Robert	bob@example.com	*Sales Consultant*
HART	Patrick	p.hart@example.com	*Production Manager*
HURST	Nicholas	n.hurst@example.com	*Engineer*
MILLBROOK	Jane	jane@example.com	*Engineer*
PROCTER	Richard	r.procter@example.com	*Managing Director*
RIPLEY	Howard	howard@example.com	*Sales Manager*
SMITH	Roger	roger@example.com	*Systems Engineer*

Figure 6-18. *The Employee Grid with grid-wide styles applied*

WebGrid Pagination

When working with large data sets, database queries can often return many more rows than can be usefully displayed on the page. To counter this problem, web developers commonly provide the user with the ability to page through the data. This can be achieved easily using the WebGrid helper by setting parameters during creation.

Amend the code used to create the WebGrid in our page to the following:

```
var employeeGrid = new WebGrid(source: result,
                               defaultSort: "Surname",
                               rowsPerPage: 3);
```

Here, we use named parameters to specify the column which will be sorted by default (`defaultSort`) and the number of rows we wish to display per page (`rowsPerPage`), in this case three.

Running or refreshing the page will show the grid displaying the first three rows, with the paging controls rendered under the table data (see Figure 6-19).

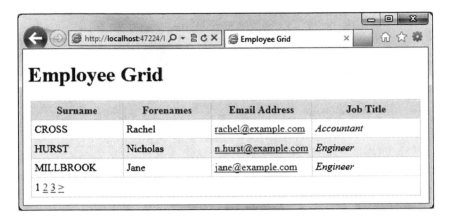

Figure 6-19. The Employee Grid set to show three records per page

The links displayed below the grid to control paging can be customized by specifying values for the firstText, previousText, nextText, lastText and mode parameters of the GetHtml() method. The firstText, previousText, nextText, and lastText properties set the text for the HTML link elements in the pager control. The mode parameter can be set to any of the WebGridPagerModes members shown here in Table 6-8.

Table 6-8. WebGridPagerMode Members

Member	Description
Numeric	Displays page numbers as links.
NextPrevious	Displays links to the next or previous pages.
FirstLast	Displays links to the first or last pages.
All	Equivalent to a combination of Numeric, NextPrevious, and FirstLast.

■ **Caution**   Note that the mode parameter must be set to a suitable value to match the values set in the firstText, previousText, nextText, and lastText properties; otherwise, an error will occur, such as, "To use this argument, pager mode "FirstLast" must be enabled."

Changing the call to GetHtml() for the employeeGrid as shown here, the pager control links will cause the pager to be rendered as seen in Figure 6-20.

```
@employeeGrid.GetHtml(
                tableStyle: "grid",
                headerStyle: "header",
                alternatingRowStyle: "alt",
                mode: WebGridPagerModes.All,
                firstText: "First",
                previousText: "Prev",
                nextText: "Next",
                lastText: "Last",
                columns: employeeGrid.Columns( ....
```

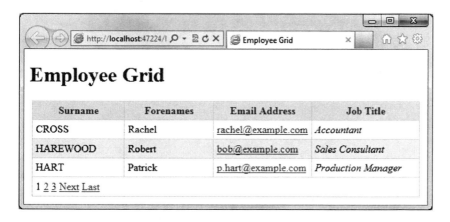

Figure 6-20. *Customizing the pager control links*

■ **Tip**   For more information on the WebGrid class and its members, visit the MDSN web site at http://msdn.microsoft.com/en-us/library/gg548335.aspx

---

The Chart Helper

The Chart helper is used to render data in graphical form. The helper can produce more than thirty different chart types, with a variety of options for formatting and labeling and, by default, renders a JPEG image to the browser.

The most common sources of data to be displayed in a chart are .NET collections and database queries, each of which we will look at in the next two sections. Once we have seen how to create charts from these two data sources, we will look at ways of customizing them and inserting them into an ASP.NET Web Page.

Creating a Chart Using a .NET Collection

A chart can be created using any .NET collection that implements the IEnumerable interface, including custom collections.

Create a new page in our project called CollectionChart.cshtml and overwrite the default markup with the following:

```
@{
    var sales = new Dictionary<string, int>()
        {
            { "Books", 10 },
            { "DVDs", 7 },
            { "Games", 12 },
            { "Music", 5 },
            { "Toys", 9 }
        };

    var myChart = new Chart(width: 600, height: 400)
        .AddTitle("Sales")
        .AddSeries(
            name: "ProductSales",
            xValue: sales.Keys,
            yValues: sales.Values)
        .Write();
}
```

The first thing we do in this code is define a new generic dictionary collection, called sales, which we populate with some data, in this case relating to the sales figures of each of five categories of products.

Next, we create a new chart and set the width and height by passing in named parameters to the constructor. To add a title to the chart, we call the AddTitle() method and pass in the title, "Sales." We then use the AddSeries() method to pass in a data series to the chart. Multiple data series can be displayed on a chart, and each must have its own unique name, in our case "ProductSales." Using the xValue and yValues parameters, we also tell the chart which set of values we wish to plot; clearly, we will be using the dictionary keys and values we have just created.

Finally, we call the Write() method to render the image to the browser which, because we didn't explicitly specify a chart type, displays the default column chart shown here in Figure 6-21.

■ **Note** We will be looking at the different types of chart and how to specify them later in the chapter.

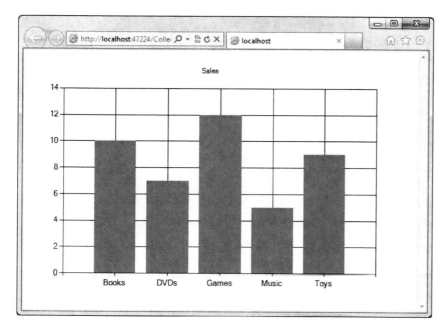

Figure 6-21. *A chart created using data from a generic dictionary collection*

Creating a Chart Using a Database Query

The most common source of data for creating charts is from the result of a database query. Fortunately, the WebMatrix **Chart** helper makes this a relatively simple task.

To start with, we will need to create some data that is suitable for graphical representation. Create a new table in our database called Products and add the three columns described here in Table 6-9.

Table 6-9. *Sales Table Schema*

Column Name	Data Type	Allow Nulls?	Other Properties
ProductId	int	False	Is Identity = true; Is Primary Key = true;
Description	nvarchar	False	Length = 100
Price	money	False	Default Value = 0.00
TotalSales	int	False	Default Value = 0

Then add some sample data, similar to that shown here, in Figure 6-22.

ProductId	Description	Price	TotalSales
1	Lawn Mower	174.99	12
2	Barbecue	69.99	24
3	Table and Chairs	94.49	20
4	Gazebo	36.99	16
5	Garden Swing	44.99	15
NULL	NULL	NULL	NULL

Figure 6-22. *Our sample products data*

Now that we have some suitable data, we can see how to display it using the `Chart` helper. Create a new page called DatabaseChart.cshtml in our project and replace the default markup with the following code.

```
@{
    var db = Database.Open("DataExample");
    var sqlCommand = "SELECT Description, TotalSales FROM Products";
    var chartData = db.Query(sqlCommand);
    var myChart = new Chart(width: 600, height: 400)
        .AddTitle("Product Sales")
        .DataBindTable(chartData, "Description")
        .Write();
}
```

This is all the code we needed to render the column chart seen in Figure 6-23. The first three lines establish a database connection, define an SQL query, and execute the query using the `Query()` method of the `Database` object, as we have seen many times before.

The fourth line creates a new Chart object and uses named parameters to pass the desired `width` and `height` for the chart into the constructor. We then set the title of the chart using the `AddTitle()` method. The data is bound to the chart using the `DataBindTable()` method, which requires two parameters: `dataSource`, which can be any `IEnumerable` object, and `xField`, which is the name of the table column to be used for the x-series axis. We pass `chartData` into the `dataSource` parameter and "Description" into the `xField` parameter.

Finally, we call the `Write()` method to output the chart to the browser.

■ **Tip**   Using the DataBindTable() method, we only have the option to specify the column to be used for the x-axis. The data column to be used for the y-axis is inferred from the dataSource, which in our case is easy as we are only returning two columns in our query.

However, if our query contains more than two columns and we need to specify both the x and y axes, we can make use of the AddSeries() method we saw in the .NET Collection Chart in the previous section. The Database.Query() method returns an IEnumerable<dynamic> collection which is compatible with the AddSeries() method.

For example, instead of binding the result of the database query to the chart using the DataBindTable(), as we have previously, we could use the AddSeries() method shown here.

```
.AddSeries("ProductSales",
    xValue: chartData, xField: "Description",
    yValues: chartData, yFields: "TotalSales")
```

In this instance, both methods return the same results.

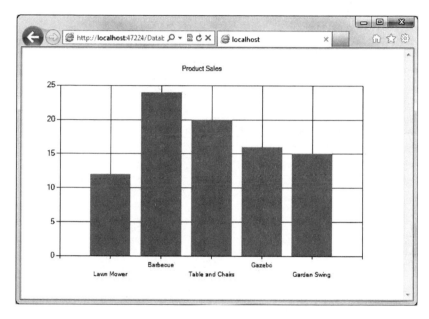

Figure 6-23. A column chart constructed from the result of a database query

Displaying a Chart in a Web Page

In both the .NET collection and database examples seen so far in the chapter, the Chart helper has rendered the chart directly to the browser as a graphic. However, we will usually want to render the chart graphic within a page containing additional markup. Placing the code we have seen so far in an existing page will result in the chart being rendered in the browser with any other markup being lost. We can prove this to our self by adding some static HTML to one of the previous Chart helper examples and running the page. None of the HTML we have added will be rendered; the browser is actually pointing to an image file created on the web server, not to a web page at all.

To solve this problem, we need to render the chart in two stages. First, we generate the Chart as we have so far, then we display the resulting image in another page using an HTML img element.

Create a new file called ChartPage.cshtml within our project and replace the default markup with the following:

```
<!DOCTYPE html>

<html lang="en">
    <head>
        <meta charset="utf-8" />
        <title>Chart Display Page</title>
    </head>
    <body>
        <h1>Chart Display Page</h1>
        <p>The chart shown on this page is rendered through the use of an
            HTML <code>img</code> tag with its <code>src</code> attribute
            set to the file which generates the chart: DatabaseChart.cshtml</p>
        <p>
            <img src="DatabaseChart.cshtml" />
        </p>
    </body>
</html>
```

The important line in this example is the one highlighted in bold, which uses the img element to display the chart we created earlier in the Creating a Chart Using a Database Query section.

When we run the ChartPage.cshtml, we will see that the graph is embedded within the rest of the markup on the page (see Figure 6-24).

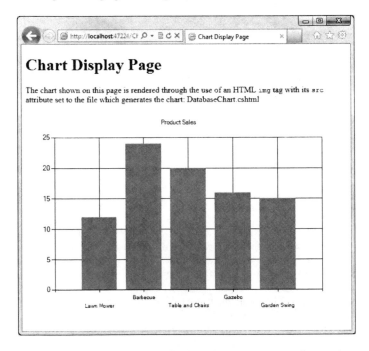

Figure 6-24. Embedding a chart within existing markup using an HTML img element

Displaying Different Chart Types

The WebMatrix Chart helper can render 35 different types of chart: Area, Bar, BoxPlot, Bubble, Candlestick, Column, Doughnut, ErrorBar, FastLine, FastPoint, Funnel, Kagi, Line, Pie, Point, PointAndFigure, Polar, Pyramid, Radar, Range, RangeBar, RangeColumn, Renko, Spline, SplineArea, SplineRange, StackedArea, StackedArea100, StackedBar, StackedBar100, StackedColumn, StackedColumn100, StepLine, Stock, and ThreeLineBreak.

To specify the type of chart to render, we set the `chartType` parameter of the `AddSeries()` method. The string passed in the `chartType` parameter can, and must, be any one of the chart types listed earlier.

The following code example renders the pie chart seen in Figure 6-25.

```
@{
    var sales = new Dictionary<string, int>()
        {
            { "Books", 10 },
            { "DVDs", 7 },
            { "Games", 12 },
            { "Music", 5 },
            { "Toys", 9 }
        };

    var myChart = new Chart(width: 600, height: 400)
        .AddTitle("Sales")
        .AddSeries(
            chartType: "Pie",
            name: "ProductSales",
            xValue: sales.Keys,
            yValues: sales.Values)
        .Write();
}
```

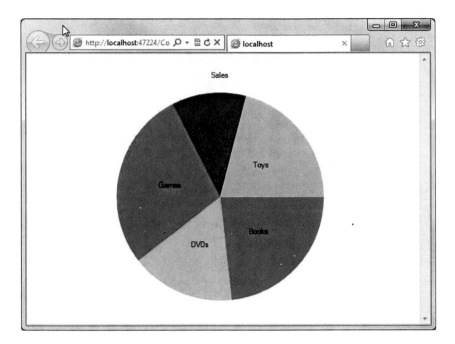

Figure 6-25. A pie chart rendered by the WebMatrix Chart helper

Styling and Formatting WebMatrix Charts

Charts rendered by the WebMatrix Chart helper can be styled in a number of ways. The easiest way to change the appearance of the whole chart is to specify one of the built-in themes. This is done by passing a `ChartTheme` name to the `theme` parameter of the Chart constructor.

The built-in themes are listed here in Table 6-10.

Table 6-10. Chart Helper Themes

ChartTheme Name	Description
Blue	Blue columns on a blue gradient background
Green	Blue columns on a green gradient background

Vanilla	Red columns on a white background
Vanilla3D	Three-dimensional red columns on a white background
Yellow	Orange columns on a yellow gradient background

It is also possible to display a legend to explain the meaning of each series in the chart. To display a legend, call the AddLegend() method of the Chart class, passing in the text to be displayed as the title of the legend and a unique name for the legend. The legend displays the text value held in the name property for each series.

The following code generates the themed chart seen in Figure 6-26.

```
@{
    var sales = new Dictionary<string, int>()
        {
            { "Books", 10 },
            { "DVDs", 7 },
            { "Games", 12 },
            { "Music", 5 },
            { "Toys", 9 }
        };

    var myChart = new Chart(width: 600, height: 400, theme: ChartTheme.Green)
        .AddTitle("Sales")
        .AddLegend("Legend:", "SalesLegend")
        .AddSeries(
            name: "Sales Per Product",
            xValue: sales.Keys,
            yValues: sales.Values)
        .Write();
}
```

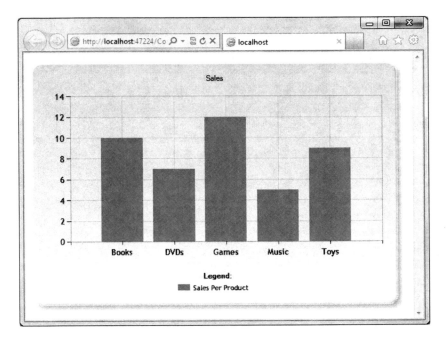

Figure 6-26. Specifying a theme and displaying a chart legend

Saving Charts

Every time we use the Chart helper in a web page, it is re-created in its entirety. That means that if the data required for any of the chart's series comes from the result of a database query, for example, that query must be re-executed every time the chart is requested. Even for a small query, this is a waste of server resources and can have an impact on the performance of the web site.

To help improve performance in this situation, we can use a number of techniques. We will look at two such techniques in this section: caching and saving the chart as an image file for later use.

Caching Charts

Caching a chart stores it in memory for a predetermined period of time. This way, if a chart is requested again within this period, it is rendered directly from the server cache, rather than being re-created. The chart is only re-created if requested again after the cache has expired. Caching is determined on a series-by-series basis and is controlled through the `AddSeries()` method of the chart.

To demonstrate caching, create a new file in the root of our example website called CachedChartPage.cshtml and replace the default markup with the following:

```
<!DOCTYPE html>
<html>
    <head>
        <title>Cached Chart Display Page</title>
    </head>
```

```
<body>
    <h1>Cached Chart Display Page</h1>
    <img src="CachedChart.cshtml?key=cacheKey" />
</body>
</html>
```

Next, create another new file in the root of our web site, this time called CachedChart.cshtml, which will contain the code to create a chart. Replace the default generated markup in CachedChart.cshtml with the following:

```
@{
    var cacheKey = Request["key"];
    if (cacheKey != null) {
        var cachedChart = Chart.GetFromCache(key: cacheKey);
        if (cachedChart == null) {

            var sales = new Dictionary<string, int>()
            {
                { "Books", 10 },
                { "DVDs", 7 },
                { "Games", 12 },
                { "Music", 5 },
                { "Toys", 9 }
            };

            cachedChart = new Chart(600, 400);
            cachedChart.AddTitle("Cached at " + DateTime.Now);
            cachedChart.AddSeries(
                name: "Sales",
                xValue: sales.Keys,
                yValues: sales.Values);
            cachedChart.SaveToCache(key: cacheKey,
                minutesToCache: 2,
                slidingExpiration: false);
        }
        Chart.WriteFromCache(cacheKey);
    }
}
```

Let's take a look at this code and how it works. First, the code attempts to get the key value from the QueryString. If a value has been passed in, the chart is retrieved from the cache.

```
var cacheKey = Request["key"];
    if (cacheKey != null) {
        var cachedChart = Chart.GetFromCache(key: cacheKey);
```

If a key value has not been passed via the QueryString, a new generic Dictionary object is created, containing the data for the chart to display (this could be replaced by code gathering data from any source). A new Chart object is then created, the series is added, and the chart title is set to the current date and time (which we will use to prove the caching later). We then call the SaveToCache() method and pass in the key, which is the ID of the chart in the cache, the minutesToCache, which is the number of minutes we wish to cache the chart for, and set the slidingExpiration to false. The slidingExpiration

217

parameter is a Boolean value which, if set to `true`, indicates that the chart's cache expiration is reset each time the cached item is accessed. By setting this to `false,` we ensure that the expiration time is based on an absolute interval time since the item was added to the cache.

```
cachedChart = new Chart(400, 300);
cachedChart.AddTitle("Cached at " + DateTime.Now);
cachedChart.AddSeries(
    name: "Sales",
    xValue: sales.Keys,
yValues: sales.Values);
cachedChart.SaveToCache(key: cacheKey,
    minutesToCache: 2,
    slidingExpiration: false);
```

Finally, instead of calling the Chart's `Write()` method, we call the `WriteFromCache()` method, passing in the key. We will notice that this method call is outside the `if` block, as we want to call it, whether the chart was available in the cache to begin with or had to be generated and saved in the cache.

```
Chart.WriteFromCache(cacheKey);
```

Now, when we run CachedChartPage.cshtml, we will see that the chart is displayed with the current date and time displayed in the chart title (see Figure 6-27).

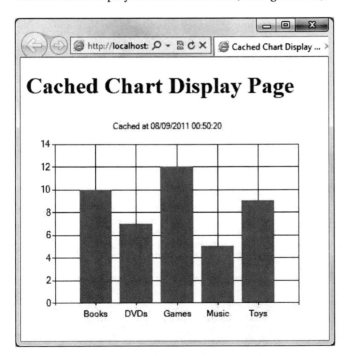

Figure 6-27. The cached chart: Note the date time displayed in the chart title.

If we close the browser and run the page again or refresh the browser, we will notice that the date and time displayed in the chart title has not changed. This proves that the chart has been cached.

To generate a new chart in the cache, click the Restart button in the WebMatrix IDE Ribbon Control (see Figure 6-28) and rerun the page (as restarting the application also resets the cache), or wait two minutes and refresh the page in the browser. This time, the date and time will change, as there is no chart currently in the cache; the chart has been re-generated using the code we supplied inside the if block, regathering any data necessary for its creation.

Figure 6-28. The Restart button in the Ribbon Control of the WebMatrix IDE

Saving Charts as Image Files

Another technique for saving a chart for later use is to save it as a standard image file on the web server. Once the image has been saved, it can then be accessed using an HTML img tag, as we would for any other graphic.

■ **Note** In order to use this technique, our web application must have read/write access to a folder on the web server.

At the root of our web site, create a folder called _Charts. Next, add a new page to the site root called SaveChart.cshtml. Replace the default markup in SaveChart.cshtml with the following:

```
@{
    var chartFileName = "_Charts/SalesChart01.jpg";
    if (!File.Exists(Server.MapPath(chartFileName))) {

        var sales = new Dictionary<string, int>()
        {
            { "Books", 10 },
            { "DVDs", 7 },
            { "Games", 12 },
            { "Music", 5 },
            { "Toys", 9 }
        };

        var chartImage = new Chart(400, 300);
```

```
        chartImage.AddTitle("Saved Chart");
        chartImage.AddSeries(
                name: "Sales",
                xValue: sales.Keys,
                yValues: sales.Values);
        chartImage.Save(path: chartFileName);
    }
}

<!DOCTYPE html>

<html lang="en">
    <head>
        <meta charset="utf-8" />
        <title>Saved Chart Example</title>
    </head>
    <body>
        <img src="@chartFileName" />
    </body>
</html>
```

In the code block at the top of the page we check to see if the chart already exists in the specified place on the web server. If the file does not exist, we generate some data in a generic Dictionary collection to display on the chart, then create a new chart, and add the collection as a chart series. Finally, we call the **Save()** method on the chart and pass in the path and filename declared on the first line to the methods **path** parameter.

In the body of the page, we simply use an HTML **img** element, pointing at the path declared in the code block, to display the chart.

The advantage of this technique is that the file is stored in the file system on the web server, rather than in a temporary cache, and so will not be lost if the web site is restarted.

Working with Other Databases

There may be occasions where we will need to connect to, and interact with, databases other than SQL Server Compact. In this section, we will see how an existing SQL Server Compact database can be migrated to a different version of SQL Server and how to connect to an SQL Server or MySQL database with ASP.NET Web Pages.

Migrating an SQL Server Database

While the SQL Server Compact database supplied with Microsoft WebMatrix is perfectly usable for small- to medium-sized web sites, it may become necessary to use one of the more powerful versions in the SQL Server family to meet performance or space requirements.

WebMatrix makes it easy to migrate an existing SQL Server Compact database from within the WebMatrix IDE.

Select the Databases workspace in the Workspace Selector and, in the Navigation Pane, highlight the database to be migrated. If the database is eligible for migration, the Migrate button will be available on the Home tab of the Ribbon Control (see Figure 6-29).

Figure 6-29. The Migrate button in the WebMatrix Ribbon Control

When we click the Migrate button, we will be presented with the Migrate Database dialog (see Figure 6-30). It is then simply a matter of entering the details of the database server we wish to migrate to and clicking the OK button.

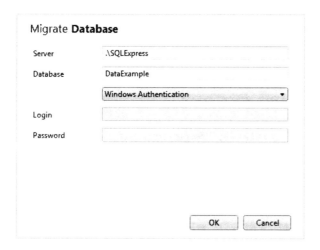

Figure 6-30. The Migrate Database dialog

When the migration has successfully completed, we will receive a success message in the notification area at the bottom of the IDE.

Connecting to an SQL Server or MySQL Database

Database interaction with WebMatrix is not solely limited to the integrated SQL Server Compact database. It may be necessary, at times, to make use of an existing database with greater capacity and performance, for example MySQL or a different version of SQL Server. In this section, we will see how WebMatrix can connect to either of these databases.

Creating a New Connection

To create a new connection to an existing database, select the Databases workspace in the Workspace Selector of the WebMatrix IDE. With the Databases workspace selected, the Ribbon Control at the top of the page will contain a New Connection icon (see Figure 6-31).

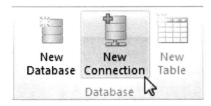

Figure 6-31. *The New Connection button in the Ribbon Control*

Click this icon to open the "Connect to Database" dialog box, shown here in Figure 6-32.

Connect to Database

Name	
Database Type	SQL Server 2005/2008 ▾
Server	
Database	
	Windows Authentication ▾
Login	
Password	

☐ Save Password
☐ Add to web.config

OK   Cancel

Figure 6-32. *The Connect to Database dialog box*

Enter a name for the connection in the "Name" textbox at the top of this dialog box. The name can be any string value but, for readability and maintenance purposes, be sure to give it a meaningful name that clearly identifies the database to which we wish to connect.

Next, select the type of database we wish to connect to, using the Database Type drop-down list. This is a choice of either SQL Server or MySQL, assuming that we have both installed on our machine.

Finally, fill in the rest of the required information, check the "Add to web.config" checkbox, and click OK.

If the connection is successful, we will see a success message in the Notification Area at the bottom of the IDE, and the database will appear in the Navigation Pane of the Database workspace. In the Navigation Pane, we will be able to browse the various objects within the database (see Figure 6-33).

Figure 6-33. The new database connection displayed in the Navigation Pane

The database can now be accessed in code in exactly the same way that we have done previously. To connect to the external database, all we need do is pass the name of our newly created database connection to the Database.Open() method.

```
var db = Database.Open("EmployeesConnection");
```

The web.config File

Because we checked the "Add to web.config" checkbox in the "Connect to Database" dialog box, the connection details have been added to a file called web.config in the root of our site. The web.config file is an XML file that can contain various configuration information regarding our site and will be created for we by WebMatrix if it does not already exist.

If we did not already have a web.config file and have connected to an SQL Server Express database, the web.config created by WebMatrix will look something like the following:

```
<?xml version="1.0" encoding="UTF-8"?>
<configuration>
    <connectionStrings>
        <add connectionString="Trusted_Connection=True;Server=.\SQLEXPRESS;Database=Employees"
            name="SqlServerConnection" providerName="System.Data.SqlClient" />
    </connectionStrings>
</configuration>
```

Each database connection that we create will be inserted as an **add** element within the **connectionStrings** section. It is useful to keep the connections in the web.config file, as they can be easily edited if necessary when deploying to a production server in the future.

We will use the web.config to store other site configuration information as we move through the later chapters of the book.

Summary

In this chapter, we have learned how to interact with databases using Microsoft WebMatrix. We have seen how we can use the WebMatrix IDE to create Microsoft SQL Server Compact databases and how to use Structured Query Language and C# Razor code to perform Create, Read, Update, and Delete (CRUD) operations.

Next, we saw how to use the in-built WebGrid and Chart helpers to easily present tabular and graphical information to the user and finished by learning how to connect to other types of external databases.

Using the information and techniques presented in this chapter, we can now create interactive, dynamic web sites which persist their data to a database for permanent storage.

In the next chapter, we will learn how to use the ASP.NET Web Pages membership functions to secure areas of our web site for access by registered and authenticated users.

■ ■ ■

CHAPTER 7

Security and Membership

It is a common requirement in the design of web applications that parts of a web site are available only to certain privileged users. In practice, this is most commonly implemented by having users log into the site to determine their identity; this process is known as *authentication*.

Once a user's identity has been established, they are then given access to the parts of the site that their user account allows; this is known as *membership*.

In this chapter, we will see how the WebMatrix WebSecurity helper can be used to implement authentication and membership functions in a web site. We will learn how to restrict areas of a site to individual and groups of authenticated users, how to allow new users to register for an account, and how to allow existing users to login and change and reset passwords.

The membership system stores its data within a set of database tables. We will see how WebMatrix can generate these tables for us in an existing database and how to plug existing user data from another source into the system. We will also see an example of how we can provide pages to carry out user administration and how to store the user information securely in a database.

Setting Up the WebSecurity Helper

In order to use the WebSecurity helper, it must first be initialized in code. To do this, we need to call the WebSecurity.InitializeDatabaseConnection() method, passing in some initialization values. The call to the InitializeDatabaseConnection() method can be made at any time before the first interaction with the helper. In most cases, it is best to do this during the initial startup of the application by placing it within the site's _AppStart.cshtml file.

The InitializeDatabaseConnection() method has a signature containing five parameters and an overload containing six parameters:

```
public static void InitializeDatabaseConnection(
        string connectionStringName,
        string userTableName,
        string userIdColumn,
        string userNameColumn,
        bool autoCreateTables
)

public static void InitializeDatabaseConnection(
        string connectionStringName,
        string providerName,
```

```
        string userTableName,
        string userIdColumn,
        string userNameColumn,
        bool autoCreateTables
)
```

Table 7-1 explains each of these parameters in detail.

Table 7-1. InitializeDatabaseConnection() Parameters

Parameter Name	Description
connectionStringName	The name of the connection string or SQL Server Compact database file (without the .sdf extension) for the database that contains user information.
providerName	Optional. The name of the ADO.NET data provider. If we are using Microsoft SQL Server, this parameter should be omitted.
userTableName	The name of the database table that contains user profile information.
userIdColumn	The name of the database column that contains user IDs. The column must be of an integer (int) type.
userNameColumn	The name of the database column that contains user names.
autoCreateTables	A Boolean value used to indicate whether user profile and membership tables should automatically be created by ASP.NET if they do not already exist. A full description of these tables appears later in this section. NOTE: Although the tables can be created automatically by the helper, the database itself must already exist before the InitializeDatabaseConnection() method is called.

The flexibility of the WebSecurity helper is one of its main features and benefits. The helper can work with either its own proprietary database tables or can be easily configured to integrate with any existing data.

Many companies, for example, will already hold employee information that could be used as the basis for a membership system. By pointing the helper at the existing database, along with the relevant columns for user IDs and user names, duplication of data can be minimized.

▓ **Tip**   ASP.NET provides an `ActiveDirectoryMembershipProvider` class that, although well beyond the scope of this chapter, could be used with ASP.NET Web Pages to authenticate users against a Windows Active Directory system. We can find more information about this on the MSDN web site at
http://msdn.microsoft.com/en-us/library/system.web.security.activedirectorymembershipprovider.aspx

---

The WebSecurity helper distinguishes between *profile* and *membership* data. The user profile data is the user name and ID, along with whatever other personal information we wish to store about our user (email addresses, contact numbers, date of birth, etc.). Membership data is the security information required by the membership system to authenticate and administer users of this particular system (passwords, last password change dates, application roles, etc.). This split between profile and membership data makes it possible for the helper to work with our present user data—our existing data providing the profile part of the system.

Let's create a new site to demonstrate the WebMatrix membership system. Create a new site using the empty site template and add a blank database called MembershipExample.sdf. Add a file called _AppStart.cshtml to the root of the site and replace the default markup with the following:

```
@{
    WebSecurity.InitializeDatabaseConnection("MembershipExample",
        "UserProfile", "UserId", "UserName", true);
}
```

Next, add a C# ASP.NET Web Page called default.cshtml to the root of the site, which will be our home page, and alter the generated markup to look like the following:

```
<!DOCTYPE html>

<html lang="en">
    <head>
        <meta charset="utf-8" />
        <title>Home Page</title>
    </head>
    <body>
        <h1>Home Page</h1>
        <p>
            Welcome to the Home Page of the Membership Example site.
        </p>
    </body>
</html>
```

When we run the site for the first time, we will see that the `InitializeDatabaseConnection()` method call in the `_AppStart.cshtml` file has created four tables in the `MembershipExample.sdf` database, as in Figure 7-1.

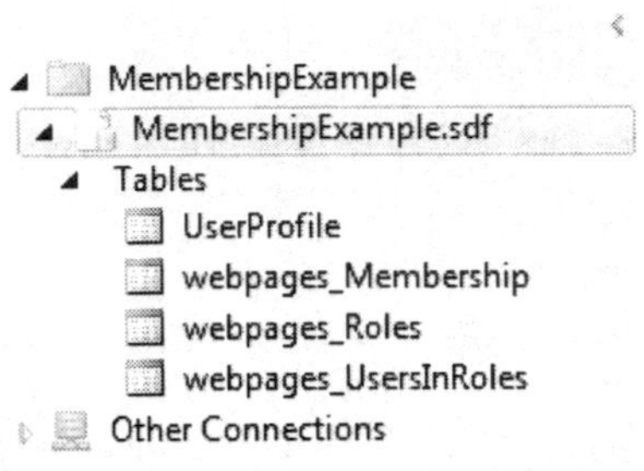

Figure 7-1. The database tables added by the InitializeDatabaseConnection() method

The `UserProfile` table contains only the two columns specified in the method call: `UserID` and `UserName`. We can customize this table to include additional personal information about the user as long as we don't alter the definitions of these two columns.

The `webpages_Membership` table contains all the detailed membership and security information required by the helper.

The `webpages_Roles` table is used by the helper to define roles that can be used to create groups of users. This table is used in conjunction with the `webpages_UsersInRoles` table, which links users to roles. Roles will be discussed in depth later in the chapter.

▨ **Caution**   Changes to the existing schema of the four database tables used by the membership system can have severe consequences, possibly resulting in the complete failure of the membership functionality of our site. The only table that is commonly changed is the UserProfile table, which can have extra columns added to it to store additional user info. This process is described in detail in the section titled "Storing Additional User Information," later in this chapter.

Now that the membership system has been initialized, we can move on and implement a registration page, which will allow new users to create accounts in our membership database.

Creating a New User Registration Page

On our user registration page, we will provide a form containing a user name textbox and two password textboxes—a standard design for this type of page. When the user submits the form, we will check that an account does not already exist with this user name and that the values of the two password textboxes match. If both these conditions are met, we will log out any current user, create the new account, log the new user in, and display a success message.

Create a new page called register.cshtml in the root of our site and add the following markup, which displays a registration form:

```
@{
    var username = "";
    var password1 = "";
    var password2 = "";
}
<!DOCTYPE html>

<html lang="en">
    <head>
        <meta charset="utf-8" />
        <title>Register</title>
    </head>
    <body>
        <h1>Register</h1>
        <form action="register" method="post">
            <div>
                @Html.Label("Username: ", "username")<br />
                @Html.TextBox("username", username)
            </div>
            <div>
                @Html.Label("Password: ", "password1")<br />
                @Html.Password("password1", password1)
            </div>
            <div>
                @Html.Label("Confirm Password: ", "password2")<br />
                @Html.Password("password2", password2)
            </div>
            <div>
                <input type="submit" value="Register" />
            </div>
        </form>
    </body>
</html>
```

Next, add code to the block at the top of the page to be run on postback. This code will do the following:

- Log out any current user (via the `WebSecurity.Logout()` method).

- Check that the username submitted in the form does not already exist (via the `WebSecurity.UserExists()` method).

- Compare the values of the two password textboxes to ensure they match.

Finally, if all the validation has passed, we'll call the `WebSecurity.CreateUserAndAccount()` method to insert the new account in the database, log the user in, and return them to the default page.

```
@{
    var username = "";
    var password1 = "";
    var password2 = "";

    if(IsPost)
    {
        WebSecurity.Logout();

        username = Request["username"];
        password1 = Request["password1"];
        password2 = Request["password2"];

        // Validation
        if (username.IsEmpty()) {
            ModelState.AddError("username", "Username is required.");
        }

        if (password1.IsEmpty()) {
            ModelState.AddError("password1", "Password is required.");
        }

        if(WebSecurity.UserExists(username))
        {
            ModelState.AddError("username", "An account with this name already exists.");
        }

        if(password1 != password2)
        {
            ModelState.AddError("password1", "The passwords do not match.");
        }

        // Create Account
        if(ModelState.IsValid)
        {
            WebSecurity.CreateUserAndAccount(username, password1, null, false);
            WebSecurity.Login(username, password1);
            Response.Redirect("default");
        }
    }
}
```

We make four method calls to the WebSecurity helper in this piece of code: Logout(), UserExists(), CreateUserAndAccount(), and Login().

The Logout() method accepts no parameters and simply logs out any current user. No error message will be shown if we call the Logout() method when there are no logged in users, so there is no need to check for this before calling it.

The UserExists() method queries the profile and membership database to see if a record can be found that has a username matching the passed in parameter. If a matching record is found, the method returns true, otherwise it returns false.

Once we are sure that the account does not already exist, we pass the `CreateUserAndAccount()` method the username and password of the account to be created and then call the `Login()` method, again passing in the username and password.

■ **Tip**   The `CreateUserAndAccount()` method can also be used to store additional information about the user. This is explained in the "Storing Additional User Information" section, later in this chapter.

Finally, we will need to add some code and markup to the page to display the results of any validation errors.

```
<!DOCTYPE html>
<html lang="en">
    <head>
        <meta charset="utf-8" />
        <title>Register</title>
        <style>
            .validation-summary-errors,
            span.field-validation-error { color: #FF0000; }
            input.field-validation-error { border: 1px solid #FF0000;
                                           background-color: #FFCCCC; }
        </style>
    </head>
    <body>
        <h1>Register</h1>
        @Html.ValidationSummary("Unable to create account. Please correct the following:")
        <form action="register" method="post">
            <div>
                @Html.Label("Username: ", "username")<br />
                @Html.TextBox("username", username)
                @Html.ValidationMessage("username")
            </div>
            <div>
                @Html.Label("Password: ", "password1")<br />
                @Html.Password("password1", password1)
                @Html.ValidationMessage("password1")
            </div>
            <div>
                @Html.Label("Confirm Password: ", "password2")<br />
                @Html.Password("password2", password2)
            </div>
            <div>
                <input type="submit" value="Register" />
            </div>
        </form>
    </body>
</html>
```

When the register.cshtml page is run, the user will be presented with the form shown here in Figure 7-2:

Figure 7-2. *The new account registration page*

When an account is successfully registered, the user will be directed back to the default page and the rows containing the relevant account information will be inserted into the UserProfile and webpages_Membership tables of our database. Take a look at these tables in the Databases workspace and we will notice that the password is stored in the webpages_Membership table as a secure hash, rather than plain text, as an aid to security.

■ **Note** By default, ASP.NET Web Pages passes data between the server and the client browser insecurely using plain text. When sending sensitive data across the internet, it is desirable to do so securely using a Secure Sockets Layer (SSL) certificate and the HTTPS protocol.

The setup for this is a server configuration process and is beyond the scope of this book. However, we can find more information on secure web communications at http://www.microsoft.com/web/post/securing-web-communications-certificates-ssl-and-https

---

Adding an Account Summary Helper

Next, we'll create a helper named AccountSummary, which we can use to display login information to the user on the pages in our site. If no user is currently logged in to the site, it will display links to the login and register pages (see Figure 7-3):

Figure 7-3. *The content displayed by the AccountSummary helper when no user is logged in*

If a user is currently logged into the site, the helper will display the current user name, which will itself be a link to a page allowing the user to change their password, and a link to log out (see Figure 7-4).

Figure 7-4. The content displayed by the AccountSummary helper when a user has already logged in

To create the AccountSummary helper, make an App_Code folder in the root of the site if one does not already exist. Inside the App_Code folder, add a file called MembershipHelpers.cshtml and replace the default markup generated by WebMatrix with the following:

```
@helper AccountSummary()
{
    <div id="accountSummary">
        @if(WebSecurity.IsAuthenticated) {
            <p>
                Welcome <a href="@Href("~/changePassword")">@WebSecurity.CurrentUserName</a> |
                <a href="@Href("~/logout")">Logout</a>
            </p>
        } else {
            <p>
                <a href="@Href("~/login")">Login</a> |
                <a href="@Href("~/register")">Register</a>
            </p>
        }
    </div>
}
```

> **Note** The AccountSummary helper is an excellent example of how helpers can be used in ASP.NET Web Pages to dramatically improve readability, quality, and maintenance through code re-use. By encapsulating this functionality in a helper, we can code it once and use it in any page within our site.
>
> For more information on the use of helpers within WebMatrix, see the Helpers section in Chapter 4.

The code inside this helper is relatively straightforward. We examine the `WebSecurity.IsAuthenticated` property to get the authentication status of the current user. If the current user is authenticated, we display the value of the `WebSecurity.CurrentUserName` property, which contains the username of the authenticated user. We display the username as a link to the changePassword page.

Next to the username, we provide a link to a page that will allow the user to log out of the site; this is an important security feature for users who may be on a shared or public computer.

If the current user is not authenticated, that is, if they are an *anonymous user*, we display links to the login and register pages.

Currently only the register page exists; we will add the login, logout, and changePassword pages as we progress through the rest of the chapter.

Finally, to display the AccountSummary helper on the home page, we need to add a call to `MembershipHelpers.AccountSummary()` in default.cshtml:

```
<body>
    @MembershipHelpers.AccountSummary()
    <h1>Home Page</h1>
    <p>
        Welcome to the Home Page of the Membership Example site.
    </p>
</body>
```

To test the functionality of the helper, close all instances of our web browser to ensure we are not still logged in, run the default page, and click the Register link. On the register page, enter a new user name and password and submit the form. The register page will then create the user, log us in, and redirect us to the home page. When we return to the home page, we will notice that the AccountSummary helper displays content similar to that shown here in Figure 7-5.

Figure 7-5. *The AccountSummary helper displayed on the home page*

Providing a Login Page

Once a user has registered with the site, they need to be able to log in on their next visit. We will achieve this by providing them with a login page, which can be accessed via the Login link displayed by the AccountSummary helper for non-authenticated users.

Add a new file to the root of the site, called login.cshtml. When login.cshtml is loaded for the first time, a simple login form will be displayed containing two textboxes, one for the username and another for the password, and a "Remember me on this computer" checkbox.

When the form is submitted, we will carry out some basic validation to ensure that the textboxes are not empty. If the validation is passed, we will attempt to log the user in using the `WebSecurity.Login()` method. If the user has checked the `rememberMe` checkbox, the `Login()` method will set the authentication token in the cookie to be persisted beyond the current session. That way, when they return to the site at a later date, they will be automatically logged in as the authentication token in the cookie will still be valid.

If the Login() method is successful, the user will be redirected to the home page; otherwise, a form error will be added to the ModelStateDictionary and a relevant error message will be shown by the ValidationSummary helper at the top of the page (see Figure 7-6).

Amend the default markup, generated by WebMatrix, in login.cshtml to the following:

```
@{
    var username = "";
    var password = "";

    if(IsPost)
    {
        username = Request["username"];
        password = Request["password"];
        var rememberMe = Request["rememberMe"].AsBool();

        // Validation
        if (username.IsEmpty()) {
            ModelState.AddError("username", "Username cannot be blank.");
        }

        if (password.IsEmpty()) {
            ModelState.AddError("password", "Password cannot be blank.");
        }

        // Attempt login
        if(ModelState.IsValid)
        {
            if(WebSecurity.Login(username, password, rememberMe))
            {
                Response.Redirect("~/default");
            }
            else
            {
                ModelState.AddFormError("Unable to log in.");
            }
        }
    }
}
<!DOCTYPE html>

<html lang="en">
    <head>
        <meta charset="utf-8" />
        <title>Login</title>
        <style>
            .validation-summary-errors,
            span.field-validation-error { color: #FF0000; }
            input.field-validation-error { border: 1px solid #FF0000;
                                            background-color: #FFCCCC; }
        </style>
    </head>
```

```
<body>
    <h1>Login</h1>
    @Html.ValidationSummary(true)
    <form action="login" method="post">
        <div>
            @Html.Label("Username: ", "username")<br />
            @Html.TextBox("username", username)
            @Html.ValidationMessage("username")
        </div>
        <div>
            @Html.Label("Password: ", "password")<br />
            @Html.Password("password")
            @Html.ValidationMessage("password")
        </div>
        <div>
            @Html.CheckBox("rememberMe", new { value = "true" })
            @Html.Label("Remember me on this computer?", "rememberMe")
        </div>

        <div>
            <input type="submit" value="Login" />
        </div>
    </form>
</body>
</html>
```

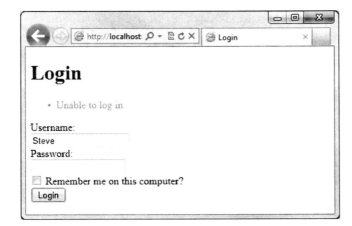

Figure 7-6. The login page showing the failure message

■ **Tip**   Later in the chapter, we will see how we can use the WebSecurity helper to deal with users who have
forgotten their password.

The Logout Page

For users who are accessing the site from a shared or public computer, it is important that we provide the ability to log out of the site when they are finished.

Add a new file called logout.cshtml to the root of the site and replace the generated markup with that shown below:

```
@{
    WebSecurity.Logout();
}
<!DOCTYPE html>

<html lang="en">
    <head>
        <title>Log Out</title>
    </head>
    <body>
        <h1>Log Out</h1>
        <p>We have been logged out from the site.</p>
        <p><a href="@Href("~/default")">Return to home page</a></p>
    </body>
</html>
```

This is a very simple page that calls the `WebSecurity.Logout()` method and displays a message to the user along with a link back to the home page (see Figure 7-7).

To test the page, log in to the site and click the Log Out link in the AccountSummary helper, which will direct we to the Log Out page. When we click the link back to the home page, we will see that we have been logged out.

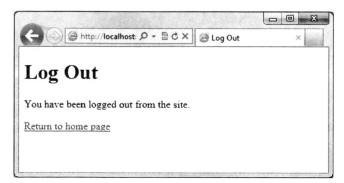

Figure 7-7. The Log Out page

Changing Passwords

The Change Password page will be accessed via the username hyperlink displayed in the AccountSummary helper. It is an essential security feature of any site that users are able to change their own passwords.

To change the password of an account, we call the WebSecurity.ChangePassword() method. The method requires three parameters—userName, currentPassword, and newPassword— and returns a Boolean value indicating whether the password change operation was successful.

Create a file called changePassword.cshtml in the root folder of our web site. Replace the default generated markup in our page with the following:

```
@{
    if (!WebSecurity.IsAuthenticated)
    {
        Response.Redirect("default");
    }

    var currentPassword = "";
    var newPassword1 = "";
    var newPassword2 = "";

    if(IsPost)
    {
        currentPassword = Request["currentPassword"];
        newPassword1 = Request["newPassword1"];
        newPassword2 = Request["newPassword2"];

        // Validation
        if (currentPassword.IsEmpty()) {
            ModelState.AddError("currentPassword", "Current Password required.");
        }

        if (newPassword1.IsEmpty()) {
            ModelState.AddError("newPassword1", "Required.");
        }

        if (newPassword2.IsEmpty()) {
            ModelState.AddError("newPassword2", "Required.");
        }

        if(newPassword1 != newPassword2)
        {
            ModelState.AddError("newPassword1", "The passwords do not match.");
        }

        // Attempt password change
        if(ModelState.IsValid)
        {
            var currentUser = WebSecurity.CurrentUserName;
```

```
            if(WebSecurity.ChangePassword(currentUser, currentPassword, newPassword1))
            {
                Response.Redirect("~/default");
            }
            else
            {
                ModelState.AddFormError("Unable to change password.");
            }
        }
    }
}
<!DOCTYPE html>

<html lang="en">
    <head>
        <meta charset="utf-8" />
        <title>Change Password</title>
        <style>
            .validation-summary-errors,
            span.field-validation-error { color: #FF0000; }
            input.field-validation-error { border: 1px solid #FF0000;
                                           background-color: #FFCCCC; }
        </style>
    </head>
    <body>
        <h1>Change Password</h1>
        @Html.ValidationSummary(true)
        <form action="changePassword" method="post">
            <div>
                @Html.Label("Current Password: ", "currentPassword")<br />
                @Html.Password("currentPassword")
                @Html.ValidationMessage("currentPassword")
            </div>
            <div>
                @Html.Label("New Password: ", "newPassword1")<br />
                @Html.Password("newPassword1")
                @Html.ValidationMessage("newPassword1")
            </div>
            <div>
                @Html.Label("Confirm New Password: ", "newPassword2")<br />
                @Html.Password("newPassword2")
                @Html.ValidationMessage("newPassword2")
            </div>
            <div>
                <input type="submit" value="Change Password" />
            </div>
        </form>
    </body>
</html>
```

Let's quickly describe how this page works.

The first thing that happens when a user lands on the page is a check to see if they are an authenticated user, that is, that they are currently logged in to the site. If they are not, they are immediately redirected to the default page. This is necessary as they may have arrived to the page via a bookmark or other link, but may not actually be currently authenticated; it makes no sense for an anonymous user to use the Change Password page. Calling the ChangePassword() method without a current, authenticated user to operate on displays an error, as we would expect.

If the page is not being displayed as a part of a post back, a form like that shown in Figure 7-8 is displayed in the user's browser. To test this page, we will first need to log in to the site, so run the default page, log in from there, and click on the user name hyperlink in the AccountSummary helper.

Figure 7-8. *The Change Password form*

When the form is submitted, we carry out some simple validation to ensure that all the necessary fields have been completed and that the two New Password fields have matching values.

Next, if the form data is valid, we get the current user name by accessing the WebSecurity.CurrentUserName property. Finally, call the WebSecurity.ChangePassword() method, passing in the required parameters.

If the password change operation is successful, the user is redirected to the default page. If the operation fails, a message is added to the form's ModelStateDictionary and the form is re-displayed.

And that is it. The basic membership functionality is complete. In the rest of the chapter, we will learn some of the other features of the ASP.NET Web Pages membership system and see how they can be integrated into our Membership Example site.

Protecting Content

As well as providing a means to register, authenticate, and administer individual user accounts, the WebMatrix membership system also provides ways to restrict access to areas of the site. In this section, we will see the various ways of achieving this at different levels, both for individual authenticated users and groups.

Restricting to Authenticated Users

The most basic form of content protection is achieved by restricting pages and folders to allow access only to authenticated users. By protecting content in this way, we are not concerned with which account a user is logged in with, only that they are logged in at all.

Page Level Access Restriction

We have already seen an example of page level access restriction in the Changing Passwords section. In the code block at the top of the page are the following lines of code:

```
if (!WebSecurity.IsAuthenticated)
{
    Response.Redirect("default");
}
```

This code simply interrogates the `IsAuthenticated` property of the `WebSecurity` class and redirects the user to the default page if it contains the value `false`. This is all the code that is necessary to restrict an individual page to only authenticated users.

Folder Level Access Restriction

By planning our site carefully, we can place all the pages we wish to restrict to only authenticated users within a specific folder or set of folders. We can then control access to that folder as a whole.

To see an example of how this works, create a new folder in the root of our site called Members. The name of this folder is not special in any way; the same technique can be applied to a folder of any name, at any level within the site structure. In the Members folder, create two new Razor files: _PageStart.cshtml and MembersPage.cshtml. The _PageStart.cshtml file is a special file that is executed when any page within that folder is requested. By placing the authentication check within the _PageStart.cshtml file, we can control access to the whole folder.

Figure 7-9 shows how the file and folder structure should now look.

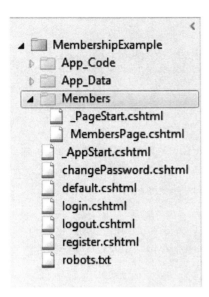

Figure 7-9. Any page in wer Members folder will be protected by the code in the _PageStart file.

In _PageStart.cshtml, replace the default markup with the following code:

```
@{
    if (!WebSecurity.IsAuthenticated)
    {
        Response.Redirect("~/default");
    }
}
```

Whenever a page is accessed within the Members folder, this code is executed first. The code uses the ASP.NET tilde (~) symbol to access the root folder of the site.

To prove this works, replace the existing markup in the MembersPage.cshtml file we just created with the following:

```
<!DOCTYPE html>

<html lang="en">
    <head>
        <meta charset="utf-8" />
        <title>Members Only</title>
    </head>
    <body>
        <h1>Members Only Page</h1>
    </body>
</html>
```

Notice that we do not need any authentication code within this page, as it is all handled for we by _PageStart.cshtml.

Run the site and browse to Members/MembersPage.cshtml without logging in. We will be redirected back to the home page. Now log in and browse again to Members/MembersPage.cshtml and we will see the page as expected. Any new page added to the Members folder will automatically be restricted to allow only authenticated users by _PageStart.

Providing a Better User Experience

When an anonymous user lands on one of our protected pages, they are redirected immediately to the home page by means of the code we have placed into _PageStart.cshtml. This is functional and certainly restricts our pages to only authenticated users, but it does leave some room for improvement with regard to the user experience.

The very best possible scenario for an unauthenticated user who tries to access a restricted page is that they land on the site at the home page, navigate through to the restricted page, and are returned back to the home page where they can click the Login link. Once they have logged in, they will be redirected again to the home page from where they can navigate their way back to the page they were originally trying to access. And that is the best scenario!

I'm sure we will agree that this provides a less than ideal experience for the user. However, the scenario gets even worse if the user browses directly to the protected page, possibly via a browser bookmark or by clicking through a hyperlink in an email. In this situation, it is quite possible that the user doesn't even know how to navigate their way to the page they wished to see in the first place.

Fortunately, this is relatively simple to fix. By making some slight alterations to the existing code in _PageStart.cshtml and login.cshtml, we can send an unauthenticated user directly to the login page and have the login page redirect them back to the page they were originally trying to visit after they have successfully logged in.

This solution will provide a vastly improved experience for the user. It is this kind of attention to detail in the user experience that is the mark of a quality web site—one that has been well designed and implemented.

Change the code in _PageStart.cshtml to the following:

```
@{
    if (!WebSecurity.IsAuthenticated)
    {
        string currentUrl = Request.Url.ToString();
        Response.Redirect("~/login?sender=" + currentUrl);
    }
}
```

This code now sends unauthenticated users directly to the login page. By interrogating the Url property of the Request object, we can get the full URL of the page the user was originally trying to visit. When we perform the redirect, we send the URL in the QueryString with a key of sender. The URL that we will redirect to will look something like the following:

```
http://localhost:1956/login?sender=http://localhost:1956/Members/MembersPage
```

243

Next, we need to make the necessary amendments to login.cshtml to redirect the user back to their initial page upon successful login. The changes necessary to the code block at the top of the page are highlighted here:

```
@{
    var username = "";
    var password = "";

    if(IsPost)
    {
        username = Request["username"];
        password = Request["password"];
        var rememberMe = Request["rememberMe"].AsBool();

        // Validation
        if (username.IsEmpty()) {
            ModelState.AddError("username", "Username cannot be blank.");
        }

        if (password.IsEmpty()) {
            ModelState.AddError("password", "Password cannot be blank.");
        }

        // Attempt login
        if(ModelState.IsValid)
        {
            if(WebSecurity.Login(username, password, rememberMe))
            {
                if (Request.QueryString["sender"] != null)
                {
                    Response.Redirect(Request.QueryString["sender"]);
                }
                else
                {
                    Response.Redirect("~/default");
                }
            }
            else
            {
                ModelState.AddFormError("Unable to log in.");
            }
        }
    }
}
```

The amended part of this code is quite straightforward and simply checks to see if a value has been passed in the QueryString with a key of sender. If it has, the user is redirected to the value passed; if not, they are redirected back to the home page.

To make this work, we need to make one final alteration to the <form> tag in login.cshtml. This alteration will pass the whole QueryString back to the page on post back, allowing us to gain access to the sender URL in the post request handler:

```
<form action="login?@Request.QueryString" method="post">
```

Now we have a much more satisfactory login system that presents a greatly improved experience to our users.

Roles

Roles are a convenient way to create groups of related users. They are the next step in granular control over access to pages and features. Whereas the examples seen up to now in this section have simply been about authenticated or anonymous users, roles allow for further break down of authenticated users into distinct groups.

For example, we may have areas of our site that are open to all users (authenticated and anonymous), areas that are open to just authenticated users, and other areas that should only be accessible by site administrators. This is where roles come in. We could create a role called "Admins" and assign that role only to the site administrators' membership accounts. Once we have done this, it is simply a matter of restricting the relevant areas of the site to only allow access to the members of the "Admins" role.

Roles and role members are stored in the webpages_Roles and webpages_UsersInRoles tables of the membership database, respectively. The schema for the database is extremely straightforward. Roles are defined in the webpages_Roles table, which contains two columns: RoleId and RoleName. Roles can be named using any valid string, but must be unique within the webpages_Roles table. The webpages_UsersInRoles table links users to roles through the use of two columns: UserId and RoleId. Each row within this table associates one user with one role. If a user has many roles, there will be a separate row for each role mapping.

Obviously, we could use the tools within the WebMatrix IDE to administer the roles and their membership by adding, deleting, and creating rows directly in the database tables. However, a much better solution is to provide this functionality within our site, so in the next four sections, we will create pages designed to carry out role administration.

The role administration section of our site will consist of two main pages. The first will list all the current roles and give the ability to add new ones. By clicking on a role name within this page the user will be taken to the second main page, which will list all users currently associated to that role and provide ways to add new users to the role and remove existing from it. We will also require two secondary pages to delete users and roles.

Listing and Adding Roles

As mentioned previously, our site will contain a page that lists all the roles in our membership database and give users the ability to add new roles. The ASP.NET Web Pages membership system provides role management functionality through the Roles class.

We'll keep all of our role administration pages in a separate folder called "Admin," which we should create in the root of the site. Within the Admin folder, create a new page called roles.cshtml and populate it with the following code:

```
@{
    if(IsPost)
    {
        var newRole = Request["roleName"];

        // Add new role
        if(!newRole.IsEmpty()) && (!Roles.RoleExists(newRole))
        {
            Roles.CreateRole(newRole);
        }
    }

    var currentRoles = Roles.GetAllRoles();
}
<!DOCTYPE html>

<html lang="en">
    <head>
        <meta charset="utf-8" />
        <title>Roles</title>
    </head>
    <body>
        <h1>Roles</h1>
        <div>
            <h2>Current Roles</h2>
            @if(currentRoles.Length > 0)
            {
                @* List all current roles *@
                <ul>
                    @foreach(var role in currentRoles)
                    {
                        <li><a href="roleDetails?roleName=@role">@role</a></li>
                    }
                </ul>
            }
            else
            {
                <p>No roles currently defined.</p>
            }
        </div>
        <div>
            @* Form to add new roles to the membership database *@
            <h2>Add New Role</h2>
            <form action="roles" method="post">
                @Html.Label("Role Name: ", "roleName")
                @Html.TextBox("roleName")
                <input type="submit" value="Add Role" name="addRole" />
```

```
            </form>
        </div>
    </body>
</html>
```

On the initial load this page gets a list of all the currently defined roles, using the
`Roles.GetAllRoles()` method, and assigns it to a variable. The `Roles.GetAllRoles()` method returns an
array of strings, with each element of the array holding a role name.

```
var currentRoles = Roles.GetAllRoles();
```

If the array is not empty, that is, there is one or more current role, we use a `foreach` loop to iterate
across the array and display each name in a bulleted list on the web page, with a hyperlink to the
`roleDetails` page, which we will create later. The hyperlink also passes the name of the role in a
QueryString key called `roleName`. If the array is empty, we simply display a message to the user to say
there are no roles to display.

```
@if(currentRoles.Length > 0)
{
    @* List all current roles *@
    <ul>
        @foreach(var role in currentRoles)
        {
            <li><a href="roleDetails?roleName=@role">@role</a></li>
        }
    </ul>
}
else
{
    <p>No roles currently defined.</p>
}
```

At the bottom of the page, underneath the list of current roles, we display a simple form that will
allow the user to add a new role. When the user clicks the submit button of this form, the code at the top
of the page checks that the textbox is not empty and that the role name entered by the user does not
already exist. If both these checks are passed, the role is added to the database by passing the new role
name into the `Roles.CreateRole()` method.

```
if(IsPost)
{
    var newRole = Request["roleName"];

    // Add new role
    if((!newRole.IsEmpty()) && (!Roles.RoleExists(newRole)))
    {
        Roles.CreateRole(newRole);
    }
}
```

An example of the page displayed to the user can be seen here in Figure 7-10:

Figure 7-10. *The role administration page, showing additional roles created through the Add New Role form*

Listing Role Members and Adding Users to Roles

When the user clicks on a role in roles.cshtml, they will be directed to a page that lists all the users currently assigned to that role. It will also be here that existing users can be assigned to the role.

Create a new file in the Admin folder called roleDetails.cshtml. Add the following code and markup to the page:

```
@{
    var roleName = Request["roleName"];

    if(IsPost)
    {
        // Assign user to role
        var userName = Request["newUser"];

        if (!Roles.IsUserInRole(userName, roleName))
        {
            Roles.AddUsersToRoles(
                new [] { userName }.ToArray(),
                new [] { roleName }.ToArray()
            );
        }
    }

    // Get all current role members
    var usersInRole = Roles.GetUsersInRole(roleName);

    // Get all users from database and create a list of SelectListItems
    var db = Database.Open("MembershipExample");
```

```
    var sqlCommand = "SELECT UserName FROM UserProfile ORDER BY UserName";

    List<SelectListItem> allUsers = new List<SelectListItem>();
    foreach(var item in db.Query(sqlCommand))
    {
        allUsers.Add(new SelectListItem { Text = item.UserName });
    }
}

<!DOCTYPE html>

<html lang="en">
    <head>
        <meta charset="utf-8" />
        <title>Role Details</title>
    </head>
    <body>
        <h1>Role Details - @roleName</h1>
        <div>
            @if(usersInRole.Length > 0)
            {
                @* List all current role members *@
                <ul>
                    @foreach(var user in usersInRole)
                    {
                        <li>@user
                            <a href="removeUserFromRole?roleName=@roleName&userName=@user">
                                [Remove]
                            </a>
                        </li>
                    }
                </ul>
            }
            else
            {
                <p>No users currently attached to this role.</p>
                <p><a href="deleteRole?roleName=@roleName">Delete this role</a></p>
            }
        </div>
        <div>
        @* Form to assign users to the current role *@
            <h2>Add User</h2>
            <form action="roleDetails" method="post">
                @Html.Hidden("roleName", roleName)
                @Html.Label("User: ", "newUser")
                @Html.DropDownList("newUser", allUsers)
                <input type="submit" value="Add User" name="addUser" />
            </form>
        </div>
    </body>
</html>
```

Let's go through the code to fully understand exactly what is happening.

When the page is requested, we get the name of the relevant role by accessing the roleName key in the Request object, which has been passed through in the URL.

```
var roleName = Request["roleName"];
```

Let's skip over the if(IsPost) post request handler code for now, we'll come back to that later. Once we have the role name, we are then able to call the GetUsersInRole() method, which returns an array of strings containing the usernames of all the members of the role passed into the method as a parameter.

```
// Get all current role members
var usersInRole = Roles.GetUsersInRole(roleName);
```

The last section of the code block at the top of the page queries the UserProfile table of the database to return a list of all users, the result of which we use to create a collection of SelectListItems to be used with a drop down list.

```
// Get all users from database and create a list of SelectListItems
var db = Database.Open("MembershipExample");
var sqlCommand = "SELECT UserName FROM UserProfile ORDER BY UserName";

List<SelectListItem> allUsers = new List<SelectListItem>();
foreach(var item in db.Query(sqlCommand))
{
    allUsers.Add(new SelectListItem { Text = item.UserName });
}
```

In the page itself we check to see if there are currently any users assigned to this role, by checking the length of the array returned by the Roles.GetUsersInRoles() method call. If there are one or more members, we iterate over the array using a foreach loop and output their names in a bulleted list. The user name in each list item is presented as a hyperlink used to facilitate the removal of users from the role. The "Remove" hyperlink directs the browser to removeUserFromRole.cshtml, which we will create later, and passes the role name and user name in the URL as a QueryString.

```
@if(usersInRole.Length > 0)
{
    @* List all current role members *@
    <ul>
        @foreach(var user in usersInRole)
        {
            <li>@user
                <a href="removeUserFromRole?roleName=@roleName&userName=@user">
                    [Remove]
                </a>
            </li>
        }
    </ul>
}
```

If there are currently no users assigned to the role, we present a message to that effect, along with a link to delete the role; a role can only be deleted when there are no related records in the webpages_UsersInRoles table, that is, the role has no members. The "Delete this role" hyperlink points to deleteRole.cshtml, which we have yet to create, passing the role name in URL.

```
else
{
    <p>No users currently attached to this role.</p>
    <p><a href="deleteRole?roleName=@roleName">Delete this role</a></p>
}
```

Finally, we display a form to the user that allows them to add a user to the role. In this form, we display a drop down list, populated using the collection of SelectListItems we created earlier from the membership database, and a button to submit the form. The form also includes a hidden field containing the role name that was earlier extracted from the URL to be passed through to the post request handler.

```
<form action="roleDetails" method="post">
    @Html.Hidden("roleName", roleName)
    @Html.Label("User: ", "newUser")
    @Html.DropDownList("newUser", allUsers)
    <input type="submit" value="Add User" name="addUser" />
</form>
```

To test this page, log in as an Admin user, click the "Roles Administration" link in the AccountSummary helper, and select a role with at least one associated user. The final page presented to the user looks like this (see Figure 7-11):

Figure 7-11. The role details page

When the "Add User" button is clicked, the post request handler checks that the user we are trying to add isn't already assigned to the role, using the Roles.IsUserInRole() method. It then uses the Roles.AddUsersToRoles() method to assign the user to the role. As the method accepts string arrays as parameters, we use the String.ToArray() method to convert our form values.

```
var roleName = Request["roleName"];

if(IsPost)
{
    // Assign user to role
    var userName = Request["newUser"];

    if (!Roles.IsUserInRole(userName, roleName))
    {
        Roles.AddUsersToRoles(
            new [] { userName }.ToArray(),
            new [] { roleName }.ToArray()
        );
    }
}
```

The final two pages in our roles administration system are concerned with the deletion of roles and role members.

Removing Users from Roles

We "Role Details" page lists all the current members of a particular role and provides the user with a "Remove" hyperlink. The hyperlink passes the name of the role and the name of the user to removeUserFromRole.cshtml, which we will create now.

The code for removeUserFromRole.cshtml is as follows:

```
@{
    var userName = Request["userName"];
    var roleName = Request["roleName"];

    if(IsPost)
    {
        // Remove user from role
        if (Roles.IsUserInRole(userName, roleName))
        {
            Roles.RemoveUsersFromRoles(
                new [] { userName }.ToArray(),
                new [] { roleName }.ToArray()
            );
        }

        Response.Redirect("roleDetails?roleName=" + roleName);
    }
}
<!DOCTYPE html>

<html lang="en">
    <head>
        <meta charset="utf-8" />
        <title>Remove User From Role</title>
```

```
        </head>
        <body>
            <h1>Remove User from Role</h1>
            <p>Are we sure we wish to remove user @userName from the @roleName role?</p>
            <p>
                <form action="" method="post">
                    @Html.Hidden("roleName", roleName)
                    @Html.Hidden("userName", userName)
                    <input type="button"
                        onclick="window.location.href='roleDetails.cshtml?roleName=@roleName';"
                        value="Cancel" />
                    <input type="submit" value="Remove" />
                </form>
            </p>
        </body>
</html>
```

When this page is first requested, we display a confirmation message to the user. This helps to ensure that the right user is going to be removed from the role and also enables we to perform the remove operation on a POST request, rather than a GET (i.e., when the user clicks the submit button on the page).

Along with a button to confirm the removal, the form also contains a simple HTML "Cancel" button with a JavaScript onclick event to send the user back to the Role Details page without submitting the form. Two HTML hidden input controls are used to pass the role name and user name from the initial URL to the POST request handler.

An example of the Remove User from Role page is seen here in Figure 7-12:

Figure 7-12. *The Remove User from Role confirmation page*

When the form is submitted, we get the user name and role name from the hidden fields, check that the user is in the role, and if so, remove them. To remove the user from the role, we use the `Roles.RemoveUsersFromRoles()` method, passing in the user name and role name. As with the `AddUsersToRoles()` method seen earlier, the `RemoveUsersFromRoles()` method accepts string arrays as parameters, so we use the `String.ToArray()` method to convert the form values to an array.

Once the user has been removed from the role, the browser is redirected to the Role Details page, passing the role name in the QueryString.

Deleting Roles

Lastly, we will implement the "Delete Role" page. The page is relatively simple and works in a similar way to the "Remove Users from Roles" page. The page is accessed via a hyperlink on the "Role Details" page.

Add a new file to the Admin folder called deleteRole.cshtml and replace the default markup with the following:

```
@{
    var roleName = Request["roleName"];

    if(IsPost)
    {
        // Delete role
        if(Roles.GetUsersInRole(roleName).Length == 0 && !roleName.IsEmpty())
        {
            Roles.DeleteRole(roleName, true);
        }

        Response.Redirect("roles");
    }
}
<!DOCTYPE html>

<html lang="en">
    <head>
        <meta charset="utf-8" />
        <title>Delete Role</title>
    </head>
    <body>
        <h1>Delete Role</h1>
        <p>Are we sure we wish to delete the @roleName role?</p>
        <p>
            <form action="" method="post">
                @Html.Hidden("roleName", roleName)
                <input type="button"
                    onclick="window.location.href='roleDetails.cshtml?roleName=@roleName';"
                    value="Cancel" />
                <input type="submit" value="Delete" />
            </form>
        </p>
    </body>
</html>
```

Again, when the user first requests the page, a confirmation message is presented. A form at the bottom of the page contains a submit button, a cancel button, and an HTML hidden field containing the role name, retrieved from the URL QueryString.

Figure 7-13 shows an example of the Delete Role page.

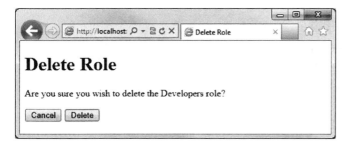

Figure 7-13. *The Delete Role confirmation page*

When the Delete submit button is clicked, the POST request handler checks that the role name is not empty and has no assigned members. This step is important as a role cannot be deleted when it has related users in the `webpages_UsersInRoles` table. Due to the nature of web applications, it is possible that another user (in another browser) has added a user to the role in the time between us requesting the Role Details page and clicking the Delete submit button on the Delete Role page. In this circumstance, we would not want to call the `Roles.DeleteRole()` method.

If the role has no member users, it is deleted using the `Roles.DeleteRole()` method and the browser is redirected to the Roles page.

Restricting Access Using Roles

Now that the role administration pages are complete, we can use them to create a role, assign users to it, and restrict pages within our site to allow access only to members of that role.

If we do not already have a role called "Administrators," create one using the Roles page or by adding it directly to the `webpages_Roles` table; be sure to add a user to the role. To create a role using the Roles page, open Admin/Roles.cshtml in the browser and use the UI to add a role named "Administrators." The page will display the new role, which we should then click on to go to the RoleDetails page. This will allow us to add users to that role.

We will restrict the access of pages within the Admin folder to users in this role. To do this, add a _PageStart.cshtml file to the Admin folder with the following code:

```
@{
    if (!Roles.IsUserInRole(WebSecurity.CurrentUserName, "Administrators"))
    {
        string currentUrl = Request.Url.ToString();
        Response.Redirect("~/login?sender=" + currentUrl);
    }
}
```

This code is run immediately before the execution of any page requested within the Admin folder. The code uses the `Roles.IsUserInRole()` method to check that the current user is in the "Administrators" role. We get the name of the current user to pass to the `Roles.IsUserInRole()` method via a call to `WebSecurity.CurrentUserName()`, which returns a string containing the user name of the currently authenticated user. If the current user is not in the "Administrators" role, they are redirected to the login page in the root folder. The URL of the requested page is appended to the URL in the QueryString, as discussed in the "Providing a Better User Experience" section.

255

Updating the AccountSummary Helper

Although the site administrators could browse directly to the Roles page by typing the URL into the address bar of their web browser, it would be much better if we could provide them with a link. The ideal place to do this is the AccountSummary helper, which already displays account information specific to the authenticated user. We will modify the AccountSummary helper to use the Roles.IsUserInRole() method to display a link to the Roles for authenticated users who are members of the "Administrators" role.

Open the MembershipHelpers.cshtml file in the App_Code folder and amend the AccountSummary helper to look like the following:

```
@helper AccountSummary()
{
    <div id="accountSummary">
        @if(WebSecurity.IsAuthenticated) {
            <p>
                Welcome <a href="@Href("~/changePassword")">@WebSecurity.CurrentUserName</a> |
                <a href="@Href("~/logout")">Logout</a>
                @if (Roles.IsUserInRole(WebSecurity.CurrentUserName, "Administrators"))
                {
                    <text>
                        | <a href="@Href("~/Admin/roles")">Roles Administration</a>
                    </text>
                }
            </p>
        } else {
            <p>
                <a href="@Href("~/login")">Login</a> |
                <a href="@Href("~/register")">Register</a>
            </p>
        }
    </div>
}
```

Now when a member of the Administrators role logs into the site, they will receive a link to the Role Administration page in the AccountSummary helper (see Figure 7-14):

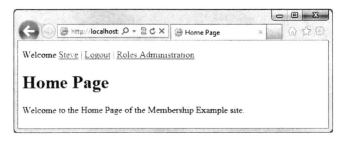

Figure 7-14. The amended AccountSummary helper showing the Roles Administration hyperlink

Advanced Membership Features

The final part of this chapter will investigate some of the more advanced features of the ASP.NET Web Pages membership system, looking at the following:

- How to use the `WebSecurity` helper to store additional information about the user gathered at registration.

- Implementing a more advanced registration system where an email is sent to the user, requiring confirmation before an account is activated.

- Adding a password reset feature for registered users who have forgotten their passwords.

Storing Additional User Information

When creating a new user account, it is often desirable to store more information than simply a user name and password. Fortunately, the `WebSecurity` helper makes this easy with an optional parameter in the `CreateUserAndAccount()` method.

To demonstrate this, we will amend our registration page and database to gather and store a user's email address. First, we will need to add an additional field to the registration form in register.cshtml:

```
<form action="register" method="post">
    <div>
        @Html.Label("Username: ", "username")<br />
        @Html.TextBox("username", username)
        @Html.ValidationMessage("username")
    </div>
    <div>
        @Html.Label("Email Address: ", "email")<br />
        @Html.TextBox("email", email)
        @Html.ValidationMessage("email")
    </div>
    <div>
        @Html.Label("Password: ", "password1")<br />
        @Html.Password("password1", password1)
        @Html.ValidationMessage("password1")
    </div>
    <div>
        @Html.Label("Confirm Password: ", "password2")<br />
        @Html.Password("password2", password2)
    </div>
    <div>
        <input type="submit" value="Register" />
    </div>
</form>
```

Next, open the Databases workspace in the WebMatrix IDE, select the `UserProfile` table in the site database, and click the "Definition" button in the Ribbon Control at the top of the screen. Now click the "New Column" button in the Ribbon Control and add a column called `EmailAddress`. This column should be a nullable `nvarchar` with a length of 100 characters (see Figure 7-15):

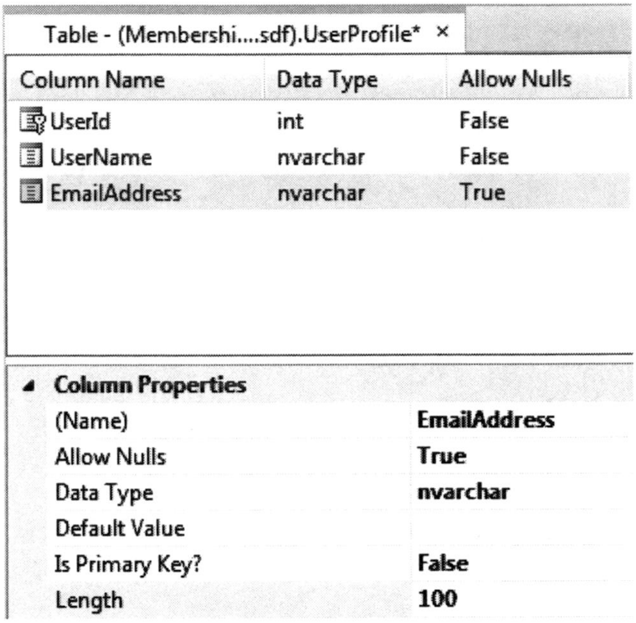

Table - (Membershi....sdf).UserProfile* ×		
Column Name	Data Type	Allow Nulls
🔑 UserId	int	False
📄 UserName	nvarchar	False
📄 EmailAddress	nvarchar	True

◢ Column Properties	
(Name)	**EmailAddress**
Allow Nulls	**True**
Data Type	**nvarchar**
Default Value	
Is Primary Key?	**False**
Length	**100**

Figure 7-15. Add an emailAddress column to the UserProfile table

Save the amended `UserProfile` table and navigate back to the register.cshtml page in the Files workspace.

When the user submits the form, we will check that they have entered an email address and then pass the value of the field into the optional `propertyValues` parameter of the `CreateUserAndAccount()` method.

■ **Caution**   This code example checks only that the user has entered a value into the emailAddress field on the form; it does not check that the email address supplied is valid. To see how WebMatrix can be used to validate email addresses, see the "Building a validation library" section of Chapter 5.

Amend the code block at the top of register.cshtml to include the following highlighted changes:

```
@{
    var username = "";
    var email = "";
    var password1 = "";
    var password2 = "";

    if(IsPost)
    {
```

```
        WebSecurity.Logout();

        username = Request["username"];
        email = Request["email"];
        password1 = Request["password1"];
        password2 = Request["password2"];

        // Validation
        if (username.IsEmpty()) {
            ModelState.AddError("username", "Username is required.");
        }

        if (email.IsEmpty()) {
            ModelState.AddError("email", "Email Address is required.");
        }

        if (password1.IsEmpty()) {
            ModelState.AddError("password1", "Password is required.");
        }

        if(WebSecurity.UserExists(username))
        {
            ModelState.AddError("username", "An account with this name already exists.");
        }

        if(password1 != password2)
        {
            ModelState.AddError("password1", "The passwords do not match.");
        }

        // Create Account
        if(ModelState.IsValid)
        {
            WebSecurity.CreateUserAndAccount(userName:username,
                                    Password: password1,
                                    propertyValues: new { emailAddress = email } );
            WebSecurity.Login(username, password1);
            Response.Redirect("default");
        }
    }
}
}
```

The propertyValues parameter accepts an object that contains additional user attributes. We simply need to create a new object and assign the value of the email variable to an entity named the same as the database column we created. When the method is called, the WebSecurity helper will attempt to match any entities in the propertyValues object to database columns and store the values held within them.

Confirming Registration by Email

In order to help prevent fraudulent registrations by humans and bots, it is a common practice to send an email to the user containing a link to a registration confirmation page following registration. Only after the user has clicked the link in the email and successfully validated their registration are they able to login to the site.

All the necessary components to accomplish this design are available within ASP.NET Web Pages. To demonstrate this technique, we will further amend our registration page from the last section using the WebSecurity and WebMail helpers.

■ **Tip**   Another useful method for the prevention of fraudulent form submission is the use of the Re-Captcha helper, which we will learn more about in Chapter 8.

The WebMail Helper

The WebMail helper takes some initial setting up, but once complete, provides a very easy way to send emails from within Razor code.

As we would expect, the WebMail helper needs some initial information about our mail server. The best place to provide this information is in the _AppStart.cshtml file, in order to make it available to the whole application.

The specific information we require here can be sought from our web hosting provider or system administrator. For the purposes of development and testing, it is often possible to use a standard web mail service. This code sample shows the _AppStart.cshtml file with WebMail helper settings for use with Google's Gmail service.

```
@{
    WebSecurity.InitializeDatabaseConnection("MembershipExample",
        "UserProfile", "UserId", "UserName", true);

    WebMail.SmtpServer = "smtp.gmail.com";
    WebMail.SmtpPort = 587;
    WebMail.EnableSsl = true;
    WebMail.UserName = "wer_username_here@gmail.com";
    WebMail.From = "wer_username_here@gmail.com";
    WebMail.Password = "wer_password_here";
}
```

Table 7-2 explains these settings in more detail.

Table 7-2. *WebMail Helper Settings*

Setting	Description
SmtpServer	The name of the SMTP server that we have access to.
SmtpPort	The port number of the SMTP server that we have access to.
EnableSsl	A Boolean value that determines if the mail properties are to be encrypted when sending to the mail server.
UserName	The username for our email account.
From	The email address that the message is to be sent from. This should be a valid email address, but does not necessarily have to be the same account as that used to send the mail.
Password	The password for our email account.

Once the initial setup is complete, sending an email is simply a matter of calling the WebMail.Send() method, passing in the email address to send to, the subject line of the email, and the body text:

```
WebMail.Send(to: "user@example.com",
             subject: "Subject line goes here",
             body: "Message text goes here" );
```

■ **Note** For more information on the WebMail helper, visit the MSDN page at http://msdn.microsoft.com/en-us/library/system.web.helpers.webmail.aspx

---

Generating and Sending the Confirmation Email

Now that we have initialized the WebMail helper, we need to generate an email to send to the user asking them to confirm their newly created account. We can use the CreateUserAndAccount() method to return a unique token, which we will send in an email to the user as part of a link to a confirmation page. The user must visit the link URL in the email in order to confirm their account.

By setting the requireConfirmationToken parameter of the WebSecurity.CreateUserAndAccount() method to **true,** we can generate a unique confirmation token that will look something like hYQSzXhwp6Se6mmPJOKFoQ==. This token is also stored against the user record in the database. The user and account is created, but in an unconfirmed state (i.e., the IsConfirmed column in the webpages_Membership table is set to false) and cannot be used to log in to the site until confirmed.

This example builds on the example in the "Storing Additional User Information" section, presented earlier in this chapter, where we amended the registration page to accept and store a user's email address in addition to the standard username and password. So, open register.cshtml and amend the post request event handler as shown here:

```
if(ModelState.IsValid)
{
    var token = WebSecurity.CreateUserAndAccount(userName: username,
                        password: password1,
                        propertyValues: new { emailAddress = email },
                        requireConfirmationToken: true);

    // Generate confirmation link URL
    var hostUrl = Request.Url.GetComponents(UriComponents.SchemeAndServer,
                                        UriFormat.Unescaped);
    var confirmAccountUrl = hostUrl +
                    "/confirmAccount?confirmationToken=" +
                    HttpUtility.UrlEncode(token);

    // Send confirmation email
    WebMail.Send(to: email,
        subject: "Thank we for registering - " + username,
        body: "Please visit <a href='" + confirmAccountUrl + "'>" + confirmAccountUrl +
            "</a> to activate wer account."
    );

    Response.Redirect("confirmSent");
}
```

In this code, we call WebSecurity.CreateUserAndAccount() and set the requireConfirmationParameter to true. We store the resulting confirmation token in a variable called token.

Next, we construct the URL of the link that the user will need to visit to confirm their account. We do this by getting the scheme, host, and port data from the Request object, which will return something like http://localhost:16458 on a local development machine using IIS Express. To that, we then append the name of the confirmation page and a QueryString containing the token. The token is URL encoded to ensure that none of the characters that form the token are misinterpreted as reserved characters in the URL.

```
// Generate confirmation link URL
var hostUrl = Request.Url.GetComponents(UriComponents.SchemeAndServer,
                                    UriFormat.Unescaped);
var confirmAccountUrl = hostUrl +
                "/confirmAccount?confirmationToken=" +
                HttpUtility.UrlEncode(token);
```

Finally, we use the WebMail helper to send an email containing a short message and the confirmation URL to the email address supplied in the form and redirect the user to confirmSent.cshtml.

The confirmSent.cshtml file merely contains a message to the user, thanking them for registering and prompting them to check their email account for further instructions. Create confirmSent.cshtml in the root of the site with the following markup:

```
<!DOCTYPE html>

<html lang="en">
    <head>
        <meta charset="utf-8" />
        <title>Confirmation Sent</title>
    </head>
    <body>
        <h1>Thanks For Registering</h1>
        <p>We have sent an email with instructions on how to activate wer account
        to the email address we supplied.</p>
    </body>
</html>
```

The Account Confirmation Page

When the user receives their confirmation email, they will be instructed to visit a URL at our site to validate their account; that URL on our site will be confirmAccount.cshtml with the unique confirmation token being passed in the QueryString with a key of confirmationToken.

When confirmAccount.cshtml is requested, we will log out any authenticated users (as there may be a user other than the one we are trying to confirm already logged in), get the confirmation token from the URL, and attempt to confirm the account by passing the token to the WebSecurity.ConfirmAccount() method. The ConfirmAccount() method returns a Boolean value that indicates whether the confirmation was successful. We will use this Boolean value to display a relevant message to the user.

Add a new file to the root of the site, called confirmAccount.cshtml, and replace the default markup with the following:

```
@{

    bool confirmed = false;
    var confirmationToken = Request["confirmationToken"];

    WebSecurity.Logout();

    // Attempt account confirmation
    if (!confirmationToken.IsEmpty()) {
        if (WebSecurity.ConfirmAccount(confirmationToken)) {
            confirmed = true;
        }
    }
}
<!DOCTYPE html>

<html lang="en">
    <head>
        <meta charset="utf-8" />
```

```
            <title>Registration Confirmation</title>
        </head>
        <body>
            <h1>Registration Confirmation</h1>

            @if (confirmed)
            {
                <p>
                    Wer registration is confirmed.
                    We can now <a href="login">login</a>.
                </p>
            }
            else
            {
                <p>Unable to confirm the registration.</p>
            }
        </body>
</html>
```

If the confirmation is successful, the user will see the page shown here in Figure 7-16:

Figure 7-16. The Registration Confirmation page

Dealing with Forgotten Passwords

The WebMatrix WebSecurity helper has a built-in scheme for dealing with forgotten passwords. In many ways, it is similar to the email registration confirmation process discussed in the last section. When a user forgets their password, an email will be sent containing a link to a URL with a unique password reset token. When they visit the URL, the code checks the token, and if valid, presents them the opportunity to reset their password.

The whole process requires two pages: one to gather the username, generate the reset token, and send the email and another to verify the token and allow the user to set a new password.

The first page will be called forgotPassword.cshtml, which we should add to the root of the example site. The code and markup for this page is listed below:

```
@{
    var username = "";
    var message = "";

    if(IsPost)
    {
        username = Request["username"];
```

```
        // Validation
        if (username.IsEmpty()) {
            ModelState.AddError("username", "Username is required.");
        }

        // Generate and send password reset email
        if(ModelState.IsValid)
        {
            // Generate confirmation link URL
            var resetToken = WebSecurity.GeneratePasswordResetToken(username);
            var hostUrl = Request.Url.GetComponents(UriComponents.SchemeAndServer,
                                                    UriFormat.Unescaped);
            var passwordResetUrl = hostUrl +
                            "/passwordReset?resetToken=" +
                            HttpUtility.UrlEncode(resetToken);

            // Get email address for user
            var db = Database.Open("MembershipExample");
            var sqlCommand = "SELECT emailAddress FROM UserProfile WHERE UserName = @0";
            var userDetails = db.QuerySingle(sqlCommand, username);

            // Send email
            WebMail.Send(to: userDetails.emailAddress,
                subject: "Password Reset for " + username,
                body: "Please visit <a href='" + passwordResetUrl + "'>" + passwordResetUrl +
                    "</a> to reset wer password."
            );

            message = "An email has been sent to wer registered email address " +
                "with a password reset link.";
        }
    }
}

<!DOCTYPE html>

<html lang="en">
    <head>
        <meta charset="utf-8" />
        <title>Forgot Password</title>
        <style>
            span.field-validation-error { color: #FF0000; }
            input.field-validation-error { border: 1px solid #FF0000;
                                        background-color: #FFCCCC; }
        </style>
    </head>
    <body>
        <h1>Forgotten Password</h1>
        @if (!message.IsEmpty()) {
            <p>@message</p>
```

```
        }
        else
        {
            <form action="forgotPassword" method="post">
                <div>
                    @Html.Label("Username: ", "username")<br />
                    @Html.TextBox("username", username)
                    @Html.ValidationMessage("username")
                </div>
                <div>
                    <input type="submit" value="Reset Password" />
                </div>
            </form>
        }
    </body>
</html>
```

On the initial request, this page displays a very simple form to the user, asking only for their username. When the form is submitted, the post request handler validates the form, and if valid, generates the URL of the password reset page, which is sent as a link in an email to the user. The password reset URL consists of the scheme and server details, the page name (passwordReset.cshtml), and a QueryString containing the unique reset token.

The reset token is a cryptographically secure string, similar to the account confirmation token we saw earlier. We generate the token by calling the `WebSecurity.GeneratePasswordResetToken()` method, passing in the username as a parameter.

Once we have generated the URL, we query the `UserProfile` table of the membership database to ascertain the email address registered against the user. We then use the WebMail helper to send an email to the user containing a short message and a link to the password reset page. Finally, we display a message to the user to let them know to look at their email account for further instructions.

When the user receives their password reset email, they will be asked to visit a particular URL to reset their password. In this case, the page they need to visit will be called passwordReset.cshtml, which we should create in the root folder of the site.

Replace the content of passwordReset.cshtml with the following:

```
@{
    var resetToken = Request["resetToken"];
    var message = "";
    var newPassword1 = "";
    var newPassword2 = "";

    if(IsPost) {
        newPassword1 = Request["newPassword1"];
        newPassword2 = Request["newPassword2"];

        // Validation
        if (newPassword1.IsEmpty()) {
            ModelState.AddError("newPassword1", "Required.");
        }

        if (newPassword2.IsEmpty()) {
            ModelState.AddError("newPassword2", "Required.");
```

```
        }

        if(newPassword1 != newPassword2)
        {
            ModelState.AddError("newPassword1", "The passwords do not match.");
        }

        // Attempt password reset
        if(ModelState.IsValid)
        {
            if (WebSecurity.ResetPassword(resetToken, newPassword1))
            {
                message = "Password changed successfully.";
            }
            else
            {
                message = "Unable to change password.";
            }
        }
    }
}

<!DOCTYPE html>

<html lang="en">
    <head>
        <meta charset="utf-8" />
        <title>Reset Password</title>
    </head>
    <body>
        <h1>Reset Password</h1>
        @if (!message.IsEmpty()) {
            <p>@message</p>
        }
        else
        {
            <form action="passwordReset" method="post">
                @Html.Hidden("resetToken", resetToken)
                <div>
                    @Html.Label("New Password: ", "newPassword1")<br />
                    @Html.Password("newPassword1")
                    @Html.ValidationMessage("newPassword1")
                </div>
                <div>
                    @Html.Label("Confirm New Password: ", "newPassword2")<br />
                    @Html.Password("newPassword2")
                    @Html.ValidationMessage("newPassword2")
                </div>
                <div>
                    <input type="submit" value="Reset Password" />
                </div>
```

```
        </form>
    }
  </body>
</html>
```

When the user clicks the link in the email sent to them by forgotPassword.cshtml, they will be taken directly to passwordReset.chtml. This page displays the form seen in Figure 7-17. The password reset token is passed in the URL as a QueryString with the key `resetToken`.

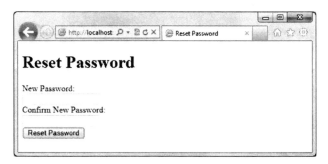

Figure 7-17. *The Reset Password form*

The user then enters the new password twice to ensure it is entered correctly and submits the form. If the form validation passes, the POST request handler attempts to reset the form by calling the `WebSecurity.ResetPassword()` method. If the method returns a Boolean value of `true`, a success message is displayed, otherwise the user receives a failure message.

All that remains is to place a link on the login page to forgotPassword.cshtml. Add the following HTML to a suitable place in login.cshtml (see Figure 7-18):

```
<div>
    </p><a href="forgotPassword">Forgotten password?</a></p>
</div>
```

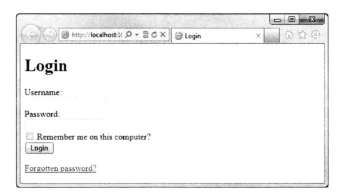

Figure 7-18. *The "Forgotten password?" link added to the Login page*

Summary

WebMatrix ships with a set of helpers designed to assist the developer in providing a comprehensive security and membership process.

In this chapter, we have learned how to initialize the membership system to work with a SQL Server Compact database and how to take advantage of user information that may already exist in a database. We also saw how to provide functionality for users to register on a site, log in, log out, and change their passwords. We created a helper to display relevant account information in any page with our site and added code to restrict individual pages and entire folders to authenticated users.

Next, we learned how roles could be used to manage groups of users and created pages to aid in their administration. We then saw how roles can be used to restrict access to specific areas of a site.

Finally, we reviewed some of the more advanced features of the ASP.NET Web Pages membership and security system, including storage of additional personal user information, registration validation by email, and dealing with users who have forgotten their password.

In the next chapter, we will get an in-depth look at the WebMatrix Package Manager and how it can be used to implement third-party helpers to integrate social networking and other features into our site.

CHAPTER 8

■ ■ ■

Using Web Helper Packages

As we saw in Chapter 4, WebMatrix helpers are self-contained packages of code and markup designed to enable and encourage reuse and rapid development. So far, we have worked with two of the three types of WebMatrix helpers. We have used built-in, native helpers, such as WebMail and WebSecurity, and created our own custom helpers. In this chapter, we will look at the third type: web helpers.

Web helpers are third-party helpers, downloaded from the Internet and "plugged in" to your site, usually in order to facilitate some sort of interaction with a third-party service. There are many examples of these helpers, some of which we will look at in this chapter, including Amazon, Twitter, Facebook, Gravatar, Google, Bing, PayPal, and Windows Azure.

The WebMatrix IDE includes an integrated Package Manager that simplifies the process of finding and installing web helper packages, which we will look at in the first part of the chapter. The latter part of the chapter will focus on the implementation of one of the more popular packages: the ASP.NET Web Helpers Library.

Accessing the Package Manager

The Package Manager is accessed via the ASP.NET Web Pages Administration button in the Content Pane of the Site Workspace (see Figure 8-1). In order for this button to be available, there must be at least one Razor file in the project. To this end, create a new WebMatrix project based on the Empty Web Site template and add a new file to the root of the site called `Default.cshtml`. Navigate to the Site Workspace, using the Workspace Selector and click the ASP.NET Web Pages Administration button.

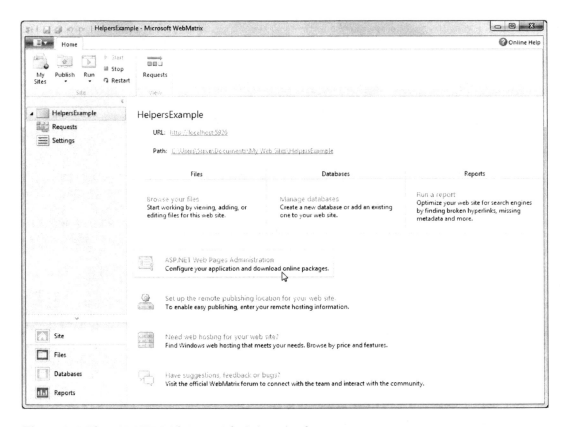

Figure 8-1. *The ASP.NET Web Pages Administration button*

The ASP.NET Web Pages Administration site opens in the default browser, as shown in Figure 8-2. The first time this site is accessed, you must create a password. Enter a suitably secure password—I would suggest a password of no fewer than eight characters that includes a combination of letters, numbers, and symbols—then click the Create Password button.

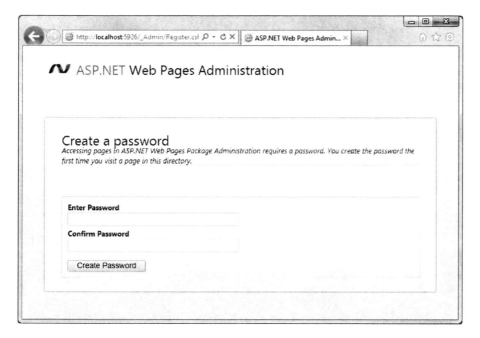

Figure 8-2. *The first time the ASP.NET Web Pages Administration site is accessed, a password must be created.*

Once the password has been created, the following message will be displayed (see Figure 8-3).

Figure 8-3. *The security check message is presented after a new password has been created.*

In order to prevent unwanted parties gaining access to your site's administration pages, whenever a new password is created, a new `_Password.config` file is created in the `/App_Data/Admin` folder containing the password hash. Before you can gain access to the administration pages via the browser you must rename this file to `Password.config` by removing the leading underscore (see Figure 8-4). This step ensures that the password cannot be set or changed by someone who does not have full access to your web server, as only users with administrative rights to the server's file system are able to rename the `_Password.config` file.

■ **Note** You may need to refresh the Navigation Pane in the Files workspace before you can see the /App_Data/Admin folder. You can do this by right-clicking the root folder and choosing Refresh from the context menu.

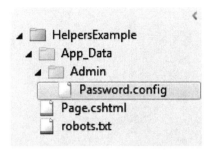

Figure 8-4. The _Password.config file must be renamed to Password.config to prove you have administrative rights to the web server before you can gain access to the ASP.NET Web Pages Administration site.

Once you have successfully renamed the file, click the "Click here" link at the bottom of the Security Check page in the browser (see Figure 8-3), and enter the password you just created into the password textbox. When you click the Login button you will be taken directly to the Package Manager (see Figure 8-5).

From this screen, you can scroll through and search the directory of available packages. As you browse through the list, you will see the vast array of web helper packages available. All the packages are listed with some descriptive text outlining the content of each package and its functionality.

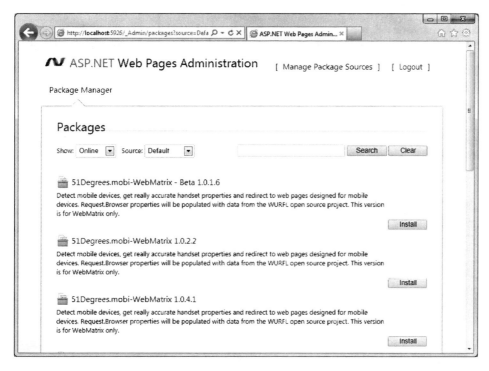

Figure 8-5. The WebMatrix Package Manager

Installing a Package

Later in the chapter, we will look at the ASP.NET Web Helpers Library package. This package contains some useful helpers to aid you in implementing some simple social networking features from platforms such as Twitter, Facebook, Bing, and Gravatar.

Search or browse the list to find the **ASP.NET Web Helpers Library** 1.15 package. Once you have located it, click the `Install` button, read the information presented, and click `Install` again to accept the license terms for the package.

The Package Manager will now automatically download the relevant package and install the necessary files and folders in your site. In the case of this package, a file called `Microsoft.Web.Helpers.dll` will be installed within a `bin` folder in the root of the site.

Once the package has been successfully downloaded and installed, the Package Manager will display a notification similar to that seen in Figure 8-6.

Figure 8-6. Notification of a successful package installation

The Package Manager can also remove previously installed packages from your site. If you search again for the package we just installed, you will notice that an Uninstall button is now available.

Close the browser instance containing the Package Manager and return to the IDE. Again, you may need to refresh the Navigation Pane within the Files workspace to see the changes made to the site file structure (see Figure 8-7).

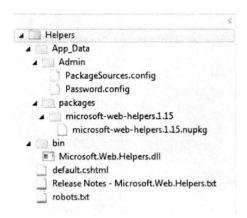

Figure 8-7. *The site file structure following installation of the ASP.NET Web Helpers Library 1.15 package*

Now that we have installed the ASP.NET Web Helpers Library to our site, we will spend the rest of the chapter exploring how it can be used to implement some useful social networking and other features.

The ASP.NET Web Helpers Library

The ASP.NET Web Helpers Library is a package of web helpers which enables you to easily add commonly used social networking functions from a number of providers, such as Facebook, Twitter, Bing, and Gravatar, into your site. The package is maintained by Microsoft. In this section, we will look at some of the most useful helpers included in the package.

Adding Search with Bing

The Bing helper makes it easy to add elementary web search capabilities to your site. The helper displays a simple interface, allowing the user to search for keywords both within your site and across the Internet as a whole, displaying results from the Microsoft Bing search engine.

To display a Bing Search Box we simply need to call the `Bing.Searchbox()` method. The helper method has two parameters, `SiteTitle` and `SiteUrl`, for which we will need to provide values. Setting the `SiteTitle` property sets the title of the search tab. The `SiteUrl` property contains the URL of the site to be searched.

We will set the values of the two properties in a code block at the top of the page and call the
Bing.Searchbox() helper method at the relevant place in the page body. Amend the contents of the
Default.cshtml file we added earlier to look like the following:

```
@{
    Bing.SiteTitle = "My Blog";
    Bing.SiteUrl = "http://blog.stevelydford.com";
}

<!DOCTYPE html>

<html lang="en">
    <head>
        <meta charset="utf-8" />
        <title></title>
    </head>
    <body>
        @Bing.SearchBox()
    </body>
</html>
```

Run this page from the WebMatrix IDE. A Bing search box is rendered in the page, like the one seen
here in Figure 8-8.

Figure 8-8. *The Bing search box rendered in the browser*

When the user enters one or more keywords and clicks the search button, they are taken to a list of
results on the Bing web site, which is opened in a new browser tab (see Figure 8-9).

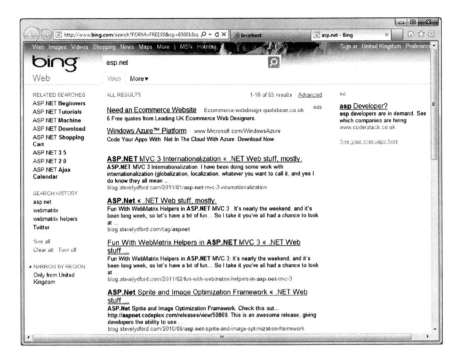

Figure 8-9. *The search results returned from the Bing site*

The helper can only return results for pages that have been indexed by the Bing search engine; these results are displayed on the Bing web site in a way that does not allow customization. Clearly, implementation of this is not appropriate for every application; however, when it is used in a suitable context, it does provide some useful functionality, particularly on sites with reasonably static content.

■ **Note** We will create our own internal search helper in Chapter 10, during the creation of our full e-commerce application, which will produce search results from a database.

Twitter

The hugely popular online social networking service, Twitter, allows users to send and receive text-based messages of up to 140 characters, known as Tweets. Tweets are by default publicly visible, but can be restricted to an individual follower or group of followers. Users can search for individual tweets using a particular keyword, or "Follow" other Twitter users to receive all their public Tweets. When a user logs in to the Twitter.com web site, they see all the public Tweets posted by the users they follow displayed in reverse-chronological order; this display is known as the timeline.

The ASP.NET Web Helpers Library contains a Twitter helper that explains a number of methods that can be used to facilitate interaction and integration with the Twitter.com application programming interface (API).

Displaying Tweets

There are four methods that can be used to display formatted Twitter data in a page: `Twitter.Search()`, `Twitter.Profile()`, `Twitter.List()`, and `Twitter.Faves()`. All four methods have a set of optional parameters, as described in Table 8-1.

Table 8-1. *Twitter Search(), Profile(), List(), and Faves() Method Optional Parameters*

Parameter	Type	Default	Description
width	int	250	The width of the Twitter panel
height	int	300	The height of the Twitter panel
backgroundShellColor	string		The background color of the top and bottom bar
shellColor	string		The top and bottom bar text color
tweetsBackgroundColor	string		The background color of the main Tweets panel
tweetsColor	string		The tweet text color
tweetsLinkColor	string		The text color of hyperlinks within tweets
numberOfTweets	int	4	Number of tweets to be displayed
scrollbar	bool	false	Toggle scrollbar
loop	bool	false	Loop results
live	bool	false	Poll for new results
hashTags	bool	true	Show hashtags in tweets
timestamp	bool	true	Show a timestamp in tweets
avatars	bool	false	Show avatars in tweets
behavior	string	"all"	Load all tweets ("all") or use a timed interval ("default")
searchInterval	int	6000	Tweet request interval in milliseconds

To use the helpers, it is simply a matter of calling the methods and setting any of the optional parameters as desired.

The Twitter helper also provides a `Search()` method to enable you to display Tweets about a particular subject, based on a keyword search. To use the `Search()` method, we pass in the search term as a `string`. In this example, we will also set the `tweetsBackgroundColor` parameter to be light grey:

```
@Twitter.Search("Football", tweetsBackgroundColor: "#eeeeee")
```

This method call will display a Twitter search widget similar to that seen in Figure 8-10.

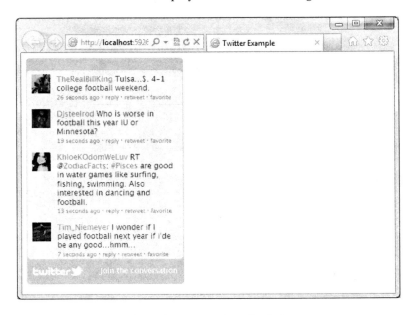

Figure 8-10. *Output from the Twitter.Search() helper*

The `Twitter.Profile()` and `Twitter.Faves()` methods require a Twitter username to be passed as a parameter, as can be seen in the following:

```
@Twitter.Profile("stevelydford")
@Twitter.Faves("stevelydford")
```

The `Twitter.List()` method requires that you pass in a Twitter username and the name of a public list associated to that user.

```
@Twitter.List("stevelydford", "web-development")
```

Twitter Buttons

Twitter buttons can be added to your web site to let users share content via Twitter, without having to leave the page. Two methods exist within the Twitter helper for displaying Twitter buttons. The first, `FollowButton()`, displays a button which, when clicked, sets the user's Twitter account to follow the specified Twitter profile.

The method has one required parameter, `username`, which is the Twitter username of the account to be followed.

```
@Twitter.FollowButton("stevelydford")
```

This displays the default Follow Me button, seen here in Figure 8-11.

Figure 8-11. *The default Follow Me button*

Six button designs are available and can be specified using the optional `followStyle` parameter. The accepted values for the `followStyle` parameter are: `follow_me`, `follow_us`, `twitter`, `t_logo`, `t_small` and `t_mini`. The following code example shows each design, with the output shown in Figure 8-12:

```
@Twitter.FollowButton("stevelydford", followStyle: "follow_me")
@Twitter.FollowButton("stevelydford", followStyle: "follow_us")
@Twitter.FollowButton("stevelydford", followStyle: "twitter")
@Twitter.FollowButton("stevelydford", followStyle: "t_logo")
@Twitter.FollowButton("stevelydford", followStyle: "t_small")
@Twitter.FollowButton("stevelydford", followStyle: "t_mini")
```

Figure 8-12. *The six Twitter Follow button styles*

Each button can also be displayed in one of three color schemes: the default blue scheme "a," a light grey scheme "b," and a dark scheme "c." Figure 8-13 shows the output of the following code example, which displays a `follow_us` style button in each of the following three color schemes:

```
@Twitter.FollowButton("stevelydford", followStyle: "follow_us", followColor: "a")
@Twitter.FollowButton("stevelydford", followStyle: "follow_us", followColor: "b")
@Twitter.FollowButton("stevelydford", followStyle: "follow_us", followColor: "c")
```

Figure 8-13. *The three Follow button color schemes*

When a user clicks the Follow button they are taken to the Twitter web site, where the specified profile information is displayed.

The second Twitter button helper method available is `TweetButton()`. When a user clicks on a Tweet button, a pre-defined Tweet, which can contain a hyperlink to a specified page, is created; the user can then send this Tweet from their personal Twitter account. This enables them to easily share a link to your site, without having to leave the current page.

The `TweetButton()` method has a number of parameters, listed in Table 8-2, all of which are optional.

Table 8-2. *TweetButton() Method Optional Parameters*

Parameter	Type	Default	Description
dataCount	string	"vertical"	Whether to display a tweet counter and, if so, its position. Accepted values: "vertical", "horizontal", or "none"
shareText	string	"Tweet"	The text displayed if button images not shown
tweetText	string	Title of page containing button	The text to be included in the Tweet
url	string	URL of page containing button	The URL to be included in the tweet
language	string		The language the button will render in. "en" = English, "fr" = French, "nl" = Dutch, etc.
userName	string		The user to be @ mentioned in the tweet
relatedUsername	string		A user to display as a follow suggestion
relatedUserDescription	string		The description to display in the follow suggestion

The following code produces the Tweet button shown in Figure 8-14.

```
@Twitter.TweetButton(tweetText: "Check this out!",
                     userName: "stevelydford",
                     relatedUsername: "Apress",
                     relatedUserDescription: "Great selection of tech books")
```

Figure 8-14. The Tweet button rendered in the browser

When the button is clicked, a new browser window is opened, allowing the user to log in to the Twitter.com web site if they are not already authenticated. Once they are logged in, they will be able to amend the message and post the Tweet (see Figure 8-15).

Figure 8-15. The tweet displayed in a new browser window on the Twitter web site

Facebook

The Facebook helper contains methods that interact with the popular social networking site. The methods fall into two categories: those that require you to register your application on the Facebook.com web site and those that do not. In this section, we will look at methods in both categories and investigate the steps required to register and initialize the application.

Using Facebook without registration or initialization

Adding a "Like Button"

When a user logs in to the Facebook.com web site, a News Feed is displayed, which shows status updates and other news stories that have been posted by the user's friends.

One of the most commonly used Facebook helper methods is the `LikeButton()`. This displays a Facebook Like button which, when clicked by the user, inserts a story into the user's friends' News Feed with a link back to your web site.

The `LikeButton()` method has one mandatory parameter, `href`, which is the URL of the page you wish the Facebook News Feed item to link back to. The following method call displays a Facebook Like button linking back to the ASP.NET web site (see Figure 8-16).

```
@Facebook.LikeButton("www.asp.net")
```

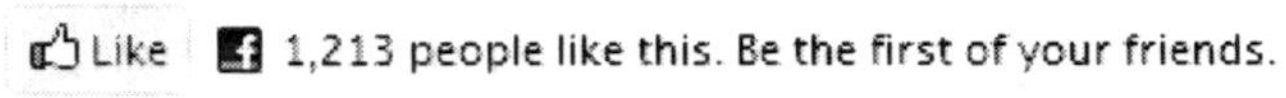

🖒 Like   ▉ 1,213 people like this. Be the first of your friends.

Figure 8-16. *The Facebook Like button*

The `LikeButton()` method also has a number of optional parameters, listed here in Table 8-3.

Table 8-3. *Facebook.LikeButton() Method Optional Parameters*

Parameter	Type	Default	Description
buttonLayout	string	"standard"	Sets the layout style for the Like button. Accepted values are "standard", "button_count", or "box_count"
showFaces	bool	true	Show profile pictures below the button
width	int	450	The width of the button in pixels
height	int	80	The height of the button in pixels
action	string	"like"	The verb to display in the button. Accepted values are "like" and "recommend"
font	string		The font-face for the button and text
colorScheme	string	"light"	The desired color scheme—"light" or "dark"
refLabel	string		A label for tracking referrals. Can be any alphanumeric string up to 50 characters. This label is appended to the URL when a user clicks a link from a Facebook stream story with the key of fb_ref

Adding an Activity Feed

The Facebook.ActivityFeed() helper displays a panel detailing recent activity on your site. The Activity Feed displays stories when users "Like" content on your site, comment on a page in your site using a Facebook Comments box (see the Enabling Facebook Comments section later in the chapter), or share content from your site on Facebook. If a user is currently logged in to Facebook, they will receive personalized content in the Activity Feed, prioritizing content from their friends.

To display an Activity Feed in your page, call the Facebook.ActivityFeed() method, passing in the domain name of your site. The following example shows an activity feed for the BBC web site, shown in Figure 8-17.

```
@Facebook.ActivityFeed("www.bbc.co.uk")
```

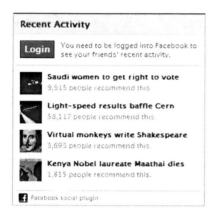

Figure 8-17. *The output of the Facebook.ActivityFeed() helper method*

The optional parameters available for the ActivityFeed() method are listed here in Table 8-4.

Table 8-4. *Facebook.ActivityFeed() Method Optional Parameters*

Parameter	Type	Default	Description
width	int	300	The width of the panel in pixels
height	int	300	The height of the panel in pixels
showHeader	bool	true	Show the Facebook header on the panel
colorScheme	string	"light"	The desired color scheme; "light" or "dark"
font	string		The font-face to be used in the panel
borderColor	string		The border color for the panel
showRecommendations	bool	false	Show Recommendations in the panel

Adding a Recommendations Feed

The Recommendations() helper method displays a panel, similar to the Activity Feed, showing personalized recommendations to users based on all the social interactions with URLs from your site.

To display a Recommendations panel, call the Facebook.Recommendations() helper, passing in your sites domain. The following code displays a Recommendations panel for the ASP.NET web site (see Figure 8-18).

```
@Facebook.Recommendations("www.asp.net")
```

Figure 8-18. *The Facebook Recommendations panel*

The Recommendations() method has a number of optional parameters, which are listed in Table 8-5.

Table 8-5. *Facebook.Recommendations() Method Optional Parameters*

Parameter	Type	Default	Description
width	int	300	The width of the panel in pixels
height	int	300	The height of the panel in pixels
showHeader	bool	true	Show the Facebook header on the panel
colorScheme	string	"light"	The desired color scheme; "light" or "dark"
font	string		The font-face to be used in the panel
borderColor	string		The border color for the panel
filter	string		Filters the URLs shown in the panel. The panel will only list URLs that contain the filter term in the first two path parameters of the URL.
refLabel	string		A label for tracking referrals. Can be any alphanumeric string up to 50 characters. This label is appended to the URL when a user clicks a link from a Facebook stream story with a key of fb_ref

▨ **Caution**   When specifying the required domain name to a relevant Facebook helper method, the domain is matched exactly. For example, if you were to specify news.example.com as the domain, results from catalog.example.com would not be shown.

Helpers requiring initialization

As mentioned previously, some Facebook helpers require initialization before they can be used. In order to initialize, you must first register your application with Facebook in order to obtain an Application ID and Application Secret.

Registering your Facebook Application

To register your Facebook Application, you will need to visit the Create Application page of the Facebook Developers site at `http://www.facebook.com/developers/createapp.php`.

Click the Create New App button, give your application a name and click Continue (see Figure 8-19).

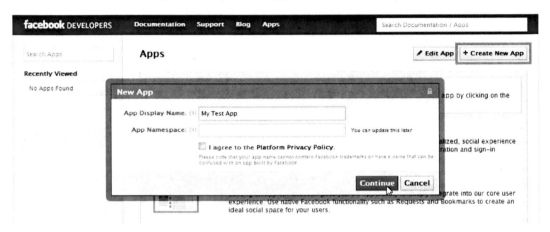

Figure 8-19. *Creating a new Facebook application*

Once you have created the application, you will be taken to the Application Summary page; here you will need to make a note of the `App ID` and `App Secret` displayed at the top of the page. Finally, choose the option that allows your app to integrate with Facebook via a web site and enter the `Site URL` (see Figure 8-20).

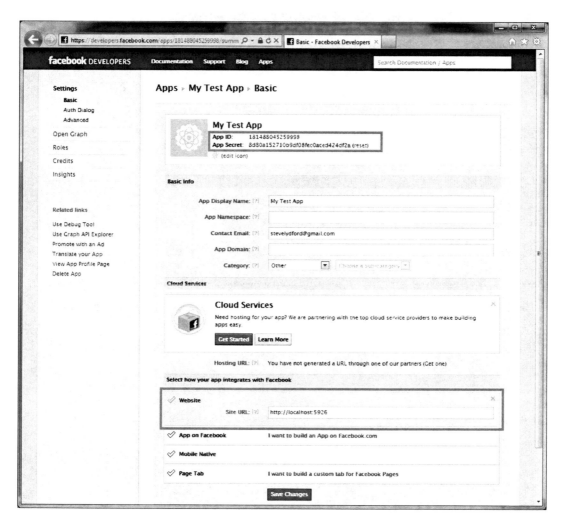

Figure 8-20. *The Facebook Application Summary page*

If you are working locally using IIS Express in WebMatrix, you will need to set the `Site URL` to the URL shown at the top of the Content Pane in the Site Workspace in the WebMatrix IDE (see Figure 8-21).

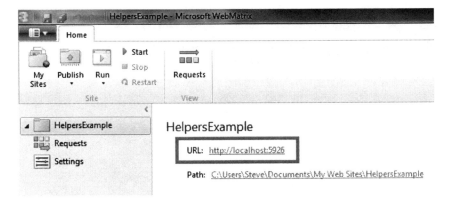

Figure 8-21. *Getting the site URL from the Site Workspace in the WebMatrix IDE*

Click the Save Changes button and close the browser.

___

■ **Note** It is possible that the port number used by WebMatrix will change when the PC is restarted or another project is opened. In order for the Facebook helpers to initialize correctly, the port number must match that specified in the Facebook Application Summary page. The port to be used by WebMatrix can be changed in the Settings area of the Site workspace.

___

Initializing the Facebook helper

To initialize the Facebook helper, create an _AppStart.cshtml page in the root of your site (if one does not already exist) and call the Facebook.Initialize() method, passing in your App ID and App Secret.

```
@{
    Facebook.Initialize("181488045259998", "8d80a152710b9df08fec0aced424df2a");
}
```

Before calling any of the Facebook methods that require initialization, you must call the GetInitializationScripts() method. This method initializes the Facebook JavaScript SDK (Software Development Kit), on which the helper relies, for the use of eXtended FaceBook Markup Language (XFBML). You only need to call the GetInitializationScripts() once per page, but it must be called before any calls are made to dependent Facebook helper methods.

___

■ **Note** More information on the Facebook JavaScript SDK and XFBML can be found at http://developers.facebook.com/docs/reference/javascript/

___

Enabling Facebook Comments

Adding a Facebook Comments Box to your page enables commenting on your site by Facebook users. If a user leaves the "Post to Facebook" check box ticked, the comment will be posted to their friends' News Feeds, which will also include a link back to your site. The Facebook Comments Box also contains a Like button and provides facilities to administer comments.

To display a Facebook Comments Box, call the `Facebook.Comments()` method, specifying any of the optional parameters listed in Table 8-6 that you may require.

Table 8-6. *Facebook.Comments() Method Optional Parameters*

Parameter	Type	Default	Description
xid	string		The unique identifier for this set of comments. XIDs can contain only alphanumeric, hyphen, percent, period, and underscore characters
width	int	550	The width of the Comments Box in pixels
numPosts	int	10	The maximum number of posts to display
reverseOrder	bool	false	Displays the comments in reverse order
removeRoundedBox	bool	false	Removes the rounded box around the comments text area

The following code displays the Comments Box shown in Figure 8-22:

```
@Facebook.GetInitializationScripts()
@Facebook.Comments()
```

Figure 8-22. *The Facebook Comments Box rendered by the Facebook.Comments() helper method*

Facepile

The Facepile helper displays the profile pictures of friends of the registered Facebook users that are either currently using your site or have "liked" it in the past. If none of the user's Facebook friends have "Liked" the site and none are currently using it, nothing will be displayed.

291

The following code displays the UI shown in Figure 8-23:

```
@Facebook.GetInitializationScripts()
@Facebook.Facepile()
```

■ **Note** The Facebook.GetInitializationScripts() method should be called once per page only. It must be called before the use of any Facebook helper methods that require initialization.

Steve Lydford is using My Test App.

Figure 8-23. *The UI presented by the Facepile helper method*

The Facepile() method exposes two optional parameters— maxRows, which determines the maximum number of profile pictures to be displayed, and width, which sets the width of the Facepile panel in pixels.

Live Stream

The Facebook Live Stream service lets users of your site share activities and comments in real time. Live Stream is designed to be used when running live real-time events, such as live video streaming of webcasts, live web chats, webinars, or online multiplayer games.

Table 8-7 details the optional parameters exposed by the Facebook.LiveStream() method.

Table 8-7. *Facebook.LiveStream() Method Optional Parameters*

Parameter	Type	Default	Description
width	int	400	The height of the Live Stream panel in pixels
height	int	500	The width of the Live Stream panel in pixels
xid	string	10	The unique identifier for this Live Stream. A value must be assigned to this parameter if more than one Live Stream is used on a single page. XIDs can contain only alphanumeric, hyphen, percent, period, and underscore characters.
viaURL	string	Site URL	The URL that users are sent to when they click your App Name within a status
alwaysPostToFriends	bool	false	Sends all user comments to their profile

To display a Live Stream panel in your page call the Facebook.LiveStream() method. The following code displays the output seen in Figure 8-24.

```
@Facebook.GetInitializationScripts()
@Facebook.LiveStream(height: 300)
```

Figure 8-24. The Facebook Live Stream panel output by the Facebook.LiveStream() helper method

---

■ **Note** Using the Facebook helper class, it is also possible to integrate Facebook Login with your site membership system. This feature allows users to login to your site using their Facebook account. We will implement this functionality in our example e-commerce site in Chapter 10.

Gravatar

Gravatar (which stands for Globally Recognized Avatar) enables users to upload a small personal image and associate it to an e-mail address. Web sites that use the Gravatar.com service can request the image associated with an e-mail address for display in a web page. This is commonly used to display user images against account information, blog posts, or comments.

In WebMatrix, you can display the Gravatar image associated to an e-mail address by calling the Gravatar.GetHtml() method. The only parameter required by the method is the e-mail address, although there are a number of optional parameters available. By default, if the e-mail address passed to the method doesn't have an associated Gravatar account, the default Gravatar image will be displayed. Table 8-8 explains each of the additional optional parameters.

Table 8-8. Gravatar.GetHtml() Method Optional Parameters

Parameter	Type	Default	Description
imageSize	int	80	Size of the displayed image in pixels (range 1 to 80)
defaultImage	string	null	URL of a GIF, JPEG, or PNG image to be returned if no associated Gravatar is available or the rating of the returned is inappropriate
rating	GravatarRating	G	The highest permitted image rating
imageExtension	string	null	The file extension to be appended to the returned image
attributes	object	null	Attributes to be added to the HTML img tag in the output, e.g., attributes: new { @class="gravatarImage" }

The following code displays the output seen in Figure 8-25:

```
@* Email address has associated Gravatar account. *@
@Gravatar.GetHtml("stevelydford@gmail.com")
```

```
@* Email address does not have an associated Gravatar
   account. Default image will be displayed instead. *@
@Gravatar.GetHtml("noSuchUser@example.com")
```

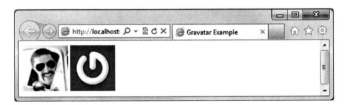

Figure 8-25. A valid Gravatar returned on the left and the default image returned on the right

Gravatar images are self-rated by the owner of the associated account. The rating property can be set to one of five values; G, PG, R, X or Default. This is the maximum permitted image rating that you wish to be displayed. By default, only G rated images are returned. To set the maximum permitted rating, assign the relevant GravatarRating enumeration to the rating property.

```
@Gravatar.GetHtml("stevelydford@gmail.com", rating: GravatarRating.G)
```

Xbox Live Gamer Card

An Xbox Live Gamer Card is an information panel that summarizes a user's profile on Microsoft's Xbox Live online multiplayer gaming service. The ASP.NET Web Helpers Library contains a `GamerCard` helper, which renders an Xbox Live Gamer Card to the browser (see Figure 8-26). The helper has one method, `GetHtml()`, which requires a one string parameter, `gamerTag`.

```
@GamerCard.GetHtml("stinky53")
```

Figure 8-26. GamerCard output

LinkShare

The LinkShare helper renders a set of flair buttons that link to various social bookmarking sites, such as Twitter, Facebook, Digg, and Reddit. To display the LinkShare helper, you call the `LinkShare.GetHtml()` method, passing in the page title.

```
@LinkShare.GetHtml("LinkShare Example")
```

The `GetHtml()` method has four optional parameters, detailed in Table 8.9.

Table 8-9. LinkShare.GetHtml() Method Optional Parameters

Parameter	Type	Description
pageLinkBack	string	The URL to be bookmarked
twitterUserName	string	The Twitter user name to be @mentioned if the user clicks the Twitter flair button
additionalTweetText	string	The text to be tweeted if the user clicks the Twitter flair button
linkSites	LinkShareSite[]	An array of LinkShareSite enumerations. Possible values are: Delicious, Digg, GoogleBuzz, Facebook, Reddit, StumbleUpon, Twitter, and All.

The linkSite's parameter accepts an array of `LinkShareSite` enumerations. For example, to display just the Digg, Facebook, Reddit, and StumbleUpon flair buttons, you could use the following code, the output of which is shown in Figure 8-27.

```
<!DOCTYPE html>

<html lang="en">
    <head>
        <meta charset="utf-8" />
        <title>LinkShare Example</title>
        <style>
            #linkshare a { text-decoration:none }
        </style>
    </head>
    <body>
        <h1>LinkShare Example</h1>
        <div id="linkshare">
            @LinkShare.GetHtml("LinkShare Example",
                        pageLinkBack: "http://www.asp.net",
                        linkSites: new LinkShareSite[] { LinkShareSite.Digg,
                                                         LinkShareSite.Facebook,
                                                         LinkShareSite.Reddit,
                                                         LinkShareSite.StumbleUpon }
            )
        </div>
    </body>
</html>
```

You will notice that this markup includes some CSS styling to tidy up the output, preventing unwanted underline characters between buttons.

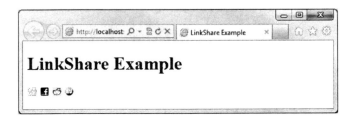

Figure 8-27. *An example of the output rendered by the LinkShare helper*

ReCaptcha

The ReCaptcha helper is used to help prevent automated programs (often called bots) submitting data to the forms in your site. The helper displays a CAPTCHA (Completely Automated Public Turing test to tell Computers and Humans Apart) test, which is validated by the reCAPTCHA service (http://www.recaptcha.net). The test displays an image of two distorted words, which the user must enter correctly in order to successfully submit the form.

In order to use the reCAPTCHA service, your web site must be registered at http://www.recaptcha.net. Once you have successfully registered, you will be assigned a public and private key. When the form is submitted, the reCAPTCHA value entered by the user is sent to the recaptcha.net service, along with the public key. If the test validates correctly, the service returns the private key against which you can validate in a post request handler.

■ **Tip** When registering on the recaptcha.net web site, requesting a global key will ensure that you can test your code locally. When you deploy your site, you should obtain new keys specific to the required domain.

The following code sample displays the form seen in Figure 8-28, displaying the ReCaptcha helper using the GetHtml() method. When the form is submitted, the POST request handler validates the ReCaptcha helper against the private key using the ReCaptcha.Validate() method and adds an error to the page ModelStateDictionary if necessary.

```
@{
    var PUBLIC_KEY = "6PqBf8gSAA1AAKjVivoiBcEWHFM94a9l-V1bVKOQ";
    var PRIVATE_KEY = "6PqBf8gSAA1AAC19mhZXPGF69t6cGfr6YG3s6lsL";

    if (IsPost)
    {
        // Validate the reCAPTCHA test
        if (!ReCaptcha.Validate(PRIVATE_KEY)) {
            ModelState.AddError("ReCatcha", "The reCAPTCHA test was answered incorrectly");
        }

        if (ModelState.IsValid)
        {
            // Process form data here...
        }
    }
}
<!DOCTYPE html>

<html lang="en">
    <head>
        <meta charset="utf-8" />
        <title>ReCaptcha Example</title>
        <style>
            form div { margin-bottom: 15px; }
            .validation-summary-errors { font-weight: bold; color: #FF0000; }
        </style>
    </head>
    <body>
        <h1>ReCaptcha Example</h1>
        @Html.ValidationSummary("Please correct the following errors:")
```

```
        <form action="" method="post">
            <div>
                @Html.Label("Email Address:", "emailAddress")<br />
                @Html.TextBox("emailAddress")
            </div>
            <div>
                @ReCaptcha.GetHtml(PUBLIC_KEY, theme: "white")
            </div>
            <div>
                <input type="submit" />
            </div>
        </form>
    </body>
</html>
```

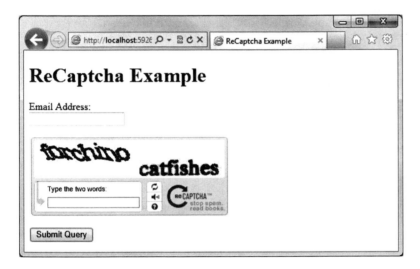

Figure 8-28. Protecting HTML forms against bots using the ReCaptcha helper

■ **Note** For more details on the reCAPTCHA service visit http://www.recaptcha.net. More information on the WebMatrix ReCaptcha helper can be found at
http://msdn.microsoft.com/en-us/library/microsoft.web.helpers.recaptcha.aspx.

Analytics

The Analytics class contains methods that generate the scripts necessary to track your page using three of the most popular free, web-based traffic analysis services.

- Google Analytics - http://www.google.com/analytics/

- Yahoo Marketing Solutions - https://marketingsolutions.login.yahoo.com/

- StatCounter - http://www.statcounter.com/

The methods are all very simple to use and simply inject some JavaScript code into your page to enable tracking by the relevant service. First you must register with the analysis service of your choice then call the relevant method (see the following code example), passing in the account details provided to you at registration.

```
// Google Analytics
@Analytics.GetGoogleHtml(your-analytics-webPropertyId-here)

// Yahoo Marketing Solutions
@Analytics.GetYahooHtml(your-yahoo-accountId-here)

// StatCounter.com
@Analytics.GetStatCounterHtml(your-statCounter-project-id-here, your-security-key-here)
```

■ **Note** The ASP.NET Web Helpers Library package also includes helpers for use with video and images. We will discuss these in depth in Chapter 12- Advanced WebMatrix.

Summary

This chapter has seen the introduction of external web helpers for use in WebMatrix applications. We have seen how to access the WebMatrix IDE Package Manager and use it to install third-party web helper packages.

In the second part of the chapter, we looked in detail at some of the more useful helpers provided within the ASP.NET Web Helpers Library package. These helpers provide easy to use integration features for several popular sites, such as Twitter, Facebook, Bing, reCAPTCHA and Gravatar.

Many other helper packages are available through the Package Manager, some of which we will make use of as we move through the next three chapters, in which we will build a complete e-commerce application using WebMatrix and ASP.NET Web Pages.

CHAPTER 9

■ ■ ■

TechieTogs:
An Example E-commerce Site

Over the last eight chapters, we have covered a lot of new technologies, skills, and techniques and seen how they can be applied to accomplish specific programming goals. Now the time has come to put WebMatrix to use in a real-world context by building a realistic e-commerce application.

The application we will build, TechieTogs, will be an e-commerce site that sells clothing. The public facing side of the site will feature all of the elements you would usually expect to find on a shopping site, such as a catalog, shopping cart, and checkout. The product catalog will be managed using a series of pages that are only accessible to site administrators, thereby providing full CRUD (create, read, update, and delete) facilities.

We will be building the site over the course of the next three chapters:

- This chapter will focus on the foundation stages: designing the core infrastructure of the site, including the database, layouts, and site structure. We will also create pages to allow the user to browse and search the product catalog and will make use of web helpers to add social networking features.

- Chapter 10 will help us add more features to the site, including processes for membership, a shopping cart, and checkout.

- The final components will be covered in Chapter 11, where we will implement the site management pages; this is where the site administrators will go to manage the catalog, as well as view and amend orders.

Along the way, we will see how best to make the most of the feature-rich environment provided by WebMatrix and ASP.NET Web Pages in order to help us develop real-world web sites. This will include the following:

- Creating a database to store the product and order data using Microsoft SQL Server Compact Edition

- Utilizing layout pages, helpers, and functions to maximize code reuse

- Using the WebMatrix membership system to authenticate users and secure parts of the site

- Using web helpers to provide interaction with popular social networking and bookmarking sites

- Making use of the ASP.NET Web Pages HTML helpers and validation in order to provide an optimal user experience.

Getting Started

To get started, we'll need to create a new web site in WebMatrix. Choose to create a site based on the Empty Site template and name it TechieTogs. Next, we'll spend a few minutes setting up the basic site infrastructure.

Page Layout

We will utilize WebMatrix layout pages to create a single template, which will contain header and footer sections, for the public-facing side of our site. The pages we subsequently create within the site will place their content between these two sections. This approach will make it easy to make changes to the site design in the future because all the public pages in the site will use a single layout.

Create a folder called 'Shared' in the root of the site. Within this folder, create two sub-folders called 'Layouts' and 'Partials'. We will use these folders to organize the layout and partial pages, respectively.

Inside the layouts folder, create a new file called _Layout.cshtml (see Figure 9-1). This file will contain the default layout for the user-facing pages within your application.

■ **Note** By default, IIS won't deliver pages named with a leading underscore (_) directly to a client browser. Here we have taken advantage of this convention by naming our layout page in just such a way. This will prevent users from browsing to them directly.

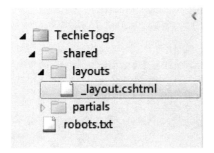

Figure 9-1. The structure of the shared folder, which will contain all our layout and partial pages

In _Layout.cshtml, replace the default markup generated by WebMatrix with the following:

```
<!DOCTYPE html>

<html lang="en">
    <head>
        <meta charset="utf-8" />
        <title>TechieTogs - @Page.Title</title>
        <link href="@Href("~/Css/Style.css")" rel="stylesheet" />

        @RenderSection("head", required: false)

    </head>
    <body>
        <div id="page">
            <div id="header">
                <p class="logo"><a href="@Href("~/")">TechieTogs</a></p>
            </div>
            <div id="content">

                @RenderBody()

            </div>
            <div id="footer">
                &copy;@DateTime.Now.Year TechieTogs. All rights reserved.
            </div>
        </div>
    </body>
</html>
```

In this markup, we have defined a header and footer section and included a call to the RenderBody()
method, where the content of our page will be inserted. Note also that we have defined a @RenderSection
called 'head' that we can use to insert code and markup into the page's <head> tags. However, as we may
not wish to make use of this section in every content page, we mark it as optional by setting the required
parameter to false:

```
@RenderSection("head", required: false)
```

In the <title> tag, we output the value stored in the Title property of the Page object. This will
enable us to set the page title separately within each content page.

The layout page relies on a CSS (Cascading Style Sheet) file to define its appearance. Create a new
folder in the root of the site called 'Css' and, within it, add a new style sheet file called Style.css. The
content of Style.css is listed below:

```
/* General Styles
--------------------------------*/
*, html, body {
    margin: 0px;
    padding: 0px;
}
```

```
body {
    background-color:#efefef;
    color: #333;
    font-family: Verdana, Helvetica, Sans-Serif;
    font-size: .75em;
}

a:link {
    color: #333399;
    text-decoration: none;
}

a:visited {
    color: #333399;
    text-decoration: none;
}

a:hover {
    color: #a70202;
    text-decoration: none;
}

h1, h2 {
    margin-bottom: 10px;
}

input, select
{
    padding: 5px;
}

input[type="text"]
{
    border: 1px solid #cdcdcd;
}

/* Layout
-------------------------------*/
#page {
    margin: 0 auto;
    width: 960px;
    background-color: #fff;
}

#header {
    height: 60px;
}

#content, #footer {
    border-top: 1px solid #cdcdcd;
    clear: both;
```

```
    margin: 0px 10px 0px 10px;
    padding: 20px;
}

#footer {
    color:#cdcdcd;
    padding: 10px;
    text-align: center;
}

.logo a {
    float: left;
    margin: 15px;
    font-size: 3em;
}
```

The combination of these two files defines the default layout page for our site. We will add additional elements to both of these files as we progress with the site's development.

■ **Note** If you are unfamiliar with the use of Cascading Style Sheets and wish to find further information, I strongly recommend Andy Budd's excellent book *CSS Mastery: Advanced Web Standards Solutions - 2nd Edition*, published by friends of ED.

Let's see the layout page in action by adding a default page to the site. Create a file called Default.cshtml in the site root and replace the default markup with a paragraph of placeholder text (notice the absence of <html>, <head>, and <body> tags here—these are supplied by the layout page, into which our content page is merged):

```
@{
    Layout = "~/Shared/Layouts/_Layout.cshtml";
    Page.Title = "Home Page";
}

<h1>Home Page</h1>

<p>
    Lorem ipsum dolor sit amet, consectetur adipiscing elit. Sed nec interdum nisi.
    Ut dui ligula, porttitor sit amet feugiat nec, sodales eget magna.
    Donec id eros et felis vulputate porttitor euismod vel est.
    Vivamus posuere interdum quam a faucibus. Mauris vestibulum cursus dictum.
    Duis blandit eleifend metus, in suscipit arcu faucibus at.
    Curabitur ipsum enim, molestie sit amet faucibus ac, vehicula ac libero.
    Class aptent taciti sociosqu ad litora torquent per conubia nostra, per inceptos
    himenaeos.
</p>
```

Notice in the code block at the top of the page that we specified the layout page and set the `Page.Title` property. We do not need to define a head section here to match the `@RenderSection` call in `_Layout.cshtml` given that we declared it as optional.

Run the page by pressing F12 or clicking the Run button in the WebMatrix IDE Ribbon Control. Figure 9-2 shows the page output to the browser:

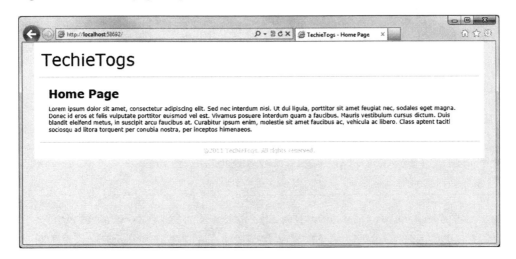

Figure 9-2. The default page containing placeholder text to test out the layout page

Now that we have a working layout page, which we will eventually use to display our product catalog, it's time to add a database to our site.

Adding a Database

In this section, we will create a new SQL Server Compact database using the WebMatrix IDE. This database will store all the data necessary for the operation of our application. This will include data related to the product catalog, orders, and account membership.

To add a database to the site, use the Workspace Selector at the bottom left-hand side of the WebMatrix IDE to navigate to the Databases workspace. Click the New Database button in the Database section of the Ribbon Control (see Figure 9-3) to add a new SQL Server Compact Edition database to the project.

Figure 9-3. Click the "New Database" button in the Ribbon Control to add a database to the project

Right-click the database in the Navigation Pane, located on the left-hand side of the IDE, and rename the database as TechieTogsData.sdf.

Creating Tables to Store the Product Catalog

Given that our first job is to create a product catalog, we will create tables for this now. We will add any additional tables we require to the database during the development process. For the product catalog, we will require two tables. The first of these two tables will contain the products; the second table will contain the categories to which each of these products can belong. On our site, each product will be assigned to a single category.

Click the New Table button in the Ribbon Control and, using the WebMatrix IDEs integrated table editor, add the fields described in Table 9-1:

Table 9-1. *Columns in the* Products *Table*

Column Name	Data Type	Allow Nulls?	Other Properties
productID	int	False	Is Identity = True; Is Primary Key = True;
title	nvarchar	False	Length = 50
description	nvarchar	False	Length = 200
price	money	False	
keywords	nvarchar	False	Length = 200
category	int	False	

- The productID column will store a unique integer, which we will use as a reference for each individual product. The value of this column will be automatically generated by SQL Server Compact when a new row is inserted into the table.

- The title column will hold a product name of up to 50 characters.

- The description column will be used to store up to 200 characters of descriptive text about each of the products in the table.

- The data type of the price column is declared as money; the column is designed to store monetary data values and will store the unit price per product.

- The keywords column will hold a string of distinct words related to the product, which may be useful for our users when they are performing a product search but which do not necessarily appear in the product title or description columns.

- The final column, category, is a foreign-key field, which is used to link an individual product to a product category.

Once you've added all the columns in the table editor, save the table by clicking the Save icon in the top left-hand corner of the IDE, and name the table 'Products' when prompted (see Figure 9-4):

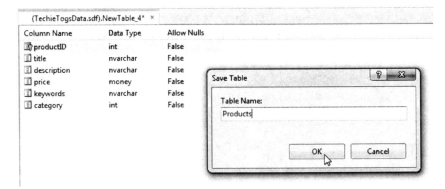

Figure 9-4. The Products *table in the WebMatrix table editor and the Save Table dialog box*

Next, we'll create the Categories table. This table will contain just two columns: the first column will be a unique category ID, which will be referenced by the category column of the Products table, and the second column will store the title of the category.

Click the New Table button on the left-hand side of the Ribbon Control and enter the two columns detailed in Table 9-2:

Table 9-2. Columns for the Categories *table*

Column Name	Data Type	Allow Nulls?	Other Properties
categoryID	int	False	Is Identity = True; Is Primary Key = True;
categoryTitle	nvarchar	False	Length = 50

Once you have created the columns, save the table as 'Categories.'

Adding Data to the Tables

In order to see the tables in the Navigation Pane, right-click the Tables node under TechieTogsData.sdf and choose Refresh from the context menu. Now, double-click the Categories table to open it in Data view.

In the Data view, the WebMatrix IDE allows us to enter values by typing them directly into the table. We will use this method for now to create some sample data, but later, in Chapter 11, we will create an interface that allows site administrators to perform this function within the site.

Enter the three categories shown in Figure 9-5. Note that entering a value into the `categoryID` column will generate an error because it is an identity column whose values can only be generated by the database.

	categoryID	categoryTitle
	1	T-Shirts
	2	Hoodies
	3	Miscellaneous
▶*	NULL	NULL

Table - (TechieTogsData.sdf).Categories ×

Figure 9-5. Values entered into the Categories table

Next, we'll add some sample data into the `Products` table by double-clicking the `Products` table in the Navigation Pane and entering the data seen below, in Figure 9-6, directly into the editor.

Table - (TechieTogsData.sdf).Products ×

	productID	title	description	price	keywords	category
▶	2	C Prompt	The ultimate DOS geeks T-Shirt. Plain black with a large command prompt in the centre.	19.99	cmd windows	1
	3	No Comment	A plain black T-Shirt for ASP.NET geeks with a Razor code comment saying "No Comment".	19.99	asp.net webmatrix	1
	5	Hex Red	Red T-Shirt with the Hexademical color code for red printed in the centre.	19.99	html web #ff0000	1
	6	ASCII Cow	A large picture of a cow printed on the front in ASCII art.	19.99	moo	1
	7	Paint Splat Hoodie	A black hoodie with a large white paint splat across the front.	29.99	splatter	2
	9	Skating Ballerina	One of our most popular hoodies. Red with a silhouette of a skateboarding ballerina.	29.99	ballet skate	2
	11	Management Tie	A tie for managers which says, "I used to be a coder".	14.99	managerial ex-coder	3
	13	Coding Hat	Wear our "Leave me alone I'm coding" hat to let your co-workers know you don't want to be disturbed.	10.99	disturb beanie	3
*	NULL	NULL	NULL	NULL	NULL	NULL

Figure 9-6. Values entered into the Products table

Now that we have some suitable sample products and categories, we can start work on our product catalog pages in order to display them to users.

Creating a Product Catalog

The product catalog can be broken down into two main components: the category list that we display on every page and another page that displays items from the selected category. Given that we want to display the list of categories on every page, the best place to accomplish this is in the layout page.

Open the `_Layout.cshtml` file we created earlier in the shared folder. Inside this file, we will insert a reference to a partial page containing the logic and presentation for the category list. The category list will be displayed in a column on the left-hand side of the page, so amend the markup inside `_Layout.cshtml` as highlighted in the listing below:

```
<!DOCTYPE html>

<html lang="en">
    <head>
        <meta charset="utf-8" />
```

309

```
        <title>TechieTogs - @Page.Title</title>
        <link href="@Href("~/Css/Style.css")" rel="stylesheet" />

        @RenderSection("head", required: false)

    </head>
    <body>
        <div id="page">
            <div id="header">
                <p class="logo"><a href="@Href("~/")">TechieTogs</a></p>
            </div>
            <div id="content">
                <div id="categories">
                    @RenderPage("~/Shared/Partials/_Categories.cshtml")
                </div>
                <div id="main">
                    @RenderBody()
                </div>
            </div>
            <div id="footer">
                &copy;@DateTime.Now.Year TechieTogs. All rights reserved.
            </div>
        </div>
    </body>
</html>
```

The content `<div>` now has two child `<div>` tags: one containing a call to `RenderPage()`, which will display a partial page containing the category list, and another containing the existing call to `RenderBody()`, where our main page content will be rendered.

The `RenderPage()` method call within the "categories" `<div>` requests a partial page called `_Categories.cshtml` from the `/Shared/Partials` folder. We will create this page in a moment.

First, we need to add a couple of styles to our CSS file in order to lay out the categories-related `<div>` in a 150-pixel-wide column to the left of the main `<div>`. Add the following to the bottom of your `/Css/Style.css` file:

```css
#categories {
    float:left;
    width:150px;
}

#main {
    float:right;
    width: 720px;
    margin-bottom: 20px;
    border-left: 1px solid #cdcdcd;
    padding-left:20px;
}
```

The Categories List

Now we are ready to create the `/Shared/Partials/_Categories.cshtml` file requested by the `RenderPage()` method in the layout page. We have named the page with a leading underscore to prevent IIS from serving the page if a user was to browse to it directly. Add the page to your project, and replace the default markup with the following:

```
@{
    var db = Database.Open("TechieTogsData");
    var sqlSelect = "SELECT * FROM Categories;";
}
<ul>
@foreach (var category in db.Query(sqlSelect))
{
    <li><a href="/Products/@category.categoryTitle">@category.categoryTitle</a></li>
}
</ul>
```

In this code, we selected all the categories from the database, then iterated through the result of the query, adding each category title to an HTML unordered list in the form of a list item.

The content of the list item `<li>` is rendered as a hyperlink pointing to the products page, which we will create in the next section. This hyperlink also passes the value of the `categoryTitle` field in the URL. By passing the `categoryTitle`, instead of the `categoryID`, in the `href` attribute of the hyperlink, we are able to provide human-readable, search-engine-friendly URLs.

For instance, to view all the products within the Hoodies category, rather than requiring the `categoryID` in the URL:

`http://domain-name/Products/2`

the user can browse directly to:

`http://domain-name/Products/hoodies`

This is clearly a neater solution, both in terms of Search Engine Optimization (SEO) and usability. However, it requires a little extra work later on, both to display the products within the category and to ensure that no duplicate category names are created.

Finally, we'll add three new CSS styles to the bottom of our style sheet at `/Css/Style.css`:

```
#categories ul {
    border-bottom: 1px solid #cdcdcd;
    margin-bottom: 20px;
}

#categories ul li {
    list-style: none;
    border-top: 1px solid #cdcdcd;
    margin: 0;
    padding: 10px;
}

#categories ul li:hover {
    background-color: #ddd;
}
```

Now when you run `Default.cshtml` in the browser, you will see the categories listed vertically on the left-hand side of the page, as shown in Figure 9-7.

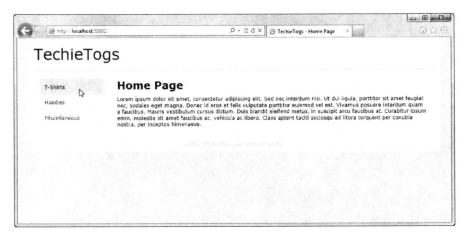

Figure 9-7. *The Default page, showing the list of category links on the left-hand side*

The content of this page is being combined from three sources (not including the style sheet) by WebMatrix before it is sent to the user's browser. The header and footer come from the layout page (`_Layouts.cshtml`), the category listing is generated by a partial page (`_Categories.cshtml`), and the content in the main part of the page is generated by `Default.cshtml`. Figure 9-8 further illustrates this point.

This layout page technique is quite useful to us because we can now display the header, footer, and categories on every page simply by setting the layout page to `/Shared/Layouts/_Layout.cshtml`. If we want to make a change to the design in the future, we can do it in this one file rather than having to change every page in the site. Remember: stay DRY—Don't Repeat Yourself!

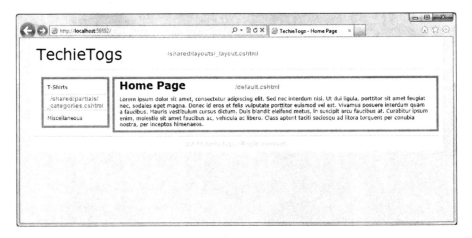

Figure 9-8. *The three files combined to render the final output*

Do not worry about the placeholder text for now. We will replace it with something more useful in Chapter 11. For now, we need to focus on creating our Product Listings page.

The Product Listings Page

The Product Listings page will display a summary of all the products within the selected category. Each product summary will contain a link to a Product Details page, where we will present the user with the ability to place an order.

Create a new file in the root of the site called `Products.cshtml`. Enter the following code block at the top of the page:

```
@{

    Layout = "~/Shared/Layouts/_Layout.cshtml";

    var categoryTitle = UrlData[0];

    if (categoryTitle.IsEmpty())
    {
        Response.Redirect("/Default");
    }

    Page.Title = categoryTitle;

    var db = Database.Open("TechieTogsData");
    var sqlSelect = "SELECT productID, title, price FROM Products " +
                "LEFT OUTER JOIN Categories ON Products.category = Categories.categoryID " +
                "WHERE Categories.categoryTitle = @0";

    var products = db.Query(sqlSelect, categoryTitle);

}
```

In this code block, we set the layout page, get the category title from the `UrlData` collection, which contains any data passed as part of the URL, and assign it to a variable, `categoryTitle`. Next, we check that the value of the `categoryTitle` variable is not empty, redirecting the user back to the Default page if this is the case:

```
var categoryTitle = UrlData[0];

if (categoryTitle.IsEmpty())
{
    Response.Redirect("/Default");
}
```

We then set the `Title` property of the `Page` to the `categoryTitle` and open a connection to the `TechieTogsData` database:

```
Page.Title = categoryTitle;

var db = Database.Open("TechieTogsData");
```

313

Following this, we create the SQL required to retrieve the `productID`, `title,` and `price` of all the products within the selected category.

In order to provide user- and SEO-friendly URLs, we pass only the category title to the page from the link in the categories list. Because we store only the category ID against each product in the `Products` table, we need to perform an SQL `LEFT OUTER JOIN` between `Products` and `Categories` in the `SELECT` statement in order to use the `Categories.categoryTitle` as the criterion in the `WHERE` clause.

■ **Note** If you have never come across SQL joins before, do not worry; just trust that the code does what it says. However, if, like me, you cannot bear not knowing how something works, take a look at the "Using Joins" page of the MSDN online library at http://msdn.microsoft.com/en-us/library/ms191472.aspx.

Finally, we call the `Query()` method against the database, passing in the SQL statement and the `categoryTitle` (which is inserted into the query in place of the `@0`) as parameters:

```
var sqlSelect = "SELECT productID, title, price FROM Products " +
        "LEFT OUTER JOIN Categories ON Products.category = Categories.categoryID " +
        "WHERE Categories.categoryTitle = @0";

var products = db.Query(sqlSelect, categoryTitle);
```

Now we'll add some markup and Razor code to the body of the page to display a summary of the products contained within the selected category. Each product summary will be displayed within an HTML unordered list and will state the title and price of the product. The product title will provide a link to a Product Details page, which we will create in the next section. From the Product Details page, the customer will be able to add the item to his or her shopping cart. We will also provide a 'More Details' link in the UI to the same page for the sake of clarity, in case the user doesn't realize that the product title is a hyperlink.

Add the following code to the page immediately underneath the code block you just added, removing any default markup:

```
<div id="contentTitle">
    <h1>@categoryTitle</h1>
</div>

@if (products.Count() == 0)
{
    <p>
        No items found in this category.
        Try browsing one of the categories listed to the left.
    </p>
}
else
{
    <ul id="productsList">
        @foreach (var item in products) {
            <li>
                <h3>
```

```
                <a href="/ProductDetails/@item.productID">@item.title</a>
            </h3>
            <p class="price">
                £@item.price
            </p>
            <p>
                <a href="/ProductDetails/@item.productID" class="detailsButton">
                    More Details
                </a>
            </p>
        </li>
    }
    </ul>
}
```

Here, we have added an <h1> header tag to the page, displaying the category title. Following this, we check the result of a call to the Count() method of the IEnumerable<dynamic> returned by the Query() method of the Database object to see if any rows have been returned (i.e., the selected category contains at least one product). If no rows have been returned, we display a helpful message to the user:

```
@if (products.Count() == 0)
{
    <p>
        No items found in this category.
        Try browsing one of the categories listed to the left.
    </p>
}
```

If at least one product has been found in the category, we iterate over the result of the query using a foreach loop, adding each product as a list item to an unordered list:

```
<ul id="productsList">
    @foreach (var item in products) {
        <li>
            <h3>
                <a href="/ProductDetails/@item.productID">@item.title</a>
            </h3>
            <p class="price">
                £@item.price
            </p>
            <p>
                <a href="/ProductDetails/@item.productID" class="detailsButton">
                    More Details
                </a>
            </p>
        </li>
    }
</ul>
```

The following CSS, to be added to the bottom of /Css/Style.css, styles the <h1> header tag and the productsList unordered list. The CSS displays the products in three columns across the page (see Figure 9-9):

315

```
#main h1 {
    border-bottom: 1px dashed #cdcdcd;
}

/* Product List
--------------------------------*/
#productsList {
    list-style: none;
    margin: 0px;
    padding: 0px;
}

#productsList li{
    float: left;
    margin: 12px;
    width: 215px;
}

#productsList h3 {
    font-size: 1.75em;
    font-weight: normal;
    margin-bottom: 5px;
    padding: 0px;
}

#productsList .price {
    font-size: 1em;
    font-style: italic;
    color: #999;
}
```

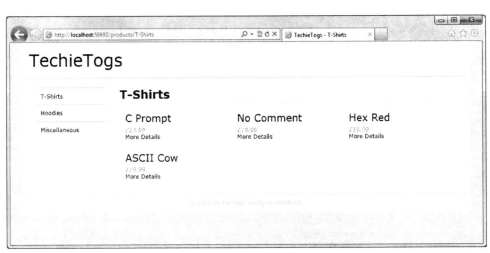

Figure 9-9. The Products page showing product summaries for the T-Shirts category

The Product Details Page

The final page in our product catalog will display the full product details and provide the user with a way to add the product to his or her shopping cart. We will be implementing the shopping cart and checkout in the next chapter, so in this section, we will simply be providing the UI in the products page to facilitate this.

The code for the page is fairly straightforward, so let's just plough straight in. Create a page called ProductDetails.cshtml in the root of the site, and replace the auto-generated content with the following code block:

```
@{

    Layout = "~/Shared/Layouts/_Layout.cshtml";

    var productID = !UrlData[0].IsEmpty() ? UrlData[0] : "0";

    var db = Database.Open("TechieTogsData");
    var sqlSelect = "SELECT * FROM Products WHERE productID = @0";

    var product = db.QuerySingle(sqlSelect, productID);

}
```

In this code, we start by setting the layout page and getting the productID from the UrlData. We use the C# Ternary Operator (?:) to assign the value of the UrlData[0] parameter to the variable productID if UrlData[0] does not contain an empty string.

If UrlData[0] does contain an empty string, i.e., no product ID has been passed in the URL, we set the productID variable to "0". Because the Products.productID column has been defined as an auto-generated identity field, we can be sure that there will never be a product row in the table with a productID of zero.

```
var productID = !UrlData[0].IsEmpty() ? UrlData[0] : "0";
```

Next, we open a database connection to TechieTogsData, and pull out the row with a matching productID, using the QuerySingle() method on the Database object, and pass in the variable containing the SQL SELECT statement and the productID.

Now we have the initial data set up, we can add some markup and Razor code to display the product details and order form. Insert the following immediately underneath the code block we just added:

```
@if (product == null)
{
    <p>
        Unable to fetch product details.
        Try browsing one of the categories listed to the left.
    </p>
}
else
{
    Page.Title = product.title;
    <text>
        <h1>@product.title</h1>
        <div id="productDetails">
```

```
            <p class="price">
                £@product.price
            </p>
            <p>@product.description</p>
        </div>
        <div id="orderForm">
            <form action="/Cart" method="post">
                <fieldset>
                    <legend>Place Order</legend>
                    <p>
                        <label for="size">Size:</label>
                        <select name="size">
                            <option value="S">Small</option>
                            <option value="M">Medium</option>
                            <option value="L">Large</option>
                            <option value="XL">Extra Large</option>
                        </select>
                    </p>
                    <p>
                        @Html.Hidden("productID", productID)
                        @Html.Hidden("price", product.price)
                        <input type="submit" value="Add to Cart" />
                    </p>
                </fieldset>
            </form>
        </div>
    </text>
}
```

The first task this code performs is to check that a product has been returned by the query. If no product has been returned, it displays a useful message to the user:

```
@if (product == null)
{
    <p>
        Unable to fetch product details.
        Try browsing one of the categories listed to the left.
    </p>
}
```

To take into account a product that has been returned, we set the page title to the value of the product title and render the product details to the page. As well as the product details, we also display an order form. The order form contains, first, a drop-down list, from which the user can select the product size he or she requires, second, two hidden fields that store the product ID and price, and, lastly, a Submit button with which the customer can add the product to his or her shopping cart. Note that the action and method attributes of the `<form>` tag specify that we wish the data to be posted to the Cart.cshtml page. We are only going to define the basic UI for the order form here; the form posts its values to Cart.cshtml, which we will be implementing in the next chapter.

All that remains is to style the page by adding the following styles to the default style sheet, /Css/Style.css:

```
/* Product Details
```

```
-------------------------------*/

#productDetails {
    float: left;
    width: 450px;
}

#productDetails .price {
    font-size: 1em;
    font-style: italic;
    color: #999;
    margin-bottom: 10px;
}

#orderForm {
    float:left;
}

#orderForm fieldset {
    width: 230px;
    margin: 0px;
    padding: 10px;
    border: 1px solid #cdcdcd;
}

#orderForm legend {
    font-weight: bold;
    padding:0px 10px 0px 10px;
}

#orderForm label {
    font-weight: bold;
    padding-right: 5px;
}

#orderForm p {
    padding: 5px 0px 5px 0px;
}

#orderForm input[type="submit"] {
    margin-top:20px;
    padding: 5px;
    width: 100%;
}
```

Run the project from the default page, choose a category and a product, and then you will be presented with a page similar to the one seen here in Figure 9-10.

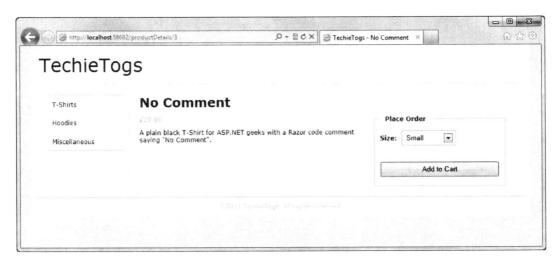

Figure 9-10. The Product Details page

Adding Social Networking Features

In this section, we will make use of ASP.NET web helper packages to add social-networking features to our product catalog. In particular, we will add Twitter, Facebook, and Google +1 buttons to the Product Details page. This will allow users to easily share a link to an item they like within our catalog with friends/followers.

Navigate to the Site workspace and open the ASP.NET Web Sites Administration site using the link in the Content Pane. Enter a password and remove the leading underscore in the filename of the /App_Data/Admin/_Password.config file when prompted.

Next, search for the ASP.NET Web Helpers Library 1.15 and Google +1 Helper 0.1.1 packages within the Package Manager and click the Install button next to both.

■ **Note** A much more detailed explanation of how to install packages using the WebMatrix Package Manager can be found in "Chapter 8 – Using Web Helper Packages." In particular, this chapter also includes detailed instructions regarding the use of the ASP.NET Web Helpers Library package.

The Google +1 Helper Package

Displaying a Google +1 button on your page enables Google+ users to publicly recommend pages across the web.

When you installed the Google +1 Helper package, the Package Manager added a single file to your project: App_Code/GooglePlusOne.cshtml. This file has just one helper method, PlusOneButton(). It has three optional parameters, which are listed below in Table 9-3. The values of the Languages, Sizes, and

DisplayTypes enumerations can be seen in the `App_Code/GooglePlusOne.cshtml` file installed by the package.

Table 9-3. *Optional Parameters of the* `GooglePlusOne.PlusOneButton()` *Method*

Parameter	Type	Default	Description
language	Languages	Languages.EnglishUS	The language to display.
size	Sizes	Sizes.Standard	The size of the button.
display	DisplayTypes	DisplayTypes.All	The type of button to display.

To insert a Google +1 button into a page called the `PlusOneButton()` method, setting any of the optional parameters is required. For example, the following code displays the button shown in Figure 9-11:

```
@GooglePlusOne.PlusOneButton(language: GooglePlusOne.Languages.EnglishUK,
                             size: GooglePlusOne.Sizes.Tall)
```

Figure 9-11. *The Google +1 button rendered by the* `PlusOneButton()` *method*

Adding Google +1, Twitter, and Facebook Buttons

Open the `ProductDetails.cshtml` file in the WebMatrix IDE and add the **<fieldset>**, highlighted in bold below, to the bottom of the orderForm <div>:

```
<div id="orderForm">
    <form action="/Cart" method="post">
        <fieldset>
            <legend>Place Order</legend>
            <p>
                <label for="size">Size:</label>
                <select name="size">
                    <option value="S">Small</option>
                    <option value="M">Medium</option>
                    <option value="L">Large</option>
                    <option value="XL">Extra Large</option>
                </select>
            </p>
            <p>
                @Html.Hidden("productID", productID)
                @Html.Hidden("price", product.price)
                <input type="submit" value="Add to Cart" />
```

321

```
            </p>
        </fieldset>
    </form>
    <fieldset>
        <legend>Share</legend>
        <p>
            @GooglePlusOne.PlusOneButton()
        </p>
        <p>
            @Twitter.TweetButton(tweetText: "Check this out on the TechieTops site!",
                                  userName: "stevelydford",
                                  dataCount: "horizontal")
        </p>
        <p>
            @{ string currentUrl = Request.Url.ToString(); }
            @Facebook.LikeButton(currentUrl,
                                 width:230,
                                 buttonLayout:"standard",
                                 height:25,
                                 showFaces:false)
        </p>
    </fieldset>
</div>
```

The Google +1 Button, Twitter TweetButton, and Facebook LikeButton will now be displayed directly under the order form (see Figure 9-12).

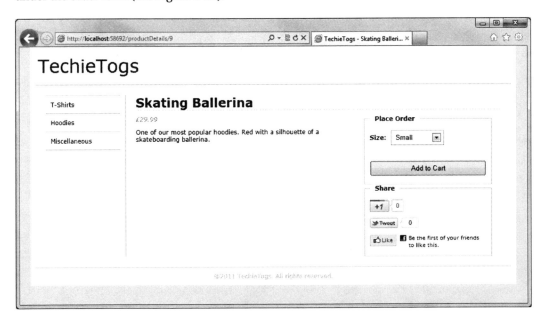

Figure 9-12. *The Google +1, Twitter, and Facebook buttons added to the Product Details page*

Searching the Catalog

As well as offering the ability to browse the catalog by category, we want the user to be able to search the database for products. In this section, we'll add this feature to our site by creating a partial page containing a search form, which we'll render in the layout page. When the user submits the search form, he or she will be taken to a separate page, which will query the database and display the search results.

So let's start by adding the search form to the layout page. Add a file called _Search.cshtml to the /Shared/Partials folder. Replace the auto-generated content with the following form:

```
<form action="/Search.cshtml" method="post">
    @Html.TextBox("searchTerm")
    <input type="Submit" value="Search" />
</form>
```

This partial page renders a very simple form, one containing only a textbox and a submit button. The form attributes are set to POST the values of the controls to our search page at /Search.cshtml.

Now let's add the search form to the layout page. Open /Shared/Layouts/_Layout.cshtml and amend the header <div> to match the following example:

```
<div id="header">
    <p class="logo"><a href="@Href("~/")">TechieTogs</a></p>
    <div id="headerRight">
        <div id="search">@RenderPage("~/Shared/Partials/_Search.cshtml")</div>
    </div>
</div>
```

We'll append the following style to our style sheet at /Css/Style.css, which positions the search form on the right-hand side of the page header (see Figure 9-13):

```
#headerRight{
    float:right;
    margin-right: 20px;
}

#search {
    margin-top: 40px;
    text-align: right;
}
```

Figure 9-13. *The search form added to the header in the layout page*

Now that we have the search form in place, add a new file, `Search.cshtml`, to the root of the site; this will be the page that accepts the form post data, queries the database, and displays the results. Delete the markup generated by WebMatrix and enter the following:

```
@{
    Layout = "~/Shared/Layouts/_Layout.cshtml";
    Page.Title = "Catalog Search";

    var db = Database.Open("TechieTogsData");

    var searchWords = Request["searchTerm"].Split(' ');
    IEnumerable<dynamic> result = Enumerable.Empty<string>();

    var sqlSelect = "SELECT productID, title FROM Products WHERE " +
                    "title LIKE @0 OR description LIKE @0 OR keywords LIKE @0";

    foreach(var word in searchWords)
    {
        result = result.Concat(db.Query(sqlSelect, "%" + word + "%").ToList());
    }

}
```

The first three lines of this code set the layout page and title and open a connection to the TechieTogsData database. The user may decide to enter more than one word into the search text box, so the next line takes the value of the `searchTerm` form item posted to the page and splits it into an array of strings, using a space character as the separator.

```
var searchWords = Request["searchTerm"].Split(' ');
```

Each element of the array returned by the call to the `Split()` method now contains an individual word.

In order to search for multiple words in the database, we will perform a separate database query for each word, selecting all rows where the word matches the `title`, `description`, or `keywords` columns. We will concatenate together all the separate query results into an IEnumerable<dynamic> variable, called `result`, and iterate over it to display the combined results to the user.

In order to achieve this, we first need to instantiate an empty IEnumerable<dynamic>:

```
IEnumerable<dynamic> result = Enumerable.Empty<string>();
```

Failure to carry out this instantiation would cause a "use of unassigned local variable" compiler error when later calling the `IEnumerable.Concat()` extension method.

We then define the SQL statement that will be used to query the Products table and iterate over the `searchWords` array, executing the SQL for each word in the array. We append the result of each separate query to the IEnumerable<dynamic> named `result` by passing the IEnumerable<dynamic> returned by the `Database.Query()` method to the `Concat()` extension method:

```
var sqlSelect = "SELECT productID, title FROM Products WHERE " +
                "title LIKE @0 OR description LIKE @0 OR keywords LIKE @0";

foreach(var word in searchWords)
{
    result = result.Concat(db.Query(sqlSelect, "%" + word + "%").ToList());
}
```

Add the following markup and Razor code under the code block, which displays the results to the user in an HTML unordered list. This is achieved by simply iterating over the result collection and rendering a hyperlink to the Product Details page:

```
<h1>Search Results</h1>

<p>@result.Count() products found matching: <em>@Request["searchTerm"]</em></p>

<ul id="searchResult">
    @foreach (var item in result)
    {
        <li>
            <a href="/ProductDetails/@item.productID">@item.title</a>
        </li>
    }
</ul>
```

Then, add the following style to /Css/Style.css in order to format the search results.

```
/* Search Results
--------------------------------*/

#searchResult li {
    margin-top: 10px;
    font-size: 1.2em;
    list-style: none;
}
```

When a user performs a search, he or she is presented with a results page similar to the one shown here in Figure 9-14.

Figure 9-14. *The search results displayed to the user*

Custom Error Pages

While it is good coding practice to attempt to deal with any likely user actions and prevent errors, it is a near-impossible task to deal with them all.

At present, if an error occurs in your application, the user will be presented with an error page similar to Figure 9-15 if the error originated from IIS or to Figure 9-16 if the ASP.NET runtime produced the error.

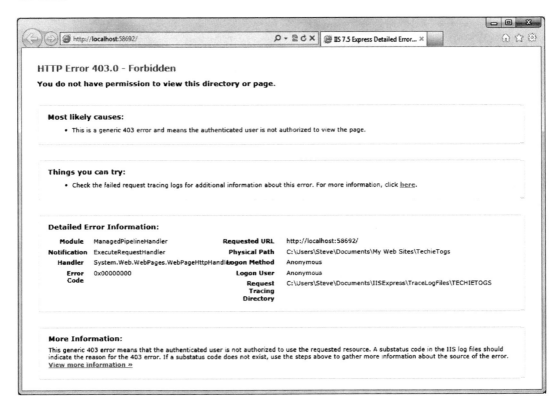

Figure 9-15. An HTTP 403 Error page produced by IIS

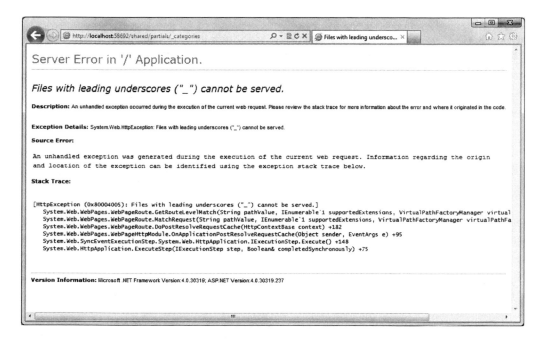

Figure 9-16. *An error page produced by the ASP.NET runtime*

While these pages can be informative during development, it would be much better to present a friendlier page to the user should they encounter an error. Fortunately, this is a relatively simple task in ASP.NET Web Pages.

Displaying a Default Error Page

First, we will need an error page to display. Create a new file called `Error.cshtml` in the root of the site and replace the default markup with the following:

```
@{
    Layout = "~/Shared/Layouts/_Layout.cshtml";
    Page.Title = "ERROR";
}

<h1>ERROR</h1>
<p>
    Unfortunately an error has occurred and
    we were unable to process your request.
</p>
<p>
    <br />Please try browsing the categories
    listed on the left to view our full
    product range.
</p>
```

327

Custom error pages are configured in the `Web.config` file of an ASP.NET web site. Given that we don't currently have a `Web.config` file in our site, add one to the root folder. You will find the `Web.Config` `(4.0)` file type listed as the last item under the 'All' tab of the New File dialog (see Figure 9-17).

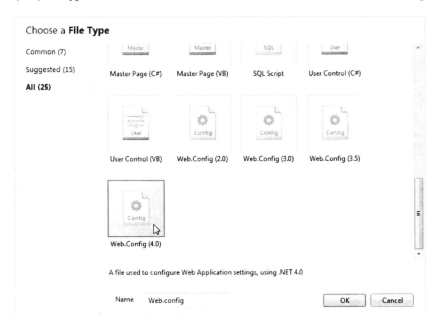

Figure 9-17. Adding a Web.config file to your application

The `Web.config` file is an XML-based file that contains information about the various configuration options available to ASP.NET web sites. The file will have been created with some base content. Amend the file to look like the following:

```
<?xml version="1.0"?>

<configuration>

    <system.web>
        <compilation debug="false" targetFramework="4.0" />
        <customErrors mode="On" defaultRedirect="/Error"/>
    </system.web>

</configuration>
```

The `customErrors` element we have just added tells the server to display the page specified in the value of the `defaultRedirect` attribute. Now, rather than receiving one of the default error pages seen in Figure 9-15 or Figure 9-16, the user will see the one shown below in Figure 9-18.

To test this page, you will need to generate an error. One way to do this is to browse to ProductDetails.cshtml, passing an invalid product ID in the URLData. For example:

```
http://localhost:<port>/ProductDetails/2h
```

Figure 9-18. *The custom error page*

The mode attribute of the `customErrors` element in Web.config can contain one of three possible values; `On`, `Off`, or `RemoteOnly`. Setting the attribute to `On` or `Off` enables or disables the custom error page respectively. However, from a development point of view, the most useful value is often `RemoteOnly`, which specifies that custom errors are shown only to remote clients and that ASP.NET errors, often showing useful debugging information, are shown to the `localhost`.

404 – Not Found Errors

The custom error page we have implemented will show the friendly error page seen in Figure 9-18 whenever an error is encountered by the web server or ASP.NET. However, if the user browses to a page that does not exist, he or she will still receive the default IIS HTTP Error 404 page, as seen here in Figure 9-19:

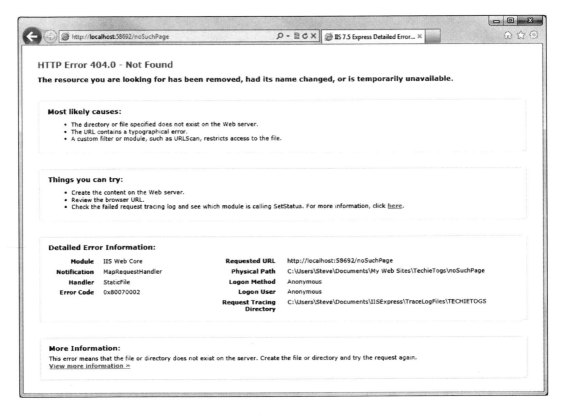

Figure 9-19. *The default IIS 404 – Not Found error page*

As with the default error page, we can instruct WebMatrix to display a custom 404 page via the Web.config file. Amend your Web.config file, adding the <system.webServer> element highlighted in the code sample below:

```
<?xml version="1.0"?>

<configuration>

    <system.web>
        <compilation debug="false" targetFramework="4.0" />
        <customErrors mode="On" defaultRedirect="/Error"/>
    </system.web>

    <system.webServer>
        <httpErrors errorMode="Custom">
            <remove statusCode="404" subStatusCode="-1" />
            <error statusCode="404" subStatusCode="-1"
                prefixLanguageFilePath=""
                path="../Error/404"
```

```
            responseMode="Redirect" />
      </httpErrors>
   </system.webServer>
```

```
</configuration>
```

This new element instructs IIS to redirect 404 errors to the ../Error.cshtml page, passing a value of 404 in the URL.

We'll make use of the UrlData by amending the Error.cshtml page to display a "File Not Found" message if relevant. Make the changes to the Error.cshtml page highlighted below:

```
@{
    Layout = "~/Shared/Layouts/_Layout.cshtml";

    var message = UrlData[0] == "404" ? "File Not Found" : "ERROR!";
    Page.Title = message;
}

<h1>@message</h1>
<p>
    Unfortunately an error has occurred and
    we were unable to process your request.
</p>
<p>
    <br />Please try browsing the categories
    listed on the left to view our full
    product range.
</p>
```

This code inspects the value of the UrlData[0] parameter and sets the value of the message variable accordingly. The value of the message variable is then used to set the page title and contents of the <h1> tag.

The resulting page is shown in Figure 9-20.

Figure 9-20. The custom 404 – Not Found error page

Summary

In this chapter, we have completed the first part of our e-commerce application, TechieTogs. We have a fully working, dynamic, data-driven product catalog linked to an SQL Server Compact Edition database, which allows the user to browse the products by category.

We have added social networking features to the Product Details page to allow the user to share links to our products on Twitter, Facebook, and Google+ and implemented search functionality to help the user find products in the catalog.

Finally, we've defined a custom error page to display friendly error and "file not found" messages to users if necessary.

In the next chapter, we will add a shopping cart, checkout features, and a membership system.

■ ■ ■

CHAPTER 10

TechieTogs:
Adding E-commerce Features

In Chapter 9, we began the implementation of our e-commerce application, TechieTogs. So far, we have built a product catalog backed by an SQL Server Compact Edition database, which the user can browse or search for products.

In this chapter, we will continue with the next stage of development, which will involve adding a shopping cart, membership system, and checkout facility. As we design and develop these features, we will see how to:

- create bespoke objects to encapsulate custom data and logic;

- make use of the browser session to maintain state;

- use the ASP.NET Web Pages membership system and its related helpers to provide user account functionality; and

- use the WebMail helper to send e-mails to users.

Our first task is to build the shopping cart, which will allow users to store a list of products to make up a single order for checkout.

The Shopping Process

The TechieTogs shopping cart and checkout will work in the traditional manner. Users will browse for products in the catalog and then add items to the cart from the product details page. The contents of users' individual shopping cart will be maintained throughout their visit to the site and a page will be available to allow them to view the contents of the cart and remove items as necessary. The shopping cart page will also display the total order price of all items in the cart.

Once users are happy with the contents of their cart, they will click the 'Proceed to Checkout' button and then provide delivery details and confirm their order. The checkout page will require users to be authenticated. If they are not already logged in, users will be redirected to a login page and then sent back to the checkout page after logging in or registering.

Figure 10-1 details the TechieTogs shopping process.

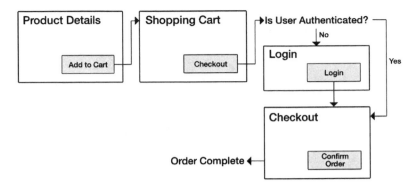

Figure 10-1. *The shopping process for our site*

The Shopping Cart

On our Product Details page, we added an order form that posts its values to `Cart.cshtml`. In this section, we will implement this page.

We need to store the contents of the shopping cart for the duration of the user's visit to the site. The browser session is an ideal place to store this information as it is maintained by the web server for the duration of the visit and can store any type of .NET object.

We will do this by creating a custom `Cart` class, which will encapsulate the data and methods required for shopping cart operations on the site.

Defining the Cart Class

Our `cart` class will need to store a list of cart items (products, sizes, and prices) and will need methods to allow us to carry out operations to add items, remove individual items, remove all items, and get the total value of all items within the cart.

To ensure the `Cart` class is available to all pages within the application, we will create it within the `App_Code` folder. Any code created with the `App_Code` folder of a site will be available to all pages within the site, but will never be served directly by IIS. So, inside the `App_Code` folder, add a class file called `Cart.cs` and enter the following code.

```
using System;
using System.Collections.Generic;

using System.Web;

/// <summary>
/// TechieTogs shopping cart
/// </summary>
public class Cart
{
    private List<CartItem> _Items = new List<CartItem>();
```

```
public List<CartItem> Items { get { return _Items; } }

public decimal TotalValue { get { return _Items.Sum(p => p.Price); } }

public void AddItem(int productID, string size, decimal price)
{
    _Items.Add( new CartItem { ProductID = productID, Size = size, Price = price } );
}

public void Clear()
{
    _Items.Clear();
}

public void RemoveItem(int index)
{
    _Items.RemoveAt(index);
}

}
```

This code defines the Cart class in its entirety. Within the class, we have a read-only public property called Items, which is backed by a private field, _Items. Items and _Items are declared as List<CartItem>.

■ **Note** The CartItem class is another separate custom class, which we will be defining later in this section. It will be used to store the ProductID, Size, and Price of individual line items within the shopping cart.

```
private List<CartItem> _Items = new List<CartItem>();

public List<CartItem> Items { get { return _Items; } }
```

We also have public property called TotalValue, which uses the List<T>.Sum() method to get the total price of all the CartItems within the _Items list.

```
public decimal TotalValue { get { return _Items.Sum(p => p.Price); } }
```

■ **Note** The TotalValue property passes a lambda expression to the _Items.Sum() method. If you have not come across lambda expressions in the past, do not worry. They are a reasonably advanced C# technique we will only use in this one instance in the book. All you need to understand for now is that the call to _Items.Sum(p => p.Price) simply returns the sum of all the values stored in the Price property of the items within the cart. A good example of the use of lambda expressions with the Sum() method can be found on the MSDN web site at http://msdn.microsoft.com/en-us/library/bb397675.aspx

Next, we define the three methods of the `Cart` class, `AddItem()`, `Clear()`, and `RemoveItem()`.

- The `AddItem()` method is used to add a new `CartItem` to the list of items in the cart. It accepts the `productID`, `size`, and `price` as parameters, which it uses to create a new `CartItem`. This is then appended to the `_Items` list.

- The `Clear()` method simply removes all items from the `_Items` list. We will call this method once an order is complete in order to empty the user's shopping cart.

- The `RemoveItem()` method removes the `CartItem` at the specified index within the `_Items` list.

Defining the CartItem Class

As mentioned above, `CartItem` is a custom class we will use to store each individual line item in a shopping cart. The class defines three public properties, `ProductID`, `Size`, and `Price`.

C# allows us to define multiple classes within the same physical file, so we now add the following code to the bottom of the `Cart.cs` file.

```
/// <summary>
/// TechieTogs shopping cart line item
/// </summary>
public class CartItem
{
    public int ProductID { get; set; }
    public string Size { get; set; }
    public decimal Price { get; set; }
}
```

This completes our custom class definitions for the shopping cart. By defining the cart in this way, we can store a `Cart` object within the browser `Session` variable, which will mean the cart is unique to each user and each individual cart's state is maintained throughout the lifetime of the user's visit.

The exact implementation and use of the `Cart` class will become much clearer as we continue to develop the shopping cart and checkout features.

The Shopping Cart Page

Now it's time to add the page that will store and retrieve values from the `Cart` object and present an overview of the cart contents to the user. This page will also allow users to remove items from their cart and will provide a button to take them to the checkout.

The shopping cart page contains some complex features that will take a little work to implement. In this section, we will walk through each stage of the implementation step-by-step.

Figure 10-2 shows the completed Shopping Cart page as displayed to the user.

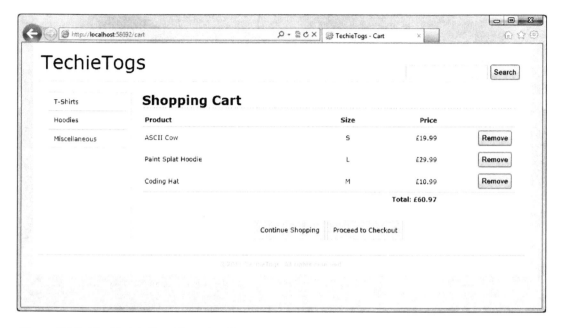

Figure 10-2. *The TechieTogs Shopping Cart page*

Create a new file in the root of the site and name it `cart.cshtml`. This page will be based on our default layout page, `Shared/Layouts/_Layout.cshtml`.

The first thing we need to do on this page is retrieve the current `Cart` object from the user's browser session. If no cart is present in the session, we will create a new empty `Cart` object and add it to the session.

Delete any markup in `Cart.cshtml` and insert the following code block.

```
@{
    Layout = "~/Shared/Layouts/_Layout.cshtml";
    Page.Title = "Cart";

    // Create a blank cart in Session if not present
    if (Session["cart"] == null)
    {
        Session["cart"] = new Cart();
    }

    // Get current cart from Session
    Cart cart = (Cart)Session["cart"];
}
```

Now that we have a `Cart` object, we'll add some markup and Razor code to iterate over the `Cart.Items` collection and output the contents in an HTML `<table>`. Add the following underneath the code block.

337

```
<table id="cartTable">
    <tr>
        <th class="product">Product</th>
        <th class="size">Size</th>
        <th class="price">Price</th>
    </tr>

    @foreach (var item in cart.Items)
    {
        <tr>
            <td class="product">@item.ProductID</td>
            <td class="size">@item.Size</td>
            <td class="price">£@item.Price</td>
        </tr>
    }

    <tr class="cartTotal">
        <td colspan="2"> </td>
        <td>Total: £@cart.TotalValue</td>
    </tr>
</table>
```

In the final row of the `<table>`, we use the `TotalValue` property of the `Cart` object to display the total price to the user.

Before we run the project and take a look at the cart, let's give it a touch of style. Add the following CSS to `Css/Style.css`.

```
/* Cart
--------------------------------*/

#cartTable {
    width: 100%;
    border: none;
    border-spacing:0px;
}

#cartTable th {
    border-bottom: 1px solid #cdcdcd;
}

#cartTable td, th {
    padding:5px;
}

#cartTable .product {
    text-align:left;
    width: 50%;
}

#cartTable .size {
    text-align:center;
```

```
        width: 10%;
}

#cartTable .price {
    text-align:right;
    width: 20%;
}

#cartTable .cartTotal td {
    margin-top: 10px;
    border-top: 1px solid #cdcdcd;
    text-align:right;
    font-weight:bold;
}
```

With the markup and CSS in place, run the project, browse to a product in the catalog, and click the 'Add to Cart' button. You'll notice two immediate problems with this page:

1. The chosen product has not been added to the cart.

2. The cart page doesn't tell the user their cart is empty.

We'll deal with the second of these issues first, as it is the easiest to remedy.

Displaying an Empty Cart

If the user's shopping cart is empty, we want to display a useful message to the user rather than just display an empty table. To do this, we'll add an if statement at the top of the page body in Cart.cshtml, which we will call the Count() method of the carts Items collection. We first check to see if the collection has any rows. If the Cart has no Items, we'll display a suitable message; otherwise, we'll display the <table> as before.

▓ **Note** We have not explicitly defined a Count() method within the Cart class. The method is utilized from List<T>, which is the generic collection type we use to store the Items collection. Hence, we have the call to cart.Items.Count() in the following code sample.

First, we add the following if statement to the top of the Cart.cshtml page directly underneath the <h1> header. Then we'll wrap the <table> inside an else block.

```
<h1>Shopping Cart</h1>

@if(cart.Items.Count() == 0)
{
    <p>There are no items in your shopping cart.</p>
}
```

339

```
else
{
    <text>
        <table id="cartTable">

            @* ... table as before ... *@

        </table>
    </text>
}
```

Now, when we run the page we'll see the message shown in Figure 10-3 instead of an empty table.

Figure 10-3. The empty shopping cart message

That resolves the empty cart display issue. Now we can take a look at how to add items to the cart from the Product Details page.

Adding Items to the Cart

The Product Details page (`ProductDetails.cshtml`) posts the values of the order form to `Cart.cshtml` in three fields, `productID`, `size`, and `price`. To add the chosen product to the cart, we'll add a post request handler to the code block at the top of the cart page.

The code inside the post request handler will simply retrieve the values of the posted form fields and pass them into the `Cart.AddItem()` method. Once the item has been added to the cart, we will save it back to the user's session.

Add the post request handler, highlighted in the code sample below, to the code block at the top of the `Cart.cshtml` page.

```
@{
    Layout = "~/Shared/Layouts/_Layout.cshtml";
    Page.Title = "Cart";

    // Create a blank cart in Session if not present
```

```
if (Session["cart"] == null)
{
    Session["cart"] = new Cart();
}

// Get current cart from Session
Cart cart = (Cart)Session["cart"];

if (IsPost)
{
    var productID = Request["productID"];
    var size = Request["size"];
    var price = Request["price"];

    cart.AddItem(productID.AsInt(), size, price.AsDecimal());
}
```
}

Now run the project again, choose an item from the catalog, and click 'Add to Cart'. When you are taken to the Shopping Cart page, you will see the item you chose has been added. If you then go and add more products to the cart, they will all be displayed.

You will, however, have noticed our next problem. The shopping cart displays the ProductID instead of the product title. We'll fix this next.

Displaying the Product Title in the Shopping Cart

We do not store the product title in the Cart object, so we'll implement a simple helper function to fetch the title from the database.

Create a new page called Products.cshtml in the App_Code folder, delete the default content, and replace it with the following.

```
@* Product Functions *@
@functions {

    public static string GetProductNameFromId(int productID)
    {
        var db = Database.Open("TechieTogsData");
        var sqlQuery = "SELECT title FROM Products WHERE productID = @0";
        return db.QuerySingle(sqlQuery, productID).title;
    }

}
```

In this code, we define a function called GetProductNameFromId(). This function accepts a Product ID as a parameter and queries the database, returning the corresponding product title.

341

> ■ **Tip**   We could easily have added the functionality of the `GetProductNameFromId()` method directly into the `Cart.cshtml` page. However, as this may be a common task, moving this logic out into a helper function makes sense because we can make it available for use in other pages.

To display the product title, we'll call this function in the `foreach` loop in `Cart.cshtml` instead of outputting the item `ProductID`. Make the highlighted amendments to your `foreach` loop in `Cart.cshtml`.

```
@foreach (var item in cart.Items)
{
    <tr>
        <td class="product">@Products.GetProductNameFromId(item.ProductID)</td>
        <td class="size">@item.Size</td>
        <td class="price">£@item.Price</td>
    </tr>
}
```

Run the project again or refresh the Shopping Cart page in the browser to see the product titles displayed correctly.

Removing Items from the Shopping Cart

If users mistakenly add an item to their shopping cart or change their minds about an order, they need to be able to remove the item easily from the cart.

To achieve this, we will place a 'Remove' button against each item in the cart (see Figure 10-2). When the user clicks the button, the item will be removed directly from the cart. No confirmation page is necessary here since it is a trivial task to re-add a mistakenly removed item.

As mentioned in Chapter 5, the W3C HTML Specification states we should not make changes to persisted data as part of an HTTP GET request. Although our cart is not stored in a database, its data is maintained within the browser session, so we must use a POST request.

As also mentioned in Chapter 5, it is quite acceptable for a single page to have multiple HTML forms, provided they are not nested or overlapping. This may be a strange concept to developers of ASP.NET Web Forms, which is restricted to one form per page, but in cases like this, it is an extremely useful capability to have. We will render a separate form on each row of the cart contents table, which will POST its data back to the cart.cshtml page. The form will consist of a hidden field storing the zero-based index of the row and a submit button. When the form is submitted, we will pass the contents of the hidden field to the `Cart.RemoveItem()` method. This method requires the item index as the sole parameter. The form, including the button, will be displayed in an additional fourth column added to the right-hand side of the existing table.

Currently, `Cart.cshtml` uses a `foreach` loop to iterate over the cart items and build the cart contents table. We need to pass in a zero-based row index to the `Cart.RemoveItem()` method, so we will need to declare a variable to store the index before we enter the loop and increment it on each iteration.

Amend the contents of the `cartTable` `<table>` within `Cart.cshtml` to include the revisions highlighted in bold type below.

```
<table id="cartTable">
    <tr>
```

```
        <th class="product">Product</th>
        <th class="size">Size</th>
        <th class="price">Price</th>
        <th> </th>
    </tr>

    @{
        // Declare and initialise index variable, i
        int i = 0;
    }

    @foreach (var item in cart.Items)
    {
        <tr>
            <td class="product">@Products.GetProductNameFromId(item.ProductID)</td>
            <td class="size">@item.Size</td>
            <td class="price">£@item.Price</td>
            <td class="remove">
                <form action="Cart" method="post">
                    @Html.Hidden("removeIndex", i)
                    <input type="submit" value="Remove" />
                </form>
            </td>
        </tr>

        // increment index
        i++;
    }

    <tr class="cartTotal">
        <td colspan="2"> </td>
        <td>Total: £@cart.TotalValue</td>
        <td> </td>
    </tr>
</table>
```

We'll also need to make some changes to the page's POST request handler since the page can now have form data posted to it from two locations, ProductDetails.cshtml via the 'Add to Cart' button and Cart.cshtml via the 'Remove' button.

If the page passes a productID in the form data, we know the POST request has come from ProductDetails.cshtml via the 'Add to Cart' button and we can call the AddItem() method, as we do presently.

However, if the POST request contains a removeIndex value, we know this request has come via a remove form in Cart.cshtml. The removeIndex form value contains the row index, stored in the hidden field value for each form. We can pass this value as an integer to the Cart.RemoveItem() method to delete the row from the cart's items collection.

Apply the highlighted amendments below to the POST request handler in Cart.cshtml.

```
if (IsPost)
{
    if (Request["productID"] != null)
```

```
        {
            // Form posted from Product Details Page
            var productID = Request["productID"];
            var size = Request["size"];
            var price = Request["price"];

            cart.AddItem(productID.AsInt(), size, price.AsDecimal());
        }
        else if (Request["removeIndex"] != null)
        {
            // Form posted by Cart Remove Item button
            var removeIndex = Request["removeIndex"].AsInt();
            cart.RemoveItem(removeIndex);
        }
    }
}
```

Finally, add the following CSS to Css/Style.css to format the Remove button column in the <table>.

```
table .remove {
    text-align:right;
    width: 20%;
}
```

Adding 'Continue Shopping' and 'Proceed to Checkout' Buttons

Now that users can successfully add and remove items from their individual shopping carts, we need to give them a choice to either continue shopping or, if their cart contains all the items they require, proceed to the checkout to finalize their order.

As the cart is stored in the user's browser session, we do not need to pass any data to the checkout page, so both of these 'buttons' can actually be hyperlinks.

Because the Shopping Cart page is now complete, the following code sample shows, for reasons of clarity, the complete listing for Cart.cshtml. The hyperlinks we need to insert are highlighted in bold.

```
@{
    Layout = "~/Shared/Layouts/_Layout.cshtml";
    Page.Title = "Cart";

    // Create a blank cart in Session if not present
    if (Session["cart"] == null)
    {
        Session["cart"] = new Cart();
    }

    // Get current cart from Session
    Cart cart = (Cart)Session["cart"];

    if (IsPost)
    {
        if (Request["productID"] != null)
```

```
        {
            // Form posted from Product Details Page
            var productID = Request["productID"];
            var size = Request["size"];
            var price = Request["price"];

            cart.AddItem(productID.AsInt(), size, price.AsDecimal());
        }
        else if (Request["removeIndex"] != null)
        {
            // Form posted by Cart Remove Item button
            var removeIndex = Request["removeIndex"].AsInt();
            cart.RemoveItem(removeIndex);
        }
    }

}

<h1>Shopping Cart</h1>

@if(cart.Items.Count() == 0)
{
    <p>There are no items in your shopping cart.</p>
}
else
{
    <text>
        <table id="cartTable">
            <tr>
                <th class="product">Product</th>
                <th class="size">Size</th>
                <th class="price">Price</th>
                <th> </th>
            </tr>

            @{
                // Declare and initialise index variable, i
                int i = 0;
            }

            @foreach (var item in cart.Items)
            {
                <tr>
                    <td class="product">@Products.GetProductNameFromId(item.ProductID)</td>
                    <td class="size">@item.Size</td>
                    <td class="price">£@item.Price</td>
                    <td class="remove">
                        <form action="Cart" method="post">
                            @Html.Hidden("removeIndex", i)
                            <input type="submit" value="Remove" />
                        </form>
```

```
                    </td>
                </tr>

                // increment index
                i++;
            }

            <tr class="cartTotal">
                <td colspan="2"> </td>
                <td>Total: £@cart.TotalValue</td>
                <td> </td>
            </tr>
        </table>
        <div id="cartButtons">
            <a href="/Default" class="linkButton">Continue Shopping</a>
            <a href="/Checkout" class="linkButton">Proceed to Checkout</a>
        </div>
    </text>
}
```

We'll use CSS to style the hyperlinks to look like buttons. Add the following to the bottom of Css/Style.css.

```
div #cartButtons {
    text-align: center;
    margin: 40px 0px 20px 0px;
}

.linkButton  {
    border: 1px solid #cdcdcd;to yet)
    background-color: #efefef;
    margin: 0px;
    padding: 10px;
}

.linkButton:hover {
    background-color: #ddd;
}
```

Now, when you run the site and use the Shopping Cart page, it has all the functionality we require (although the 'Proceed to Checkout' button doesn't actually have a checkout page to go to yet) and it looks like the one in Figure 10-2.

At present, short of typing the URL into the browser address bar, the user can only get to the cart when they add an item from the product details page. Don't worry, I haven't overlooked this. We will provide a link to the cart in the layout page during the course of the next section, User Accounts.

User Accounts

When we defined 'The Shopping Process' for the TechieTogs site at the beginning of the chapter, we decided a user must be authenticated before they can progress to the checkout page. We are therefore clearly going to have to implement a membership system on the site. This section will cover that implementation.

Why Bother?

We could easily allow users simply to proceed to the checkout without having them log in or register for an account, so why are we making it a requirement? Well, there are several benefits to this process, including the following.

- The e-mail addresses of registered users can be used at a later date for marketing purposes.

- The users' perception of security on the site improves, thus increasing the trust level.

- Site administrators have the ability to view orders per unique user.

- The account system has the scope to be extended in future versions to provide additional functionality to users, such as storing a default delivery address, viewing past orders, and viewing the delivery status of current orders.

Initializing the Membership System

As we saw in Chapter 7, the ASP.NET Web Pages membership system must first be initialized by calling the `WebSecurity.InitializeDatabaseConnection()` method.

This method tells the membership system which database we wish to use to store the profile and membership information, which table should store the user profile data, and the column names used to identify the unique user ID and password fields. Because the user name must be unique within the table and we wish to collect the user's e-mail address for later use, it makes sense to use the e-mail address as the user name throughout the application.

Add a new file, `_AppStart.cshtml`, to the root of the TechieTogs site and replace the default markup with the following method call.

```
@{
    WebSecurity.InitializeDatabaseConnection("TechieTogsData",
        "UserProfile", "UserId", "Email", true);
}
```

Any code declared within the `_AppStart.cshtml` file will be run when the site is run for the first time, making it an ideal place to call the `WebSecurity.InitializeDatabaseConnection()`, which must be called before any interaction with the ASP.NET Web Pages membership system.

▓ **Note** An in-depth explanation of the ASP.NET Web Pages membership system can be found in this book in Chapter 7.

Registering New Accounts

Now we have initialized the membership system, which has created the necessary tables in our database, we need to provide a page to allow new users to register on the site.

Create a new folder in the root of the site called **Account**. We will use this folder to help us organize the pages within our site by placing all pages that contain membership functionality inside it. Inside this new folder, create a file called **Register.cshtml**. The code listing below contains the complete code and markup required for this page.

```
@{
    Layout = "~/Shared/Layouts/_Layout.cshtml";
    Page.Title = "Register";

    var email = "";
    var password1 = "";
    var password2 = "";

    if(IsPost)
    {
        WebSecurity.Logout();

        email = Request["email"];
        password1 = Request["password1"];
        password2 = Request["password2"];

        // Validation
            if (email.IsEmpty()) {
            ModelState.AddError("email", "Email Address is required.");
        }

        if (!Validation.IsValidEmail(email))
        {
            ModelState.AddError("email", "Invalid Email Address.");
        }

        if (password1.IsEmpty()) {
            ModelState.AddError("password1", "Password is required.");
        }

        if(WebSecurity.UserExists(email))
        {
            ModelState.AddError("email", "An account with this name already exists.");
        }

        if(password1 != password2)
        {
            ModelState.AddError("password1", "The passwords do not match.");
        }

        // Create Account
```

```
        if(ModelState.IsValid)
        {
            WebSecurity.CreateUserAndAccount(email, password1, null, false);
            WebSecurity.Login(email, password1);
            if (Request.QueryString["sender"] != null)
            {
                // Return user to the URL sent in the "sender" key of the QueryString
                Response.Redirect(Request.QueryString["sender"]);
            }
            else
            {
                // Return the user to the home page
                Response.Redirect("~/Default");
            }
        }
    }
}

}

<h1>Register New Account</h1>
<form action="Register?@Request.QueryString" method="post" class="accountForm">
    <p>
        @Html.Label("Email Address: ", "email")<br />
        @Html.TextBox("email", email)
        @Html.ValidationMessage("email")
    </p>
    <p>
        @Html.Label("Password: ", "password1")<br />
        @Html.Password("password1", password1)
        @Html.ValidationMessage("password1")
    </p>
    <p>
        @Html.Label("Confirm Password: ", "password2")<br />
        @Html.Password("password2", password2)
    </p>
    <p>
        <input type="submit" value="Register" />
    </p>
</form>
```

When this page loads for the first time (that is, as the result of an HTTP GET request), an empty registration form is displayed to the user. The registration form consists of an e-mail address textbox and two password fields. Two password fields are displayed to minimize the chance of password typos being submitted to the database.

When the user submits the form, we log out any current user and perform validation on the submitted form values. This validation includes checks to ensure that none of the fields are empty, the two password fields have matching values, and a user with the requested name does not already exist in the membership database.

Because we are using an e-mail address as the required unique user name, we also need to perform validation to check the e-mail address is in a valid format. To do this, we will make use of the validation library we built in Chapter 5. For convenience, this code is repeated in full, as follows, and should be stored in a file called `Validation.cshtml` in the `App_Code` folder.

```
@* Validation Functions *@
@functions {

    @* Comparisons *@
    public static bool IsEqualTo<T>(T value, T comparator) where T : IComparable
    {
        return value.Equals(comparator);
    }

    public static bool IsGreaterThan<T>(T value, T comparator) where T : IComparable
    {
        return value.CompareTo(comparator) > 0;
    }

    public static bool IsLessThan<T>(T value, T comparator) where T : IComparable
    {
        return value.CompareTo(comparator) < 0;
    }

    public static bool IsGreaterThanOrEqualTo<T>(T value, T comparator) where T : IComparable
    {
        return value.CompareTo(comparator) >= 0;
    }

    public static bool IsLessThanOrEqualTo<T>(T value, T comparator) where T : IComparable
    {
        return value.CompareTo(comparator) <= 0;
    }

    @* Range Validation *@
    public static bool IsBetween<T>(T value, T minValue, T maxValue) where T : IComparable
    {
        return (value.CompareTo(minValue) >= 0 && value.CompareTo(maxValue) <= 0);
    }

    @* Pattern Matching *@
    public static bool IsNumbersOnly(string value)
    {
        string expression = @"^[0-9]+$";

        return System.Text.RegularExpressions.Regex.IsMatch(value, expression);
    }

    public static bool IsLettersOnly(string value)
    {
        string expression = @"^[A-Za-z]+$";

        return System.Text.RegularExpressions.Regex.IsMatch(value, expression);
```

```
    }

    public static bool IsAlphaNumeric(string value)
    {
        string expression = @"^[A-Za-z0-9]+$";

        return System.Text.RegularExpressions.Regex.IsMatch(value, expression);
    }

    public static bool IsValidEmail(string value)
    {
        string expression = @"^([a-zA-Z0-9_\-\.]+)@((\[[0-9]{1,3}" +
                @"\.[0-9]{1,3}\.[0-9]{1,3}\.)|(([a-zA-Z0-9\-]+\." +
                @".)+))([a-zA-Z]{2,4}|[0-9]{1,3})(\]?)$";

        return System.Text.RegularExpressions.Regex.IsMatch(value, expression);
    }

}
```

We will make further use of this validation library as we continue to develop the TechieTogs site.

■ **Tip**   A full explanation of this code can be found toward the end of Chapter 5.

If any of the validations fail, the relevant error information is displayed to the user via the `Html.ValidationMessage()` helper.

Once a valid form has been submitted successfully, the account is created by passing the user name and password to the `WebSecurity.CreateUserAndAccount()` method and the user is logged in. The browser is then either redirected back to the Default page or to a URL passed in via the `sender` key of the QueryString. We will use this key in the QueryString when registering directly from the checkout page to return the user to it.

As with all the pages in the TechieTogs site, formatting for the registration page is conducted exclusively via CSS. Add the following, which styles both the form and the output of the validation helpers, to the bottom of your `Css/Style.css` file.

```css
/* Account Forms
--------------------------------*/
.accountForm label {
    font-weight: bold;
    padding-right: 5px;
}

.accountForm p {
    padding: 5px 0px 5px 0px;
}

input[type="password"]
```

```
{
    border: 1px solid #cdcdcd;
}

/* Validation
--------------------------------*/
.validation-summary-errors,
span.field-validation-error {
    color: #FF0000;
}

input.field-validation-error  {
    border: 1px solid #FF0000;
    background-color: #FFCCCC;
}
```

Running the site and browsing to the `Account/Register.cshtml` page will display the registration form seen in Figure 10-4.

Figure 10-4. The account registration page

▦ **Tip**   To minimize the chances of accounts being registered by automated bots or cross-site scripting, you may wish to use the ReCaptcha helper on your registration form. Complete instructions for the use of this helper can be found in Chapter 8.

Alternatively, you could implement an e-mail confirmation process, such as the one described in the Confirming Registration by E-mail section in Chapter 7.

The Account Summary Helper

In this section, we will add an account summary panel to the layout page. The account summary will display different content to users depending on their current authentication status, that is, whether they are logged in to the site.

If the user is not currently logged in (that is, they are an anonymous user), the account summary will display a link to their shopping cart along with links to the login and registration pages. However, if the user is logged in, they will see their username displayed, which will be a link to the Change Password page, a link to their shopping cart, and a link to allow them to log out from the site.

We'll implement this functionality in a helper, so add a new file to the App_Code folder called MembershipHelpers.cshtml and delete the default markup.

Inside the MembershipHelpers.cshtml file, add the following code.

```
@helper AccountSummary()
{
    if(WebSecurity.IsAuthenticated) {
        <text>
            Welcome <a href="@Href("~/Account/ChangePassword")">
                        @WebSecurity.CurrentUserName
                </a> |
            <a href="@Href("~/Cart")">Cart</a> |
            <a href="@Href("~/Account/Logout")">Logout</a>
        </text>
    } else {
        <text>
            <a href="@Href("~/Account/Login")">Login</a> |
            <a href="@Href("~/Cart")">Cart</a> |
            <a href="@Href("~/Account/Register")">Register</a>
        </text>
    }
}
```

This code is fairly straightforward and simply checks the WebSecurity.IsAuthenticated property to see if the user is currently logged into the site and displays the appropriate set of content. The helper currently renders hyperlinks to some pages that we have yet to implement, Login, Logout, and ChangePassword. We will create all these pages during the remainder of this chapter.

To display the account summary helper to the user in every page, we will call it from within the layout page. Open Shared/Layouts/_Layout.cshtml and add the call to the helper, highlighted in the following code sample, within the "header" <div>.

```
<div id="header">
    <p class="logo"><a href="@Href("~/")">TechieTogs</a></p>
    <div id="headerRight">
        <div id="accountSummary">@MembershipHelpers.AccountSummary()</div>
        <div id="search">@RenderPage("~/Shared/Partials/_Search.cshtml")</div>
    </div>
</div>
```

We'll position the "accountSummary" <div> in the top right-hand side of the page by adding the following CSS in the "Layout" section of our stylesheet at Css/Style.css.

```
#accountSummary {
    float:right;
    margin-top: 10px;
    text-align: right;
}
```

Now when we run the site, we will see the helper rendered in the top right-hand corner of the page header. Figure 10-5 and Figure 10-6 show the account summary helper as displayed to non-authenticated and authenticated users, respectively.

Figure 10-5. The account summary as displayed to anonymous users

Figure 10-6. The account summary as displayed to an authenticated user

Showing the Number of Items in the Cart

This is great, but wouldn't it be nice if we could display some more useful user-specific information? Let's make use of the Cart object we created and display the number of items currently in the user's shopping cart.

Make the amendments to the AccountSummary() helper in MembershipHelpers.cshtml, as highlighted below.

```
@helper AccountSummary()
{
    var cartItemCount = 0;

    if (Session["cart"] != null)
    {
        cartItemCount = ((Cart)Session["cart"]).Items.Count;
    }

    if(WebSecurity.IsAuthenticated) {
```

```
        <text>
            Welcome <a href="@Href("~/Account/ChangePassword")">
                    @WebSecurity.CurrentUserName
                </a> |
            <a href="@Href("~/Cart")">Cart - @cartItemCount item(s)</a> |
            <a href="@Href("~/Account/Logout")">Logout</a>
        </text>
    } else {
        <text>
            <a href="@Href("~/Account/Login")">Login</a> |
            <a href="@Href("~/Cart")">Cart - @cartItemCount item(s)</a> |
            <a href="@Href("~/Account/Register")">Register</a>
        </text>
    }
}
```

With these changes, we get the current number of items in the user's cart by calling the `Cart.Items.Count()` method and we display the number to the user as part of the cart hyperlink. Figure 10-7 shows the result.

Figure 10-7. *The account summary helper, showing the number of items in the user's cart*

Displaying a Gravatar Image

The final flourish to our account summary helper will be to display the user's Gravatar image if they have associated an image to their e-mail address at Gravatar.com. A Gravatar, or Globally Recognized Avatar, is an image that can be associated with your e-mail address at www.gravatar.com. Web sites that use the Gravatar service will be able to display the associated image against your name when you do things like comment or post on a blog. In our case, we'll display the Gravatar image in the AccountSummary, next to the user name.

We'll use the `Gravatar()` web helper from the ASP.NET Web Helpers Library package and pass in the user's e-mail address. Add the following method call to the `AccountSummary()` helper in `MembershipHelpers.cshtml` just before the word 'Welcome' and the user name will be displayed to an authenticated user.

```
@Gravatar.GetHtml(WebSecurity.CurrentUserName,
                    imageSize:24,
                    defaultImage:"mm")
```

Here, we have passed the user's e-mail address to the method and set the image size to 24 by 24 pixels.

355

In addition to the option of loading a default image from a specified URL, the Gravatar service provides a number of default image options that can be returned if no image is associated with the requested e-mail address. Table 10-1 shows the built-in options for Gravatar default images.

Table 10-1. The built-in options available for the Gravatar defaultImage parameter

defaultImage Value	Example Image	Description
not specified		The default Gravatar icon
404	none	An HTTP 404 (File Not Found) response
mm		A "mystery-man" silhouetted outline of a person
identicon		A geometric pattern based on the e-mail hash
monsterid		A generated "monster" based on the e-mail hash
wavatar		A generated cartoon face based on the e-mail hash
retro		An 8-bit arcade game style pixelated face based on the e-mail hash

By passing "mm" to the defaultImage parameter, we instruct the helper to load the "mystery-man" image if none is associated with the e-mail address passed.

To align the image in the vertical middle of the account summary, we'll add the following CSS style to the "Layout" section of our stylesheet at Css/Style.css.

```
#accountSummary img {
    vertical-align: middle;
}
```

Figure 10-8 shows the finished account summary helper displayed on the page.

Figure 10-8. The final version of the account summary helper, displaying the Gravatar image associated with the user's e-mail address.

The Login Page

The Login page is used to authenticate users and will be accessed either from the account summary helper or via a redirect from the Checkout page if the current user is anonymous.

Create a new page, called `Login.cshtml`, within the `Account` folder and replace any existing default markup with the code listed below.

```
@{
    Layout = "~/Shared/Layouts/_Layout.cshtml";
    Page.Title = "Login";

    var email = "";
    var password = "";

    if(IsPost)
    {
        email = Request["email"];
        password = Request["password"];
        var rememberMe = Request["rememberMe"].AsBool();

        // Validation
        if (email.IsEmpty()) {
            ModelState.AddError("email", "Username cannot be blank.");
        }

        if (password.IsEmpty()) {
            ModelState.AddError("password", "Password cannot be blank.");
        }

        // Attempt login
        if(ModelState.IsValid)
        {
            if(WebSecurity.Login(email, password, rememberMe))
            {
                if (Request.QueryString["sender"] != null)
                {
                    Response.Redirect(Request.QueryString["sender"]);
                }
```

```
                else
                {
                    Response.Redirect("~/Default");
                }
            }
            else
            {
                ModelState.AddFormError("Unable to log in.");
            }
        }
    }
}
```

```
<h1>Login</h1>
@Html.ValidationSummary(true)
<form action="Login?@Request.QueryString" method="post" class="accountForm">
    <p>Please log in. If you do not have an exisiting account please <a
href="../Account/Register?@Request.QueryString">register</a>.</p>
    <p>
        @Html.Label("Email Address: ", "email")<br />
        @Html.TextBox("email", email)
        @Html.ValidationMessage("email")
    </p>
    <p>
        @Html.Label("Password: ", "password")<br />
        @Html.Password("password")
        @Html.ValidationMessage("password")
    </p>
    <p>
        @Html.CheckBox("rememberMe", new { value = "true" })
        @Html.Label("Remember me on this computer?", "rememberMe")
    </p>

    <p>
        <input type="submit" value="Login" />
    </p>
    <p>
        <a href="ForgottenPassword">Forgotten Password?</a>
    </p>
</form>
```

When the page is loaded for the first time, the user is presented with a blank login form consisting of e-mail address (user name) and password textboxes, a 'Remember Me?' checkbox, and a submit button. The page also provides hyperlinks to the Account Registration and Forgotten Password pages.

Figure 10-9 shows the page displayed to the user. Note we do not need to declare any additional CSS styles since we are reusing the formatting styles we created when developing the registration page.

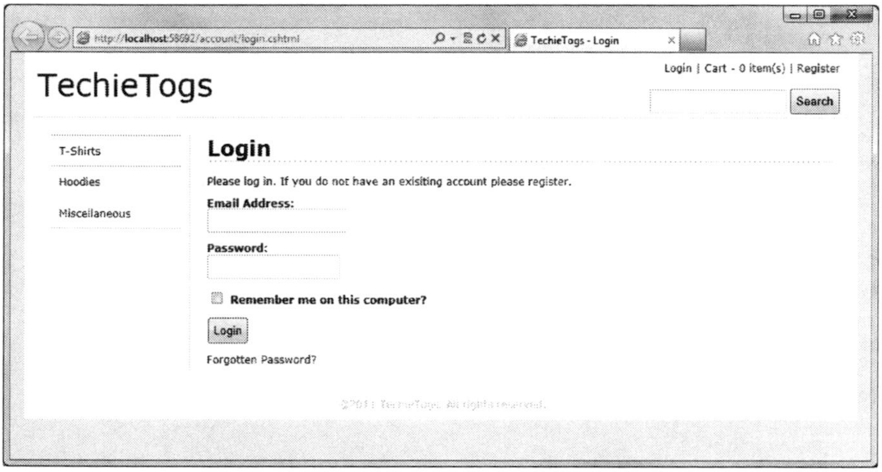

Figure 10-9. *The user login page*

When the form is submitted, the form values are validated and error messages are shown to the user, if relevant. If the submitted data are valid, we attempt a login by passing the values of the `email`, `password`, and `rememberMe` form controls to the `WebSecurity.Login()` method.

As mentioned in Chapter 7, the `persistCookie` parameter, to which we pass the Boolean value of the `rememberMe` checkbox, specifies whether the user wishes to persist the authentication cookie beyond the current session.

If the login attempt fails, that is, the `Login()` method returns `false`, we add a form error to the `ModelState` and re-display the form. If the login is successful, we redirect the user to the URL passed in the `sender` key of the `QueryString` if one is present; otherwise, we return them to the home page.

The Logout Page

The logout page is very simple and requires little explanation. When a user lands on the page, the `WebSecurity.Logout()` method is called, which removes the authentication cookie. Users are then shown a message informing them this has happened and they are given a hyperlink back to the home page.

Create `Logout.cshtml` in the `Account` folder and replace any existing content with the following.

```
@{

    Layout = "~/Shared/Layouts/_Layout.cshtml";
    Page.Title = "Log Out";

    WebSecurity.Logout();

}

<h1>Log Out</h1>
<p>You have been logged out from the site.</p>
<p><a href="@Href("~/Default")">Return to home page</a></p>
```

The Change Password Page

The Change Password page is accessed by clicking the user name in the account summary helper. It is essential for security purposes that we provide this facility to users.

The page, called ChangePassword.cshtml, should be created in the Account folder and should contain the following code and markup.

```
@{
    Layout = "~/Shared/Layouts/_Layout.cshtml";
    Page.Title = "Change Password";

    if (!WebSecurity.IsAuthenticated)
    {
        Response.Redirect("~/Default");
    }

    var currentPassword = "";
    var newPassword1 = "";
    var newPassword2 = "";

    if(IsPost)
    {
        currentPassword = Request["currentPassword"];
        newPassword1 = Request["newPassword1"];
        newPassword2 = Request["newPassword2"];

        // Validation
        if (currentPassword.IsEmpty()) {
            ModelState.AddError("currentPassword", "Current Password required.");
        }

        if (newPassword1.IsEmpty()) {
            ModelState.AddError("newPassword1", "Required.");
        }

        if (newPassword2.IsEmpty()) {
            ModelState.AddError("newPassword2", "Required.");
        }

        if(newPassword1 != newPassword2)
        {
            ModelState.AddError("newPassword1", "The passwords do not match.");
        }

        // Attempt password change
        if(ModelState.IsValid)
        {
            var currentUser = WebSecurity.CurrentUserName;

            if(WebSecurity.ChangePassword(currentUser, currentPassword, newPassword1))
```

```
                {
                    Response.Redirect("~/Default");
                }
                else
                {
                    ModelState.AddFormError("Unable to change password.");
                }
            }
        }
}


<h1>Change Password</h1>
    @Html.ValidationSummary(true)
    <form action="ChangePassword" method="post" class="accountForm">
        <p>
            @Html.Label("Current Password: ", "currentPassword")<br />
            @Html.Password("currentPassword", currentPassword)
            @Html.ValidationMessage("currentPassword")
        </p>
        <p>
            @Html.Label("New Password: ", "newPassword1")<br />
            @Html.Password("newPassword1", newPassword1)
            @Html.ValidationMessage("newPassword1")
        </p>
        <p>
            @Html.Label("Confirm New Password: ", "newPassword2")<br />
            @Html.Password("newPassword2", newPassword2)
            @Html.ValidationMessage("newPassword2")
        </p>
        <p>
            <input type="submit" value="Change Password" />
        </p>
    </form>
</body>
```

The first time users land on the page as the result of an HTTP GET request, they are presented with a form containing three textboxes and a submit button. The first textbox requires they enter their current password; this is to prevent malicious changing of passwords on an account that has been left logged in. The other two textboxes require users to enter the new password twice; this is done to help prevent them from submitting a password with a typographical error. If users unknowingly submitted a misspelled password, they would be effectively locking the account until a password reset is performed (see the next section, Dealing with Forgotten Passwords).

When the form is submitted, the form values are validated and appropriate validation messages are displayed to the user, using the page ModelState and Html.ValidationMessage() helper if necessary (see Figure 10-10). Once an entirely valid form has been submitted, we call the WebSecurity.ChangePassword() method, passing in the current user name and password along with the new password to be stored. If the attempted password change is successful, the user is sent to the home page; otherwise, an error message is added to the page ModelState and the form is redisplayed.

Figure 10-10. *The Change Password page showing a validation error message*

Forgotten Passwords

The last membership process to implement for our site is the one that deals with forgotten passwords. If users have forgotten their password, they can click the Forgotten Password link on the Login page to request a password reset e-mail, which will be sent to their registered e-mail address (in our case, this is the same as the user name).

In the password reset e-mail, they will receive a hyperlink to the Password Reset page (Account/PasswordReset.cshtml) on our site. This hyperlink will contain a unique password reset token, stored in the URL QueryString with a key of "passwordReset". When they visit the Password Reset page, they will be prompted to enter a new password. If both the new password entered and the password reset token are valid, the password entry in the database will be changed for that user.

Sending E-mail

In order to send the password reset e-mail to the user, we will first need to configure the site to send e-mail. Open your _AppStart.cshtml file and add the WebMail initialization code highlighted in bold type below. You will need to enter the details of your specific e-mail server/account.

■ **Tip** The section The WebMail Helper in Chapter 7 covers this topic in much greater detail and includes some default settings for sending e-mail from a Google Gmail account.

```
@{
```

```
WebSecurity.InitializeDatabaseConnection("TechieTogsData",
    "UserProfile", "UserId", "Email", true);

WebMail.SmtpServer = "<smtp server address>";
WebMail.SmtpPort = <port number>;
WebMail.EnableSsl = <true or false>;
WebMail.UserName = "<email account user name>";
WebMail.From = "<email account to send mail from>";
WebMail.Password = "<email account password>";

}
```

Now that we have initialized the WebMail helper, we can build our Forgotten Password page.

The Forgotten Password Page

Add a new page called ForgottenPassword.cshtml to the Account folder. Inside this file, delete any existing markup and replace it with the following.

```
@{
    Layout = "~/Shared/Layouts/_Layout.cshtml";
    Page.Title = "Forgotten Password";

    var email = "";
    var message = "";

    if(IsPost)
    {
        email = Request["email"];

        // Validation
        if (email.IsEmpty()) {
            ModelState.AddError("email", "Email Address is required.");
        }

        // Generate and send password reset email
        if(ModelState.IsValid)
        {
            if(WebSecurity.UserExists(email))
            {
                // Generate confirmation link URL
                var resetToken = WebSecurity.GeneratePasswordResetToken(email);
                var hostUrl = Request.Url.GetComponents(UriComponents.SchemeAndServer,
                                                    UriFormat.Unescaped);
                var passwordResetUrl = hostUrl +
                                "/Account/PasswordReset?resetToken=" +
                                HttpUtility.UrlEncode(resetToken);

                // Send email
```

```
            WebMail.Send(to: email,
                subject: "TechieTogs Password Reset for " + email,
                body: "Please visit <a href='" + passwordResetUrl + "'>" +
                    passwordResetUrl +
                    "</a> to reset your TechieTogs account password."
            );

            message = "An email has been sent to your registered email address " +
                "with a password reset link and further instructions.";
        }
        else
        {
            message = "Unable to find matching account.";
        }
    }
  }
}


<h1>Forgotten Password</h1>
@if (!message.IsEmpty()) {
    <p>@message</p>
}
else
{
    <form action="ForgottenPassword" method="post" class="accountForm">
        <p>Please enter your registered email address to be sent a password reset link:</p>
        <p>
            @Html.Label("Email Address: ", "email")<br />
            @Html.TextBox("email", email)
            @Html.ValidationMessage("email")
        </p>
        <p>
            <input type="submit" value="Reset Password" />
        </p>
    </form>
}
```

The user is asked for an e-mail address (see Figure 10-11). Once submitted, we check to see if it already exists in our database. If the e-mail address exists, we generate a unique password reset token using the `WebSecurity.GeneratePasswordResetToken()` method. This token is stored automatically by the method against the user record in the database. We also use the generated token to construct the URL for the password reset link sent by e-mail to the user. Finally, the e-mail is assembled and sent using the WebMail helper and a message is displayed to the user instructing them to check their e-mail inbox.

Figure 10-11. *The Forgotten Password page*

That completes the Forgotten Password page. Now we'll create the page the user will land on when they click the link in the password reset e mail.

The Reset Password Page

The user is sent an e-mail by the Forgotten Password page that contains a link similar to the following.

```
http://localhost:58692/Account/PasswordReset?resetToken=0dogNPAJewCD%2b1MQIe%2fXOQ%3d%3d
```

The link sends the user to `Account/PasswordReset.cshtml`, which you should create now in your site. The page will contain a form with two password textboxes and a submit button (see Figure 10-12).

Figure 10-12. *The Reset Password page, where the user is sent by the hyperlink in the Forgotten Password e-mail.*

365

When the user submits a valid form, a password reset is attempted by passing the token, retrieved from the resetToken key of the QueryString, and the new password to the WebSecurity.ResetPassword() method. If the token matches the one stored in the database, the password is reset and a 'Success' message is displayed to the user; otherwise, a failure message is shown.

The code below is the complete listing for the Account/PasswordReset.cshtml page.

```
@{
    Layout = "~/Shared/Layouts/_Layout.cshtml";
    Page.Title = "Reset Password";

    var resetToken = Request["resetToken"] ?? "";
    var message = "";
    var newPassword1 = "";
    var newPassword2 = "";

    if(IsPost) {
        newPassword1 = Request["newPassword1"];
        newPassword2 = Request["newPassword2"];

        // Validation
        if (newPassword1.IsEmpty()) {
            ModelState.AddError("newPassword1", "Required.");
        }

        if (newPassword2.IsEmpty()) {
            ModelState.AddError("newPassword2", "Required.");
        }

        if(newPassword1 != newPassword2)
        {
            ModelState.AddError("newPassword1", "The passwords do not match.");
        }

        // Attempt password reset
        if(ModelState.IsValid)
        {
            if (WebSecurity.ResetPassword(resetToken, newPassword1))
            {
                message = "Password changed successfully.";
            }
            else
            {
                message = "Unable to change password.";
            }
        }
    }
}

<h1>Reset Password</h1>
@if (!message.IsEmpty()) {
```

```
    <p>@message</p>
}
else
{
    <form action="PasswordReset" method="post" class="accountForm">
        @Html.Hidden("resetToken", resetToken)
        <p>
            @Html.Label("New Password: ", "newPassword1")<br />
            @Html.Password("newPassword1", newPassword1)
            @Html.ValidationMessage("newPassword1")
        </p>
        <p>
            @Html.Label("Confirm New Password: ", "newPassword2")<br />
            @Html.Password("newPassword2", newPassword2)
            @Html.ValidationMessage("newPassword2")
        </p>
        <p>
            <input type="submit" value="Reset Password" />
        </p>
    </form>
}
```

That concludes the implementation of the TechieTogs membership system. Now that we have created a fully functional membership system in our application, it is time to complete the final task of this chapter, the Checkout process.

The Checkout Process

The checkout process of our site will require users to enter their shipping details and to confirm the order. Once they have done these things, the order will be stored in the database, a confirmation e-mail will be sent, and they will be redirected to an 'Order Complete' page.

Our first task then is to create the database tables necessary to store the completed orders.

Preparing the Database

We will add two new tables to the site database to store our orders. The first table, called Orders, will store the header details of the order, including the shipping address and User ID. The second table, OrderItems, will be used to store the individual line items that make up each order.

In the Databases workspace, right-click the Tables node within the TechieTogsData.sdf database in the Navigation Pane and choose 'New Table' from the context menu. Add the columns listed below in Table 10-2 and save the table as Orders.

Table 10-2. *The columns in the* Orders *table*

Column Name	Data Type	Allow Nulls?	Other Properties
OrderId	int	False	Is Identity = True; Is Primary Key = True;
UserId	int	False	
OrderShipped	bit	False	Default Value = 0
OrderTotal	money	False	
OrderDateTime	datetime	False	
Address1	nvarchar	False	Length = 100
Address2	nvarchar	False	Length = 100
Town	nvarchar	False	Length = 50
Region	nvarchar	False	Length = 50
PostalCode	nvarchar	False	Length = 20
Country	nvarchar	False	Length = 50

Next, add the columns listed in Table 10-3 to a new table called OrderItems.

Table 10-3. *The columns in the* OrderItems *table*

Column Name	Data Type	Allow Nulls?	Other Properties
OrderItemId	int	False	Is Identity = True; Is Primary Key = True;
OrderId	int	False	
ProductId	int	False	
Size	nvarchar	False	Length = 2
Price	money	False	

Now that we have the required database tables in place, let's build our checkout page.

The Checkout Page

On the Checkout page, we will display the contents of the user's shopping cart and ask them to supply the shipping details for the order (see Figure 10-13). When the user clicks the 'Place Order' button, the following process will take place.

1. The order details will be inserted into the database.

2. A confirmation e-mail will be sent to the user.

3. All current items will be removed from the shopping cart.

4. The user will be redirected to an 'Order Complete' page.

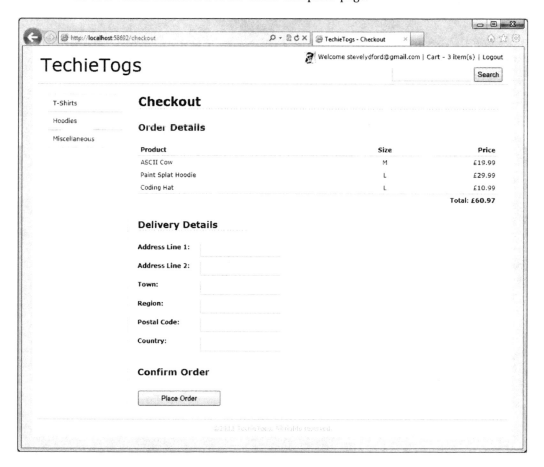

Figure 10-13. The TechieTogs Checkout page

Create a new page called Checkout.cshtml in the root of the TechieTogs site and remove any auto-generated content.

369

Add the following code and markup to the page to display the Checkout page to the user.

```
@{
    if (!WebSecurity.IsAuthenticated)
    {
        string currentUrl = Request.Url.ToString();
        Response.Redirect("~/Account/Login?sender=" + currentUrl);
    }

    Layout = "~/Shared/Layouts/_Layout.cshtml";
    Page.Title = "Checkout";

    var address1 = "";
    var address2 = "";
    var town = "";
    var region = "";
    var postalCode = "";
    var country = "";

    // Redirect to Cart.cshtml if no cart exists in Session
    if (Session["cart"] == null)
    {
        Response.Redirect("Cart");
    }

    // Get current cart from Session
    Cart cart = (Cart)Session["cart"];

    // Redirect to cart.cshtml if cart has no items
    if(cart.Items.Count() == 0)
    {
        Response.Redirect("Cart");
    }

    // POST REQUEST HANDLER GOES HERE

}

<h1>Checkout</h1>
<div id="checkout">
    <h2>Order Details</h2>
    <table id="cartTable">
        <tr>
            <th class="product">Product</th>
            <th class="size">Size</th>
            <th class="price">Price</th>
        </tr>

        @foreach (var item in cart.Items)
        {
            <tr>
```

```
                <td class="product">@Products.GetProductNameFromId(item.ProductID)</td>
                <td class="size">@item.Size</td>
                <td class="price">£@item.Price</td>
            </tr>
        }

        <tr class="cartTotal">
            <td colspan="2"> </td>
            <td>Total: £@cart.TotalValue</td>
        </tr>
    </table>

    <h2>Delivery Details</h2>
    <form action="Checkout" method="post">
        <p>
            @Html.Label("Address Line 1: ", "address1")
            @Html.TextBox("address1", address1, new { maxlength = "100" } )
            @Html.ValidationMessage("address1")
        </p>
        <p>
            @Html.Label("Address Line 2:", address2)
            @Html.TextBox("address2", address2, new { maxlength = "100" } )
        </p>
        <p>
            @Html.Label("Town: ", "town")
            @Html.TextBox("town", town, new { maxlength = "50" } )
            @Html.ValidationMessage("town")
        </p>
        <p>
            @Html.Label("Region: ", "region")
            @Html.TextBox("region", region, new { maxlength = "50" } )
            @Html.ValidationMessage("region")
        </p>
        <p>
            @Html.Label("Postal Code: ", "postalCode")
            @Html.TextBox("postalCode", postalCode, new { maxlength = "20" } )
        </p>
        <p>
            @Html.Label("Country: ", "country")
            @Html.TextBox("country", country, new { maxlength = "50" } )
        </p>

        <h2>Confirm Order</h2>
        <p>
            <input type="submit" value="Place Order"/>
        </p>
    </form>
</div>
```

The first action performed by the page is to check that the current user is logged in to the site. We do this by checking the Boolean property, WebSecurity.IsAuthenticated. If users are not authenticated,

371

they are redirected immediately to the Login page. By passing the current URL in the sender key of the URL QueryString, we instruct the Login page to send the user back to the Checkout once they have logged in successfully.

Next, we set the layout page and title and declare a set of variables to store the data from the shipping details form. If at this point users currently have no shopping cart in their browser session, we redirect them to Cart.cshtml. If a cart is present in the session, we retrieve it and get the count of items, again redirecting users to Cart.cshtml if the cart is empty.

On the page, we then define an HTML <table> and iterate over the Items collection of the cart and display a summary of each item, adding one as a row to the table. In the final row, we display the total order value of all items in the cart from the Cart.TotalValue property.

Underneath the cart summary table, we display a form to collect the shipping details. This is a straightforward HTML form containing six textboxes and a submit button. The maxlength attribute of each textbox is set to match the length of the corresponding database columns in the Orders table.

To provide some formatting to the page, we will need to add some additional CSS styles to our Css/Style.css stylesheet. Add the following section immediately above the 'Validation' section.

```
/* Checkout
---------------------------------*/
#checkout h2 {
    width: 30%;
    border-bottom: 1px dashed #cdcdcd;
    margin: 25px 0px 20px 0px;
}

#checkout label {
    font-weight: bold;
    padding-right: 5px;
    width: 10em;
    float:left;
}

#checkout p {
    padding: 5px 0px 5px 0px;
}

#checkout input[type="submit"] {
    padding: 5px 45px 5px 45px;
}
```

With the Checkout page displaying correctly, we'll add a POST request handler to carry out the actions described earlier when the user clicks the 'Place Order' button. Insert the following code into the page in place of the // POST REQUEST HANDLER GOES HERE comment.

```
if (IsPost)
{
    address1 = Request["address1"];
    address2 = Request["address2"];
    town = Request["town"];
    region = Request["region"];
    postalCode = Request["postalCode"];
    country = Request["country"];
```

```
// Validate Delivery Details
if (address1.IsEmpty()) {
    ModelState.AddError("address1", "Address Line 1 is required.");
}

if (town.IsEmpty()) {
    ModelState.AddError("town", "Town is required.");
}

if (region.IsEmpty()) {
    ModelState.AddError("region", "Region is required.");
}

if(ModelState.IsValid)
{
    // Save Order
    var UserID = WebSecurity.GetUserId(WebSecurity.CurrentUserName);

    var db = Database.Open("TechieTogsData");
    var orderSql = "INSERT INTO Orders (UserId, OrderShipped, OrderTotal, " +
                   "OrderDateTime, Address1, Address2, Town, " +
                   "Region, PostalCode, Country) " +
                   "VALUES ( @0, @1, @2, @3, @4, @5, @6, @7, @8, @9 )";
    db.Execute(orderSql,
                UserID,
                false,
                cart.TotalValue,
                DateTime.Now,
                address1,
                address2,
                town,
                region,
                postalCode,
                country);

    var orderId = db.GetLastInsertId();

    foreach(var item in cart.Items)
    {
        orderSql = "INSERT INTO OrderItems (OrderID, ProductID, Size, Price) VALUES (" +
                   "@0, @1, @2, @3)";
        db.Execute(orderSql, orderId, item.ProductID, item.Size, item.Price);
    }

    // Send confirmation email
    WebMail.Send(to: WebSecurity.CurrentUserName,
        subject: "TechieTogs Order Confirmation",
        body: "Many thanks for your order. Your items will be " +
        "dispatched shortly and should arrive within 3-5 working days."
    );
```

```
    // Clear shopping cart
    cart.Clear();

    Response.Redirect("OrderComplete");
    }
}
```

In the POST request handler, we retrieve the values of the shipping details form fields, assign them to the variables declared earlier, and validate the necessary fields. If any form fields contain invalid data, we add an error to the `ModelState` and display the relevant error message in the form.

If all the form data are valid, we insert the order header details into the `Orders` table, setting the `UserId` field to the `UserId` of the authenticated user, by calling the `WebSecurity.GetUserId()` method. We set the `OrderShipped` field to `false` and the `OrderTotal` field from the `Cart.TotalValue` property. Finally, the `OrderDateTime` field is populated with `DateTime.Now` and the remaining fields to the values submitted by the user.

Once we have executed the insert into the `Orders` table, we get the `OrderId` created by calling the `GetLastInsertId()` method. Then we iterate over the contents of the cart, inserting the details of each item into the `OrderItems` table using the `OrderId` we just retrieved.

■ **Tip**　This POST request handler is the best place to insert code to take an online payment. Web helper packages for taking payments via PayPal and Amazon are available in the WebMatrix Package Manager, although any online payment system can be integrated with WebMatrix.

Next, we send an e-mail to the user thanking them for their order and advising them of the expected delivery timescales. To finish, we clear the contents of the shopping cart and redirect the user to the Order Complete page.

The Order Complete Page

The Order Complete page simply displays a message to the user thanking them for their order and informing them that a confirmation e-mail has been sent.

Insert the following code into a new page in the root of the site called `OrderComplete.cshtml`.

```
@{
    Layout = "~/Shared/Layouts/_Layout.cshtml";
    Page.Title = "Order Complete";
}

<h1>Order Complete</h1>
<p>Many thanks for your order. An email confirmation has been sent.</p>
<br />
<p>Your order will be dispatched shortly and should arrive in 3-5 working days.</p>
```

And that's it! Our checkout process is complete.

Summary

In this chapter, we have added the e-commerce features to the TechieTogs web site. These features included a fully-featured shopping cart, a checkout process, and membership system.

In the next chapter, we will add some final features to the site, including uploading, storing, and displaying product images, generating some dynamic content for the home page to show featured and popular products, and creating administration pages to facilitate the management of the site.

CHAPTER 11

■ ■ ■

TechieTogs: Site Administration and Finishing Touches

Now that we have completed the public-facing side of the site, it is time to turn our attention to the administrative functionality that is essential for maintaining the site and dealing with customer orders. The administrative processes that we will deal with in this chapter include:

- Creating a secure area for administrators to manage users, orders and the product catalog

- Adding and removing administrative users

- Viewing customer orders

- Adding and editing categories and products

In addition to these processes, we will add some final finishing touches to the public side of the site to improve the user experience; including:

- Uploading and displaying product images

- Creating dynamic content for the home page

We have a significant amount of content to cover in this chapter. In the majority of cases, the code will be familiar to you by now and will require little explanation. For each page we add, I will describe the function and workflow of the page. I will only provide detailed explanations of the code where I present a new or particularly complex concept.

Creating an Admin Area

We'll need to create an area that can only be accessed by the site administrators. There we will manage the web site. We'll achieve this by creating an 'Admin' folder, which will contain all of our administration pages. This folder will be secured by allowing access only to members who have an 'Admin' role. Let's start by creating that role.

Creating the Admin Role

Open the Databases workspace in the WebMatrix IDE. In the Navigation pane, open the webpages_Roles table in the TechieTogsData.sdf database. Add a new record, inserting the value 'Admin' into the RoleName field (see Figure 11-1). The RoleId field is an identity field that is automatically populated by the database, so do not enter a value in this column.

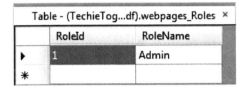

Figure 11-1. *Insert an Admin role in to the* webpages_Roles *table*

Next, if you do not currently have a registered user in the database, run the site and create an account using the Account/Register.cshtml page. Once you have a registered user, return to the WebMatrix IDE, open the UserProfile table, and make a note of their UserId.

Open the webpages_UsersInRoles table and create a new record, inserting the relevant UserId and RoleId (see Figure 11-2). In this table, both columns are Foreign Keys so they are not generated by the database (i.e., you should enter a value in both columns).

Table - (TechieTog...pages_UsersInRoles ✕	
UserId	RoleId
1	1

Figure 11-2. *Assign a user to the Admin role in the* webpages_UsersInRoles *table*

Since this is one of the first administrative functions that will get a user interface built for it on the site, this is the only time we will have to carry out this action. In the future, site administrators will be able to do this through the UI in the site.

■ **Note** For more information on the use of roles as part of the ASP.NET Web Pages membership system, see the 'Roles' section in Chapter 7 – Security and Membership.

Creating and Securing the Admin Folder

All of the administration pages within the site will be stored within an 'Admin' folder. We will only allow access to this folder to members of the Admin role we just created.

In the WebMatrix IDE, create a new folder called 'Admin' within the site root and to it add a new page called _PageStart.cshtml. Inside the _PageStart.cshtml file add the following code, removing any default markup:

```
@{
    if (!Roles.IsUserInRole(WebSecurity.CurrentUserName, "Admin"))
    {
        string currentUrl = Request.Url.ToString();
        Response.Redirect("~/Account/Login?sender=" + currentUrl);
    }
}
```

This code checks to see that the current user is a member of the Admin role, and returns them to the login page if they are not. By convention, the _PageStart.cshtml file will be executed before any other page in the containing folder (in our case, the 'Admin' folder), or its sub-folders, thereby securing all of our admin pages.

The Site Administration Home Page

The pages within the admin area will all use the same layout page. Let's create that page before we start to develop any pages that might rely on it.

The Admin Layout Page

Create a new page called _AdminLayout.cshtml within the Shared/Layouts folder. The page will be very similar to the layout page used for the public-facing side of the site, but will present a menu on the left hand side that facilitates navigation to the various administration pages, in place of the categories menu.

The content of the _AdminLayout.cshtml page, in its entirety, is as follows:

```
<!DOCTYPE html>

<html lang="en">
    <head>
        <meta charset="utf-8" />
        <title>TechieTogs - @Page.Title</title>
        <link href="@Href("~/Css/Style.css")" rel="stylesheet" />
        <link href="@Href("~/Css/AdminStyle.css")" rel="stylesheet" />

        @RenderSection("head", required: false)

    </head>
    <body>
        <div id="page">
```

```
        <div id="header">
            <p class="logo"><a href="@Href("~/")">TechieTogs</a></p>
            <div id="headerRight">
                <div id="accountSummary">@MembershipHelpers.AccountSummary()</div>
            </div>
        </div>
        <div id="content">
            <div id="adminMenu">
                @RenderPage("~/Shared/Partials/_AdminMenu.cshtml")
            </div>
            <div id="main">
                @RenderBody()
            </div>
        </div>
        <div id="footer">
            &copy;@DateTime.Now.Year TechieTogs. All rights reserved.
        </div>
    </div>
</body>
</html>
```

You will notice that the admin layout page requires two files that do not yet exist: `_AdminMenu.cshtml`
and `AdminStyle.css`. We'll create these files next.

The Admin Menu

The Admin Menu is simply a partial page that provides navigation to the various pages within the
administration section of the site. Create the file `_AdminMenu.cshtml` in the `Layouts/Partials` folder and
enter the following markup:

```
<p class="title">
    <a href="@Href("~/Admin/")">Site Administration</a>
</p>
<ul>
    <li><a href="@Href("~/Admin/Orders/")">Orders</a></li>
    <li><a href="@Href("~/Admin/Categories/")">Categories</a></li>
    <li><a href="@Href("~/Admin/Products/")">Products</a></li>
    <li><a href="@Href("~/Admin/Products/Featured")">Featured Product</a></li>
    <li><a href="@Href("~/Admin/Users/")">Admin Users</a></li>
</ul>
```

You can see that the admin pages will be stored within subfolders that relate to their function. We'll
create these subfolders and pages as we move through the chapter and implement the various parts of
the site administration interface.

The Admin Stylesheet

Any CSS styles that are required solely for use in the administration area of the site will be defined within a separate stylesheet. By doing this, we ensure that non-admin users do not have to download the styles required only for the administration area of the site. This saves us some page load time and bandwidth.

Create a file called `AdminStyle.css` within the `Css` folder. For ease, we will add all of the CSS we need for the administration pages here, in one go. We'll make use of these pages throughout the chapter.

Add the following CSS to `/Css/AdminStyle.css`:

```
/* General Styles
-------------------------------*/
h2 {
    width: 30%;
    border-bottom: 1px dashed #cdcdcd;
    margin: 25px 0px 20px 0px;
}

textarea {
    font-family: Verdana, Helvetica, Sans-Serif;
}

/* Menu
-------------------------------*/
#adminMenu {
    float:left;
    width:150px;
}

#adminMenu ul {
    border-bottom: 1px solid #cdcdcd;
    margin-bottom: 20px;
}

#adminMenu ul li {
    list-style: none;
    border-top: 1px solid #cdcdcd;
    margin: 0;
    padding: 10px;
}

#adminMenu ul li:hover {
    background-color: #ddd;
}

#adminMenu .title {
    margin-bottom: 20px;
    text-align:center;
    font-size: 12px;
    font-weight: bold;
```

```css
}
/* Grid
-------------------------------*/
.grid {
    margin-top: 20px;
    border-collapse: collapse;
    width: 100%;
}

.grid td {
    padding: 5px;
 }

.gridHeader {
    background-color: #fff;
    font-weight: bold;
    text-align: left;
    border-bottom: 1px solid #cdcdcd;
}

.gridAlt {
    background-color: #f7f7f7;
}

.gridFooter {
    border-top: 1px solid #cdcdcd;
}

.grid tr #mainColumn {
    width: 100%;
}

/* Forms
-------------------------------*/
#shippedForm, #deleteForm {
    margin-top: 15px;
}

#productForm
{
    float: left;
    width: 350px;
}
#productFormImage
{
    float: left;
    width: 330px;
}
```

```
#productForm label {
    font-weight: bold;
}

#productForm p {
    padding: 5px 0px 5px 0px;
}
```

The Site Administration Home Page

The Admin Home Page will be based on the `_AdminLayout.cshtml` layout page. The page itself will contain little content, although you may wish to add some content later to provide summaries of important site data, such as number of registered users, unshipped orders, overall order values, etc. This is left as an exercise for the reader.

Create a file called `Default.cshtml` inside the `Admin` folder and replace the default markup with the following:

```
@{
    Layout = "~/Shared/Layouts/_AdminLayout.cshtml";
    Page.Title = "Administration";
}

<h1>Site Administration</h1>
<p>Select an administration task from the menu.</p>
```

Now run the site, log in as the user you assigned to the 'Admin' role, and browse to the `/Admin/Default.cshtml` page. You will see the Site Administration Home Page, based on the admin layout page, including the admin menu, shown in Figure 11-3:

Figure 11-3. The Site Administration Home Page

Amending the Account Summary Helper

Although the site administrators can gain access to the Site Administration Home Page by browsing directly to the URL, it would be much better to provide them with a link after login. We'll do this by adding a new section to the Account Summary Helper, displayed in the top right hand corner of every page.

Open the App_Code/MembershipHelpers.cshtml file and add the code highlighted in bold in the following listing:

```
@helper AccountSummary()
{
    var cartItemCount = 0;

    if (Session["cart"] != null)
    {
        cartItemCount = ((Cart)Session["cart"]).Items.Count;
    }

    if(WebSecurity.IsAuthenticated) {
        <text>
            @Gravatar.GetHtml(WebSecurity.CurrentUserName,
                              imageSize:24,
                              defaultImage:"mm")

            Welcome <a href="@Href("~/Account/ChangePassword")">
                      @WebSecurity.CurrentUserName
                  </a> |
            <a href="@Href("~/Cart")">Cart - @cartItemCount item(s)</a> |
            <a href="@Href("~/Account/Logout")">Logout</a>
            @if (Roles.IsUserInRole(WebSecurity.CurrentUserName, "Admin"))
            {
                <text>
                    | <a href="@Href("~/Admin/Default")">Admin</a>
                </text>
            }
        </text>
    } else {
        <text>
            <a href="@Href("~/Account/Login")">Login</a> |
            <a href="@Href("~/Cart")">Cart - @cartItemCount item(s)</a> |
            <a href="@Href("~/Account/Register")">Register</a>
        </text>
    }
}
```

This new section of code displays an additional hyperlink in the account summary, providing a link to the Site Administration Home Page for authenticated users who are members of the Admin role (see Figure 11-4).

Figure 11-4. *The Account Summary Helper showing the 'Admin' hyperlink*

User Administration

Now that we have the infrastructure in place for the secure admin area of our site, we'll need a way to add users to, and remove existing users from, the Admin role.

Create a new subfolder within the admin folder called 'Users', and within it a page called `Default.cshtml`.

This page will list all current Admin role members, with a button to remove them from the role, and provide a form to allow new members to be added. Figure 11-5 shows the completed page:

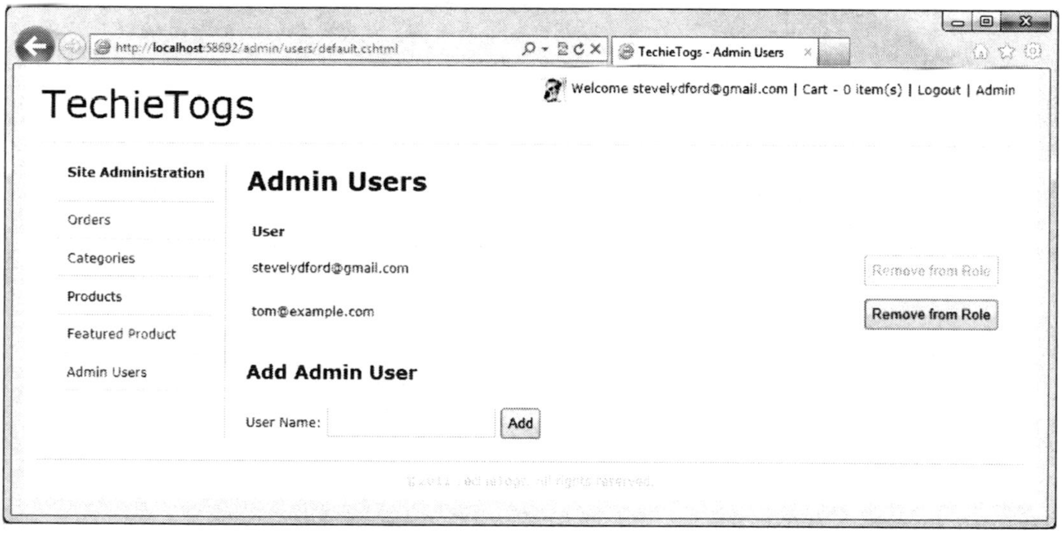

Figure 11-5. *The Admin Users page*

Replace any existing markup within the `Admin/Users/Default.cshtml` page with the following:

```
@{
    Layout = "~/Shared/Layouts/_AdminLayout.cshtml";
    Page.Title = "Admin Users";

    var userToAdd = "";
```

```
    var role = "Admin";

    if(IsPost)
    {
        userToAdd = Request["userToAdd"];

        if(userToAdd != null)
        {
            // Add User to Role
            if (WebSecurity.UserExists(userToAdd) &&
                !Roles.IsUserInRole(userToAdd, role))
            {
                Roles.AddUsersToRoles(
                    new [] { userToAdd }.ToArray(),
                    new [] { role }.ToArray()
                );
            }
            else
            {
                ModelState.AddError("userToAdd", "Unable to add user");
            }
        }
        else if (Request["userToRemove"] != null)
        {
            // Remove User from Role

            var userToRemove = Request["userToRemove"];
            if (Roles.IsUserInRole(userToRemove, role))
            {
                Roles.RemoveUsersFromRoles(
                    new [] { userToRemove }.ToArray(),
                    new [] { role }.ToArray()
                );
            }
        }
    }

    var users = Roles.GetUsersInRole(role);
}

<h1>Admin Users</h1>

<table class="grid">
    <tr>
        <th colspan="3" class="gridHeader">User</th>
    </tr>
    @foreach (var user in users)
    {
        <tr>
```

```
            <td id="mainColumn">
                @user
            </td>
            <td>
                @{
                    var buttonState = "";
                    if(user == WebSecurity.CurrentUserName)
                    {
                        buttonState = "disabled=disabled";
                    }
                }
                <form action="" method="post">
                    @Html.Hidden("userToRemove", user)
                    <input type="submit" value="Remove from Role" @buttonState />
                </form>

            </td>
        </tr>
    }
</table>

<h2>Add Admin User</h2>
<form action="" method="post">
    <p>
        User Name:
        @Html.TextBox("userToAdd", userToAdd)
        <input type="submit" value="Add" />
        @Html.ValidationMessage("userToAdd")
    </p>
</form>
```

The POST request handler checks to see if a userToAdd field has been passed back in the posted form values. If it has, we know that the user has submitted the 'Add Admin User' form, so we attempt to add the user to the role. Otherwise, if a userToRemove field has been submitted, we know that the user clicked a 'Remove from Role' button, so we attempt to remove the relevant user. We have used a mechanism similar to this before, on the Shopping Cart page.

▓ **Note** For an explanation of the methods used to add and remove role members, see the 'Roles' section in Chapter 7 – Security and Membership.

There are two further points of interest on this page. First, we disable the remove button in the row containing the currently authenticated user. Although not foolproof, this will at least help to ensure that at least one user can always gain access to the administrative section of the site.

Second, we require the user to actually type in the user name of the account they wish to add to the Admin role, even though we could easily have provided a dropdown list of registered users. This approach would be fine while the site has a small number of users, but when the site goes live and starts to dominate the worldwide ecommerce marketplace, as we expect it to do, we would soon have page loading issues when we are trying to load thousands of user names in to a dropdown list. A good solution to this, although beyond the scope of this book, would be to implement an auto-complete textbox using AJAX.

Orders Administration

We'll need an area on our site where we can view customers' orders and mark them as shipped. The Orders Administration process will consist of two pages. The first page will list a summary of all orders in a WebGrid. Each row in the WebGrid will display a hyperlink to take the user to the second page, which displays the complete details of the order.

We'll start by creating the Orders Summary page.

The Orders Summary Page

We will use the WebGrid helper to display the summary of orders, as it gives us the ability to easily add paging and sorting functionality to the grid. We will also include a small form above the grid to allow the user the choice to view either shipped or unshipped orders. Figure 11-6 shows the completed Order Summary page:

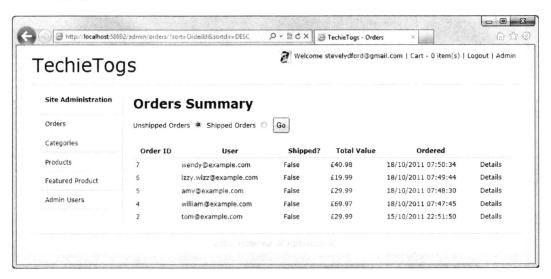

Figure 11-6. The Order Summary Page

To create the page in your site, add a new subfolder called 'Orders' within the 'Admin' folder and add a page inside it called Default.cshtml. The following listing contains the complete code and markup for Admin/Orders/Default.cshtml:

```
@{
    Layout = "~/Shared/Layouts/_AdminLayout.cshtml";
    Page.Title = "Orders";

    var showShippedOrders = false;

    if(IsPost)
    {
        showShippedOrders = Request["showShippedOrders"].AsBool();
    }

    var db = Database.Open("TechieTogsData");
    var sqlCommand = "SELECT Orders.OrderId, Orders.OrderShipped, Orders.OrderTotal, " +
                     "Orders.OrderDateTime, UserProfile.Email FROM Orders " +
                     "INNER JOIN UserProfile ON Orders.UserId = UserProfile.UserId " +
                     "WHERE OrderShipped = @0 " +
                     "ORDER BY OrderDateTime DESC";

    var result = db.Query(sqlCommand, showShippedOrders);

    var ordersGrid = new WebGrid(source: result,
                                 rowsPerPage: 20);

}

<h1>Orders Summary</h1>
<form action="Default" method="post">
    <p>
        Unshipped Orders @Html.RadioButton("showShippedOrders", "false", !showShippedOrders)
        Shipped Orders @Html.RadioButton("showShippedOrders", "true", showShippedOrders)
        <input type="submit" value="Go"/>
    </p>
</form>
<div class="grid">
    @ordersGrid.GetHtml(
        tableStyle: "grid",
        headerStyle: "gridHeader",
        alternatingRowStyle: "gridAlt",
        footerStyle: "gridFooter",
        columns: ordersGrid.Columns(
            ordersGrid.Column("OrderId",
                              "Order ID"),
            ordersGrid.Column("Email",
                              "User",
                              format: @<text>
```

389

```
                                        <a href="mailto:@item.Email">
                                                @item.Email
                                        </a>
                                    </text>),
        ordersGrid.Column("OrderShipped",
                        "Shipped?"),
        ordersGrid.Column("OrderTotal",
                        "Total Value",
                        format: @<text>
                                        £@item.OrderTotal
                                </text>),
        ordersGrid.Column("OrderDateTime",
                        "Ordered"),
        ordersGrid.Column(null,
                        null,
                        format: @<text>
                                        <a href="OrderDetails/@item.OrderId">
                                            Details
                                        </a>
                                    </text>)
        )
    )
</div>
```

Looking through the code, you can see that the SQL statement to get the data for the WebGrid contains an INNER JOIN between the Orders and UserProfile tables. This allows us to retrieve the user name (Email) of the user, based on the UserId stored against each order.

The WHERE clause of the SQL statement filters the results based on the OrderShipped column. By default this is set to False, but is changed to the value of the radio button group on post back.

The body of the page under the form contains our WebGrid, which is populated from the results of the SQL query mentioned previously. The grid is fairly standard, except that the last column is not bound to a data column but instead displays a hyperlink to the Order Details page, passing the OrderId in the URL.

■ **Note** A full explanation of the WebGrid helper and its use can be found in Chapter 6 – Working with Data, in the 'Displaying Data with WebMatrix Helpers' section.

The Order Details Page

The Order Details page displays the comprehensive details of any specific order, including the date and time of order, shipping details, details of all items within the order, and shipping status.

The page includes an 'Order Shipped?' checkbox, which the administrator can check to say that the order has been dispatched. This will set the OrderShipped field to true, which will place it onto the 'Shipped Orders' list on the Order Summary page.

Create a new page called `OrderDetails.cshtml` in the `Admin/Orders` folder and enter the following code, in place of the default markup generated by WebMatrix when the page was created:

```
@{
    Layout = "~/Shared/Layouts/_AdminLayout.cshtml";
    Page.Title = "Order Details";

    // Get orderID from URL, or set to 0 if not present
    var orderID = !UrlData[0].IsEmpty() ? UrlData[0] : "0";

    var db = Database.Open("TechieTogsData");

    if (IsPost)
    {
        orderID = Request["orderID"];
        var shipped = Request["shipped"].AsBool();

        var sqlUpdate = "UPDATE Orders SET OrderShipped = @0 WHFRF OrderId - @1";
        db.Execute(sqlUpdate, shipped, orderID);

        Response.Redirect("~/Admin/Orders/");
    }

    // Get Order header details
    var sqlCommand = "SELECT Orders.*, UserProfile.Email FROM Orders " +
                     "INNER JOIN UserProfile ON Orders.UserId = UserProfile.UserId " +
                     "WHERE OrderId = @0 ";

    var order = db.QuerySingle(sqlCommand, orderID);

    // Get Order items
    var itemsSql = "SELECT * FROM OrderItems WHERE OrderID = @0";
    var orderItems = db.Query(itemsSql, orderID);

}

@if (order == null)
{
    <p>
        Unable to fetch order details.
    </p>
}
else
{
    <text>
        <h1>Order Details</h1>
        <p><strong>Order ID:</strong> @order.OrderId</p>
        <p><strong>User:</strong> <a href="mailto:@order.Email">@order.Email</a></p>
```

```
        <p><strong>Ordered: </strong>@order.OrderDateTime</p>

        <h2>Shipping Details</h2>
        <p><strong>Address 1:</strong> @order.Address1</p>
        <p><strong>Address 2:</strong> @order.Address2</p>
        <p><strong>Town: </strong>@order.Town</p>
        <p><strong>Region:</strong> @order.Region</p>
        <p><strong>Postal Code:</strong> @order.PostalCode</p>
        <p><strong>Country: </strong>@order.Country</p>
        <p>
            <form action="OrderDetails" method="post" id="shippedForm">
                @Html.Hidden("orderId", order.OrderId)
                    Order Shipped?
                    @Html.CheckBox("shipped", order.OrderShipped, new { value = "true" })
                    <input type="submit" value="Update" />
            </form>
        </p>
        <h2>Order Items</h2>
        <table id="cartTable">
            <tr>
                <th class="product">Product</th>
                <th class="size">Size</th>
                <th class="price">Price</th>
            </tr>

            @foreach (var item in orderItems)
            {
                <tr>
                    <td class="product">@Products.GetProductNameFromId(item.ProductID)</td>
                    <td class="size">@item.Size</td>
                    <td class="price">£@item.Price</td>
                </tr>
            }

            <tr class="cartTotal">
                <td colspan="2"> </td>
                <td>Total: £@order.OrderTotal</td>
            </tr>
        </table>
    </text>
}
```

When the page initially loads, the `OrderId` is retrieved from the URL and two database queries are run. The first query populates the top half of the page, including the Shipping Details section. The second query retrieves all of the individual items that form part of the order and is iterated over to produce the Order Items section at the bottom of the page.

If the user checks the 'Order Shipped?' checkbox and clicks the 'Update' button, the value of the `Orders.OrderShipped` field in the database is updated to reflect the value of the checkbox and the user is returned to the Orders Summary page. When performing this action, you will note that the order is now listed only under the "Shipped Orders" list on the Orders Summary page.

Figure 11-7 shows the completed Order Details page:

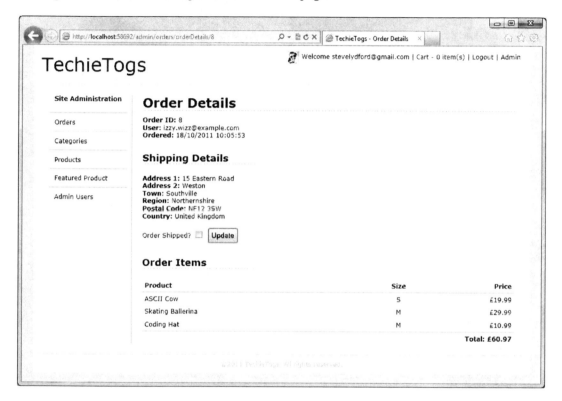

Figure 11-7. *The Order Details page*

Product Categories

The products within the TechieTogs catalog are organized into categories. All products must be assigned to a category.

The product categories are stored within the `Categories` table of our database and are used to dynamically build the menu (`Shared/Partials/_Categories.cshtml`) seen on the left hand side of every page of the public-facing side of the site.

Clearly we need a way to add, edit, and delete items from the `Categories` table so that we can keep the product catalog well organized. Therefore, add a new subfolder called `Categories` within the main Admin folder and inside it create a new page called `Default.cshtml`. This page will be used to list all of the categories in the table and will allow administrators to add a new category record (see Figure 11-8).

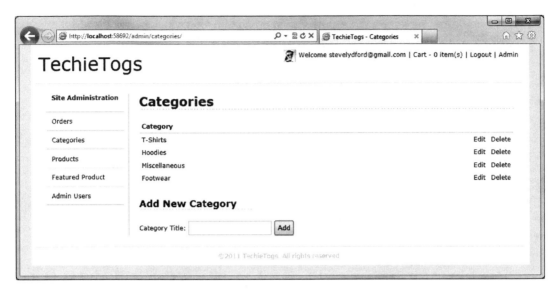

Figure 11-8. *The Categories administration default page*

The complete listing for the `Admin/Categories/Default.cshtml` page is as follows:

```
@{
    Layout = "~/Shared/Layouts/_AdminLayout.cshtml";
    Page.Title = "Categories";

    var categoryTitle = "";

    var db = Database.Open("TechieTogsData");

    if(IsPost && !Request["categoryTitle"].IsEmpty())
    {
        categoryTitle = Request["categoryTitle"];
        if(!Admin.CategoryExists(categoryTitle))
        {
            var sqlInsert = "INSERT INTO Categories (CategoryTitle) VALUES (@0)";
            db.Execute(sqlInsert, categoryTitle);
        }
        else
        {
            ModelState.AddError("categoryTitle", "Category already exists");
        }
    }

    var sqlCommand = "SELECT * FROM Categories";
    var categories = db.Query(sqlCommand);
```

```
}

<h1>Categories</h1>

<table class="grid">
    <tr>
        <th colspan="3" class="gridHeader">Category</th>
    </tr>
    @foreach (var category in categories)
    {
        <tr>
            <td id="mainColumn">
                @category.categoryTitle
            </td>
            <td>
                <a href="EditCategory/@category.categoryId">Edit</a>
            </td>
            <td>
                <a href="DeleteCategory/@category.categoryId">Delete</a>
            </td>
        </tr>
    }
</table>

<h2>Add New Category</h2>
<form action="" method="post">
    <p>
        Category Title:
        @Html.TextBox("categoryTitle", categoryTitle)
        <input type="submit" value="Add" />
        @Html.ValidationMessage("categoryTitle")
    </p>
</form>
```

On its initial load, the page retrieves all of the categories from the database and displays them in a table, with two links next to each category to send the user to the Edit and Delete pages.

Underneath the list of categories, an HTML form is displayed to allow the user to add a new item into the Categories table.

When this form is posted back to the server, the `Admin.CategoryExists()` method is called to ensure that no duplicate categories are created. If the method returns `false`, the record is inserted into the `Categories` table and the page displayed again. If the category already exists, an error is added to the `ModelStateDictionary`, to be displayed to the user via a call to the `Html.ValidationMessage()` helper method in the Add New Category form.

The `Admin.CategoryExists()` method is a custom Razor function that we will create. We are creating it as a function, rather than just adding the code directly into the page, as we will want to call the same code again later from the Edit Categories page. Yet again, we are doing our best to stay DRY!

Add a new file called `Admin.cshtml` inside the site's `App_Code` folder. Replace any existing content within the file with the following Razor function:

395

```
@* Admin Functions *@
@functions {

    public static bool CategoryExists(string categoryTitle)
    {
        var db = Database.Open("TechieTogsData");
        var sqlQuery = "SELECT categoryID FROM Categories WHERE categoryTitle = @0";
        return db.Query(sqlQuery, categoryTitle).Count() > 0;
    }

}
```

You can see here that the CategoryExists() method simply accepts a string parameter, categoryTitle, and returns a Boolean. The value of the categoryTitle parameter is searched for in the database; if no rows are returned, the method returns false.

Editing Categories

The Edit Category page simply displays a textbox to allow an administrator to change the title of a category. The code within the post request handler is very similar to that of the default Categories page. When the form is posted back, we call the Admin.CategoryExists() Razor function to ensure that no duplicate categories will be created, before submitting the update query to the database. Note that the call to the Admin.CategoryExists() function is not case sensitive.

Add a new file at Admin/Categories/EditCategory.cshtml and replace the auto-generated content with the following code and markup:

```
@{
    Layout = "~/Shared/Layouts/_AdminLayout.cshtml";
    Page.Title = "Edit Category";

    // Get categoryId from URL, or set to 0 if not present
    var categoryId = !UrlData[0].IsEmpty() ? UrlData[0] : "0";
    var categoryTitle = "";

    var db = Database.Open("TechieTogsData");

    if(IsPost)
    {
        categoryId = Request["categoryId"];
        categoryTitle = Request["categoryTitle"];

        // Validation
        if (categoryTitle.IsEmpty())
        {
            ModelState.AddError("categoryTitle", "Category Title cannot be blank");
        }

        if(Admin.CategoryExists(categoryTitle))
```

```
        {
            ModelState.AddError("categoryTitle", "Category already exists");
        }

        if(ModelState.IsValid)
        {
            var sqlUpdate = "UPDATE Categories SET CategoryTitle = @0 WHERE CategoryId = @1";
            db.Execute(sqlUpdate, categoryTitle, categoryId);

            Response.Redirect("~/Admin/Categories/");
        }
    }
    else
    {
            var sqlCommand = "SELECT * FROM Categories WHERE CategoryID = @0";
            categoryTitle = db.QuerySingle(sqlCommand, categoryId).CategoryTitle;
    }

}

<h1>Edit Category</h1>

<form action="" method="post">
    <p>
        Category Title:
        @Html.Hidden("categoryId", categoryId)
        @Html.TextBox("categoryTitle", categoryTitle)
        <input type="submit" value="Update" />
        @Html.ValidationMessage("categoryTitle")
    </p>
</form>
```

Deleting Categories

When deleting categories, we need to be careful that we do not delete any category that has products currently associated with it. The code for this page is fairly simple and calls a helper function to ensure that the category is empty before we carry out the delete. The delete is executed on the database using the CategoryId passed in the URL from the Categories page.

When users first land on the Delete Category page, and if the category is empty, they are presented with a confirmation message and two buttons. One of these buttons submits the form (i.e., to proceed with the deletion), which is then processed by the post request handler in the code block at the top of the page. The second button is a 'Cancel' button, which uses JavaScript in the onclick attribute to send the user directly back to the Categories page without submitting the form. The Delete Category page is shown in Figure 11-9:

Figure 11-9. *The Delete Category page*

If the user lands on the page and the category is not empty, a message is displayed to the user to say that the category cannot be deleted as it has associated products.

Add a new file called DeleteCategory.cshtml to the Admin/Categories folder and replace any existing markup with the following code:

```
@{
    Layout = "~/Shared/Layouts/_AdminLayout.cshtml";
    Page.Title = "Delete Category";

    var categoryId = UrlData[0];
    if (categoryId.IsEmpty()) {
        Response.Redirect("~/Admin/Categories/");
    }

    var db = Database.Open("TechieTogsData");

    if (IsPost)
    {
        var sqlDelete = "DELETE FROM Categories WHERE CategoryId = @0";
        db.Execute(sqlDelete, categoryId);
        Response.Redirect("~/Admin/Categories/");
    }

    var sqlSelect = "SELECT * FROM Categories WHERE categoryId = @0";
    var category = db.QuerySingle(sqlSelect, categoryId);
}

<h1>Delete Category</h1>
```

```
@if (!Admin.CategoryIsEmpty(categoryId))
{
    <p>
        Unable to delete the @category.CategoryTitle category as it has associated products.
    </p>
}
else
{
    <p>
        Are you sure you want to delete the @category.CategoryTitle category?
    </p>
    <p style="margin:">
        <form action="" method="post" id="deleteForm">
            <input type="button"
                onclick="window.location = '@Href("~/Admin/Categories/")';"
                value="Cancel" />
            <input type="submit" value="Delete" />
        </form>
    </p>
}
```

As mentioned previously, the page calls a custom Razor function that checks that the category is empty before deletion. This function must now be added within the App_Code/Admin.cshtml page, which we created earlier to contain our CategoryExists() method. Open the App_Code/Admin.cshtml file and insert the function highlighted in bold in the following code sample:

```
@* Admin Functions *@
@functions {

    public static bool CategoryExists(string categoryTitle)
    {
        var db = Database.Open("TechieTogsData");
        var sqlQuery = "SELECT categoryID FROM Categories WHERE categoryTitle = @0";
        return db.Query(sqlQuery, categoryTitle).Count() > 0;
    }

    public static bool CategoryIsEmpty(string categoryId)
    {
        var db = Database.Open("TechieTogsData");
        var sqlQuery = "SELECT ProductID FROM Products WHERE category = @0";
        return db.Query(sqlQuery, categoryId).Count() == 0;
    }

}
```

This method simply queries the database for products within the specified category and returns true if no matching records are found.

Product Administration

As the product catalog is generated entirely dynamically from the TechieTogsData database, we will need to provide facilities to administer it.

The Product Administration part of our site will consist of two pages. The first page will list a summary of all products within the catalog, showing the product ID, title, and category. Alongside each product will be a link to the second page, which will display the product details in full, enabling the user to update them. The Products Summary page will also display a link to allow the user to add a new product to the catalog.

The Products Summary Page

The Products Summary page presents a list of all of the products held within the database. For this task we will use the WebGrid helper, which gives us built-in sorting and paging functionality.

Figure 11-10 shows the Products Summary page running in the browser:

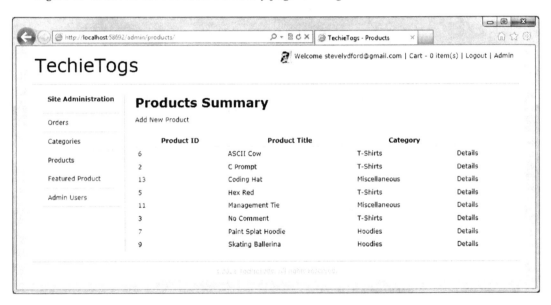

Figure 11-10. The Products Summary page

The page is straightforward and requires little explanation, so go ahead and create a new `Products` subfolder within the main `Admin` folder and add to it a new file called `Default.cshtml`. The following listing shows the complete code for the `Admin/Products/Default.cshtml` page:

```
@{
    Layout = "~/Shared/Layouts/_AdminLayout.cshtml";
    Page.Title = "Products";
```

```
    var db = Database.Open("TechieTogsData");
    var sqlCommand = "SELECT Products.ProductId, Products.Title, Categories.CategoryTitle " +
                     "FROM Products " +
                     "INNER JOIN Categories ON Products.Category = Categories.CategoryId " +
                     "ORDER BY title";

    var result = db.Query(sqlCommand);

    var productsGrid = new WebGrid(source: result,
                                   rowsPerPage: 20);
}

<h1>Products Summary</h1>
<a href="productDetails">Add New Product</a>
<div class="grid">
    @productsGrid.GetHtml(
        tableStyle: "grid",
        headerStyle: "gridHeader",
        alternatingRowStyle: "gridAlt",
        footerStyle: "gridFooter",
        columns: productsGrid.Columns(
            productsGrid.Column("ProductId",
                                "Product ID"),
            productsGrid.Column("Title",
                                "Product Title"),
            productsGrid.Column("CategoryTitle",
                                "Category"),
            productsGrid.Column(null,
                                null,
                                format: @<text>
                                            <a href="ProductDetails/@item.ProductId">
                                                Details
                                            </a>
                                        </text>)
        )
    )
</div>
```

You will no doubt have noticed that the 'Add New Product' link points to the same page as the individual product details links. This is done intentionally so that we can use the same page for both tasks, as the UI is identical. We'll deal with the Product Details page next.

The Product Details Page

The Product Details page will be used to create new products and edit existing products. If a Product ID is passed in the UrlData, the product details are retrieved from the database and the form is populated. If no Product ID is present in the URL, an empty form is displayed to allow the creation of a new product.

If we are to create a new product, we store the value "new" in the productID hidden field. This enables us to identify it as a new product in the post request handler and to perform a SQL INSERT command, rather than an UPDATE.

Create a new file called ProductDetails.cshtml in the Admin/Products folder and replace any existing content with the following code:

```
@{
    Layout = "~/Shared/Layouts/_AdminLayout.cshtml";
    Page.Title = "Edit Category";

    var productId = "new";
    var title = "";
    var price = "";
    var description = "";
    var keywords = "";
    var category = "";

    var db = Database.Open("TechieTogsData");

    // Retrieve product details associated to the Product ID passed in the URL
    if (!UrlData[0].IsEmpty())
    {
        productId = UrlData[0];

        var sqlCommand = "SELECT * FROM Products WHERE productID = @0";
        var product = db.QuerySingle(sqlCommand, productId);

        title = product.title;
        price = product.price.ToString();
        description = product.description;
        keywords = product.keywords;
        category = product.category.ToString();
    }

    if(IsPost)
    {
        productId = Request["productId"];
        title = Request["title"];
        price = Request["price"];
        description = Request["description"];
        keywords = Request["keywords"];
        category = Request["category"];

        // Validation
```

```
        if (title.IsEmpty())
        {
            ModelState.AddError("title", "Product Title cannot be blank");
        }

        if (price.IsEmpty())
        {
            ModelState.AddError("price", "Price is required");
        }

        if (description.IsEmpty())
        {
            ModelState.AddError("description", "Description cannot be blank");
        }

        if(ModelState.IsValid)
        {
            var sql = "";
            if (productId == "new")
            {
                // Insert new product record
                sql = "INSERT INTO Products (title, price, description, " +
                        "keywords, category) VALUES (@0, @1, @2, @3, @4)";
            }
            else
            {
                // Update existing product record
                sql = "UPDATE Products SET title = @0, price = @1, " +
                        "description = @2, keywords = @3, category = @4 " +
                        "WHERE productId = @5";
            }

            db.Execute(sql, title, price, description,
                        keywords, category, productId);

            Response.Redirect("~/Admin/Products/");
        }
    }
}

}

<h1>Product Details</h1>

<div id="productForm">
    <form action="" method="post">
        <p>
            @Html.Hidden("productId", productId)
            @Html.Label("Title:", title)<br />
            @Html.TextBox("title", title)
```

```
            @Html.ValidationMessage("title")
        </p>
        <p>
            @Html.Label("Price:", price)<br />
            @Html.TextBox("price", price, new { @class="short" })
            @Html.ValidationMessage("price")
        </p>
        <p>
            @Html.Label("Description:", description)<br />
            @Html.TextArea("description", description, 10, 40, null)
            @Html.ValidationMessage("description")
        </p>
        <p>
            @Html.Label("Keywords:", keywords)<br />
            @Html.TextBox("keywords", keywords)
        </p>
        <p>
            @Html.Label("Category:", category)<br />
            @Products.CategoriesDropDownList("category", category)
        </p>
        <p>
            <input type="submit" value="Update" />
        </p>
    </form>
</div>
```

This page uses a helper, `Products.CategoriesDropDownList()`, to display a dropdown list of categories. Add the following helper code to the App_Code/Products.cshtml file we created earlier:

```
@helper CategoriesDropDownList(string name, string selectedValue)
{
    var optionList = new List<SelectListItem>();
    var db = Database.Open("TechieTogsData");

    var sqlCommand = "SELECT categoryId, categoryTitle FROM Categories " +
                    "ORDER BY categoryTitle";
    var result = db.Query(sqlCommand);

    foreach(var item in result)
    {
        optionList.Add(new SelectListItem { Value = item.categoryId.ToString(),
                                            Text = item.categoryTitle });
    }

    @Html.DropDownList(name, null , optionList, selectedValue, null)
}
```

This helper retrieves a list of categories from the database and uses it to output an HTML `<select>` control. The name of the `<select>` control and the item selected within it are set by the parameter values.

The completed Product Details page is shown here in Figure 11-11:

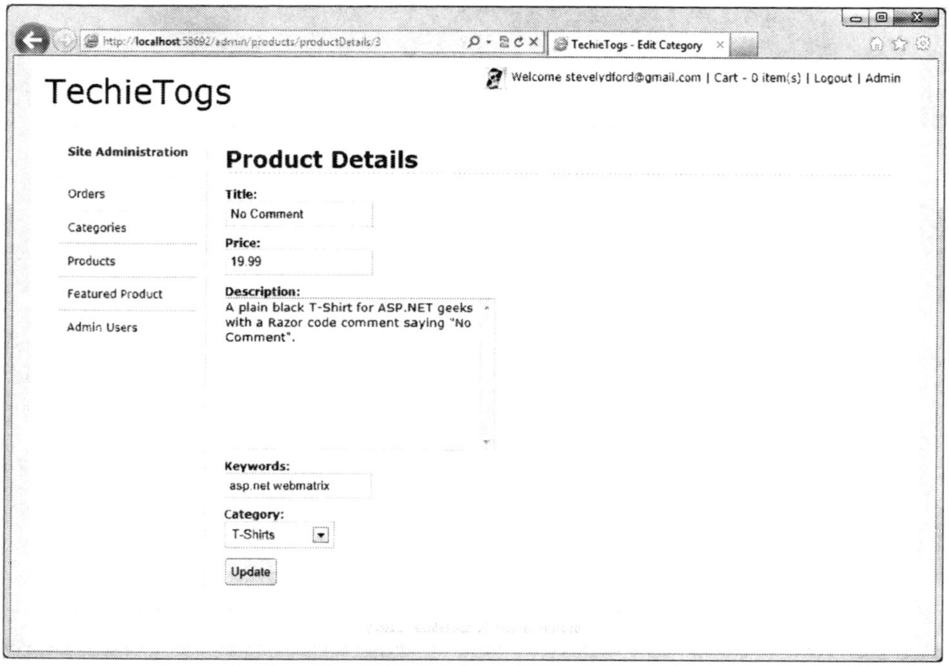

Figure 11-11. *The Product Details page*

Adding Product Images

Our product catalog is complete and works well, but it we are much more likely to sell products if customers can see an image of the product before they buy. In this section, we'll amend the Product Details administration page to allow site administrators to upload a picture of the product. We'll then display thumbnails of the product image in the catalog, with a full-size image on the Product Details page.

Let's make the changes to the Product Details administration page first, to give the site administrator the option of uploading a product image.

Open the `Admin/Products/ProductDetails.cshtml` page we created earlier and make the changes to the body of the page, shown in bold in the following listing:

```
<h1>Product Details</h1>
<div id="productForm">
    <form action="" method="post" enctype="multipart/form-data">
        <p>
            @Html.Hidden("productId", productId)
            @Html.Label("Title:", title)<br />
```

405

```
        @Html.TextBox("title", title)
        @Html.ValidationMessage("title")
    </p>
    <p>
        @Html.Label("Price:", price)<br />
        @Html.TextBox("price", price, new { @class="short" })
        @Html.ValidationMessage("price")
    </p>
    <p>
        @Html.Label("Description:", description)<br />
        @Html.TextArea("description", description, 10, 40, null)
        @Html.ValidationMessage("description")
    </p>
    <p>
        @Html.Label("Keywords:", keywords)<br />
        @Html.TextBox("keywords", keywords)
    </p>
    <p>
        @Html.Label("Category:", category)<br />
        @Products.CategoriesDropDownList("category", category)
    </p>
    <p>
        @Html.Label("Product Image:", "productImage")<br />
        <input type="file" name="productImage" />
    </p>
    <p>
        <input type="submit" value="Update" />
    </p>
    </form>
</div>
```

The first change is to insert the enctype="multipart/form-data" attribute into the <form> tag. The addition of this attribute is necessary to be able to gather the file information submitted in the file control.

The other change to the page is the addition of a file input control. This will present the user with the UI necessary to select a file from their local file system for upload.

We will store the uploaded files in a folder in the site root called ProductImages, which you should create now. Next we'll add some code to the post request handling code to grab the file from the user's machine and upload it into this folder. Make the following changes seen in bold type:

■ **Note** When deploying this site to a public-facing server, you may have to alter the default permissions of the ProductImages folder to allow write access. Your system administrator or web hosting provider will be able to help you with this.

```
if(IsPost)
{
    productId = Request["productId"];
    title = Request["title"];
    price = Request["price"];
    description = Request["description"];
    keywords = Request["keywords"];
    category = Request["category"];

    // Validation
    if (title.IsEmpty())
    {
        ModelState.AddError("title", "Product Title cannot be blank");
    }

    if (price.IsEmpty())
    {
        ModelState.AddError("price", "Price is required");
    }

    if (description.IsEmpty())
    {
        ModelState.AddError("description", "Description cannot be blank");
    }

    if(ModelState.IsValid)
    {
        var sql = "";
        if (productId == "new")
        {
            // Insert new product record
            sql = "INSERT INTO Products (title, price, description, " +
                "keywords, category) VALUES (@0, @1, @2, @3, @4)";

            db.Execute(sql, title, price, description,
                    keywords, category, productId);

            productId = db.GetLastInsertId().ToString();
        }
        else
        {
            // Update existing product record
            sql = "UPDATE Products SET title = @0, price = @1, " +
                "description = @2, keywords = @3, category = @4 " +
                "WHERE productId = @5";

            db.Execute(sql, title, price, description,
                    keywords, category, productId);
        }
```

```
    // Product image
    var productImage = WebImage.GetImageFromRequest();
    if(productImage != null)
    {
        // Save main product image
        var savePath = @"~\ProductImages\" + productId;
        productImage.Save(filePath: savePath + ".png",
                          imageFormat: "png",
                          forceCorrectExtension: true );

        // Resize and save thumbnail
        productImage.Resize(height: 120, width: 120,
                          preserveAspectRatio: true);
        productImage.Save(filePath: savePath + "_thumb.png",
                          imageFormat: "png",
                          forceCorrectExtension: true );
    }
    Response.Redirect("~/Admin/Products/");
}
}
```

In this code, we make use of the WebImage helper to process and upload the image file.

■ **Note** A full explanation of the WebImage helper and its use can be found in Chapter 12 – Additional Techniques and Features.

First, if this is a new product, we need to get the ID of the product inserted using the Database.GetLastInsertId() method. This is necessary because we will be using the Product ID to create the file name that we are going to use to store the images in the productImages folder.

We then use the WebImage.GetImageFromRequest() method to retrieve the image, whose path is passed in via the file control, from the user's local file system. We then construct the path and file name we wish to use to store the file on our web server. In our case, we are going to store all of the images in the ProductImages folder, using the Product ID as the filename, which will ensure that each file name is unique. The call to the Save() method stores the file at the specified path, with the imageFormat parameter telling the WebImage helper to save the image file in the Portable Network Graphics (PNG) format, regardless of the format of the original image.

We want to display thumbnail images in the product catalog. Rather than asking the user to provide an additional thumbnail image, we use the WebImage.Resize() method to produce a thumbnail from the uploaded product image. When the Resize() method is called, we specify maximum width and height and set the preserveAspectRatio parameter to true, to ensure that the aspect ratio of the original image is maintained. Finally, we save the thumbnail, appending "_thumb" to the Product ID to produce the file name.

Displaying Product Images

When it comes to displaying the image on the page, we could simply point an HTML `<img>` tag at the uploaded image in the `ProductImages` folder. However, if for any reason a product image has not been uploaded, the browser will display an ugly "missing image" graphic, such as the one seen in Figure 11-12 displayed by Internet Explorer:

Figure 11-12. A missing image, as seen in Internet Explorer 9

Obviously, this behavior is not desirable, so we'll write some code to display a default image wherever a specific product image is not available. In the interest of code reuse, we'll implement this code inside a helper method so that we can make use of it wherever we want to display a product image in the application.

Open the file at `App_Code/Products.cshtml` and insert the following helper method, called `ShowProductImage()` at the bottom of the file:

```
@helper ShowProductImage(string productId)
{
    var imagePath = @"~/ProductImages/" + productId + ".png";
    if (!File.Exists(Server.MapPath(imagePath)))
    {
        imagePath = "~/ProductImages/noImage.png";
    }
    <img src="@Href(imagePath)" alt="Product Image"/>
}
```

This product uses the .NET `File.Exists()` method to determine the existence of a product image matching the Product ID. The `Server.MapPath()` method is used to map the specified URL to the corresponding physical directory on the server.

■ **Note** More information on the File.Exists() and Server.MapPath() methods can be found on the following two pages of the MSDN web site:

http://msdn.microsoft.com/en-us/library/system.io.file.exists.aspx

http://msdn.microsoft.com/en-us/library/system.web.httpserverutility.mappath.aspx

If the requested image file can be found, it is displayed using an HTML `<img>` tag. If the relevant image file does not exist, a default image, `noImage.png`, which we you should create and store in the `ProductImages` folder, will be displayed.

The first page we will change to display our product image is `/Admin/Products/ProductDetails.cshtml`. Add the following `<div>` and method call to the bottom of the page:

```
<div id="productFormImage">
    @Products.ShowProductImage(productId)
</div>
```

Now, when we visit the Product Details administration page for a product that does not yet have an associated image, we will see the following (see Figure 11-13):

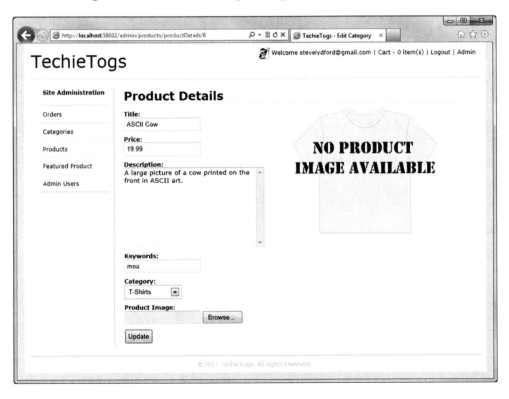

Figure 11-13. The Product Details administration page showing a product that has no associated image

Now we'll upload an image and move on to make amendments to the Product Details page within the catalog to display the image to the user.

Open the `ProductDetails.cshtml` page in the root of the site and add the following highlighted paragraph and method call within the `productDetails` `<div>`:

```
<div id="productDetails">
    <p class="price">
        £@product.price
    </p>
    <p>@Products.ShowProductImage(productID)</p>
    <p>@product.description</p>
</div>
```

Now, when we run the page and browse to the Product Details page of a product with an uploaded image, we will see the image rendered in the browser (see Figure 11-14):

Figure 11-14. *The Product Details page of the catalog showing a product image*

Finally, we want to display the thumbnail images that we have created on the products summary page of the catalog. For this, we will need to add the following `ShowProductThumbnail()` helper method to the bottom of the `App_Code/Products.cshtml` file:

```
@helper ShowProductThumbnail(string productId)
{
    var imagePath = @"~/ProductImages/" + productId + "_thumb.png";
```

411

```
    if (!File.Exists(Server.MapPath(imagePath)))
    {
        imagePath = "~/ProductImages/noThumb.png";
    }
    <img src="@Href(imagePath)" alt="Product Image"/>
}
```

This method works in exactly the same way as the `ShowProductImage()` helper that we created earlier, except that it displays the product thumbnail.

Amend the unordered list, populated with a `foreach` loop, in the `Products.cshtml` file in the site root folder to include the method call to `ShowProductThumbnail()`, as highlighted in the following listing:

```
<ul id="productsList">
    @foreach (var item in products) {
        <li>
            <h3>
                <a href="/ProductDetails/@item.productID">@item.title</a>
            </h3>
            <p>
                @Products.ShowProductThumbnail(item.productID.ToString())
            </p>
            <p class="price">
                £@item.price
            </p>
            <p>
                <a href="/ProductDetails/@item.productID" class="detailsButton">
                    More Details
                </a>
            </p>
        </li>
    }
</ul>
```

Now, when we run the site and browse to a category, the product thumbnails will be displayed in the catalog (see Figure 11-15):

Figure 11-15. The product thumbnail images displayed in the catalog

Displaying Dynamic Content on the Home Page

The last job to perform on the TechieTogs web site is to produce some dynamic content for the Home Page. We will create this content in this section.

Displaying a 'Featured Product'

You will have noticed that we have included a menu item in the administration menu for 'Featured Product'. We will create a page where the site administrator can choose one item to 'feature' on the Home Page.

First, we will need to create a database table to store the Product ID of the featured item. Create a new table in the TechieTogsData database called Settings. For now, the Settings table will have only one column, featuredProduct, although you may wish to add more 'settings' at a later date, as you develop the site further. Figure 11-16 shows the details of the Settings table that you will need to add to your site's database:

413

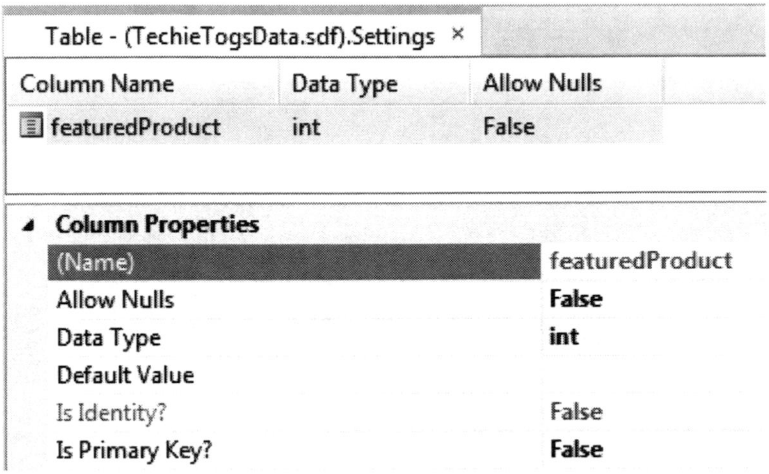

Figure 11-16. *The details of the Settings table*

Now that the necessary database table is in place, add a new page to the Admin folder at
Admin/Products/Featured.cshtml. Replace any existing page content with the following code and
markup:

```
@{
    Layout = "~/Shared/Layouts/_AdminLayout.cshtml";
    Page.Title = "Featured Product";

    var featuredProduct = "";

    var db = Database.Open("TechieTogsData");

    if(IsPost)
    {
        featuredProduct = Request["featuredProduct"];
        var sqlUpdate = "UPDATE Settings SET featuredProduct = @0";
        db.Execute(sqlUpdate, featuredProduct);

        Response.Redirect("~/Admin");
    }

    var sqlCommand = "SELECT featuredProduct FROM Settings";
    featuredProduct = db.QuerySingle(sqlCommand).featuredProduct.ToString();
}

<h1>Featured Product</h1>

<form action="Featured" method="post">
```

```
    <p>
        Featured product:
        @Products.ProductsDropDownList("featuredProduct", featuredProduct)
        <input type="submit" value="Save" />
    </p>
</form>
```

This code requires very little explanation. It simply displays a dropdown list of all of the products in the database using the `Products.ProductsDropDownList()` helper that we created earlier and it stores the value of that dropdown list to the `featuredProduct` column of the `Settings` table on post back.

Now we'll make some changes in the Home Page to display the featured product. Open `Default.cshtml` in the site root folder and replace the entire current content with the following:

```
@{
    Layout = "~/Shared/Layouts/_Layout.cshtml";
    Page.Title = "Home Page";

    var db = Database.Open("TechieTogsData");
    var sqlSelect = "SELECT * FROM Products " +
                    "INNER JOIN Settings ON Products.ProductID = Settings.featuredProduct";

    var product = db.QuerySingle(sqlSelect);
}

@if (product != null)
{
    <h1 class="homePageHeading">Featured Product</h1>
    <div id="featuredProductImage">
        <p>@Products.ShowProductImage(product.productID.ToString())</p>
    </div>
    <div id="featuredProductDetails">
        <a href="/ProductDetails/@product.productID">
            <h2>@product.title</h2>
        </a>
        <p>
            @product.description
        </p>
        <p class="price">
            £@product.price
        </p>
        <p>
            <a href="/ProductDetails/@product.productID" class="detailsButton">
                More Details
            </a>
        </p>
    </div>
}
```

This page uses a SQL INNER JOIN to get the details of the featured product from the Products table, and uses the result to display the product details on the page. The information displayed includes a link to the Product Details page, from where the customer can place an order.

Add the following CSS to Css/Style.css, to format the Featured Product on the Home Page:

```
/* Home Page
--------------------------------*/
#featuredProductImage {
    float: left;
    width: 380px;
}

#featuredProductDetails
{
    float:left;
    width: 250px;
}

#featuredProductDetails h3
{
    margin-bottom: 20px;
}

#featuredProductDetails .price {
    font-size: 1em;
    font-style: italic;
    color: #999;
    margin: 10px 0px 10px 0px;
}
```

Popular Products

In addition to the Featured Product, we'll also display the four most popular products on the Home Page of the site. We can get this information from the OrderItems table by finding the four productIDs that occur most often in the table. Add the following code to the bottom of the Default.cshtml page in the site root folder:

```
@{
    sqlSelect = "SELECT TOP 4 COUNT(productID) AS productCount, productId " +
                "FROM OrderItems GROUP BY productID ORDER BY productCount DESC";
    var mostPopular = db.Query(sqlSelect);
}
@if (mostPopular.Count() > 0)
{
    <div id="popularProducts">
        <h1 class="homePageHeading">Most Popular Products</h1>
        <ul id="popularProductsList">
            @foreach (var item in mostPopular) {
```

```
            <li>
                <a href="/ProductDetails/@item.productID" class="detailsButton">
                    @Products.ShowProductThumbnail(item.productID.ToString())
                </a>
            </li>
        }
    </ul>
    </div>
}
```

This code uses the SQL COUNT function to count the number of occurrences of each productID in the OrderItems table. In the same query, we also use the SQL TOP function to return just the first four records. It is then simply a matter of using a foreach loop to iterate over the results of the query and output the thumbnail image of each of the four most popular products to the page.

Add the following CSS to Css/Style.css to style the Most Popular Products section:

```
#popularProducts {
    clear:both;
    padding-top:25px;
}

#popularProductsList {
    list-style: none;
    margin: 0px;
    padding: 0px;
}

#popularProductsList li {
    float: left;
    margin: 12px 32px 12px 32px;
    text-align: center;
}

#popularProductsList li a img {
    border: none;
}
```

This is now our Home Page—and our site—complete. Now, when the user lands on the TechieTogs Home Page, they will be presented with something similar to that shown in Figure 11-17:

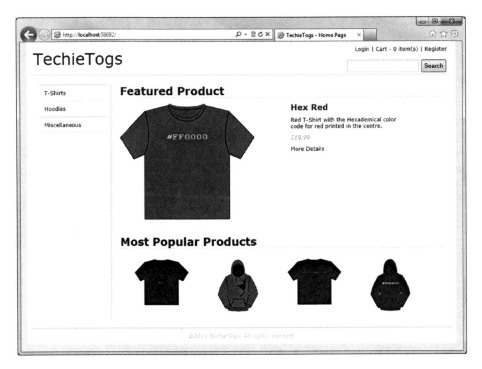

Figure 11-17. The completed TechieTogs Home Page, displaying dynamic content

---

■ **Tip** The dynamic content we have generated here for the Home Page is a prime candidate for performance enhancement using caching. See Chapter 12 – Additional Techniques and Features, for more information on caching using WebMatrix.

Summary

Over the last three chapters, we have seen how WebMatrix can be used to produce a fully functional e-commerce application. The creation of the TechieTogs site has demonstrated the real-world use of many of the features and techniques that we have covered in earlier chapters of the book, and it has introduced some new ones.

CHAPTER 12

Working with Images and Video

As Internet connection speeds have improved over the last few years, images and video have become an increasingly important part of the modern web site. In this chapter, we'll take a look at how WebMatrix helpers can be used to greatly improve the ease with which we can work with images and video.

Let's start this chapter with a discussion about uploading and manipulating images in ASP.NET Web Pages.

Working with Images

WebMatrix ships with a WebImage helper that is designed to assist with the manipulation of images on your website. We already saw it in action in the last chapter, when we used it to upload product images to the TechieTogs example website. In this section, we will look at the helper in more detail and see how it can be used to:

- Let users upload images

- Resize and crop images

- Flip and rotate images

- Add a textual watermark to an image

- Overlay another image as a watermark

Create a new WebMatrix site in order to work through the examples in this section. Within the root of the site, you should create a new folder called 'images'. It is important that you create this folder in the correct place, with the correct name, because you may receive error messages if you try to manipulate an image that is not in the correct path, or try to save an image to a folder that doesn't exist, when working through the examples later in the chapter.

Uploading Images

To allow users to upload images, we will need to provide them with a form containing an HTML `file` `<input>` control and a submit button. When they submit the form, we will use the `WebImage.GetImageFromRequest()` method to retrieve the file from their local file system. Next, we'll construct a unique file name using a Globally Unique Identifier (GUID) and save the image to the images folder using the `WebImage.Save()` method.

The `WebImage.Save()` method has three parameters, detailed in Table 12-1:

Table 12-1. *WebImage.Save() Parameters*

Parameter Name	Type	Description
filePath	string	The path where the image will be saved.
imageFormat	string	The format to use when saving the file, such as gif, jpeg, or png
forceCorrectExtension	bool	A Boolean value used to indicate whether the file extension used to save the image should be forced to match the image type indicated in the imageFormat parameter. If set to true, the correct file extension will be appended to the file name.

In the following example, we output the uploaded image to the page underneath the form to verify that it has worked. Enter the following code into a new page called `UploadingImages.cshtml`:

```
@{
    WebImage image = null;
    var imageFileName = "";

    if(IsPost)
    {
        image = WebImage.GetImageFromRequest();
        if(image != null)
        {
            imageFileName = Guid.NewGuid().ToString() + "_" +
                Path.GetFileName(image.FileName);

            image.Save(@"~\images\" + imageFileName);
        }
    }
}

<!DOCTYPE html>

<html lang="en">
<head>
    <meta charset="utf-8" />
    <title>Uploading Images</title>
</head>
    <body>
        <form action="" method="post" enctype="multipart/form-data">
            @Html.Label("Image to upload:", "imageUpload")
```

```
            <input type="file" name="imageUpload" /><br/>
            <input type="submit" value="Upload Image" />
        </form>

        <h1>Uploaded Image</h1>
        @if(imageFileName != "")
        {
            <div>
                <img src="images/@imageFileName" alt="Uploaded Image" />
            </div>
        }
    </body>
</html>
```

You will see that the enctype="multipart/form-data" parameter has been included in the <form> tag. This additional attribute is necessary in order to be able to retrieve the value of the file <input> control. The attribute allows uploading of file content that would not otherwise be submitted with the form data.

We use a GUID to create a unique file name for storing the image in our images folder. By constructing a unique file name, we ensure that an image will never be overwritten in the images folder. Without this, if two images were to be saved in the same folder with identical file names, one would overwrite the other.

GUIDs

A GUID is a 128-bit Globally Unique Identifier and looks something like this:

90a565be-f8a5-4dd9-8076-24abb40a8e08

A new GUID can be created at any time using the .NET Guid.NewGuid() method. The GUID-creation algorithm practically guarantees a unique number every time (the chances of a duplicate are so incredibly small that such numbers are usually treated as unique). This uniqueness makes GUIDs ideal for applications, such as our file upload example, where we need to ensure that two objects never receive the same name. Obviously, a GUID is not the most user-friendly identifier, so we tend to use them only in code.

Figure 12-1 shows the image-upload example in action:

Figure 12-1. *Uploading an image using the WebImage helper*

■ **Note** As noted when you were developing the image-upload functionality of the TechieTogs example web site in Chapter 11, when deploying this site to a public-facing server, you may have to alter the default permissions of the images folder to allow read–write access. Your system administrator or web hosting provider will be able to help you with this.

Resizing Images

The WebImage helper also exposes a `Resize()` method, which allows us to alter the size of an image. The `Resize()` method has four parameters, listed in Table 12-2:

Table 12-2. *WebImage.Resize() Parameters*

Parameter Name	Type	Description
width	int	The maximum image width (pixels)
height	int	The maximum image height (pixels)
preserveAspectRatio	bool	Indicates whether the aspect ratio of the original image should be maintained
preventEnlarge	bool	A Boolean value used to indicate whether image enlargements should be prevented if the original image is smaller than the height and width specified

The following code sample allows the user to upload an image, which is then saved and displayed back to the user both in its original size and as a thumbnail image. The thumbnail image is stored with 'thumb_' prefixed to the file name, a preserved aspect ratio, and a maximum width and height of 120 pixels.

Add the following code to a new page called ResizingImages.cshtml:

```
@{
    WebImage originalImage = null;
    WebImage thumbnailImage = null;
    var imageFileName = "";

    if(IsPost)
    {
        originalImage = WebImage.GetImageFromRequest();
        if(originalImage != null)
        {
            imageFileName = Guid.NewGuid().ToString() + "_" +
                Path.GetFileName(originalImage.FileName);

            originalImage.Save(@"~\images\" + imageFileName);

            thumbnailImage = originalImage.Resize(width: 120,
                                                  height:120,
                                                  preserveAspectRatio: true);

            thumbnailImage.Save(@"~\images\thumb_" + imageFileName);
        }
    }
}

<!DOCTYPE html>

<html lang="en">
<head>
    <meta charset="utf-8" />
    <title>Resizing Images</title>
</head>
    <body>
        <form action="" method="post" enctype="multipart/form-data">
            @Html.Label("Image to upload:", "imageUpload")
            <input type="file" name="imageUpload" /><br/>
            <input type="submit" value="Upload Image" />
        </form>

        <h1>Uploaded Images</h1>
        @if(imageFileName != "")
        {
            <div>
                Original Image: <br />
                <img src="images/@imageFileName" alt="Original Image" />
            </div>
```

```
        <div>
            Thumbnail Image: <br />
            <img src="images/thumb_@(imageFileName)" alt="Thumbnail Image" />
        </div>
    }
  </body>
</html>
```

Figure 12-2 shows an example of the output produced by the ResizingImages.cshtml page:

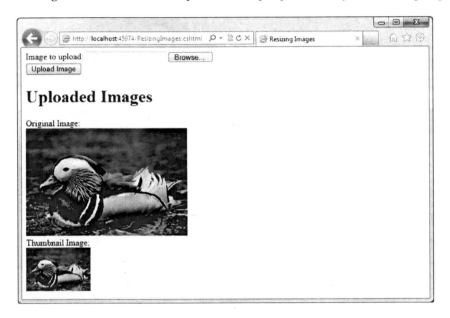

Figure 12-2. Resizing an image using the WebImage.Resize() method

Cropping Images

The WebImage.Crop() method allows us to remove a specified number of pixels from each side of an image. The method itself is very simple to use and is best demonstrated with example code.

Add a new file called CroppingImages.cshtml and insert the following code, which removes 50 pixels from each side of an image:

```
@{
    WebImage originalImage = null;
    WebImage croppedImage = null;
    var imageFileName = "";

    if(IsPost)
    {
        originalImage = WebImage.GetImageFromRequest();
        if(originalImage != null)
```

```
        {
            imageFileName = Guid.NewGuid().ToString() + "_" +
                Path.GetFileName(originalImage.FileName);

            originalImage.Save(@"~\images\" + imageFileName);

            croppedImage = originalImage.Crop(top: 50, left: 50,
                                              bottom: 50, right: 50);

            croppedImage.Save(@"~\images\cropped_" + imageFileName);
        }
    }
}
```

```html
<!DOCTYPE html>

<html lang="en">
<head>
    <meta charset="utf-8" />
    <title>Cropping Images</title>
</head>
    <body>
        <form action="" method="post" enctype="multipart/form-data">
            @Html.Label("Image to upload:", "imageUpload")
            <input type="file" name="imageUpload" /><br/>
            <input type="submit" value="Upload Image" />
        </form>

        <h1>Uploaded Images</h1>
        @if(imageFileName != "")
        {
            <div style="float:left; margin-right: 10px;">
                Original Image: <br />
                <img src="images/@imageFileName" alt="Original Image" />
            </div>
            <div>
                Cropped Image: <br />
                <img src="images/cropped_@(imageFileName)" alt="Cropped Image" />
            </div>
        }
    </body>
</html>
```

425

Figure 12-3 shows this code in action:

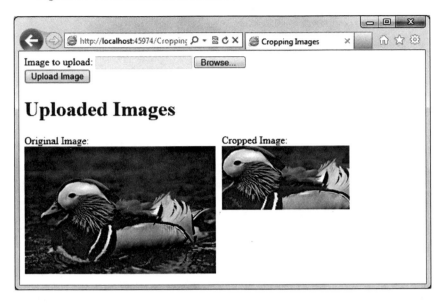

Figure 12-3. *Using the WebImage.Crop() method*

Flipping and Rotating Images

Four methods are exposed by the WebImage helper for flipping and rotating images, listed in Table 12-3:

Table 12-3. *WebImage flipping and rotating methods*

Method Name	Description
FlipHorizontal()	Flips an image horizontally
FlipVertical()	Flips and image vertically
RotateLeft()	Rotates an image 90 degrees counter-clockwise
RotateRight()	Rotates an image 90 degrees clockwise

The following example is similar to the Resizing Images example except that this time the image is rotated 90 degrees to the right and flipped horizontally.

Create a new page called FlipAndRotate.cshtml and replace any existing markup with the following:

```
@{
    WebImage originalImage = null;
    WebImage flippedAndRotatedImage = null;
```

```
    var imageFileName = "";

    if(IsPost)
    {
        originalImage = WebImage.GetImageFromRequest();
        if(originalImage != null)
        {
            imageFileName = Guid.NewGuid().ToString() + "_" +
                Path.GetFileName(originalImage.FileName);

            originalImage.Save(@"~\images\" + imageFileName);

            flippedAndRotatedImage = originalImage.RotateRight().FlipHorizontal();

            flippedAndRotatedImage.Save(@"~\images\flippedAndRotated_" + imageFileName);
        }
    }
}

<!DOCTYPE html>

<html lang="en">
<head>
    <meta charset="utf-8" />
    <title>Resizing Images</title>
</head>
    <body>
        <form action="" method="post" enctype="multipart/form-data">
            @Html.Label("Image to upload:", "imageUpload")
            <input type="file" name="imageUpload" /><br/>
            <input type="submit" value="Upload Image" />
        </form>

        <h1>Uploaded Images</h1>
        @if(imageFileName != "")
        {
            <div style="float:left; margin-right: 10px;">
                Original Image: <br />
                <img src="images/@imageFileName" alt="Original Image" />
            </div>
            <div>
                Flipped and Rotated Image: <br />
                <img src="images/flippedAndRotated_@(imageFileName)" alt="Manipulated Image"
/>
            </div>
        }
    </body>
</html>
```

Figure 12-4 shows the output of this example in the browser:

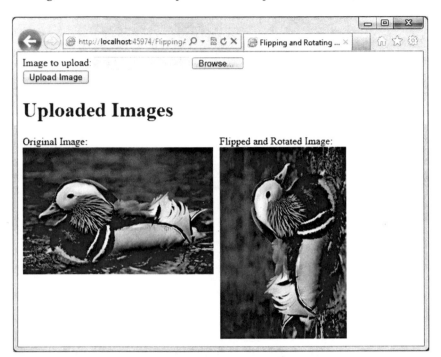

Figure 12-4. Rotating and flipping images using the WebImage helper

Adding Watermarks to Images

The WebImage helper offers two ways to add watermarks to images. The first method overlays text onto the image as a watermark, whereas the second overlays another image on top of the original as a watermark. We'll look at each one in turn.

Adding Text as a Watermark

Text can be added as a watermark to an image through the use of the `WebImage.AddTextWatermark()` method. The method has several parameters used to style the watermark. Table 12-4 lists these parameters in detail:

Table 12-4. *WebImage.AddTextWatermark() Parameters*

Parameter Name	Type	Description
text	string	The text to be used as a watermark
fontColor	string	The color of the watermark text. This can be either defined as a named color or in standard hex RGB color notation
fontSize	int	The font size of the watermark text
fontStyle	string	The style of the text to be used as a watermark (i.e., normal, italic, oblique, inherit—as per the CSS font-style element)
fontFamily	string	The font family to be used for the watermark text. The font required must be one already installed on the server because the watermark is applied server-side.
horizontalAlign	string	The horizontal alignment for the watermark. Can be "Left", "Right", or "Center". Default value = "Right"
verticalAlign	string	The vertical alignment for the watermark. Can be "Top", "Middle", or "Bottom". Default value = "Bottom"
opacity	int	The opacity of the watermark text. Specified as an integer value between 0 and 100.
padding	int	The number of pixels to be applied as padding to the watermark text

Add a new file to your example site, and name it `TextWatermark.cshtml`. Our example page will allow the user to upload an image, to which we will apply a textual watermark and render it back to the browser. Add the following code to the page, replacing any existing content:

```
@{
    WebImage originalImage = null;
    WebImage watermarkedImage = null;
    var imageFileName = "";

    if(IsPost)
```

429

```
    {
        originalImage = WebImage.GetImageFromRequest();
        if(originalImage != null)
        {
            imageFileName = Guid.NewGuid().ToString() + "_" +
                Path.GetFileName(originalImage.FileName);

            originalImage.Save(@"~\images\" + imageFileName);

            watermarkedImage = originalImage.AddTextWatermark("Sample Watermark",
                                                    fontColor:"#00FFFF",
                                                    fontSize: 20,
                                                    fontFamily: "Tahoma",
                                                    horizontalAlign: "Center",
                                                    verticalAlign: "Top",
                                                    padding: 15);
            watermarkedImage.Save(@"~\images\watermarked_" + imageFileName);
        }
    }
}

<!DOCTYPE html>

<html lang="en">
<head>
    <meta charset="utf-8" />
    <title>Text Watermark</title>
</head>
    <body>
        <form action="" method="post" enctype="multipart/form-data">
            @Html.Label("Image to upload:", "imageUpload")
            <input type="file" name="imageUpload" /><br/>
            <input type="submit" value="Upload Image" />
        </form>

        <h1>Uploaded Images</h1>
        @if(imageFileName != "")
        {
            <div style="float:left; margin-right: 10px;">
                Original Image: <br />
                <img src="images/@imageFileName" alt="Original Image" />
            </div>
            <div>
                Watermarked Image: <br />
                <img src="images/watermarked_@(imageFileName)" alt="Watermarked Image" />
            </div>
        }
    </body>
</html>
```

Figure 12-5 shows the watermark applied by this code:

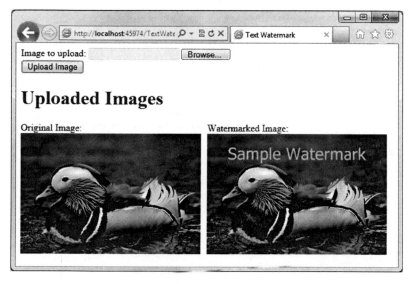

Figure 12-5. *A watermark applied using the AddTextWatermark() method*

Using Another Image as a Watermark

The other way to add a watermark to an image is by overlaying another image on top of the original. To do this, wecall the `AddImageWatermark()` method.

The `AddImageWatermark()` method can overlay either an image stored on file or a specified `WebImage` object onto another image. In our example here, we will create a page that accepts two images for upload, stores both, and displays one as a watermark on top of the other.

Create a new page called `ImageWatermark.cshtml`, and replace the default markup with the following code sample:

```
@{
    WebImage originalImage = null;
    WebImage watermarkImage = null;
    WebImage watermarkedImage = null;
    var originalFileName = "";
    var watermarkFileName = "";

    if(IsPost)
    {
        originalImage = WebImage.GetImageFromRequest("originalImage");
        watermarkImage = WebImage.GetImageFromRequest("watermarkImage");
        if((originalImage != null) && (watermarkImage != null))
        {
            originalFileName = Guid.NewGuid().ToString() + "_" +
                Path.GetFileName(originalImage.FileName);
```

431

```
                originalImage.Save(@"~\images\" + originalFileName);

                watermarkFileName = Guid.NewGuid().ToString() + "_" +
                    Path.GetFileName(watermarkImage.FileName);
                watermarkImage.Save(@"~\images\" + watermarkFileName);

                watermarkedImage = originalImage.AddImageWatermark(watermarkImage,
                                                        width: 150, height: 50,
                                                        horizontalAlign:"Right",
                                                        verticalAlign:"Top",
                                                        opacity:100,  padding:10);

                watermarkedImage.Save(@"~\images\watermarked_" + originalFileName);
        }
    }
}

<!DOCTYPE html>

<html lang="en">
<head>
    <meta charset="utf-8" />
    <title>Image Watermark</title>
</head>
    <body>
        <form action="" method="post" enctype="multipart/form-data">
            @Html.Label("Original image:", "originalImage")
            <input type="file" name="originalImage" /><br/>
            @Html.Label("Watermark image:", "watermarkImage")
            <input type="file" name="watermarkImage" /><br/>
            <input type="submit" value="Upload Images" />
        </form>

        <h1>Uploaded Images</h1>
        @if(originalFileName != "")
        {
            <div style="float:left; margin-right: 10px;">
                Original Image: <br />
                <img src="images/@originalFileName" alt="Original Image" />
            </div>
            <div>
                Watermark Image: <br />
                <img src="images/@watermarkFileName" alt="Watermark Image" />
            </div>
            <div style="clear:both;">
                Watermarked Image:<br />
                <img src="images/watermarked_@(originalFileName)" alt="Watermarked Image" />
            </div>
        }
    </body>
</html>
```

When you run the page, you will be asked for an original image and a watermark image. When you click the Upload Images button, the watermark image will be applied to the original image and will be displayed in the browser, as shown here in Figure 12-6:

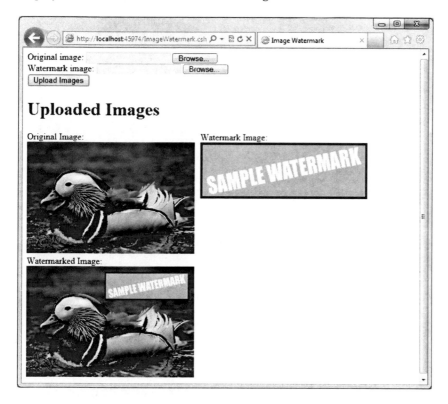

Figure 12-6. *Using an image as a watermark*

The AddImageWatermark() method has a number of parameters for customizing the output. They are listed in Table 12-5:

Table 12-5. *WebImage.AddImageWatermark() Parameters*

Parameter Name	Type	Description
watermarkImage	string or WebImage	Either the path of the file that contains the watermark image, or a WebImage object, to be used as the watermark
Width	int	The width of the watermark image in pixels
Height	int	The height of the watermark image in pixels

433

horizontalAlign	string	The horizontal alignment for the watermark image. Can be "Left", "Right", or "Center". Default value = "Right"
verticalAlign	string	The vertical alignment for the watermark image. Can be "Top", "Middle", or "Bottom". Default value = "Bottom"
Opacity	Int	The opacity of the watermark image. Specified as an integer value between 0 and 100.
Padding	Int	The number of pixels to apply as padding to the watermark image

Working with Video

The ASP.NET Web Helpers Library package includes a Video helper that lets you embed Adobe Flash (.swf), Windows MediaPlayer (.wmv), and Microsoft Silverlight (.xap) videos into your web pages. The helper simplifies the process of embedding video in a web page by automatically generating the <object> and <embed> HTML tags and associated attributes that are normally used to embed video.

To use the helper, you will first need to install the ASP.NET Web Helpers Library package using the WebMatrix Package Manager.

Navigate to the Site workspace and open the ASP.NET Web Sites Administration site using the link in the Content Pane. Enter a password and remove the leading underscore in the filename of the /App_Data/Admin/_Password.config file when prompted. Next, search for the ASP.NET Web Helpers Library 1.15 package within the Package Manager, and click the Install button to add it to your site.

■ **Note** For full instructions about installing the ASP.NET Web Helpers Library package using the WebMatrix Package Manager, see "Chapter 8 – Using Web Helper Packages."

Once the ASP.NET Web Helpers Library has been successfully installed in your project, you can embed video into the page by using one of the three methods exposed by the Video object: Video.Flash(), Video.MediaPlayer, and Video.Silverlight().

The next three sections look at each of these in turn.

Embedding Flash Video

Adobe Flash video can be embedded into a page using the Video.Flash() helper method. The method has several parameters, listed here in Table 12-6:

Table 12-6. *Video.Flash() Parameters*

Parameter Name	Type	Default	Description
path	string		The URL of the video to be embedded
width	string	*null*	Video width—either in pixels or as a percentage value
height	string	*null*	Video height—either in pixels or as a percentage value
play	bool	true	Indicates whether to play the video automatically once loaded
loop	bool	true	Specifies whether the video should repeat from the start when the final frame is reached
menu	bool	true	Determines whether to display a full menu, including movie-playback controls
bgColor	string	*null*	Sets the background color of the .swf content—expressed as a hexadecimal RGB color
quality	string	*null*	Specifies the video-rendering quality. Possible values: low, autolow, medium, high, or best.
scale	string	*null*	Determines how the Flash Player scales to fit the content area defined by the height and width settings if not an exact fit. Possible values: default, noborder, exactfit, or noscale.
windowMode	string	*null*	Sets the Window Mode property of the .swf file for transparency, layering positioning, and rendering in the browser. Possible values: window, direct, opaque, transparent, or gpu.
baseUrl	string	*null*	Specifies the base URL used to resolve all relative path statements in the .swf file
Version	string	*null*	The version of the Flash Player to be used
options	object	*null*	A list of options added as attributes to the <embed> tag and as child <param> elements of the <object> tag
htmlAttributes	object	*null*	Additional HTML attributes to be added to the <object> tag.
embedName	string	*null*	Sets the name attribute of the <embed> tag

435

Create a new folder in the root of your web site called Media, and place a Flash video (.swf) file inside it.

The following code sample embeds a Flash video located at Media/wildlife.swf into a web page:

```
<!DOCTYPE html>

<html lang="en">
    <head>
        <meta charset="utf-8" />
        <title>Flash Video</title>
    </head>
    <body>
        <h1>Flash Video</h1>
        @Video.Flash(path: "Media/wildlife.swf",
                width: "640",
                height: "360",
                play: true,
                loop: true,
                menu:  true,
                quality: "best",
                scale: "exactfit",
                windowMode: "transparent")
    </body>
</html>
```

Figure 12-7 shows the resulting page in the browser:

Figure 12-7. Embedding Flash video with the Video helper

Note More information about Flash video attributes can be found on the Adobe web site at
http://kb2.adobe.com/cps/127/tn_12701.html

Embedding Windows MediaPlayer Video

Windows MediaPlayer videos can be embedded into a page using the Video.MediaPlayer() helper method. Videos embedded using the Video helper will play once they are completely downloaded; there is no facility within the helper for streaming video. The method parameters are detailed in Table 12-7:

Table 12-7. *Video.MediaPlayer() Parameters*

Parameter Name	Type	Default	Description
path	string		The URL of the video to be embedded
width	string	*null*	Video width—either in pixels or as a percentage value
height	string	*null*	Video height—either in pixels or as a percentage value
autoStart	bool	true	Specifies whether the video should play automatically once loaded
playCount	int	1	Specifies the number of times the video will play
uiMode	string	*null*	Specifies which controls are shown in the user interface. Possible values: invisible, none, mini, full, or custom.
stretchToFit	bool	false	Specifies whether to automatically stretch the video to match the content area specified by the width and height parameters
enableContextMenu	bool	true	Specifies whether to enable the right-click context menu
mute	bool	false	Set to true to mute all audio
volume	int	-1	Sets the volume ranging from 0 to 100. A value of -1 sets it to the default level.
baseUrl	string	*null*	Specifies the base URL used to resolve all relative path statements embedded in the media script commands
options	object	*null*	A list of options added as attributes to the <embed> tag and as child <param> elements of the <object> tag

| htmlAttributes | object | *null* | Additional HTML attributes to be added to the <object> tag. |
| embedName | string | *null* | Sets the name attribute of the <embed> tag |

The following code sample embeds a MediaPlayer video, Media/wildlife.wmf, in a web page.

■ **Note** All three of the video types that the Video helper is capable of playing require the relevant plug-in to be installed in the user's browser. Users who do not have the relevant plug-in installed will receive a message in the browser to this effect. The actual message displayed depends on the combination of the user's browser and the required plug-in.

```
<!DOCTYPE html>

<html lang="en">
    <head>
        <meta charset="utf-8" />
        <title>MediaPlayer Video</title>
    </head>
    <body>
        <h1>MediaPlayer Video</h1>
        @Video.MediaPlayer(
            path: "Media/wildlife.wmv",
            width: "640",
            height: "480",
            autoStart: true,
            playCount: 1,
            uiMode:  "full",
            stretchToFit: false,
            enableContextMenu: true,
            mute: false,
            volume: 75)
    </body>
</html>
```

Figure 12-8 shows the MediaPlayer plug-in displaying the video in the browser.

Figure 12-8. Embedding a .wmv movie in a web page with the MediaPlayer() helper method

---

■ **Note** More information about MediaPlayer's parameters can be found on the Windows Media web site at
http://msdn.microsoft.com/en-us/library/aa392321(VS.85).aspx

Embedding Microsoft Silverlight Video

The final method of the Video helper class allows you to embed Microsoft Silverlight (.xap) videos into a
web page. The Video.Silverlight() method's parameters are listed here in Table 12-8:

Table 12-8. Video.Silverlight() Parameters

Parameter Name	Type	Default	Description
path	string		The URL of the video to be embedded
width	string		Video width—either in pixels or as a percentage value
height	string		Video height—either in pixels or as a percentage value
bgColor	string	*null*	The background color. Specified as a hexadecimal RGB color.
initParameters	string	*null*	Sets user-defined initialization parameters
minimumVersion	string	*null*	Specifies the earliest version of the Silverlight runtime that can be used to play the video.
autoUpgrade	bool	true	Indicates whether to automatically upgrade the browser's Silverlight plug-in if it is earlier than the value specified by the minimumVersion parameter.
options	object	*null*	A list of options added as attributes to the <embed> tag and as child <param> elements of the <object> tag
htmlAttributes	object	*null*	Additional HTML attributes to be added to the <object> tag.

The following code sample embeds a Silverlight video into a web page. Figure 12-9 shows the page rendered to the browser:

```
<!DOCTYPE html>

<html lang="en">
    <head>
        <meta charset="utf-8" />
        <title>Silverlight Video</title>
    </head>
    <body>
        <h1>Silverlight Video</h1>
        @Video.Silverlight(
            path: "media/wildlife.xap",
            width: "640",
            height: "360")
    </body>
</html>
```

Figure 12-9. A Silverlight movie embedded using the `Video.Silverlight()` *helper*

■ **Note** More information about the Silverlight plug-in parameters can be found on the MSDN web site at:
`http://msdn.microsoft.com/en-us/library/cc838259(v=VS.95).aspx`

Summary

This chapter has been entirely concerned with the embedding of images and videos into web pages by making use of the helper classes provided by Microsoft WebMatrix: `WebImage` and `Video`.

In addition to simply embedding images, we have also seen how the WebImage helper can be used to upload images and manipulate them on the web server.

In the final chapter, we will discuss how WebMatrix can be used to debug your web pages and deploy the finished site to a public-facing web server. We'll also see how caching can be used to improve the performance of the site, and we'll look at the tools provided as part of the WebMatrix IDE for improving your site's placement in search engines.

■ ■ ■

CHAPTER 13

Debugging, Caching, and Deployment

In this, the final chapter, we'll take a look at a range of topics, including:

- Debugging ASP.NET Web Pages

- Improving performance through caching

- Search Engine Optimization (SEO)

- Publishing your WebMatrix site to the World Wide Web.

By the end of this chapter, and therefore the end of this book, you will have gained all the knowledge necessary to build and deploy dynamic, data-driven web sites using Microsoft WebMatrix.

Let's start the chapter with a discussion about debugging: the art of finding and removing errors.

Debugging ASP.NET Web Pages

Debugging really is an art. It is the combination of a number of different techniques that assist the developer in finding and fixing errors in his or her code.

■ **Note** It's even harder to find and fix errors in someone else's code, which is why it is so important for you to keep your code readable and well documented: you may not be the only one who maintains your code in the future.

Whole books have been written about debugging. The art of debugging is a skill that you will hone over time as you gain experience tracking down and fixing bugs. You will learn which techniques work best in certain situations and which tools can be used to identify problems.

The best debugging technique is performed before any code is ever executed. Through a combination of experience and logical thought, you can eliminate most bugs before they ever become a problem.

By using code to deal with a user entering unexpected or unusual values, for example, you can prevent a lot of errors. Specifically, if you are developing code that retrieves a database record about a customer based on the user entering a valid customer ID, you should anticipate what would happen if no matching record is found. Should we let the web server display an error message, such as a NullReferenceException, or should we write code to deal with it in a better way, such as having the program display a helpful message to the user and provide links to useful pages?

As you gain more and more experience writing code in any language, you will become better able to identify and eliminate potential bugs and errors as well as write code to deal with or prevent them. However, no matter how good you are, you will never be able to write bug-free working code the first time, every time.

In this section, we'll look at some of the ways that WebMatrix can help with the process.

Displaying Server Information

Sometimes, in order to track down a bug, it is useful to be able to view information about the environment in which the web site is running. Rather than having to interrogate individual server properties, WebMatrix provides the ServerInfo helper class, which gives a broad overview of what is typically considered the most useful information, including data about the server hardware, operating system, current user, server variables, and HTTP runtime.

The information provided by the ServerInfo class is shown in the browser and is split across four tables. The list below describes the kind of information you can expect to see in each table:

- **Server Configuration**: Local time at the server, culture, server machine name, operating system, current user name, ASP.NET version, operating system version, etc.

- **ASP.NET Server Variables**: Physical path of the web application, path of the current page, information about any currently authenticated user, HTTP request method (i.e., GET or POST), server name, etc.

- **HTTP Runtime Information**: Path of important directories, such as the .NET Framework CLR directory and the ASP.NET installation directory, as well as information about the cache.

- **Environment Variables**: Information about the server hardware, such as processor information; paths of important system folders, such as Program Files and Windows installation; value of the path environment variable on the server.

■ **Note** Readers with previous experience using PHP will no doubt notice similarities between the output of the WebMatrix ServerInfo helper and the phpinfo() function.

To display the output of the `ServerInfo` helper, you must call its `GetHtml()` method. The following code produces the output seen in Figure 13-1:

```
<!DOCTYPE html>

<html lang="en">
    <head>
        <meta charset="utf-8" />
        <title>ServerInfo Example</title>
    </head>
    <body>
        @ServerInfo.GetHtml()
    </body>
</html>
```

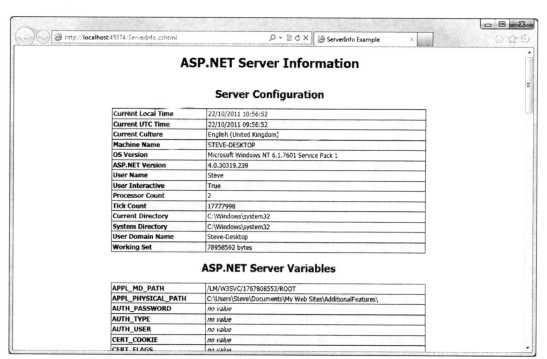

Figure 13-1. The output produced by the ServerInfo.GetHtml() helper method

---

▓ **Caution** The ServerInfo helper class displays important and detailed information about the web server, some of which may be useful to people with malicious intent. For that reason, you must ensure that any calls to the ServerInfo helper are removed from your pages before you deploy them to a public-facing site. This same rule applies to any of the diagnostic debugging code discussed in this chapter.

Displaying Object Information

WebMatrix includes an `ObjectInfo` helper class, which displays the type and value of each object passed to it. It can be used to view variables and objects in your code and to display data-type information about the object. If an object contains multiple values, such as an array, or an object is returned as the result of a database query, the helper displays each property and its value.

The best way to demonstrate this is with an example. The following code example sets up various objects and uses the `ObjectInfo` helper class to display their information by calling the `ObjectInfo.Print()` method for each. Figure 13-2 shows the output.

```
@{
    var message = "This example shows the ObjectInfo helper at work.";
    var activityDate = DateTime.Now;
    var cars = new List<String>() { "Ferrari",
                                    "Aston Martin",
                                    "Porsche",
                                    "Lamborghini",
                                    "McLaren" };
}
<!DOCTYPE html>

<html lang="en">
    <head>
        <meta charset="utf-8" />
        <title>ObjectInfo Example</title>
    </head>
    <body>
        <p>
            @message
        </p>
        @ObjectInfo.Print(message)
        @ObjectInfo.Print(activityDate)
        @ObjectInfo.Print(cars)
    </body>
</html>
```

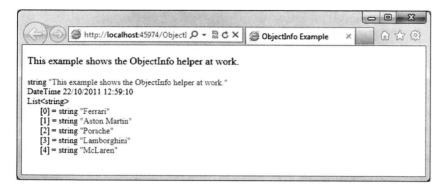

Figure 13-2. *The output produced by the ObjectInfo.Print() helper method*

Notice that even though we used the **var** keyword to declare the objects instead of declaring them as explicit types in the first place, the actual type of the object created is displayed by the **ObjectInfo** helper. This feature alone can be an incredibly useful debugging tool.

Output Expressions

The use of code to output expressions to the browser can be tremendously useful when debugging code. This enables you to see the value of important variables or the results of calculations in real-time at the point of evaluation.

Values can be output from the body of the page using Razor markup, as you would expect. This technique is often particularly useful when you need to check a value at a certain point in the page execution.

■ **Note** Much more sophisticated debugging tools are available in the Visual Studio development environment. See the "Debugging with Microsoft Visual Studio" section later in this chapter to learn how to launch a WebMatrix project in Visual Studio.

For example, we could output the value of a **for** loop index to check that we were looping through it the number of times we would expect. This could be used to diagnose a common bug known as an "off-by-one" error. Off-by-one errors occur when an iterative loop iterates one time too many or too few; this can often occur when there is confusion in the code between the actual number of elements in a collection and a zero-based index of elements. For example, the following code and resulting screenshot in Figure 13-3 show an example of an output expression being used to diagnose an "off-by-one" error in which the last element of the array, **"McLaren"**, is never output to the page.

```
@{
    var cars = new string[] { "Ferrari",
                              "Aston Martin",
                              "Porsche",
```

```
                              "Lamborghini",
                              "McLaren" };
}
<!DOCTYPE html>

<html lang="en">
    <head>
        <meta charset="utf-8" />
        <title>Output Expression Example</title>
    </head>
    <body>
        <ul>
            @for (int i = 0; i < cars.GetUpperBound(0); i++)
            {
                <li>
                    @cars[i]

                    @* Output "for loop" indexer for debugging *@
                    @i

                </li>
            }
        </ul>
    </body>
</html>
```

■ **Caution** This is *not* a good example of how to iterate over an array. In fact, this is a good example of how *not* to do it. I have included it to show how outputting expressions to the page can help identify bugs, in this case an "off-by-one" error.

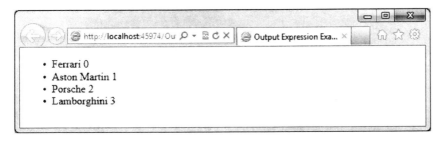

Figure 13-3. Output expressions used to diagnose an "out-by-one" error while iterating over a collection

We can see that by outputting the index of the loop next to the array content, it is much easier to identify the problem.

If you wish to output the value of a variable from within a code block, you can do so using the Response.Write() method. For example, the following code outputs the value stored against the username key of the Session variable:

```
@{
    Session["username"] = "wendy";
    Response.Write(Session["username"]);
}
<!DOCTYPE html>

<html lang="en">
    <head>
        <meta charset="utf-8" />
        <title>Output Expression Example</title>
    </head>
    <body>
        <h1>Home Page</h1>
        <p>Welcome to the Home Page.</p>
    </body>
</html>
```

Figure 13-4 shows the output sent to the browser:

Figure 13-4. Output sent to the browser using the Response.Write() method

■ **Caution** Again, for security reasons it is important that you remove all debugging output from a page before it is made publicly available.

Browser Debugging Tools

Most modern web browsers provide tools for debugging web pages, some natively and some via plug-ins. These tools allow you to see in-depth information about the data sent to the browser. In this section, we'll see how to access the tools available in three of the most popular browsers: Microsoft Internet Explorer, Google Chrome, and Mozilla Firefox.

Internet Explorer Developer Tools

The developer tools within Microsoft's Internet Explorer 8 and Internet Explorer 9 browsers can be accessed simply by pressing F12 or by choosing the Developer Tools item from the Tools menu (see Figure 13-5).

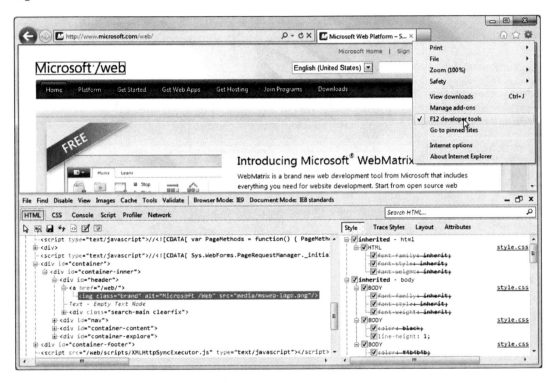

Figure 13-5. *Internet Explorer Developer Tools*

The Developer Tools panel allows you to explore elements of the page such as HTML, JavaScript, and CSS.

Open Internet Explorer 8 or Internet Explorer 9 and browse to the official ASP.NET web site at http://www.asp.net. Now press the F12 key to open the Developer Tools panel and explore the page content.

The left-hand side of the Developer Tools panel shows the page source, with sets of nested tags being displayed hierarchically. As you move through the source, clicking the plus signs to expand nodes containing nested elements, you can highlight any HTML tags to display the actual CSS rules applied to them. The CSS applied to any highlighted element is displayed on the right-hand side. The check boxes next to each item allow you to temporarily un-apply a style.

■ **Note** Information and tutorials regarding Internet Explorer Developer Tools can be found online at
http://msdn.microsoft.com/en-us/ie/aa740478

Google Chrome Developer Tools

Google's Chrome browser also comes with an excellent set of built-in developer tools, and they too can be accessed by pressing F12. These tools (seen here in Figure 13-6) offer functionality similar to that of the Internet Explorer Developer Tools.

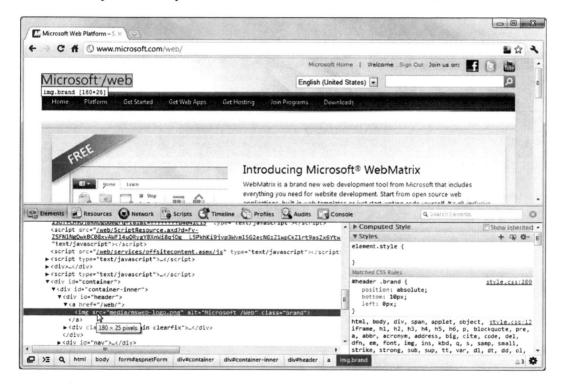

Figure 13-6. Google Chrome Developer Tools

■ **Note** More information about the Google Chrome Developer Tools can be found online at
http://code.google.com/chrome/devtools/

Mozilla Firefox Firebug

Excellent in-browser debugging tools are provided for the Firefox browser via the Firebug add-on. Firebug does not come as part of the standard Firefox installation but can be downloaded free of charge from www.getfirebug.com or via the Firefox Add-ons Manager. The Add-ons Manager can be accessed by pressing Ctrl+Shift+A while in the browser or through the "Firefox" menu at the top, left-hand corner of the browser window. Once the add-on has been installed, restart the browser and press F12 to open Firebug (see Figure 13-7).

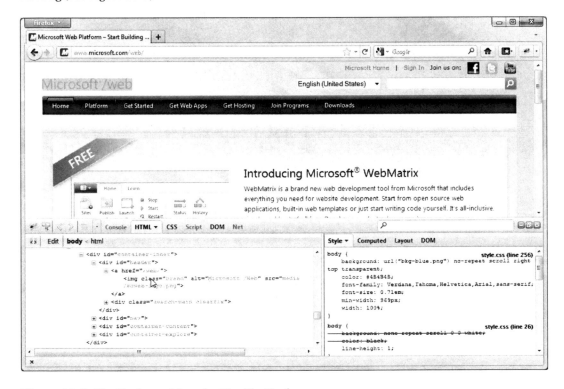

Figure 13-7. *The Firebug add-on for Mozilla Firefox*

Analyzing HTTP Requests

The WebMatrix IDE has a built-in tool for analyzing requests to your web site by letting you view the status of requests in real time. The tool displays useful information about each request, including the HTTP verb (GET or POST), URL requested, time elapsed, and status. This information can be used to help diagnose bugs that may have resulted from HTTP errors, such as 404 – File Not Found.

To access this tool in WebMatrix, click Site in the workspace area and then click Requests in the Navigation pane.

By using the toggle buttons in the Ribbon Control, the tool can be set to capture all requests or to capture only errors and to ignore or list requests for image files.

Clicking on an item in the list displays more information about the request. Figure 13-8 shows the built-in WebMatrix Requests tool.

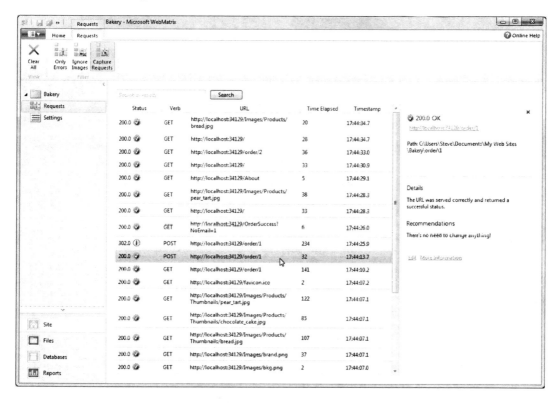

Figure 13-8. The WebMatrix Requests tool

■ **Tip** If you would find it useful to see more information about each request than what is shown by the WebMatrix Requests tool, I highly recommend the Fiddler tool. Fiddler can be downloaded completely free of charge from `www.fiddler2.com`.

Debugging with Microsoft Visual Studio

Visual Studio has an excellent suite of de-bugging (and general development) tools that are far more comprehensive than those found in the WebMatrix IDE.

If you have a version of Microsoft Visual Studio 2010 installed on your system, including the free Web Developer Express 2010, you can launch it from within the WebMatrix environment. To do this, click Files in the workspace area and then take a look in the Ribbon—the Launch section now has a button to launch Visual Studio (see Figure 13-9). Doing this allows you to take full advantage of the more mature and capable development environment offered by the Visual Studio suite of products.

Figure 13-9. The Launch Visual Studio button found in the Ribbon Control of the Files workspace

---

■ **Tip**   If you would like more information about how to use the excellent debugging tools provided with Visual Studio, visit the "Debugging in Visual Studio" section of the MSDN web site at `http://msdn.microsoft.com/en-us/library/sc65sadd.aspx`

Improving Performance Using Caching

Each dynamic page that is requested from a web site requires that the server perform various tasks in order to construct the final output that is then sent to the requesting client's browser. If the construction of the final output requires the completion of a comparatively slow task, such as retrieving data from a database or external web service, the performance of the site can be adversely affected. Although during the development cycle the task may not have appeared to take a particularly long time to complete, if the live site experiences a lot of traffic, the time taken to complete these slow tasks can add up. Heavy traffic such as this can ultimately affect the overall speed at which the server can deal with page requests.

ASP.NET Web Pages provides an output caching mechanism to deal with this situation. If the data on a page does not necessarily need to be re-requested for each visit and is not time-sensitive, instead of fetching it or re-calculating it each time the page is requested, we can store the page in a cache in the web server's memory. This means that when the data is requested by another user, the page can be retrieved straight from the cache rather than being generated from scratch. The data added to the cache can be any type of object, including complex types and collections.

As a rule, the server should cache information that it accesses frequently but that doesn't change often. A good example of a page that would benefit from caching is the home page of the TechieTogs example web site we created in Chapter 11. This page retrieved and displayed a single featured product and the top four most popular products from the database. Because this page is frequently visited, the data on this page is not time-critical, and the database queries involved are comparatively slow tasks, we could store the data in the cache for a period of time with absolutely no adverse effect to the user.

The default expiration time for an item stored in the cache is twenty minutes. However, you can adjust this length of time in code for each item cached, the period ranging from minutes to days.

When you retrieve an item from the cache, you must check that it still exists, even if you are certain that you are requesting it within the cache-expiration period. Entries in the web server's cache may be removed for reasons outside your control, even within the expiration period. For example, if the web server is running low on memory for any reason, it may empty items from the cache in order to reclaim some memory. A server restart will also clear the cache.

ASP.NET Web Pages includes a WebCache helper class to simplify the process of working with the server cache. The helper class exposes three methods, detailed here in Table 13-1:

Table 13-1. *WebCache Helper Methods*

Method Name	Description
Set()	Inserts an item into the cache
Get()	Retrieves an item from the cache
Remove()	Removes an item from the cache

When we add an item to the cache using the Set() method, we need to provide a number of parameters. Table 13-2 explains these in detail:

Table 13-2. *WebCache.Set() Parameters*

Parameter Name	Type	Description
key	string	A string literal used to identify the item
value	object	The data to be stored in the cache
minutesToCache	int	Optional. The number of minutes that the item should be kept in the cache. The maximum expiration period is one year. The default setting is twenty minutes.
slidingExpiration	bool	Optional. Indicates whether the cache expiration period should be start over each time the item is accessed. Default = true

The Get() and Remove() methods simply accept a string parameter that specifies the key of the cache item to be retrieved or deleted.

To demonstrate the WebCache helper class in action, we'll create a page that caches the current date and time for one minute.

■ **Note** The date and time is not a good candidate for caching in the real world. It is both quick to calculate and definitely time sensitive! However, it does provide an excellent demonstration of caching in action.

Create a page called CachingExample.cshtml, and insert the following code in place of any that may have been created automatically by WebMatrix:

```
@{
    var dateTime = WebCache.Get("dateTime");
    if (dateTime == null)
    {
        dateTime = DateTime.Now;
        WebCache.Set("dateTime", dateTime, 1, false);
    }
}

<!DOCTYPE html>

<html lang="en">
    <head>
        <meta charset="utf-8" />
        <title>Caching Example</title>
    </head>
    <body>
        <h1>Caching Example</h1>
        <p>
            Current Date and Time: @DateTime.Now
        </p>
        <p>
            Cached Date and Time: @dateTime
        </p>
    </body>
</html>
```

When the page is requested, the value of the **"dateTime"** item in the cache is retrieved. If the item is **null**, the current date and time is set into the cache, with an expiration time of one minute.

In the page body, we display the current date and time and the date and time stored in the cache. On initial load, both values will be the same. However, when the page is refreshed within the one minute expiration limit, the current date and time will change while the cached value remains static. If the page is refreshed once the minute has elapsed, the cached value will be updated.

Figure 13-10 shows the output of the code sample in which the cached time is different from the actual current time:

***Figure 13-10.** The Caching Example demonstrating the use of the WebCache helper class*

Search Engine Optimization (SEO) with WebMatrix

Before you deploy your web site to the World Wide Web, you will want to ensure that your site is optimized for search-engine placement. For a newly launched web site, traffic from search engines can mean the difference between success and failure. It is therefore vitally important that the content of your site is formatted in such a way that it can be easily indexed by the automated search-engine "spiders" that "crawl" the World Wide Web, autonomously indexing sites and pages. The process of customizing a web site's content and structure to appeal to these spiders is known as Search Engine Optimization (SEO).

WebMatrix ships with a built-in tool that imitates a search-engine spider—such as that deployed by Google, Yahoo, or Bing—by crawling your web site and noting any SEO issues it encounters. The tool prepares a report detailing any issues with your site as well as helpful pointers that suggest potential remedies.

To see the SEO Reporting Tool in action, create a new site, based on the Empty Web Site template, called SEOExample. Inside the site, create a new page called default.cshtml and insert the following code:

```
<!DOCTYPE html>

<html lang="en">
    <head>
        <meta charset="utf-8" />
        <title></title>
    </head>
    <body>
        <p><em>This is the home page.</p></em>
        <p>
            <a href="about.cshtml">About Us</a>
        </p>
    </body>
</html>
```

Once you have created and saved the page, navigate to the Reports workspace by clicking the bottom icon, labeled Reports, in the Workspace Selector. On entering the Reports workspace, you will be presented with a screen similar to that shown in Figure 13-11:

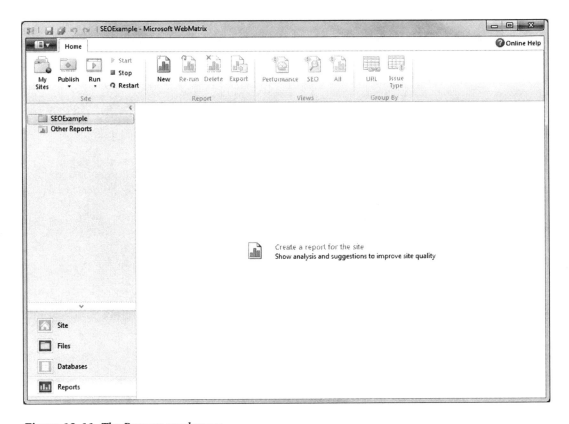

Figure 13-11. The Reports workspace

Click the New button in the Report section of the Ribbon Control to open the New Report dialog. Enter a suitable name for the report and the full URL of the page from which the Reporting Tool spider should start crawling. In our case, we will accept the default URL, which is the default document for the web site because it is hosted locally by IIS Express.

Clicking the arrow to show the Advanced Settings panel will allow you to set a number of preferences, including the maximum number of pages to crawl and the maximum download size (see Figure 13-12). In our case, we only have one page to crawl, so these settings are essentially irrelevant. However, in the future, if you need to run the tool on a large site, these settings will be useful for keeping the size of the report manageable.

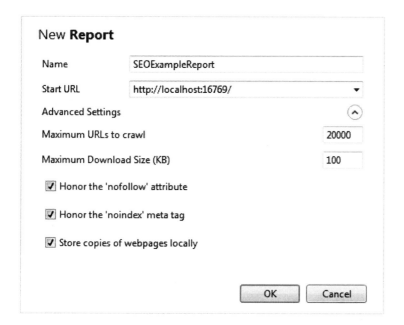

Figure 13-12. The New Report dialog showing the Advanced Settings panel

Table 13-3 explains the options available in the Advanced Settings panel of the New Report dialog:

Table 13-3. Advanced Settings Options in the New Report Dialog

Option	Description
Maximum URLs to crawl	The maximum number of unique URLs to crawl during the analysis
Maximum Download Size (KB)	The maximum number of kilobytes to be downloaded per URL and stored on the local file system
Honor the 'nofollow' attribute	Allows you to override "nofollow" metatags and attributes to allow analysis of hyperlinked pages that wouldn't normally be processed by search-engine spiders
Honor the 'noindex' meta tag	Allows you to override "noindex" attributes to allow analysis of pages that wouldn't normally be processed by search-engine spiders
Store copies of web pages locally	Determines whether to store the content of the analyzed web pages on the local hard disk. If this box is unchecked, some analysis features will not be available.

Click OK to run the report, which will produce the output seen in Figure 13-13:

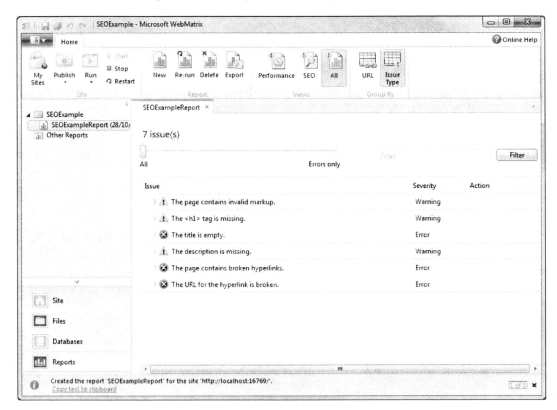

Figure 13-13. The report produced for our test site

Each issue identified by the Reporting Tool is categorized as either an error, a warning, or information. We can see that for our test page, six warnings and errors have been identified. The slider control at the top of the report can be moved to show all issues, only errors and warnings, or errors only.

By clicking on an item in the report, we can see details of where exactly in the site this issue has occurred; in fact, the issue may be present in more than one place. Clicking on a specific violation displays more information, including recommended remedies. Click the "The page contains invalid markup" warning to see the information shown in Figure 13-14:

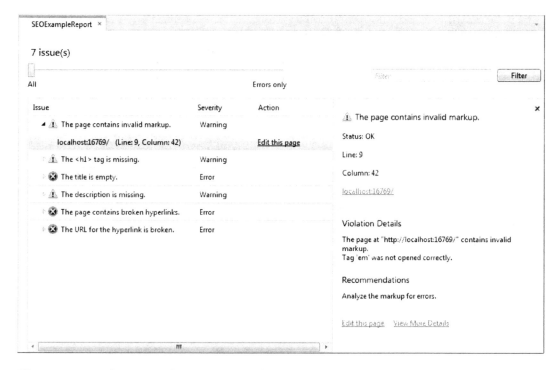

Figure 13-14. Information that is more specific can be viewed by selecting individual violations.

This specific warning tells us that there was a problem with our <em> tag, so click the "Edit this page" link at the bottom, right-hand side and fix the markup, as highlighted below:

```
<!DOCTYPE html>

<html lang="en">
    <head>
        <meta charset="utf-8" />
        <title></title>
    </head>
    <body>
        <p><em>This is the home page.</em></p>
        <p>
            <a href="about.cshtml">About Us</a>
        </p>
    </body>
</html>
```

Now we can save the default.cshtml file, go back to the Reports workspace, and click the Re-run icon in the Ribbon Control to determine if the warning has disappeared.

Looking in the Navigation pane, you will see that WebMatrix generated an entirely separate report when you clicked Re-run. It is useful to be able to go back and see the effect that code changes have on your site, particularly for performance, but after a while you will want to remove some of the older reports. To do this, simply right-click the report you wish to remove in the Navigation pane, and choose Delete from the context menu. A dialog box will be shown asking you to confirm the deletion.

When addressing your SEO issues, it may be easier to fix the violations on a page-by-page basis. To make this easier, the report can be grouped by URL rather than by issue type. This can be done by clicking the URL button in the Group By section of the Ribbon Control. Clicking a specific URL will list all the associated violations (see Figure 13-15):

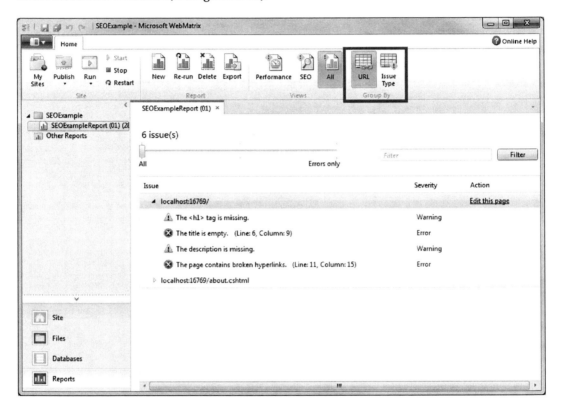

Figure 13-15. Grouping SEO violations by URL

The Performance Report

When the spider crawls your site to produce the SEO Report, it also notes the amount of time taken for each page to be served. This information can be seen by clicking the Performance button in the Views section of the Ribbon Control (see Figure 13-16):

Figure 13-16. *Accessing the Performance Report*

Given that we have run this report on the local IIS Express web server, the actual timings are only an indication; real-world page-load times will depend on various other factors, including bandwidth, server performance, database performance, traffic, etc. However, the timings will help us to identify potential performance issues in pages before they go live.

Figure 13-17 shows the Performance Report for your test site:

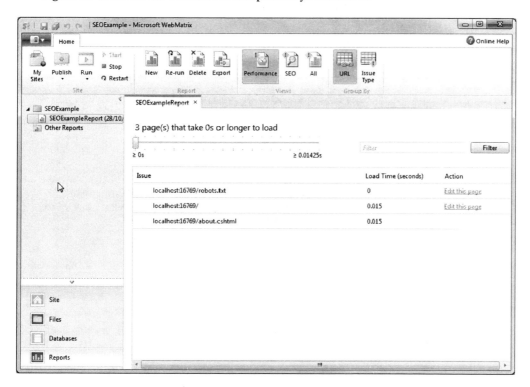

Figure 13-17. *The WebMatrix Performance Report*

The slider at the top of the report allows us to filter the report to show only pages that take more than a specified time period to load. This is useful when analyzing a large site, for example, and you want to only see pages that take over five seconds to load.

Analyzing Other Web Sites

If you want to run an SEO Report on a site other than the one you currently have open, choose New from the Report section of the Ribbon Control and enter the URL of the site you wish to spider. Bear in mind that if you are planning to analyze a large commercial site, you should specify a sensible value for the "Maximum URLs to crawl" setting in the Advanced Settings panel.

Once the report is complete, you will be able to view the SEO issues, but obviously you will not be able to edit the violating pages.

■ **Tip** Microsoft offers a great tool called the "IIS Search Engine Optimization (SEO) Toolkit" as a free download. This tool is similar in functionality to the WebMatrix Reports workspace but has greatly enhanced capabilities. It is more complicated to use but provides a much greater level of detail and sophistication if that is what you require. To download the tool, visit `http://www.iis.net/download/SEOToolkit`

Deploying Your Web Site

Once you are satisfied that your site is ready for the World Wide Web, WebMatrix can help you deploy your site to a production web server.

Finding a Hosting Provider

WebMatrix has a built-in facility to help you find a suitable web host for your site. If you already have an account with a web-hosting provider, you may want to skip to the next section, "Publish Settings."

To get started with finding suitable web hosting for your project, click the "Need web hosting for your site?" button found in the Content Pane of the Site workspace (see Figure 13-18).

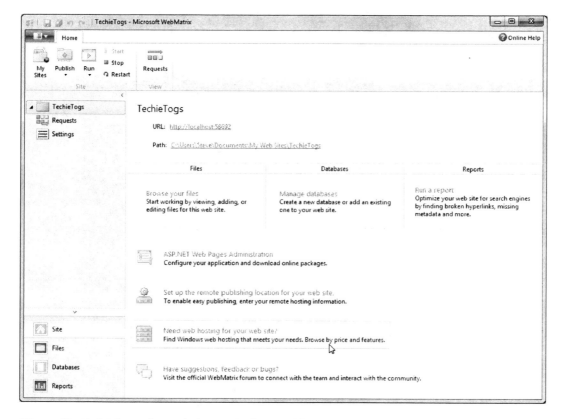

Figure 13-18. WebMatrix can help you find a suitable hosting provider for your site.

Clicking the button will take you to the "Find Web Hosting..." page of the Microsoft web site, as shown here in Figure 13-19:

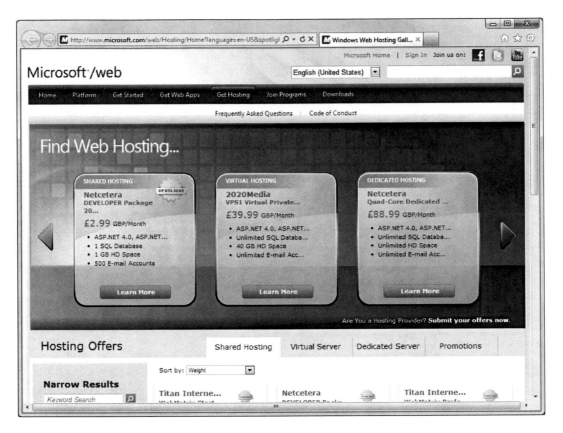

Figure 13-19. The "Find Web Hosting..."page of the Microsoft web site

WebMatrix passes some basic information about your site to this page to help narrow down the list of hosting packages, thereby only showing those that are suitable for hosting your application. You can filter this list further using the tools on the page (see Figure 13-20).

Take care when changing these settings, particularly the Scripting Language setting, to ensure that you do not end up purchasing an unsuitable hosting package. The settings for storage (GB), number of SQL databases, number of email accounts, and bandwidth per month can be set using the sliders. There are a number of factors to consider when setting these criteria:

- **Storage**: The initial size of your web site can be found by viewing the folder properties of your site in Windows Explorer on your development machine. However, this is only a starting point. If your site has the potential to grow over time—for example if it has the facility for users to upload documents—you should bear this in mind. If you are using an SQL Server Compact Edition database, the disk space required to hold this database (up to 4GB) will also be included when calculating storage capacity.

- **Number of SQL Databases**: If you are planning to use an SQL Server Compact Edition database for your site, there is no need to choose a host with additional database capabilities, as SQL Server Compact Edition is file-based and requires no additional software to be installed on the server. However, if you are planning to use a different edition of SQL Server, you will need a host that can provide these facilities. WebMatrix can automatically produce SQL scripts to create tables and can insert data to replicate this schema on your development computer. You will need to run these scripts on the database provided by your hosting provider, usually through the host's control panel.

- **Bandwidth per month**: To calculate roughly how much bandwidth your site requires, you can use the following formula:

    Monthly bandwidth =
        Average page size x (Average monthly visitors x Average page views per visit)

    Remember to add a substantial contingency amount (about 50 percent) for sudden peaks in traffic as a result of popular links to your site or successful marketing campaigns. If your site provides downloadable content for users, your bandwidth calculations should also take this into account. Average monthly usage statistics can be easily obtained through a web-based analysis tool such as Google Analytics or StatCounter.

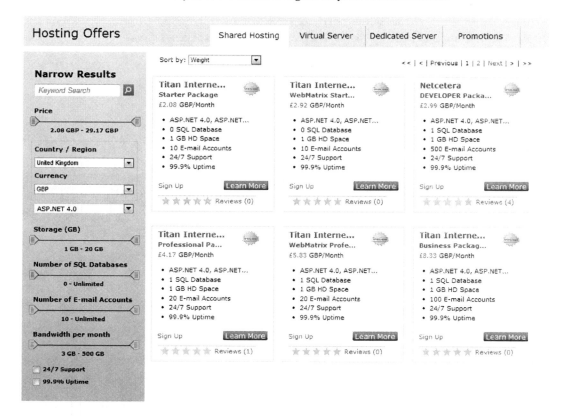

Figure 3-20. Choosing a web-hosting provider

To find more information about a particular hosting package, click one of the green Learn More buttons. Once you have found a package that meets your criteria, click the Sign Up link on the relevant company's web site.

Publish Settings

Once you have chosen and purchased a suitable hosting plan, your chosen provider will typically send you an email containing the details of your account and connection information. This connection information will be provided either as a list of settings or as a file with a .PublishSettings extension.

WebMatrix can publish your site using either of these methods; once the initial setup is complete, they both work in exactly the same way. In the next two sections, we'll look at each of these methods.

Open the Site workspace and click the "Set up remote publishing location for your web site" button found in the Content Pane (see Figure 13-21).

Set up the remote publishing location for your web site.
To enable easy publishing, enter your remote hosting information.

Figure 13-21. *Click the button in the Site workspace to open the Publish Settings dialog*

Clicking this button opens the Publish Settings dialog seen in Figure 13-22:

Publish Settings

Protocol :	Web Deploy ▼
Server:	*e.g. server1.acmepublishing.com*
User name:	
Password:	
Site name:	*e.g. www.microsoft.com*
Destination URL:	*e.g. http://www.contoso.com*

☐ Save password

Validate Connection

Common **Tasks**

▢ Find web hosting

↗ Import publish settings

Save   Cancel

Figure 13-22. *The Publish Settings dialog*

Using a .PublishSettings File

A .PublishSettings file is an XML-based file that contains connection and publishing information specific to your web-hosting account. If your web host has provided you with a .PublishSettings file, it can be used to configure site deployment using WebMatrix.

Click the "Import publish settings" link, located under Common Tasks on the right-hand side of the Publish Settings dialog; this will allow you to browse for your .PublishSettings file. Once you have located the file, click Open to allow WebMatrix to retrieve the necessary settings from the file. The Publish Settings dialog will be populated for you using the information stored in the .PublishSettings file, including connection strings for any non-SQL Server Compact Edition databases you may be using.

Once you are happy with the settings, click the Validate Connection button to have WebMatrix test the settings (see Figure 13-23), and if they are successful, click Save.

Figure 13-23. *Click the Validate Connection button to have WebMatrix test the specified settings.*

Manual Configuration

If you have not received a .PublishSettings file from your web hosting provider, you can configure the Publish Settings dialog manually using the host settings, usually sent as part of your account confirmation email or available through the host's control panel.

If you selected your web-hosting package via the WebMatrix IDE, you can enter the host settings directly into the Publish Settings dialog, as seen in Figure 13-22, leaving the Protocol drop-down set to "Web Deploy." If you did not choose your hosting package through WebMatrix and your web host does not support Web Deploy, you should follow the instructions in the section titled "Configuring Publish Settings using FTP."

The following list explains the settings required by the Publish Settings dialog for Web Deploy projects:

- **Server:** This is often referred to by web hosts as the "Server Name" or "Service URL".

- **User name and Password**: These are usually chosen by you when you sign up for the hosting account, although alternatives may be provided by the hosting company for publishing purposes.

- **Site Name:** This is typically referred to as the "Site" or as "Site/Application" in the list of settings provided by hosting companies.

- **Destination URL:** This is the URL that will be used to browse to your site (i.e., the site's web address).

Once you have entered all the necessary settings, click the Validate Connection button (see Figure 13-23) to verify that WebMatrix can successfully connect to your hosting account, and then click Save.

Configuring Publish Settings using FTP

If your web host does not support Web Deploy, WebMatrix can be configured to publish using the File Transfer Protocol (FTP). Choosing FTPfrom the Protocol drop-down in the Publish Settings dialog will present you with a slightly different set of options, explained below:

- **Server**: Web-hosting companies often call this the "Server Name" or "Service URL."

- **Site Name**: This is often referred to in the list of settings provided by hosting companies as the "Site Root" or "Default Directory." This setting is optional.

- **User name and Password**: Typically, these are chosen by you when you sign up for the hosting account. However, alternatives for publishing may be set by the hosting provider.

- **Destination URL**: This is the URL that will be used to browse to your site (i.e., the site's web address).

Again, once you have entered all of the necessary information, click the Validate Connection button, seen in Figure 13-23, to have WebMatrix test the settings, and then click Save.

Configuring External Database Connections

If your web site uses a database other than the built-in SQL Server Compact Edition, your site will have one or more database connection strings stored in the `web.config` file, which specifies the details of each database connection.

During development, these settings will be different to those required to point the site at the live database on the public-facing site. By clicking the Connection String textbox next to each database listed at the bottom of the Publish Settings dialog, you can specify the live-database connection settings (see Figure 13-24).

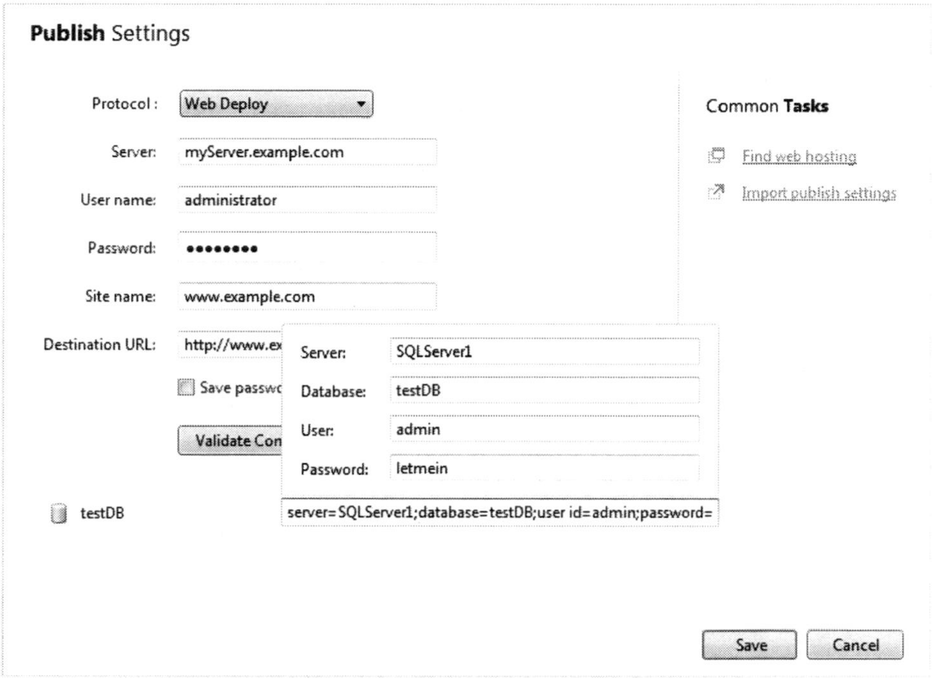

Publish Settings

Protocol : Web Deploy ▼

Server: myServer.example.com

User name: administrator

Password: ••••••••

Site name: www.example.com

Destination URL: http://www.ex

Server: SQLServer1

Database: testDB

User: admin

Password: letmein

☐ Save passwo

Validate Con

server=SQLServer1;database=testDB;user id=admin;password=

▢ testDB

Common **Tasks**

Find web hosting

Import publish settings

Save   Cancel

Figure 13-24. Configuring database connections in the Publish Settings dialog

These settings tell WebMatrix to build a connection string so that it knows how to connect to the live data. This overwrites the `web.config` settings only on the live server.

Publishing Your Web Site

With your Publish Settings correctly configured, you are now in a position to upload your site to the World Wide Web. You can do this at any time by clicking the Publish button on the left-hand side of the Ribbon Control.

The first time you click the Publish button, a Publish Compatibility dialog will appear, shown here in Figure 13-25. This dialog gives you the opportunity to have WebMatrix test your publish settings and make adjustments to .NET settings on the server if necessary. Click Yes to proceed with the test.

Figure 13-25. The Publish Compatibility dialog

Once the test is complete, the Publish Preview dialog will be displayed. Figure 13-26 shows the Publish Preview dialog shown for the first upload of the TechieTogs site we developed in chapters 9, 10, and 11.

Publish Preview

	Name	Action	Date modified	Size	
☑	account/login.cshtml	Add	14 October 06:50	2 KB	
☑	account/passwordReset.cshtml	Add	15 October 06:31	1 KB	
☑	admin/categories/default.cshtml	Add	16 October 14:49	1 KB	
☑	admin/categories/editCategory.cshtml	Add	16 October 09:13	1 KB	
☑	admin/orders/default.cshtml	Add	18 October 07:52	2 KB	
☑	admin/products/default.cshtml	Add	19 October 08:05	1 KB	
☑	admin/products/productDetails.cshtml	Add	21 October 15:52	4 KB	
☑	admin/_PageStart.cshtml	Add	16 October 03:49	215 B	

Changed Files (107) — Total: 7.3 MB

Don't see all your files? Click here to learn more

Databases (1)

☐ TechieTogsData.sdf   Copy as file

Publishing will overwrite any remote databases   ✕

Continue   Cancel

Figure 13-26. The Publish Preview dialog

The Publish Preview dialog shows all the files that have changed since the last upload to the site. The dialog gives you the opportunity to check the list of changed files to be published and to remove them from the list as necessary; this is done by un-ticking the check box next to the file name.

If this is the first time you have uploaded the site, then all files will be shown and ticked. On subsequent uploads, only changed files will appear in this dialog.

Databases will never be ticked by default, so if you wish WebMatrix to upload your SQL Server Compact Edition database, you should be sure to check the box next to the database file.

Once you have selected all the necessary files for upload, click Continue to publish your site. The notification bar across the bottom of the WebMatrix IDE will inform you of its progress (see Figure 13-27).

Figure 13-27. Site-publishing progress shown in the WebMatrix IDE notification bar

The initial publishing of a site can take several minutes, particularly if databases are to be uploaded. Once the process is complete, a success message, such as the one seen in Figure 13-28, will be displayed in the notification bar:

Figure 13-28. The message seen in the notification bar once publishing is complete

Now that the initial upload is complete, you can view the site in a web browser at your chosen URL. You can continue to safely develop the site on your local PC and only need to upload changed files to the web server as necessary. This makes the whole publishing process much quicker and enables you to keep the development site completely separate from the live production site.

Summary

In this chapter we have covered a lot of the features of WebMatrix that go beyond ASP.NET Web Page development. We have seen how WebMatrix can be used to help debug pages and fix errors and how further debugging tools can be accessed in modern web browsers and through Visual Studio.

We have also seen how the performance of a web site can be improved by caching data in the memory of the web server for faster retrieval. Search Engine Optimization (SEO) was also discussed, and we learned how WebMatrix can "crawl" your web site by mimicking a search engine spider, identifying issues that may affect how your pages are indexed and placed by search engines.

Finally, we saw how WebMatrix can help us choose a hosting provider and publish our completed sites to the World Wide Web.

This brings us to the end of the book! So, thanks for reading; I really hope you enjoyed learning, and I wish you every success with all your future WebMatrix projects.

Index

B

C

X, Y, Z

CPSIA information can be obtained at www.ICGtesting.com
Printed in the USA
LVOW130337231211

260829LV00011B/2/P